THE CHARTERED INSTITUTE OF BANKERS
cib

Law and Practice

3rd edition

BANKERS WORKBOOK SERIES

PAUL COWDELL DipFS, FCIB, MCT

Published in association with
Sheffield Hallam University

First published in 1991
2nd edition 1994
3rd edition 1996

BANKERS BOOKS LIMITED
c/o The Chartered Institute of Bankers
10 Lombard Street
London EC3V 9AS

CIB Publications are published by The Chartered Institute of Bankers, a non-profit making registered educational charity, and are distributed exclusively by Bankers Books Limited which is a wholly owned subsidiary of The Chartered Institute of Bankers.

ISBN 0–85297–411–6

Contents

Table of Cases

Table of Statutes

Introduction

The Concept of the Course

This is a practical workbook written for students studying for banking and finance qualifications and also for practitioners in the financial services who are looking for a practical refresher.

Each unit is divided into sections and contains:

- Learning objectives;
- Clear, concise topic-by-topic coverage;
- Examples and learning activities to reinforce learning, confirm understanding and stimulate thought;
- Often, past examination questions to try for practice;
- Self-assessment questions to test your knowledge, understanding and skills.

Learning activities

Learning activities are provided throughout. These come in a variety of forms. For example, they:

- Test your ability to recall information, your ability to analyse material, or assess whether you have appreciated the full significance of a piece of information.
- Require discussion with colleagues, friends or fellow students.
- Require you to do some research.

Virtually all require you to record something in writing and you should keep your notes/answers for later reference.

Where the activity comprises a series of short questions, a reference is given to the precise part of the preceding text where you can find the answer. For others, where appropriate, a suggested answer/response/solution is given, but often in abbreviated form to help you avoid the temptation of merely reading the 'answer'! You will find our suggestions in the Appendix.

At the end of each unit there are self-assessment questions. These usually comprise a number of short answer questions and multiple-choice questions and, often, a full specimen examination question. The answers to all of these questions are also to be found in the Appendix.

Syllabus

The key sections of the Law and Practice syllabus are:

- The Banker-Customer Relationship

- Building Society-Investor Relationship
- Types of Customer
- Regulated Lending
- Financial Services Regulation
- Cheques and Payments Systems
- Insolvency
- Security
- External Regulation of Banks and Building Societies

Your contribution

Although this workbook is designed to stand alone, as with most topics, certain aspects of this subject are constantly changing. Therefore it is very important that you keep up-to-date with these key areas.

We anticipate that you will study this course for one academic year, reading through and studying approximately two units every three weeks. However, note that as topics vary in size and as knowledge tends not to fall into uniform chunks, some units are unavoidably longer than others.

The masculine pronoun 'he' has been used in this workbook to encompass both genders and to avoid the awkwardness of the constant repetition of 'he and/or she'.

Study Guide

Below we offer advice and ideas on studying, revising and approaching examinations.

Studying

As with any examination, there is no substitute for preparation based on an organised and disciplined study plan. You should devise an approach which will enable you to complete this workbook and still leave time for revision of this and any other subject you are taking at the same time. Many candidates find that about six weeks is about the right period of time to leave for revision, enough time to get through the revision material, but not so long that it is no longer fresh in your mind by the time you reach the examination.

This means that you should plan how to get to the last chapter by, say, the end of March for a May sitting or the end of August for an October sitting. This includes not only reading the text, but making notes, working through the student activities and answering any illustrative examination questions which are included.

We offer the following as a starting point for approaching your study.

- *Plan time each week* to study a part of this workbook. Make sure that it is 'quality' study time: let everyone know that you are studying and that you should not be disturbed. If you are at home, unplug your telephone or switch the answerphone on; if you are in the office, put you telephone on 'divert'.

- Set a *clearly defined objective* for each study period. You may simply wish to read through a unit for the first time or perhaps you may want to make notes on a unit you have already read a couple of times. Don't forget the student activities, self-assessment questions and any examination questions.
- *Review your study plan.* Devise a study checklist and/or timetable so that you can schedule and monitor your progress. Don't panic if you fall behind, but do think how you will make up for lost time.
- Look for *relevant examples* of what you have covered in the 'real' world. If you work for a financial organisation, this should provide them. If you don't, then think about your experiences as an individual bank or building society customer or perhaps about your employer's position as a corporate customer of a bank. Keep an eye on the quality press for reports about banks and building societies and their activities.

Revising

The period which you have earmarked for revision is a very important. Now it is even more important that you plan *time each week for study* and that you set *clear objectives* for each revision session. So ...

- *Make use of a timetable.*
- *Use time sensibly.* How much revision time do you have? Remember that you still need to eat, sleep and fit in some leisure time!
- *How will you allocate the available time between subjects?* What are your weaker subjects? You will need to focus on some topics more than others. You will also need to plan your revision around your learning style. By now, you should know whether, for example, early morning, early evening or late evening is best.
- *Take regular breaks.* Most people find they can absorb more if they attempt to revise for long uninterrupted periods of time. Award yourself a five minute break every hour or so. Go for a stroll or make a cup of coffee, but don't turn the television on!
- *Believe in yourself.* Are you cultivating the right attitude of mind? There is absolutely no reason why you should not pass the exam if you adopt the correct approach. Be confident, you have passed exams before so you can pass this one.

The examination

Passing examinations is half about having the required knowledge, understanding and skills, and half about doing yourself justice in the examination. You must have the right *technique.*

The day of the exam

- Set at least one alarm (or get an alarm call) for a morning exam.
- Have something to eat but don't eat too much; you may feel sleepy if your system is digesting a large meal.
- Don't forget pens, pencils, rulers, erasers and anything else you will need.
- Avoid discussion about the exam with other candidates outside the exam hall.

Tackling the examination paper

First, make sure that you satisfy the examiner's requirements

- *Read the instructions on the front of the exam paper carefully.* Check that the exam format hasn't changed. It is surprising how often examiners' reports remark on the number of students who attempt too few – or too many – questions, or who attempt the wrong number of questions from different parts of the paper. Make sure that you are planning to answer the right number of questions.
- *Read all the questions on the exam paper before you start writing.* Look at the weighting of marks to each part of the question. If part (a) offers only four marks and you can't answer the 12 marks part (b), then don't choose the question.
- *Don't produce irrelevant answers.* Make sure you answer the question set, and not the question you would have preferred to have been set.
- *Produce an answer in the correct format.* The examiner will state the format in which the question should be answered, for example in a report or memorandum. If a question asks for a diagram or an example, give one. If a question does not specifically asks for a diagram or example, but it seems appropriate, give one.

Second, observe the following simple rules to ensure that your script is acceptable to the examiner.

- *Present a tidy paper.* You are a professional and it should always show in the presentation of your work. Candidates may be penalised for poor presentation and so you must make sure that you write legibly, label diagrams clearly and lay out your work professionally. Assistant examiners each have dozens of papers to mark; a badly written scrawl is unlikely to receive the same attention as a neat and well laid out paper.
- *State the obvious.* Many candidates look for complexity which is not required and consequently overlook the obvious. Make basic statements first. Plan your answer and ask yourself whether you have answered the main parts of the question.
- *Use examples.* This will help to demonstrate to the examiner that you keep up-to-date with the subject. There are lots of useful examples scattered through this workbook and you can read about others if you dip into the quality press or take notice of what is happening in your working environment.

Finally, Make sure that you give yourself the opportunity to do yourself justice.

- *Select questions carefully.* Read through the paper once, then quickly jot down any key points against each question in a second read through. Reject those questions against which you have jotted down very little. Select those where you could latch on to 'what the question is about' – but remember to check carefully that you have got the right end of the stick before putting pen to paper.
- *Plan your attack carefully.* Consider the order in which you are going to tackle questions. It is a good idea to start with your best question to boost your morale and get some easy marks 'in the bag'.
- *Read the question carefully and plan your answer.* Read through the question

again very carefully when you come to answer it.

- *Gain the easy marks.* Include the obvious if it answers the question and do not spend unnecessary time producing the perfect answer. As we suggested above, there is nothing wrong with stating the obvious.
- *Avoid getting bogged down in small parts of questions.* If you find a part of a question difficult, get on with the rest of the question. If you are having problems with something the chances are that everyone else is too.
- *Don't leave the exam early.* If you finish early, use your spare time to check and recheck your script.

Don't worry if you feel you have performed badly in the exam. It is likely that the other candidates will have found the exam difficult too. As soon as you get up and leave the exam hall, forget the exam and think about the next – or, if it is the last one, celebrate!

Don't discuss an exam with other candidates. This is particularly the case if you still have other exams to sit. Put it out of your mind until the day of the results. Forget about exams and relax.

Unit 1

The Banker-Customer Relationship

Objectives

After studying this unit, you should be able to:

- **define the terms 'banker' and 'customer';**
- **explain the nature of the banker-customer relationship;**
- **list and explain the legal duties which exist between banks and their customers;**
- **explain the system of bankers' references and a bank's liability to the recipient of status replies;**
- **state the requirements and evaluate the impact of the Data Protection Act 1984 and the Code of Banking Practice on banking operations.**

1 What is a bank and who is a customer?

Student Activity 1

Before you read further, write down your definitions of a bank and of a customer and compare these with the definitions which follow. (Use any spare pages at the end of the units, a section of your personal study folder or some spare paper for your written responses to this and the other activities in this workbook – depending on whether or not you need to keep your notes as part of your study material. You will find the answers to all the self-assessment questions and, where appropriate, the student activities in the Appendix.)

What is a bank?

1.1 Two separate statutes and one leading case have considered this point. In chronological order they are:

- The Bills of Exchange Act 1882;
- *United Dominions Trust v Kirkwood* (1966);
- The Banking Act 1987.

The Bills of Exchange Act 1882

1.2 This defines a bank as 'a body of persons ... who carry on the business of banking'.

United Dominions Trust v Kirkwood (1966)

1.3 This case defined a bank as an organisation which:

- Accepts money from, and collects cheques for, customers;
- Honours cheques or other withdrawal authorities given by customers;
- Maintains current accounts or accounts of a similar nature;

or, as an alternative:

- had the reputation of being a bank within the financial community.

1.4 Clearly, on this basis many building societies and other similar financial services groups would apparently be classed as banks. However, under the Banking Act 1987, they would fail to gain 'banking status'.

The Banking Act 1987

1.5 Today only an organisation which is recognised by the Bank of England as an authorised deposit taker under the 1987 Banking Act can use the word 'bank' in its title. Thus, any organisation which is authorised to use the word 'bank' in its title under the 1987 Banking Act can be classed as a bank, and it would seem that any other financial services organisation which carries out what are generally considered to be banking activities could also be legally classed as a bank.

1.6 In certain transactions concerning cheques, the issue of whether or not an organisation is a bank can have important legal consequences. (These matters are fully covered in Units 9–12 where collection and payment of cheques and similar instruments are considered.)

Who is a customer?

1.7 It is important to be able to decide whether or not a person is a customer because banks have various obligations which they must carry out for customers but which they need not always carry out for non-customers. In addition, the term 'customer' has important legal implications in connection with payment and collection of cheques. These aspects are examined later.

1.8 At one time a customer was defined as anyone who had an account with the bank. The number of transactions or the length of time the account had been opened was immaterial: *Commissioners of Taxation v English, Scottish and Australian Banks* (1920). In more recent times, the growth of financial services provided by banks has inevitably widened the definition of 'customer'. In *Woods v Martins Bank and Another* (1958) it was held that a bank which gave investment advice to someone who did not have an account had the same contractual duty of care as if that person had held an account with that bank.

1.9 Under the voluntary Code of Banking Practice a personal customer is defined as:

> A private individual who maintains an account (including a joint account with another private individual or an account held as an executor or trustee, but excluding the accounts of sole traders, clubs and societies) or who takes other services from a bank or building society.

1.10 To sum up, a person who has an account with a bank is certainly a customer. A person to whom the bank provides financial services without including a bank account is a customer as regards the duty of care owed by the bank regarding that service.

1.11 Note: the importance of defining a customer is seen in Units 9 to 12 which cover the paying and collecting of cheques and other similar instruments.

2 The basis of the banker-customer relationship and how this can be affected by special authorities

Contract

2.1 The rights and duties of bankers and customers have evolved from custom and practice, as amended by various court decisions and statutes such as the Consumer Credit Act 1974 and the Financial Services Act 1986. These implied rights and duties are amended whenever a customer completes a standard form or facility letter, each of which is an express written contract.

2.2 There are a wealth of forms signed by customers in connection with the various banking activities, for example:

- Mandates – signed when opening account (see Units 4 and 5);
- Charge forms (see Units 13–17);
- Payment instructions (see Units 9–12);
- Consumer credit agreement forms (see Unit 19);
- Customer agreement forms required under the Financial Services Act 1986 (see Unit 18).

2.3 Finally, the second edition of the voluntary Code of Banking Practice has important implications for the banker-customer relationship. Banks will provide new customers with a written summary of the key features of the more common services. This may form the basis of the banker-customer contract.

Student Activity 2

Find out whether your bank has a form of contract signed by customers when they open an account. If your bank does have such a contract, keep a copy. When you have completed the whole of this unit, assess the extent to which your bank's contract might vary the normal duties of banks to customers and vice versa.

The effect of special authorities on the normal banker-customer contractual relationship

2.4 The bank can vary the normal banker-customer relationship if specially authorised to do so by the customer. A typical example is seen when a business customer completes a standard authority for disclosure of information to the auditors. This authority varies the normal duty of secrecy.

2.5 In addition, banks can include special clauses in their customer agreements covering specific services. For example, Thomas Cook included a clause in their travellers' cheque agreement that there was no obligation to refund lost travellers' cheques if the loss had been caused by the purchaser's negligence and the court upheld the clause. Note, however, that under the Unfair Contract Terms Act 1977, a court can invalidate any clause which seems unfair or inequitable, especially if imposed by a party with much the stronger bargaining power.

Other aspects, apart from contract, which govern the banker-customer relationship

2.6 In *Foley v Hill* (1848), confirmed in *Joachimson v Swiss Bank Corporation* (1921), it was held that the normal relationship between a bank and customer is that of debtor and creditor. However, when the bank is a debtor, there is no obligation to seek out the customer and repay him, this is the opposite of the usual position. A bank is only under an obligation to repay its customer when the customer makes demand.

2.7 This position is still valid for current accounts, but practice varies with special accounts such as fixed-term money market deposits. Here the bank's normal practice is to seek the customer's instructions for disposal of the balance once the fixed term has ended.

2.8 Other aspects which govern the banker-customer relationship tend to apply only to particular transactions:

- Agency applies whenever the bank acts as an agent, for instance in the purchase of stocks and shares.
- Bailment – the relationship of bailor and bailee arises in safe custody transactions.
- Trustee law applies when the bank carries out specialised trustee services – but note that a bank is not a trustee of its customer's normal credit balances.

2.9 In *Joachimson v Swiss Bank Corporation* (1921) other terms were implied.

- That the bank undertakes to receive money and collect bills and cheques for its customer's account, and the bank will pay the customer such monies held in his account.
- The bank promises to repay money held at the branch of the bank where the account is kept during normal banking hours. Note that the bank does not promise to make such repayments at another branch.
- The bank promises to repay any part of the customer's balance against the order of the customer at the branch where he banks.
- The bank promises not to cease to do business with the customer except on giving reasonable notice.
- The customer promises to exercise reasonable care in executing his written orders so as not to mislead the bank or to facilitate forgery

3 The duties of a bank to its customer

Student Activity 3

From your day-to-day experience, write down the items which you think come under the heading of a bank's duty to its customer and then compare your list with the list which follows.

3.1 A bank owes the following duties to its customer.

- To receive a customer's *cash and cheques and other instruments for collection*: *Joachimson v Swiss Bank Corporation* (1921).
- To *pay a customer's cheques*, or allow him to withdraw cash, to the extent of his balance on receipt of a proper written authority during banking hours at the account-holding branch, or at another bank or branch subject to suitable arrangements, e.g. cheque guarantee card.

  Note: a bank's duty to pay its customer's cheques which are properly drawn up to the balance of the account or to the agreed overdraft facility is not absolute. If the bank knows the cheques are drawn for an unlawful purpose (or should have known so from the facts at its disposal) it must not pay the cheques.
- To maintain the *duty of secrecy* regarding the customer's affairs.
- To give *reasonable notice before closing a credit account*. In *Prosperity v Lloyds* (1923) one month was considered unreasonable for a business with complex banking affairs. However, one month should be sufficient for a private account.
- To *honour the word of its authorised officials*. In *Box v Midland Bank* (1979), the branch manager told a customer that head office sanction would be a mere formality provided that an ECGD policy was obtained. The manager failed to explain the difference between an ECGD policy (which could be obtained) and an ECGD bills and notes guarantee (which could not be obtained from ECGD because of the customer's poor financial situation). Head office would not accept the ECGD policy, only an ECGD guarantee. Head office refused to accept the ECGD policy obtained by the customer and because the borrowing facility was not granted the customer got into financial difficulties and was made bankrupt.

  It was held that the bank had failed to take reasonable care, i.e. the level of care to be expected of a competent bank manager and the bank was liable in tort to the plaintiff.
- To *follow up all obligations* under the Consumer Credit Act 1974, and the Financial Services Act 1986 (see Units 18 and 19).
- To inform a customer if his *signature has been forged* on a cheque or other instruction.
- Under the *Code of Banking Practice*, a bank will provide personal customers with full written details of the basis on which charges and interest are to be calculated, and will deal fairly with customers.

4 Notice of trust and the bank's duty to honour its customers' authorities to withdraw money

The duty of a bank when paying a customer's cheques

4.1 The bank must exercise reasonable skill and care in carrying out its customer's instructions. Hence the bank must not pay cheques which the bank knows, or should know, are drawn for an illegal purpose. If the bank pays such cheques it will be liable to refund the money, as payment is a breach of trust: *Selangor United Rubber Estates v Craddock* (1968). Obviously, if a bank knows of the illegal purpose, it will refuse payment. However the issue which causes difficulty is the problem of deciding in what circumstances a court would say a bank 'should have known' of the illegal purpose.

Lipkin Gorman

4.2 In *Lipkin Gorman v Karpnale Ltd* (1989) partner in a firm of solicitors was known by the branch manager to be a compulsive gambler. The partner, over a period of time, withdrew £323,000 from the firm's client account and used the money to pay off gambling debts at the Playboy Club. The withdrawals were made in accordance with the mandate. When the facts became known, the other partners sued the bank for reimbursement on the basis that the bank was a constructive trustee of the sums withdrawn and therefore liable to them, because it should have known the funds were being withdrawn for a unauthorised purpose.

4.3 On the facts the bank was not liable to refund because:

- Although the bank knew of the partner's gambling addiction, it did not know the purpose of the withdrawals.
- If the bank had passed on its knowledge of the gambling to the other partners this would have been a breach of its duty of secrecy towards the partner concerned, the partner maintained his own account with the bank.
- If the bank had refused to allow the withdrawals it would have been in breach of its duty to honour the mandate if there are sufficient funds since, on the facts, the withdrawals were not sufficiently unusual to warrant investigation.
- Mere suspicion or unease is insufficient grounds to justify refusal to allow withdrawals which are in accordance with the mandate. The bank could be liable for wrongful dishonour if it refused to honour cheques etc on mere suspicion.
- The bank is not expected to be a private detective agency.

4.4 Note that the principles applied in the decision apply:

- Not only apply to cheques but also to all other authorities, e.g. transfers from solicitors' or estate agents' client accounts.
- Only when the cheque or authority is validly authorised. If the signature of the customer is forged, then the bank must refuse payment. If the bank pays against a forged signature it must refund: *Tai Hing Cotton Mill* (1985) unless estopped: *Greenwood v Martins Bank* (1933).
- If an endorsement is forged on a cheque, this is of no concern to the paying bank unless it knows or should have known of the forgery.

5 The extent to which a bank has a duty to advise its customer

5.1 A bank has no duty to warn a customer against the risks inherent in any transaction unless the customer asks for advice: *Redmond v Allied Irish Banks* (1987) where the court held that the bank had no duty to warn its customer of the effect of a 'not negotiable' crossing on a cheque.

5.2 *Spindler & Verity v Lloyds Bank* (1995) establishes some modern principles for the liability of banks who give advice. The facts were that after discussions between S&V and a local branch manager, Lloyds agreed to lend S&V £152,000 to cover the purchase and renovation costs of a house. S&V purchased the property for £126,500, with a view to renovating it and then selling at a profit. Unfortunately, the proposition did not work out as anticipated because the property market prices began to fall, the cost of the renovation (£26,000) exceeded the original estimate by £16,000, and interest rates began to rise. In May 1990 S&V sold the property for £135,000 at a time when the amount owing to the bank had risen to £208,000 due to interest costs.

5.3 S&V instigated proceedings against Lloyds Bank claiming, *inter alia*, that:

- Lloyds had acted negligently in advancing the £152,000;
- The couple had suffered emotional distress and loss of earnings;
- They had lost money on the forced sale of another property which had been sold to help meet the obligations to Lloyds on the advance for the house at the centre of the dispute.

5.4 The court ruled that in ordinary circumstances there is *no duty for a bank to give advice*, thereby upholding *Redmond*. However, when a customer asks for advice and the bank is *aware, or ought to be aware, that the customer is relying on that advice*, then a duty of care will arise.

5.5 Based on the facts, the court ruled that the local branch manager had assumed the role of financial advisor and that a duty of care had therefore arisen. The judge ruled that the bank had been in breach of its duty because if the branch manager had exercised reasonable care and skill, he would have told S&V that 'the project was not a sensible thing for them to do and they should forget about it'.

5.6 The question was then whether S&V had acted as they did in reliance on the advice. To answer this the judge examined the Lloyds Bank leaflets on *Starting Your Business* which contained sentences such as 'Your bank manager will help you decide how much you can really afford to invest', 'Do not hesitate to ask your manager for advice'. On the facts of the case, the judge ruled that S&V had acted on the advice of the Bank.

5.7 The final question was what was S&V's loss on the transaction and had the reliance on the bank's advice caused the loss? On this question the judge ruled that as the loss on the house came about as a result of the bank's advice, damages should be calculated as if the transaction had never been entered into. Although emotional distress had been suffered, there was no basis for any award of damages. The loss on the forced sale of the other property was not a valid claim for damages and the claim for loss of earnings was adjourned.

5.8 The conclusion from the case is that if banks give the impression that they are giving advice, then they are under a duty to exercise reasonable care and skill when doing so. Failure to exercise that care and skill will leave banks vulnerable to claims in damages if that advice is relied upon. It is therefore very likely that banks will review the wording on their promotional literature so as to make it clear that a decision to lend does not necessarily mean that the bank has checked that the project is viable and beneficial from the customer's point of view.

Student Activity 4

Examine the promotional literature of your bank in connection with small business start ups. Consider whether your bank could still be held to be acting in an advisory capacity to small businesses.

6 The bank's duty of secrecy

Student Activity 5

When you joined the bank you had to sign a declaration of secrecy regarding your customers' affairs. Why does the bank require this to be done? When you have thought through and written down your answer, compare it with the text which follows which explains the legal reasons.

The *Tournier* case

6.1 The basic duties of the bank in this respect are set out in *Tournier v National Provincial and Union Bank of England* (1924). *Tournier* establishes that a bank must maintain a duty of secrecy except in the following circumstances.

- *Compulsion of law*. This can take the form of a court order or it can be derived from a specific statute.
- *Public duty*. This only applies in the case of serious crime, large scale fraud, drugs, terrorism or similar situations.
- *Bank's interest*. If a bank sues, it must state the amount owing by the customer in its writ, an action to enforce a guarantee is a good example.
- *Customer's authority*. This can be expressed, i.e. in writing or by word of mouth, or it can be implied. An example of' implied authority occurs in the case of status enquiries.

Other cases and laws which have widened the principles set out in *Tournier*

Barclays v Taylor (1989)

6.2 If a court orders a bank to disclose information to the police, the bank must divulge the information and must not inform its customer of any aspects of this matter. The bank has no duty to contest the court order, except in the unlikely instance that the bank knows some relevant facts which are not known to the police or court. In *Taylor*, the court order was obtained under the Police and Criminal Evidence Act 1984. This PACE order meant that the bank was acting under compulsion of law, thus had no duty to contest the PACE order or to inform the customer of the receipt of such an order.

Statutes dealing with money laundering

6.3 Money laundering is the process whereby criminals attempt to conceal the true origin of the proceeds of their criminal activities. Generally speaking the process involves three stages.

- The placement of the proceeds of criminal activity with a financial institution.
- By a process sometimes known as 'layering', the proceeds are moved around the financial system by a succession of financial transactions.
- After the origin of the dirty money has been suitably disguised, the laundered money is reintegrated into the financial system in the guise of legitimate business funds.

6.4 Banks and building societies are particularly vulnerable at the placement stage, but because of these organisations' ever widening range of financial services, they become vulnerable to layering and reintegration in connection with products such as unit trusts.

6.5 The EU directive on money laundering (Directive No 91/308) has been implemented in the UK through the relevant provisions of:

- The Criminal Justice Act 1993
- The Drug Trafficking Act 1994

In addition there are *Guidance Notes* issued by the Joint Money Laundering Steering Group.

6.6 This legislation overall aims to cover under its provisions the proceeds of drug trafficking, terrorism and violent crime. For example, it is an offence to:

- Assist a money launderer to obtain, conceal, retain or invest funds, if the person assisting knows or suspects (or should have known or suspected in the case of terrorist offences) that the funds represent the proceeds of criminal conduct: s.29, Criminal Justice Act 1993.
- Fail to disclose knowledge or suspicion of money laundering. Anyone who in the course of his profession or trade knows or suspects that another person is engaged in money laundering must report this knowledge or suspicion to the police as soon as it is reasonably practical to do so after it has come to his attention. This reporting obligation is restricted to terrorism and drug related offences, rather than general crime: s.18, Criminal Justice Act 1993.
- Fail to disclose knowledge or suspicion of money laundering. Anyone who in the course of his profession or trade knows or suspects that another person is engaged in money laundering must report this knowledge or suspicion to the police as soon as it is reasonably practical to do so

after it has come to his attention. This reporting obligation is restricted to terrorism and drug related offences, rather than general crime: s.18, Criminal Justice Act 1993.

In practice in the case of suspicion, it can be difficult to decide whether the suspicion is justified or not. The Criminal Justice Act provides a defence of reasonable excuse (not defined). In practice always report any suspicions via your own internal procedures (many banks have a compliance officer or inspection department). The Criminal Justice Act expressly provides that an employee reporting suspicions via the employer's internal procedures will have a defence under the reporting provisions of the Act.

- Under ss.18 and 32, Criminal Justice Act 1993 it is an offence to disclose to a customer or to a third party that information on money laundering has been passed to the police, or that a money laundering investigation is being carried out or planned.

6.7 It is implied in the Criminal Justice Act 1993 that a bank/building society or other financial institution making a disclosure in good faith under the money laundering provisions will be protected from any potential liability under the normal duty of secrecy. There are as yet no decided cases in this matter.

Student Activity 6

Check on your employer's internal procedures for dealing with the money laundering provisions. In particular, find out the name of the person or department to which suspicions must be reported.

7 The duties of a customer and the various cases which apply

Student Activity 7

From your day-to-day experience, think about this and then list the duties which you consider a customer might owe to his bank. Compare your list with the following text.

The duties listed

7.1 A customer owes a duty to:

- Exercise *reasonable care in drawing his cheques* or other authorities so as not to mislead the bank or facilitate fraud: *London Joint Stock Bank Ltd v MacMillan and Arthur* (1918).
- Advise the bank immediately if he discovers his *signature has been forged* on a cheque: *Greenwood v Martins Bank* (1933).
- *Repay any overdraft on demand.* In *Williams and Glyn's Bank Ltd v Barnes* (1981) it was held that when money is lent on overdraft by a bank, and there is no agreed date for repayment and no special terms which could imply the repayment is not due on demand, then the overdraft is repayable

on demand. (It is recommended that banks add the words 'subject to normal banking terms and conditions which include the right of the bank to demand repayment at any time' to any correspondence regarding overdraft facilities being granted.)

- To *pay 'reasonable' charges* for the work involved in handling the account, and to pay all charges set out in any regulated agreement under the Consumer Credit Act 1974 or in any published tariff.

Illustrative cases

London Joint Stock Bank v MacMillan and Arthur (1918)

7.2 In this case the customer did not write any amount in words on his cheque, and simply inserted £2 against the amount in figures. There was ample space between the £ and the 2 for a fraudulent alteration of the amount to £120 in figures, by simply inserting the figures 1 and 0 in the appropriate place. The alteration was nonapparent and had been assisted by the customer's carelessness. It was held that the paying bank was not liable to refund the excess to its customer since the customer had been in breach of his duty of care in drawing the cheque.

7.3 From this decision we we can see that a customer has a duty to draw his cheques in such a way so as not to facilitate fraud. This duty applies to all instructions, and is not restricted to cheques. Any losses caused because the amount has been increased without authority will be the customer's responsibility provided:

- The customer's signature is genuine;
- The alteration is nonapparent and has been facilitated by the customer's carelessness. For example, a customer should not use pencil as this can be easily erased and the alteration would be nonapparent to the bank.

Greenwood v Martins Bank (1933)

7.4 A customer has a duty to inform the bank as soon as he becomes aware that his signature on cheques is being forged. Failure to report the forgery immediately will mean that the customer must stand the loss caused by any cheques debited subsequently. It will also protect the bank against cheques debited before the customer became aware of the fraud, if this delay has prevented the bank from seeking redress from the forger.

7.5 This case is based on the doctrine of 'estoppel'. Greenwood had given the impression, by his conduct, that matters were in order. In such cases the person giving that impression is subsequently estopped (prevented) from denying that impression.

Tai Hing Cotton Mill v Liu Chong Hing Bank and Others (1985)

7.6 *Tai Hing*, decided according to English law, held that if a bank pays cheques on which the customer's signature has been forged, the bank must reimburse the customer provided the customer was previously unaware of the forgeries and provided the customer reported the forgery as soon as he became aware of the problem. The fact that the customer's own incompetence has aided the fraud is immaterial. There is no implied duty on a customer to exercise care in the supervision of his banking affairs to prevent fraud.

7.7 In *Tai Hing*, the court was satisfied that the company's system of internal financial control was lax and was inadequate from the point of view of detecting fraud. Nevertheless, it held that there is no duty on a customer to take precautions in the general course of his business to prevent forgeries on the part of his servants.

7.8 This case also ruled that banks must refund interest as well as principal on any amounts debited without authority.

7.9 Finally, the case confirmed that a customer is under no obligation to examine his bank statement. If the customer finds a mistake on his statement and fails to notify the bank promptly, he is not estopped from bringing the mistake to the bank's attention at a later date. In such a case the bank must correct the mistake. In other words, the onus is on the bank to ensure the statement is correct.

7.10 In *Tai Hing*, the bank had incorporated a clause into its contract with the customer which purported to impose an obligation on the customer to check bank statements, report to the bank any disputed transactions and to sign a confirmation slip that the statement was correct. The court held that such a clause, which was a major variation of the normal banker-customer relationship, was invalid because its terms had not been communicated clearly and firmly to the customer.

8 Banker's references (status enquiries)

Student Activity 8

List the procedures that apply in your bank when one person wants to make a status enquiry on another person. Do you know why these procedures are carried out? Read the following text to see how the law covers status enquiries.

Code of Banking Practice

8.1 Under the Code banks and building societies will, on request:

- Advise customers as to whether or not they will provide banker's references in reply to status enquiries on their customers; and
- Explain how the system works.

8.2 Assuming that authority to reply is held, the procedure is that a:

- Standard enquiry form is received;
- Standard response form is sent to the enquirer (see specimen formats in both cases).

Customer's consent

8.3 Banks used to rely on the implied authority exception under *Tournier*. Indeed it used to be standard banking practice to respond to enquiries without the need to obtain express authority. Current practice is not to respond unless there is an 'omnibus' authority to do so, or specific express authority regarding the enquiry in question. The British Bankers' Association has stated that the 'implied authority' view is out of touch with modern views of the banker-customer relationship.

Customer's approval to the wording

8.4 Banks have never submitted a status reply to a customer for his consent to the wording. The Code makes no reference to this aspect at all.

Advice of receipt of a status enquiry

8.5 The bank will need to advise its customer in order to obtain authority to reply. This however, will not be necessary if the enquiry form itself contains a completed authority to reply, or if there is an omnibus authority.

Disclosure of information

8.6 When banks have authority to reply, they must still be careful not to disclose any information regarding the state of the account, or other confidential details that are not publicly available.

8.7 The answers given to a status enquiry appear to an outsider to be rather vague. However banks have certain ways of answering replies which will be understood by the recipient.

8.8 If the answer is 'considered good for your figures', or 'he is considered reliable and trustworthy', the recipient will know that the customer is likely to repay any borrowing, based on present information. A reply such as 'we confirm he has an account with us' or 'we cannot speak for your figures' would tend to warn the recipient that the customer may have difficulties repaying the borrowing. These replies do not suggest that the customer is unreliable, just that the bank is unable to reply through lack of knowledge of its customer, or that there have been no serious problems in the past. In the case of a limited company customer where the bank knew that there were charges registered against the company, the reply would state 'there are charges registered'. This is not breaking the secrecy rules, because these charges are registered at Companies House and therefore in the public domain. There is no suggestion in this reply of the lack of ability on the part of the company to repay any further borrowing.

The modern enquiry form system

8.9 The system relies upon the express authority of the person being enquired upon and standard forms are available (see sample format below). The enquirer sends the form directly to the bank of the person being enquired upon. If the authority is in order, the recipient bank will formulate its reply which will be sent directly to the enquirer, relying on the express authority to disclose information.

8.10 Banks may make a charge to the enquirer for this service.

8.11 The enquiry form does not always specify an amount of money. Some enquiries are made for purposes other than granting a loan. If a customer wishes to open an account at another bank, or take up a job requiring a reference, he may give the name of his bank as referee.

Sample standard enquiry form

XYZ Limited

Private and Confidential

The Manager
ABC Bank Plc
Town Branch
Town
County
AB12 3CD

Your Ref:
Our Ref:

Date: April 1994

Dear Sir

STATUS ENQUIRY REQUEST

I/We request your opinion as to the means and standing of:

(Name) A/C No

(Address)

and their/his/her trustworthiness in the way of business/normal business engagements to the extent of:

£

CONSENT

I/We consent to Bank Plc providing a reference on me/us to

Signed Date

(For and on behalf of)

I/We enclose our cheque for £ in payment of your tariff for this service.

Yours faithfully,

Director
XYZ LTD

UNIT 7, BUSINESS PARK, INDUSTRIAL ROAD, WORKPLACE, SHIRE TU7 6VW

The status reply form

Standard bank reply form

Name and address of enquirer	Name and address of replying bank

Dear Sir,

Re: Your enquiry dated

(Details of reply)

The bank is not a credit reference agency within the terms of s.145(8), Consumer Credit Act 1974. Disclosure of the sources and content of this opinion is not required.

This information is given without responsibility on the part of the bank or its officials.

8.12 The name of the customer is *never* stated on the reply form. The customer's initials are inserted where the form says 'Re'. This is to prevent any disclosure problem if the reply should fall into the wrong hands.

8.13 The note that the bank is 'not a credit reference agency within the terms of s.145(8), Consumer Credit Act 1974' is to notify the recipient that the bank is not carrying out the business of furnishing information relating to the financial standing of individuals or companies. If the bank were a credit reference agency anyone, on payment of a small fee, could ask for full details of any information held by the bank upon them. The only information that an individual can ask the bank to supply about himself is that which is held in the form of computer records. The Data Protection Act 1984 relates to this area.

8.14 The disclaimer should protect the bank if it makes any mistakes in giving the reply. Whilst it is possible that the disclaimer clause could be overturned under the Unfair Contract Terms Act 1977, the bank is thought to be safe if it can show that the reply is fair and reasonable enough to enable the recipient to rely upon it.

9 Liability of the bank to the recipient of a status reply

9.1 Provided the bank always states the disclaimer when giving a status reply (including a reply over the phone), it should be protected even if it has made innocent errors in the reply.

9.2 In *Hedley Byrne and Co Ltd v Heller and Partners Ltd* (1963) it was held that banks are not liable in tort to the recipient of a status enquiry for any errors in the reply, provided that the reply was made honestly and provided that the bank expressly declines to accept any responsibility when making that reply. The standard bank status enquiry reply form contains a disclaimer, and this disclaimer protects the bank from being sued for negligence. (Note that but for the disclaimer the House of Lords held that the bank would have been liable and the case established important principles applying to liability for negligent statements generally.)

9.3 The disclaimer applies to the recipient of the reply. It does not apply to the customer about whom the reply has been made and cannot protect the replying bank from an action for breach of contract or defamation by that customer.

9.4 In *Commercial Banking Co of Sydney Ltd v R H Brown and Co* (1972) a branch manager gave an obviously over-optimistic reply to a status enquiry despite the fact that his head office had advised him that they were worried about the account. On the facts the disclaimer clause had no effect and the bank was liable to the recipient of the reply because the court held that the reply was reckless and unjustifiably given that it amounted to a fraudulent misrepresentation. (This is a commonwealth case and thus not binding on English courts. However the English courts would take the decision into consideration and would be influenced by it.)

9.5 The Statute of Frauds Amendment Act 1828 provides that liability for *fraudulent misrepresentation* of a person's creditworthiness only arises if the statement is in writing and signed by the maker of the statement. Whatever the merits of a specific situation, by simply ensuring that a status reply is initialled the bank can take advantage of the protection afforded by this old Act.

9.6 In *London Association for the Protection of Trade v Greenlands Ltd* (1916) it was held that there is a social duty to answer a status enquiry from a business about the character and creditworthiness of a person with whom it has, or proposes to have, dealings. If the bank makes a reply that contains information which is untrue and defamatory, the bank is protected provided that:

- It believed that the information given was true;
- The person making the enquiry has a justifiable interest in receiving the information.

10 Data Protection Act 1984

10.1 If any organisation holds information about an individual on computer (including personnel records or salaries) the individual concerned is entitled to have access to that information on payment of a small fee.

10.2 Thus, any information a bank holds on its customers on a computer file must be given to the customer upon payment of the fee. This information usually consists of the name and address, financial information as shown on bank statements, and possibly other information. Any information held on manual records is not available to customers.

10.3 If there is any error in computer-based information the nature of which is harmful to the customer, he would be entitled to sue the bank for negligence or more simply for defamation. Negligence requires the customer to prove lack of reasonable care on the part of the bank – which would be difficult. Defamation requires the customer to show that the publication of the information held lowered his standing in the eyes of right-minded people. In order to avoid liability the bank would need to prove that what it said was true.

10.4 Banks must register with the Data Protection Registrar so that members of public can see the:

- Source of the data held by the bank;
- Purpose for which it has been obtained;
- Persons to whom the information can be disclosed.

Data protection principles

10.5 Banks must comply with the data protection principles set out in the 1984 Act, for example:

- *Principle One*: Personal information must be obtained and processed lawfully;
- *Principle Two*: Personal data shall be used only for the lawful purposes which are shown on the Register. Banks will therefore register all possible lawful purposes for which they may wish to use computerised information.

10.6 These principles and rules govern information disclosure in connection with activities such as status replies.

11 The Code of Banking Practice

11.1 The major clearing banks have subscribed to the Code of Banking Practice. The Code, which is overseen by the Banking Ombudsman, has no statutory standing. However, if a subscribing bank wilfully disregards it, then the Ombudsman will publicly state that the bank in question no longer subscribes to the Code. The second edition of the Code came into effect in March 1994, apart from the section on pre-notification of charges which came into force on 31 December 1996. The Code applies only to personal customers, as defined by the code.

Main points of the Code

11.2 The main points are that

- Banks will deal fairly with their customers.
- Customers will have a maximum liability of £50 for unauthorised withdrawals under cash cards, debit cards and credit cards when these withdrawals have arisen prior to notification to the bank (more properly called the 'card issuer').

  The only exception to the £50 maximum will arise if the bank can prove fraud or gross negligence on the part of the customer. An example of gross negligence would be the writing of the PIN number on the card itself by the card holder.
- Banks will always satisfy themselves as to the identity of prospective customers when opening accounts.
- Written explanations of key features of the more common services will be provided.
- Full written details of the basis of charges and interest will be provided.
- Banks will give reasonable notice when closing credit accounts.
- Banks will provide on request details of how they deal with status enquiries.
- Banks and building societies will provide new customers with a written summary or explanation of the key features of the more common services that they provide. This will include an explanation, when accounts

are held in the names of more than one customer, of the rights and responsibilities of each customer.

- Written terms and conditions of a banking service will be expressed in plain language and will provide a fair and balanced description of the relationship between the customer and bank or building society.
- Banks and building societies will tell customers how any variation of the terms and conditions will be notified. Banks and building societies will give customers reasonable notice before any variation takes effect.
- Banks and building societies will ensure that they will give no less than 14 days' notice of the amount to be deducted from their customers' current and savings accounts in respect of interest and charges for account activity accumulated during the charging period. Banks and building societies which have not introduced such systems will disregard the charges to be applied to customers' accounts for any charging period if those were incurred solely as a result of the application of charges for the previous charging period.
- Each bank and building society will have its own internal procedures for handling customers' complaints fairly and expeditiously.
- Banks and building societies will inform their customers that they have a complaints procedure. Customers who wish to make a complaint will be told how to do so and what further steps are available if they believe that the complaint has not been dealt with satisfactorily either at branch or more senior level within the bank or building society.
- Banks and building societies will ensure that all their staff who deal directly with customers are made aware of their institution's internal complaints procedure and are able to help customers by giving correct information about it.

11.3 Banks subscribing to the code will be expected to belong to one or other of the following, the:

- Banking Ombudsman Scheme;
- Finance and Leasing Association Conciliation and Arbitration Scheme;
- Consumer Credit Trade Association Arbitration Scheme;
- Building Societies Ombudsman Scheme.

11.4 *Note*: The Code applies to banks, building societies and card issuers such as Visa.

The significance of the code

11.5 The Code of Banking Practice forms the basis on which the Banking Ombudsman will determine good practice in order to rule in disputes submitted to him. Since the Banking Ombudsman can make binding awards of up to £100,000 against a bank subscribing to the scheme, personal customers, as defined by the Code, will no doubt prefer to take disputes to the Ombudsman rather than to the courts. Thus, it will probably be more important for banks to comply with the Code, in the case of personal customers, than to comply with strict legal requirements, especially in the case of cash and debit cards where there is very little case law.

Summary

Now that you have studied this unit, you should be able to:

- **appreciate what is meant by the terms 'banker' and 'customer';**
- **understand the contractual basis of the banker-customer relationship and how this contract can be affected by special authorities;**
- **list the duties of a bank to its customer;**
- **understand how notice of trust can affect the bank's duty to repay deposits;**
- **appreciate the extent to which a bank has a duty to advise a customer in special situations;**
- **understand a bank's duty of secrecy and how this is affected by case and statute law;**
- **list the obligations of a customer to his bank and know the various cases which govern these obligations;**
- **understand the nature of banker's references;**
- **understand a bank's liability to the recipient of a status reply;**
- **understand the implications of the Data Protection Act 1984 to banks;**
- **understand the significance of the voluntary Code of Banking Practice.**

Self-assessment questions

1 A cheque is presented which is properly drawn, not stopped and backed by adequate funds. However, you know the cheque was drawn for an illegal purpose. Which of the following is correct?

(a) The cheque can be paid so long as it is not 'stopped'.

(b) The cheque must be dishonoured.

(c) The bank can pay the cheque so long as there are sufficient funds in the account.

(d) The bank can pay the cheque so long as the customer's signature is valid.

2 An unsatisfactory account is in credit and the bank wishes to close the account.

(a) The bank must give 'reasonable' notice.

(b) The bank can close the account at once.

(c) The bank can close any account by giving one week's notice.

(d) The bank can close any account by giving one month's notice.

3 (i) Which case supports your answer for Question 2?

(a) *Tournier.*

(b) *Tai Hing Cotton Mill.*

(c) *MacMillan & Arthur.*

(d) *Williams and Glyn's v Barnes.*

(e) *Prosperity v Lloyds.*

(ii) Name any other authority, apart from the relevant case, which might apply.

4 A bank has a duty of secrecy to its customer but *Tournier* states that the duty ends in certain circumstances.

(i) Which circumstances apply?

(a) Compulsion of law.

(b) Customer's authority.

(c) In the bank's interest.

(d) Public duty.

(e) All of the above.

(ii) Give another, non-statutory, authority which governs the duty of secrecy.

5 Which of the following cases covers the implied terms of the banker-customer relationship?

(a) *Joachimson v Swiss Bank Corporation.*

(b) *Box v Midland.*

(c) *Lipkin Gorman v Karpnale Ltd.*

(d) *Barclays v Taylor.*

6 The bank paid a cheque on which the customer's signature was forged. The customer admitted to being careless in the custody of the cheque book. The customer was unaware of the forgery.

(i) Which case applies?

(a) *MacMillan & Arthur.*

(b) *Greenwood v Martins Bank.*

(c) *Tai Hing Cotton Mill.*

(ii) What is the position?

(a) The bank must refund.

(b) The customer must stand the loss.

(c) Estoppel applies.

7 Study the facts in Question 6 but assume that the customer knew of the loss of the cheque book well before the fraud happened. The customer did not report the loss.

(i) Which case applies?

(a) *MacMillan & Arthur.*

(b) *Greenwood v Martins Bank.*

(c) *Tai Hing Cotton Mill.*

(ii) What is the position?

(a) The bank must refund because estoppel applies.

(b) The customer must stand the loss because estoppel applies.

8 What is the position under the Code of Banking Practice regarding status replies on personal customers?

(a) Banks will respond to status enquiries on their customers only with the customer's express authority.

(b) Banks will always respond, under the implied terms of the banker-customer contract.

9 Which clauses appear on the standard status reply form?

(a) Disclaimer.

(b) Note on the Unfair Contract Terms Act.

(c) Note that the bank is not a credit reference agency.

(d) Note on Tournier.

10 Which case protects the bank if it acts in good faith but gives a 'wrong' reply to a status enquiry?

(a) *Commercial Banking Co of Sydney v Brown and Co.*

(b) *Hedley Byrne and Co Ltd v Heller and Partners Ltd.*

(c) *London Joint Stock Bank v MacMillan and Arthur.*

(d) *Tai Hing Cotton Mill.*

11 (i) Which case governs the bank's duty of secrecy when answering status enquiries?

(a) *Commercial Banking Co of Sydney v Brown and Co.*

(b) *Tournier.*

(c) *Banbury v Bank of Montreal.*

(d) *London Association for the Protection of Trade v Greenlands Ltd.*

(ii) What non-statutory authority applies in the case of personal customers?

12 Which case in question 11, whilst not binding in English law, would influence a decision in English courts if the bank manager gave an obviously over-optimistic or fraudulent reply to a status enquiry?

13 Which Act means that it is safer for the bank not to sign status replies?

14 Which case held that a signed status reply given fraudulently or deceitfully would render the bank liable on the reply?

15 Which Act influences whether a bank keeps information on customers on computer or on manual records?

16 Which Act could overturn the disclaimer clause on a status reply form?

17 What is the maximum award which the Banking Ombudsman can make to personal customers?

18 You recently gave the following reply to a status enquiry on your customer which came from another bank: 'Considered respectable and should prove good for your figures and purpose (36 monthly instalments of £100).'

As a result of your reply, the hire purchase company lent the customer £2,500 excluding interest. This customer has now defaulted and disappeared.

It now transpires that on making the reply, the bank inadvertently looked at the record of another customer with a similar name. If the bank had looked at the records of the customer concerned, it would have given an unfavourable reply.

The hire purchase company now hold you responsible for this bad debt. What is the position?

Further reading

- Laidlaw, A and Roberts, G — Chapter 1, *Law Relating to Banking Services*, 2nd edition 1992, Bankers Books.
- Milnes Holden, J — Chapter 1, *The Law and Practice of Banking*, Vol 1, 5th edition 1991, Pitman
- Raby, P — Chapter 1, *Law Relating to Banking Services*, 2nd edition 1992, Pitman
- Morris, S — Chapter 17, *Financial Services: Regulating Investment Business*, 2nd edition 1995, FT Law & Tax

Unit 2

Building Society-Investor Relationship

Objectives

After studying this chapter, you should be able to:

- **define a building society;**
- **describe the main functions of a building society;**
- **understand how building society law has evolved;**
- **outline the current legal framework within which building societies operate;**
- **understand the automatic and adoptable powers available to a building society;**
- **describe the constitutional basis of an individual building society, with special reference to its memorandum and rules, statutory limits which apply to assets and liabilities and the duties of directors and officers;**
- **understand the Building Societies' Investor Protection Scheme;**
- **describe how mergers and takeovers take place between building societies;**
- **describe how a building society can transfer its business to a public limited company.**

1 What is a building society?

1.1 Building societies originated as non-profit making, self-help institutions in the early part of the Industrial Revolution. The earliest records of a building society are those relating to Ketley's Building Society, founded in Snow Hill, Birmingham in 1775. There were almost certainly similar earlier bodies.

Terminating societies

1.2 The 18th and early 19th century building societies were *terminating societies*. Their functions were simple. There would be a fixed number of members who would elect officers to act on their behalf and agree a set of rules. All would agree to save regularly in order to fulfil their ambition of home ownership. Once the fund had grown sufficiently to build a number of houses, the members would hold a ballot to determine those to get the first houses available. The process would continue and further ballots would be held until all the members had a house, at which stage the society would terminate, its purpose having been fulfilled.

1.3 The early societies grew rapidly, with demand for their services fuelled by the need for housing in the new urban areas. Their growth was greatest in the Midlands and North of England, where industrial activity was greatest.

1.4 In 1836 the Benefit Building Societies Act was the first formally to recognise societies, requiring them to have their rules registered with the Certifying Barrister. The title of this official was eventually to become the Chief Registrar of Friendly Societies, and the Chief Registrar's office continued to be responsible for supervision and regulation until 1986.

Permanent societies

1.5 In the mid-19th century, permanent building societies began to evolve. Their founders recognised that there was a need for financial institutions which would be able to facilitate savings and create mortgages on an ongoing basis, without an upper limit on the number of members. This model of operation soon came to supersede the terminating society.

Mutual status

1.6 One key aspect of building societies was that they started as (and remain) mutual institutions, owned by their members. With the exception of one Dublin based society founded whilst the Republic of Ireland was part of the UK, all societies operate on the basis of 'one member, one vote'.

Core purpose

1.7 Building societies to this day retain their core purpose – that of raising a stock or fund from members and depositors and making secured advances on residential land. Until 1986, this was their only purpose. The Building Societies Act 1986 Act broadened their powers but still stated (s.5(1)) that this would continue to be their 'principal purpose'.

1.8 Essentially, a building society is a simple organisation. It receives mostly retail savings from the public and makes loans, mainly on residential mortgages. About 80% of liabilities raised are channelled into mortgages, with the remainder in liquidity (15–18%) and fixed assets.

2 Background to building society legislation

2.1 The statutory operational basis was originally laid down in Victorian times. In 1871 a Royal Commission found that there were over 2,000 building societies trading in the UK, which implied a need for formal regulation. With the Chief Registrar as regulator, building societies were obliged for the first time to make formal accounting returns. More importantly, the Building Societies Act 1874 recognised societies as separate 'bodies corporate' with limited liability, though they have never been permitted to use the word 'limited' in their names.

2.2 The 1874 Act was clearly inadequate to control a fast growing movement. Though the majority of institutions were sound, abuses of funds became apparent and in some cases fairly large institutions lurched out of control. In

1891 the largest building society, the Liberator Permanent, stopped withdrawals and inevitably collapsed in the following year. The crisis grew as six more societies went under. The total assets of the industry fell for three consecutive years as the industry's largest ever crisis of confidence brought a run on funds. The Building Societies Act 1894 brought matters under control, requiring societies to produce much more detailed accounts and prohibiting them from lending on anything other than mortgages secured by first charge. This regime was to continue until the provisions of the 1874 and 1894 Acts were repealed by the 1986 Act (having first been consolidated by the Building Societies Act 1962).

2.3 The progress of building societies continued into the first part of the 20th century. Their increasing profile was boosted by several mergers, notably those creating the Halifax and Abbey National, both during the interwar years. Branch offices were opened for the first time in the 1920s. Many societies which had operated on a part-time basis started to recruit full-time staff. The interwar years were a golden period for societies, despite the prolonged depression of the 1930s.

2.4 The number of societies fell rapidly after the 1939–45 War, though their assets increased continuously. There was a tendency towards larger units, operating in wider geographical catchment areas.

2.5 In 1958 another scandal rocked the industry with the failure of the State Building Society. It transpired that this had been used to fund property speculation. The Building Societies Act 1960 tightened legislation to prevent a recurrence, with societies limited to lending a maximum of 10% of their funds on 'special advances' (mainly corporate loans and higher value loans). This requirement is the earliest version of what is termed 'nature limits'.

2.6 Nearly all the Acts relating to societies were consolidated in 1962.

2.7 By the 1970s, building societies were large players in the financial sector. The largest five societies resembled banks, with national networks of branches and agency offices. The industry had a dominant position in the savings market, mainly accepting money on a instant access basis. They also monopolised mortgage provision. The latter occurred due to government monetary controls on banks in pursuit of economic objectives, but was reinforced by the existence of a Building Societies Association 'recommended interest rate' structure – in effect, a cartel, tolerated by the government as something which stabilised the mortgage market. The effects of this were to keep mortgage rates down to create a situation where demand for funds almost constantly exceeded supply. The cartel broke down in 1983.

2.8 By the late 1970s there was a strong drive in many sectors for deregulation. The Wilson Committee was set up to look at the workings of the financial system. It felt that building societies could do more if freed from the constraints of legislation. It also favoured a 'level playing field' to bring about competition on an equal basis between different types of institution. The building societies were lobbying in their own right for greater powers to move into mainstream banking services and in the early 1980s the Spalding Report became the focal point of their drive for new legislation.

2.9 These forces, together with a government committed to bring about greater choice and competition, led eventually to the Building Societies Act 1986, most of which came into effect on 1 January 1987.

Student Activity 1

Recap on the previous sections and consider what might be the benefits and drawbacks of deregulation and the abolition of the building society interest rate cartel.

3 The Building Societies Act 1986

3.1 The Act introduced both *enabling* provisions and *regulatory* constraints. The enabling provisions brought building society powers more in line with those enjoyed by retail banks. The regulatory constraints set down a thorough regulatory and supervisory regime with the main intention of ensuring that the deposits of customers would be protected in a higher risk environment.

3.2 The Act stopped short of giving building societies the same powers as banks for several reasons. Although the larger societies were considered to be able to operate safely and securely with existing structures in place, or at least 'buy in' expertise where necessary, the building society industry as a whole was in 1986 made up of a wide range of organisations from the very large to the very small, some of the latter with less than a dozen staff. The Act therefore has to cater for a diverse group of institutions. When difficult business conditions arose in the late 1980s and early 1990s, it was not only the smaller societies that made mistakes. This perhaps justifies the thinking behind the legislation.

3.3 The Act provided for building societies retaining their *mutual* status. Mutuality implies 'interdependence' – two groups (savers and borrowers) facilitating their needs through an organisation of which most were members. For those societies disappointed at not being brought into the banking arena, the Act also conferred powers to *transfer business to a public limited company* – in effect to shed mutual status and become a bank, regulated by the Bank of England.

3.4 As mentioned above, the pre-1986 only purpose of a building society became the *principal purpose*, admitting new purposes if the society, with the agreement of members, so desired. To ensure that societies complied with this principal purpose, the regulator was given specific powers and *nature limits* were laid down, mainly in respect of commercial assets.

3.5 To bring societies more in line with company requirements, the Act introduced the need for each society to have a *memorandum*. This has to contain the name and registered address of the society as well as its powers, both automatic and those adopted by special resolution of the members. In addition, the constitution of societies would be laid down in the *rules*, as was the case prior to 1986. The rules are a contract of membership between the members and the society and are broadly equivalent to the articles of association of a limited company. The Act lays down minimum requirements for the content of both the memorandum and the rules.

3.6 The Act established a new regulator called the *Building Societies Commission*. This new body replaced the Chief Registrar of Friendly Societies, though the Central Office of the Chief Registrar retains responsibility for (mainly) administrative duties and registration of constitutional matters. (The Building Societies Commission is considered in more detail in Unit 20.)

3.7 Building societies' *liabilities* are regulated in two ways. There is a limit on the amount of funding which can be raised from 'non-retail' sources. This was originally set at 20% but has been increased successively by statutory instrument to the present limit of 50%. In addition, at least 50% of the share and deposit capital must be in shares: s.8.

3.8 Building societies assets are also subject to controls through 'nature limits' (discussed below) and a maximum liquidity requirement laid down by the Building Societies Commission, currently 33.3%.

3.9 Minimum capital adequacy requirements are laid down by the Building Societies Commission.

3.10 Under s.34, building societies may provide a range of financial services, with six categories of service set out in Schedule 8, also discussed below. To adopt some of these powers, a society must have a 'qualifying asset holding' – currently minimum £100 million total assets.

3.11 Until the 1986 Act, societies were unable to own or have equity in subsidiary or associated companies. The Act empowers societies to do so, within prescribed limits.

3.12 The membership basis of building societies was largely unchanged by the 1986 Act. Building societies continue to have shareholders, who are part-owners and have voting rights, and depositors, who are creditors with no membership rights. It did, however, create a new type of member called a 'borrowing member'. In practice, borrowing members have few rights in comparison with investing members.

3.13 A building society remains a distinct legal entity. It is a unique type of body corporate. It must have the words 'building society' (or Gaelic or Welsh equivalent) in its name. The Act also prohibits any business from calling itself a building society if it is not registered as such with the Central Office.

4 Nature limits

4.1 All lending involves risk. Traditional mortgage lending for residential homes is far less risky than other types of lending, such as credit cards and unsecured personal loans. The government wanted to allow building societies into a broader lending market but was keen to establish a regime whereby the temptation of high margins on high risk business would be tempered somewhat. To achieve this, the Act lays down requirements on the composition of commercial assets.

4.2 Section 10(1), Building Societies 1986 Act states:

A building society may make advances to members (in this Act referred to as 'advances secured on land') secured by:

(a) a mortgage of a legal estate or, as provided under subsection 6 below, an equitable interest in land in England and Wales or Northern Ireland, or

(b) a heritable security over land in Scotland ...

4.3 Equitable interests referred to above are laid down by statutory instrument and are extremely restrictive. (You are not expected to know these.)

Commercial assets

4.4 Commercial assets are the total assets of the society less liquidity and fixed assets. The bulk of commercial assets is in mortgage advances.

4.5 The Act created three categories of commercial asset:

- Class 1 – there are four criteria to be satisfied for an asset to be a class 1 advance: s.11(2):
  - loans to individuals (which includes joint mortgages)
  - fully secured (that is, the loan to value must not exceed 100%)
  - on land for residential use (at least 40% for owner-occupation of the mortgagor or a dependant relative)
  - first charge only.
- Class 2 includes any loan secured on land which does not satisfy one or more of the class 1 criteria and is either a first or second charge. Class 2 is mainly commercial mortgages in practice: s.11(2).
- Class 3 is any commercial asset not included in classes 1 and 2. This includes, *inter alia*, unsecured loans and overdrafts, loans on mobile homes, bridging loans and the value of subsidiary bodies: ss.15 and 16. Unsecured loans can only be made to private individuals and total indebtedness cannot exceed £25,000 (£15,000 on mobile homes – this has to be aggregated with any other class 3 borrowings). (Very few, if any, societies consider loans on mobile homes.)

4.6 The maximum and minimum proportions of assets in each category have been varied since the Act was passed. Societies are currently required to have no less than 75% of commercial assets in class 1 (basically, orthodox residential lending business), no more than 25% in class 2 and no more than 15% in class 3.

4.7 In practice, the nature limits have worked well. In a tighter lending market during the 1990s, most of the societies which encountered difficulties have been those who have moved into class 2 and 3 business too willingly. Nevertheless, there is a strong lobby for reform of the limits, which are considered by some to comprise a regulatory strait jacket on larger institutions.

Student Activity 2

1 Why did the 1986 Act fall short of providing societies with the same powers as retail banks? *(Paragraph 3.2)*

2 What are the purposes of the memorandum and rules of a building society? *(Paragraph 3.5)*

3 What are the criteria for class 1 advances? *(Paragraph 4.5)*

4 Classify the following as class 1, 2 or 3 assets.

(a) An overdraft.

(b) A 70% loan to the dependant mother of a borrower who wants to buy a bungalow.

(c) A loan on a factory to XYZ Limited, to be fully secured on the land.

(d) A bridging loan to an individual. *(Paragraph 4.5)*

5 Provision of services

5.1 Schedule 8 of the 1986 Act sets down six categories of services which can be provided by societies in addition to their core business.

5.2 To offer any of these services the society must adopt the power to do so by special resolution passed by at least 75% of those voting at a general meeting. Many societies adopted the full range of powers shortly after the Act came into effect whether they were contemplating offering them or not. This removes the need to return to the members each time new powers are required.

5.3 The six categories are:

- Banking services;
- Investment services;
- Insurance services;
- Land services;
- Trusteeship services;
- Executorship services.

Banking services

5.4 Banking services must be offered by the building society and not through a subsidiary. These include money transmission and both secured and unsecured lending, as well as foreign exchange. Banking services can be provided to individuals but not to companies, though this is to change in 1996.

5.5 This power enabled societies to compete more directly for current account business, and most of the larger societies have such accounts, though some aim deliberately to attract higher net worth (and therefore lower risk) customers.

Investment services

5.6 Investment services include unit trusts, investment management, portfolio planning and a full range of related activities. Only the very largest societies have moved into this field, though most societies sell financial products regulated by the Financial Services Act 1986 as 'tied agents' of insurance companies.

Insurance services

5.7 Insurance services include the power to wholly own a life insurance company. Many large societies, such as Halifax, Nationwide and Woolwich, set up companies of their own. Some moved into this area by buying an existing company. Britannia acquired FS Assurances and renamed it Britannia Life. Halifax bought Clerical and Medical but operates the company as a separate brand.

5.8 The Act permitted societies to own a maximum 15% equity stake in a general insurer. Since 1993, they have been able to wholly own a captive insurance company solely for the purpose of writing mortgage indemnity guarantee (MIG) policies. In 1996, societies were empowered to wholly own a 'personal lines' general insurance company, providing, for example, motor and travel policies.

Land services

5.9 Land services includes estate agency, property listing and survey/valuation services. Many societies encountered problems due to either acquiring or setting up estate agency networks prior to the property slump of the 1990s. Some have divested themselves of these holdings, whilst others claimed to have 'ridden the storm'.

Trusteeship and executorship services

5.10 Very few societies have entered trusteeship or executorship service provision.

6 Constitutional matters

Memorandum

6.1 Each building society must have a memorandum. This is similar to the requirement under the Companies Act 1985 for a limited company to have a memorandum of association.

6.2 A building society memorandum must include the:

- Name of the society;
- Address of the principal office;
- Principal purpose, which must be consistent with s.5(1) of the 1986 Act;
- Adoptable powers which have been adopted by the members.

6.3 A building society memorandum does not have to state that the society's members have limited liability or any statement with regard to capital. These are both requirements of limited companies' memoranda.

Rules

6.4 Every society must have a set of rules and these must be made available to members on request. The rules are the contract of membership and the constitutional framework of the society.

6.5 The 1986 Act lays down minimum requirements for the content of the rules (Schedule 2):

- Name of society and principal office;
- The manner in which the stock or fund will be raised;
- The manner in which the terms are to be determined on which shares are to be issued and how shareholders will be informed of changes in the terms on which shares are held;
- Whether preference or deferred shares are to be issued (they are not usually offered, except (curiously) in the North East of England;
- The manner in which advances are made and repaid and conditions of loans;
- The manner in which losses are to be ascertained and provided for;
- How membership may cease;
- How auditors are to be remunerated;
- Matters concerning election, co-option, removal, remuneration and compensation for directors;
- The powers and duties of the directors and other officers;
- Custody of title deeds and other documents of security;
- The form, custody and use of the society's common seal;
- Rights of members relating to calling, attending and voting at meetings;
- Distributions relating to winding up or dissolution.

6.6 The rules will generally set out very broad terms of business so that changes are not necessary. Most sets of rules follow a standard format, and the Building Societies Association publishes a set of 'model rules'.

6.7 Only the investing members can vote on new rules or rule changes. This requires a special resolution at a general meeting. Borrowing members can only do so if they also have a qualifying investment. To avoid a conflict arising, if the mortgage deed is at odds with the rules, the former takes precedence, being a legal contract between the society and its borrower.

Student Activity 3

1 To what extent may a building society own (a) a life insurance company and (b) a general insurance company? *(Paragraphs 5.7 and 8)*

2 Consider whether the power to diversify into insurance areas is beneficial to the society and to its members.

Membership

6.8 A building society has two types of member. These are investing members and borrowing members. The Act lays down minimum requirements for each, although a building society can make additional provisions in the rules.

6.9 *Investing members* are those with share accounts. These can be various types of account from instant access and notice accounts to term shares. Traditionally, most building society accounts offered were share accounts, but this has become less common in recent times. The main reason for societies offering retail savings accounts without voting rights is to prevent speculative investments from those seeking 'free shares' if the society decides to convert to public limited company status.

6.10 The minimum shareholding for membership varies from society to society. Prior to 1986 it was £1, but in most societies was this increased to £100 once the legislation was enacted.

6.11 Members have various rights, including entitlement to:

- Receive notices of general meetings;
- Attend and speak at general meetings;
- Vote at general meetings;
- Receive a summary financial statement.

6.12 In practice, the majority of members do not exercise their rights and indeed, few are aware of them. Various battles have been fought at general meetings including:

- Opposition to the takeover of the Hastings and Thanet Building Society by Anglia Building Society in the 1970s;
- Opposition to removal of the 'teetotal' pledge (through which directors had to be abstainers) at the Temperance Permanent Building Society, also in the 1970s;
- Contests for positions on the boards of the former Leeds Permanent and Nationwide by former executives.

6.13 Borrowing members may only vote on matters relating to mergers and plc conversion resolutions.

7 Directors

7.1 Boards of directors of building societies are charged with various duties and responsibilities under the 1986 Act. Failure to comply with these provisions is a criminal offence.

79.2 The directors can be full-time employees (or executive directors) or part-time directors (non-executive directors). The majority of building society directors are non-executive directors. It is common for various senior executives to be members of the board. The Act makes no distinction between executive and non-executive directors.

Directors' duties

7.3 Under the 1986 Act, the duties of a director are to:

- Be satisfied regarding adequacy of arrangements for assessment of security for any advance: s.13;
- Ensure that the chief executive and secretary have the requisite knowledge and experience necessary: s.59;
- Disclose interests in contracts into which the society is to enter: s.63;
- Not accept commissions in respect of loans or insurances: s.67;
- Disclose income from related activities: s.69;

- Ensure that the society keeps proper books of account and has satisfactory systems of control, inspection and report: s.71;
- Report to the Commission within three months of the financial year end that the last requirement has been met: s.71;
- Prepare each year:
  - an income and expenditure account
  - a balance sheet
  - a source and application of funds statement
  - group accounts if applicable (section 72);
- Sign the balance sheet – two directors and the chief executive must: s.80;
- Prepare an annual business statement: s74;
- Prepare a directors' report for submission to the AGM: s.75;
- Prepare a summary financial statement for members and depositors: s.76;
- Lay the accounts before the AGM and send copies to the Commission: s.81;
- Determine where the register of member will be kept: Schedule 2.

Statutory powers

7.4 The statutory powers of directors are to:

- Authorise linking of the society with a qualifying corporate body: s.18;
- Inspect the accounting records at any time: s.71;
- Petition for winding up of the society: s.89;
- Accept a transfer of engagements (takeover of a smaller society) where the Building Societies Commission waives the requirement for a special resolution: s.94;
- Authorise another person to countersign the receipt on the redemption of a mortgage: Schedule 4.

Statutory liability

7.5 Under s.112, directors incur liability if they:

- Accept deposits before authorisation: s.9;
- Attempt to alter, suppress, conceal, destroy or refuse to produce any document required by the Treasury: s.48;
- Provide false or misleading information to the Building Societies Commission: s.52;
- Supply false or misleading information to support an application for authorisation: Schedule 3.

8 Amalgamations and takeovers

Amalgamations

8.1 Section 93 provides a framework by which two or more societies may amalgamate to form a new society. Here the constituent organisations cease to exist and a new one is constituted. The new society has to have its own memorandum and set of rules.

8.2 To establish the new society there must be:

- Agreement on purpose or principal purpose and extent of powers to be contained in the memorandum;
- Agreement on the rules;
- Approval by each society of the terms of the amalgamation by:
    - a special resolution passed by 75% of those voting
    - a borrowing members' resolution passed by simple majority.

  Prior to this being done, each society must issue a statement to members concerning the proposal. The prescribed content of this statement is laid down in Schedule 16.
- Application to the Building Societies Commission for confirmation of the amalgamation; and
- The Central Office must be sent four copies of the memorandum and rules, each signed by the secretary.

8.3 If the Commission approves the amalgamation (s.95) the amalgamation can then go ahead. A certificate of incorporation is issued – this is effectively the new society's birth certificate.

8.4 Amalgamations are rare. It is much more common for one society to take over another.

Transfer of engagements

8.5 The takeover of one society by another is called a *transfer of engagements*. The transferor is the society being taken over. Historically, some transfers of engagements have been carried out, at least on paper, by the small society taking over the larger one. This has usually been to secure tax advantages – 'reverse takeovers' are rare in the building society industry.

8.6 The 1986 Act lays down requirements for transfers of engagements under s.94 and Schedule 16.

8.7 A transfer of engagements differs conceptually from an amalgamation in that the transferor society ceases to exist but the transferee continues. There is therefore no need for a new memorandum or rules.

8.8 The transferor society must pass a special resolution and a borrowing members' resolution under the same conditions as in 10.2 above.

8.9 In the event of a partial transfer of engagements, where only part of a society's operation is being transferred, only those affected have to vote (an 'affected shareholders' resolution' and an 'affected borrowing members' resolution'). These are only of theoretical importance, as no partial transfers have taken place since the Act was passed.

8.10 To accept the engagements of another society, the transferee society must either pass the same resolutions as those required for the transferor, or pass a resolution of the board instead, subject to Commission approval. The latter course of action is often deemed expedient when a very large society wishes to take over a very small one.

8.11 The transfer is subject to the approval of the Commission. Once this has occurred, Central Office registers the particulars. The property, rights and liabilities of the transferor then pass to the transferee.

9 Conversion to plc status

11.1 This is a highly topical issue, with 10 societies either having converted or proposing to do so. The first to become a plc was the Abbey National. Since then, Cheltenham and Gloucester has converted to join the Lloyds-TSB Group and others have followed to remain independent but operate under the Banking Acts rather than the Building Societies Act 1986. Most significant of all is the proposal of the Halifax Building Society, the largest in the UK, to convert in 1997. In addition to the obvious effects on the industry, there has been considerable public interest in proposed conversions, not least because it is now common to expect a free distribution of shares to existing members once the conversion takes place. The 'something for nothing' instinct will probably drive a strong lobby for further conversions in future.

9.2 A 'conversion' is really a transfer of engagements to a limited company. This can be to a new company established specially for this purpose or to an existing company.

9.3 The effect of a conversion is that the society ceases to be a mutual institution regulated by the 1986 Act. At law it becomes a bank, though several former societies which have converted avoid the use of the term 'bank' quite deliberately.

9.4 The drive towards conversion seems to originate in the dissatisfaction with the relatively restrictive regulatory regime in building societies compared with banks. This affects:

- Asset structure, particularly as nature limits do not exist under banking law;
- Restrictions on the ability to raise capital;
- Other statutory provisions contained in the Building Societies Act 1986, plus the enormous number of prudential notes and statutory instruments which affect their business complexion.

9.5 The conversion provisions are set out in ss.97–102 and Schedule 17 of the 1986 Act. The provisions are that:

- A building society may transfer the whole of its business to a company (its successor);
- The successor company must be:
  - formed for the purpose of assuming and conducting the society's business, or
  - an existing company which is to do the same;
  - if the successor company is especially formed for the purpose, the articles of association must contain the necessary 'protective provisions' (see below);
- The society must agree with its successor in a transfer agreement the terms of the transfer – these must comply with statute;

- The transfer must be approved by:
  - a requisite shareholders' resolution, and
  - a borrowing members' resolution;
- In the case of a new successor company, the requisite shareholders' resolution must be passed as a special resolution and passed on a poll where no less than 20% of those eligible to vote actually do so;
- In the case of an existing successor company, the requisite shareholders' resolution requires:
  - a 50% majority in favour by those qualified to vote, and
  - a vote in favour by members holding 90% of the value of shares of members who are qualified to vote.

9.6 As in the case of an amalgamation, a statement to members is required regarding the proposal. Confirmation by the Commission is also required.

9.7 Once the transfer is ratified, s.101, Building Societies Act 1986 states that no person can own more than 15% of the equity in the company for a period of five years. This effectively serves as a protective clause to prevent an immediate hostile takeover.

9.8 The transfer terms can allow distributions of funds to members or confer share rights in the new company. This effectively serves as a distribution of accumulated profits (reserves). To maintain stability of funding, most societies which have proposed conversion have announced a 'cut off' date retrospectively for such distributions, laying down a:

- Minimum balance requirement;
- Latest date by which this balance requirement would have to be invested.

9.9 These measures have not prevented speculative investments by so-called 'carpet baggers', many of whom have placed a minimum investment necessary for a vote with dozens of building societies.

Student Activity 4

1 What is the difference between an amalgamation and a transfer of engagements? *(Paragraphs 8.1–6)*

2 List the duties of directors under the 1986 Act. *(Paragraph 7.3)*

3 If the Nationwide Building Society proposed to take over a small, single office local society (with its approval), would the former have to propose a special resolution to do so? *(Paragraph 8.10)*

4 Explain some of the motives which have persuaded some societies to convert to plc. *(Paragraph 9.4)*

Summary

Now you have studied this unit, you should understand:

- **the origins of building societies, what they are and their traditional activities;**
- **the background to modern legislation and the main provisions of the Building Societies Act 1986;**
- **the regulatory framework, including the restrictions on liabilities and assets and powers to provide services;**
- **the constitutional structure of a society, with particular regard to the memorandum and rules;**
- **the role, duties and responsibilities of the directors of a society;**
- **how mergers take place;**
- **how conversion to plc status takes place.**

Self-assessment questions

1 The maximum indebtedness in respect of an unsecured loan to an individual is:

(a) £10,000.

(b) £15,000.

(c) £25,000.

(d) No limit laid down.

2 Which of the following are directly regulated by the 1986 Act?

(a) The maximum amount of class 1 assets.

(b) The maximum amount of class 2 assets.

(c) The minimum liquidity level of a society.

(d) The maximum liquidity of a society.

3 In order to adopt new powers, a building society must:

(a) Have a special resolution sanctioned by at least 50% of investing members.

(b) Have a special resolution sanctioned by at least 75% of investing members.

(c) Have a special resolution sanctioned by at least 50% of investing members and borrowing members.

(d) Have a special resolution sanctioned by at least 75% of investing members and borrowing members.

4 Which of the following require confirmation by the Building Societies Commission?

(a) A transfer of engagements.

(b) An amalgamation.

(c) A transfer to a new successor company.

(d) A transfer t[illegible] existing successor company.

5 A breach of duty by a director is:

(a) A criminal offence.

(b) A civil offence.

(c) Unlawful – the director will be required to comply forthwith.

(d) None of these, but considered unethical.

6 The equivalent of the rules of a building society in a limited company is:

(a) The memorandum.

(b) The articles of association.

(c) The certificate of incorporation.

(d) There is no equivalent.

7 What is the purpose of nature limits on the commercial assets of building societies?

8 For many years banks were required to have a minimum liquid assets figure, yet the building societies have a maximum liquidity figure laid down. Why do you think this is the case?

9 To what extent have building societies used the powers available to them under Schedule 8?

10 Having read through this unit, do you consider that the 1986 Act is too restrictive? Do you think that mutuality will survive?

11 Explain the process which a building society wishing to convert to plc has to follow.

12 (a) Define what is meant by building society membership and explain the relationship between mutuality and membership.

(b) Explain the rights and liabilities of building society members.

(c) Compare and contrast the positions of shareholders and depositors in building societies.

Further reading

- Boleat, M, Armstrong, R French, C and Coogan, M — Chapters 1–8, *Building Societies, the Regulatory Framework*, The Building Societies Association

Unit 3

Agency

Objectives

After studying this unit, you should be able to:

- **define the terms 'agent' and 'principal';**
- **explain how agency is created;**
- **differentiate between the types of agent;**
- **list and explain the rights and duties of a principal and agent each to the other;**
- **explain the position of an undisclosed principal;**
- **understand how agency may be terminated;**
- **explain the effects of the Powers of Attorney Act 1971 and the Enduring Powers of Attorney Act 1985;**
- **explain how a bank acts as an agent for its customers.**

1 Introduction

1.1 Agency underpins a number of aspects of the banker-customer relationship, and an understanding of basic agency principles is an essential prerequisite to understanding certain banker-customer situations.

Student Activity 1

Think about the words 'principal' and 'agent' and write down your definitions. Compare your definitions with the information below. In particular, note specific 'legal' ways in which your definitions differ from ours.

1.2 An agent is someone who acts on another's behalf, the other person being known as his principal. An agent can make *binding contracts* on behalf of his principal, which means that the principal must honour the contractual obligations entered into on his behalf by duly authorised agents. An agent does *not normally incur any rights or liabilities* in contracts entered into on behalf of his principal.

1.3 An undischarged bankrupt, a minor, or anyone who lacks contractual capacity can still be an agent, provided his principal has contractual capacity.

2 Types of authority

2.1 There are two types of authority:

- Actual authority;
- Ostensible authority.

Actual authority

2.2 Actual authority may be:

- Express;
- Implied.

Express authority

2.3 Express authority arises where the principal has given the agent clear instructions as to his duties. For example, the principal instructs the agent to purchase a specific machine at a specific price from a specific supplier. This is express authority as the agent has totally clear instructions from his principal which set out the extent of his authority.

Implied authority

2.4 Implied authority arises when the principal intends the agent to have authority, but has not stated this clearly in words. Certain situations exist where there is a considerable degree of implied authority, e.g. a company director is an agent of the company and has implied authority to bind the company; a partner is an agent of the partnership and has implied authority to bind the partnership in most aspects of its business. Note, however, that a bank will usually take express authority in the form of a mandate even where the required implied authority would be held to exist.

Ostensible authority

2.5 Even if the agent has no actual authority, there may have been a representation by words or deeds that a person is an agent of the principal. This can arise where:

- The principal by his words or deeds implies that someone is his agent: *Armagas Ltd v Mundogas SA, The Ocean Frost* (1986).
- Other authorised agents of the principal may by their words or deeds imply that someone else is also an agent of their principal.

2.6 Thus, in the second situation, if a third party is influenced by the behaviour of the 'principal' and acts upon the presumption that the agent actually is an agent, then the principal is estopped from denying the agency because of his conduct. The only time the principal can deny the agency is if the third party knew or ought to have known of limitations on the agent's authority.

2.7 Ostensible authority cannot exist if the third party does not know that the agent is acting for the principal: *McLaughlin v Gentles* (1919).

3 Creation of agency

3.1 Agency can be created by:

- Express agreement;
- Operation of law.

Express agreement

3.2 The agent may be appointed:

- Orally;
- By written contract;
- By deed:

By word

3.3 If appointed orally the agent can act for his principal in all matters except those involving him in the execution of a deed. Only an agent appointed by deed can execute a deed.

By written contract

3.4 The agent and principal can enter into a contract whereby the agent is empowered to act on behalf of his principal for a fee. Alternatively the contract need not be in writing, but can come into being by implication from the conduct of the parties. When a bank collects cheques for a customer, there is no formal contract, yet the bank is acting as the customer's agent. However, the bank will usually have opened the account with a signed mandate.

By a power of attorney

3.5 An agent who has to execute a deed on behalf of his principal must be appointed by deed. A power of attorney is a deed which appoints someone to act on behalf of someone else. Powers of attorney are regulated by the Powers of Attorney Act 1971 and, in the event of the mental incapacity of the principal, under the Enduring Powers of Attorney Act 1985.

Operation of law

3.6 This situation arises where the two parties concerned had no intention of acting as 'agent' and 'principal', or where in certain circumstances, the agent has had to exceed his authority without the principal's consent.

Agency from cohabitation

3.7 A wife living with a husband is entitled to pledge his credit for necessaries, e.g. food and clothing, which fall within her normal domestic responsibilities.

Agency of necessity

3.8 This applies when an agent acts in excess of his authority in an emergency when he cannot contact his principal for permission, e.g. a ship's master may need to perform certain acts to save a ship. In today's conditions, with methods of communication such as fax and e-mail, it is much easier to communicate and it is less likely in practice that there will be no contact between the parties.

3.9 The person claiming agency of necessity must show that:

- It was impossible to obtain the principal's instructions: *Springer v Great Western Railway Company* (1921) and *Great Northern Railway Company v Swaffield* (1874).
- There was a real commercial necessity for his action, e.g. livestock would

be at risk, perishable goods would be in danger of perishing, or lives would be at risk, and that he acted to protect these items in good faith: *Prager v Blatspiel, Stamp and Heacock Ltd* (1924).

- The actions taken were those reasonably necessary to save the principal's property or interests, and that (probably) the agent and principal were not strangers but had some preexisting, and probably contractual, relationship: *Jebara v Ottoman Bank* (1927).

By estoppel

3.10 When a principal from his words or conduct makes it appear to third parties that someone who is not in fact his agent is his agent, the principal cannot later reject the contract. The principal is estopped (prevented) from denying his agent's authority.

3.11 For agency by estoppel to arise:

- The principal must by his conduct or words make it seem that the 'agent' is his authorised agent.
- The third party must have considered that the agency existed.
- The third party must then have relied upon the agency existing, and altered his position relying on that fact.

By ratification

3.12 Ratification occurs when a principal confirms and adopts a contract made on his behalf by someone who had no authority to bind the principal, or someone who was exceeding his authority at the time the contract was made.

3.13 For ratification to occur:

- The principal must ratify the whole of the contract;
- Ratification must take place within a reasonable period of time after the transaction unless the principal and third party agree to the contrary: *Metropolitan Asylums Board Managers v Kingham and Sons* (1890).
- The principal must be aware of all the details of the contract, unless he deliberately chooses to ratify regardless of the details. Provided there is no fraudulent agreement between the principal and third party, choosing to ratify in total ignorance of the details will be binding: *Marsh v Joseph* (1897).
- The third party must have been aware that the agent was acting on behalf of his principal at the time the contract was arranged. An undisclosed principal cannot ratify: *Keighley, Maxsted and Co v Durant* (1901).
- The purpose of the contract must be legal.
- The principal must exist and have had contractual capacity both at the time of the original contract and at the time of ratification.

3.14 Whilst a contract is unlikely to be made on behalf of a natural person who did not exist but later does, i.e. an unborn child, existence is of particular importance in relation to limited companies. A limited company only comes into existence when it has received a certificate of incorporation issued by the Registrar of Companies. This can create a problem as the incorporation process can be a lengthy one (especially in the case of a public limited company) and the directors of the company to be formed may need to enter into certain contracts prior to incorporation. Because the company does not exist at this time, it cannot ratify the contract: *Kelner v Baxter* (1866). Thus, in order to bind the company, the contract must be adopted as a new contract after the company is incorporated. If the contract is not so adopted, the agent who entered into it is personally liable: Companies Act 1989.

3.15 Other situations arise where an individual will have limited or no contractual capacity:

- A minor, although a minor can ratify a contract after attaining majority;
- An enemy alien;
- A mentally incapacitated person.

4 Types of agent

Universal

4.1 Such agents are appointed by a power of attorney and can act on behalf of their principals in all matters.

Special agent

4.2 This is an agent appointed to act on behalf of his principal in a particular transaction which is not part of his normal business activities.

4.3 The principal is bound only by the authorised acts of his special agent and third parties should always check that the special agent has proper authority. Examples of special agents are estate agents, auctioneers and stockbrokers.

General agent

4.4 A general agent has authority to act on behalf of his principal in all business of a particular kind, e.g. a company director is a general agent of a limited company and a partner is a general agent of a partnership.

4.5 A general agent has implied authority to bind his principal in all matters in the ordinary business of the agent's business: *Watteau v Fenwick* (1893). A third party is not affected by any limitation of authority unless he knew of it.

Factor

4.6 A factor is defined in s.1, Factors Act 1889 as an agent who:

> ... has in the customary course of his business as such an agent authority either to sell goods, or to consign goods for the purpose of sale, or to buy goods, or to raise money on the security of goods.

4.7 Even if a factor who is in possession of goods with the principal's consent exceeds his authority, a sale will be valid so long as the third party does not know that the factor is exceeding his authority: s.2, Factors Act 1889.

Broker

4.8 A broker acts as a middleman between buyers and sellers and does not have possession of any goods of the principal.

Del credere agent

4.9 A *del credere* agent is one who undertakes responsibility for the payments due under the contract by the third party whom he has introduced to his principal.

4.10 For example, where a UK exporter is introduced to an overseas buyer by a confirming house, the confirming house will be responsible for indemnifying the UK exporter if the buyer does not pay. In this instance the exporter is the principal and the confirming house is a *del credere* agent. A *del credere* agency is usually, but not necessarily, evidenced in writing: *Galenel and Sons v Churchill and Sons* (1914).

Student Activity 2

Consider the various types of agent and consider which of the various types are likely to be encountered in a banking situation.

5 Duties of the agent to the principal

5.1 An agent must:

- Obey lawful instructions;
- Exercise skill and diligence;
- Personally perform the contract;
- Account to his principal for all money received;
- Not make a secret profit or taker a bribe;
- Avoid a conflict of interests;
- Maintain secrecy about his principals' affairs;
- Act in good faith.

Lawful instructions

5.2 The agent must act in accordance with his principal's lawful instructions and not exceed his authority: *Turpin v Bilton* (1843).

Skill and diligence

5.3 The agent must carry out his tasks with reasonable skill and diligence. What is reasonable depends upon whether or not the agent is paid. A paid agent, or one who holds himself out to have special skills, must exercise professional competence: *Beal v South Devon Railway Company* (1864). An unpaid agent (a gratuitous agent) is only liable to his principal for negligence committed in the course of agency, but cannot be sued if he fails to carry out his agency at all.

Personal performance

5.4 *Delegates non potest delegare*: literally 'a delegate cannot delegate'. Thus the agent must perform his task personally and not delegate it to someone else: *McCann and Co v Pow* (1975).

5.5 However, delegation is allowed where:

- The principal specifically authorises delegation: *De Bussche v Alt* (1878).

- Delegation is necessary for the proper performance of the task, e.g. when a customer asks his bank to buy shares, the bank must delegate the task to a stockbroker as the bank cannot deal on the Stock Exchange.
- The task does not require any particular skills or judgement, e.g. signing documents or sending notices: *Allam and Co Ltd v Europa Poster Services Ltd* (1968).
- An unforeseen emergency makes delegation necessary.

Account

5.6 The agent must pay over any money received from third parties to his principal.

Secret profit

5.7 The agent must not make a secret profit or to take a bribe or gain an advantage from his position: *Turnbull v Garden* (1869). If a secret profit is made, the principal can:

- Claim if from the agent: *Thompson v Meade* (1891);
- Dismiss the agent without notice: *Bulfield v Fournier* (1895);
- Refuse to pay the agent any agreed commission on the transaction in question;
- Repudiate the contract within a reasonable time of discovering the secret profit: *Oliver v Court* (1820);
- Take action for damages against the agent if he has suffered a loss due to the agent's actions – but he cannot take both the secret profit and sue for damages, it has to be one or the other: *Mahesan v Malaysia GOCHS* (1979); and
- Both parties to the bribe are liable to prosecution (under the Prevention of Corruption Act 1906) if the bribe is seen to be a criminal offence.

Conflict of interests

5.8 The agent must avoid a conflict of interest between two principals; an agent cannot be the agent of another principal without the prior permission of the original principal: *Fullwood v Hurley* (1928).

Secrecy

5.9 The agent must maintain secrecy regarding his principal's affairs. The agent must not disclose information to others, nor to use it for his own benefit: *Weld-Blundell v Stephens* (1920). If the agent does use information for his own benefit, the profit belongs to the principal: *Peter Pan Manufacturing Corporation v Corsets Silhouette Ltd* (1963).

Good faith

5.10 The agent must act in good faith and not to allow his own interests to conflict with those of his principal: *Boardman v Phipps* (1967).

Note: These are the duties *any* agent owes to his principal. The specific duties a bank owes to its customer are dealt with in sections 12 and 13.

6 Duties of the principal to the agent

6.1 The principal must:

- Pay the agreed fees and commission;
- Indemnify the agent.

Fees and commission

6.2 The principal must pay fees and commission to the agent as agreed and on the date agreed. If the agent commits a serious breach of contract where payment is due on completion, then he is not entitled to payment: *Mason v Clifton* (1863). If the agent commits only a minor breach of contract, i.e. if he performs the contract but not exactly according to its terms, then the agent is entitled to the agreed sum, less damages for the breach.

Indemnity

6.3 The agent is entitled to be indemnified for liabilities or losses, or reimbursement of expenses incurred in the proper performance of his agency: *Hichens, Harrison, Woolston and Co v Jackson and Sons* (1943).

An agent's lien

6.4 In addition to the right to fees/commission and an indemnity – considered above as *duties* of the principal – the agent may exercise a lien (a creditor's right to retain the goods of his debtor until the debt is repaid) over his principal's goods if his commission has not been paid.

6.5 A lien may be 'particular' or 'general'. A particular lien only extends to the specific debt in connection with which the goods are held. A general lien entitles the agent to retain possession of goods in connection with all monies owed and, at common law, also gave a qualified right to sell the goods if repayment was not made. This general lien applies to banks and in such cases is often called a 'banker's lien'.

6.6 *Note:* Under the EU Commercial Agent Directive, which came into force in the UK in January 1994, agents have a number of new rights. However, these rights apply only in the case of an agent for goods. As this book is primarily concerned with services, the EU directive is not covered.

7 Liabilities of an agent

7.1 Because an agent merely acts as a middleman between the principal and third party, he would not normally incur any liabilities to third parties. However an agent incurs liability to a *third party*:

- By agreement;
- For breach of warranty of authority;
- By signing a contract without indicating his status as an agent;
- By trade custom;
- where the principal is undisclosed;

and to his principal:

- For exceeding his authority where loss results;
- Through failure to exercise proper care and skill.

Agreement

7.2 The agent agrees to be personally liable, e.g. if he is a *del credere* agent.

Breach of warranty of authority

7.3 The agent must compensate any third party for loss caused when he asserts authority he lacks. This can apply when the principal does not actually have contractual capacity, or does not exist at the time the contract is made.

7.4 Furthermore, if the principal dies or becomes mentally incapable, the agent will be liable on any contracts entered into after the event, even though the agent does not know of the event. The agent is liable because he warrants to the third party that he has the authority to enter into a contract: *Yonge v Toynbee* (1910).

Signing without indicating his status

7.5 If the agent signs a cheque or a bill of exchange or contract without any indication that he is acting as an agent of the principal, then the agent may be personally liable on the cheque/bill/contract.

7.6 With a contract, if the agent identifies his principal and makes it clear that he is signing on behalf of his principal but then simply signs his own name, then the agent will not be personally liable: *Universal Steam Navigation Co Ltd v J McKelvie and Co* (1923).

7.7 With a bill of exchange, the agent is personally liable if he signs it without indicating his principal's name: s.26, Bills of Exchange Act 1882. However, if a cheque is printed with the name of a company that is the principal, the agent is not personally liable even if he does not sign with the addition of 'per pro' or 'for and on behalf of': *Bondina Ltd v Rollaway Shower Blinds Ltd* (1986). Thus, if a director signs a cheque the payee would have no rights against the director in the event of the cheque's dishonour. (Normally the words 'per pro' or 'for and on behalf of' would appear beside the company's name.)

Trade custom

7.8 If it is the custom of the trade that the agent undertakes personal liability, then the agent will be personally liable unless there are special circumstances.

Undisclosed principal

7.9 Where the agent does not disclose his agency, a third party may chose to enforce the contract against either the agent or the principal (when discovered) but not both (see section 9).

Exceeding his authority

7.10 The agent must compensate his principal when he exceeds his authority and renders his principal contractually liable to third parties.

Proper care and skill

7.11 The agent must compensate his principal when he is a paid agent who has not exercised proper skill.

8 Liability of the principal for the agent's torts

8.1 If an agent commits a fraudulent act whilst acting on his principal's behalf within the scope of his authority, then the principal will be jointly and severally liable with his agent. This applies even if the principal was unaware of the fraudulent act and gained no personal benefit from that act: *LLoyds v Grace Smith and Co* (1912).

9 The doctrine of the undisclosed principal

9.1 Where an agent has given the impression that he is acting on his own behalf, the third party may enforce the contract against either the agent or the principal once he knows the facts but cannot enforce the contract against both, the third party must choose one or the other: *Scarf v Jardine* (1882). However if the principal has paid the agent for the goods or services in good faith, the third party can only sue the agent: *Armstrong v Stokes* (1872). Once the third party has commenced an action against either the agent or principal, he cannot then go on and sue the other party if his first action is unsuccessful.

9.2 When an agent does not disclose his principal and acts outside his authority, the 'principal' is not liable at all; not can an undisclosed principal cannot ratify. The agent is personally liable to the third party.

9.3 When it is clear that the agent is actually acting as an agent, but when he does not disclose the identity of the principal, then the agent is not liable. This is because it is clear that he is the agent of someone else.

9.4 Unless the agent acted without authority or the principal's identity is a material factor in the contract, the principal can enforce the contract against the third party. For example, if a principal used an undisclosed agent to purchase theatre tickets for him from a theatre from which he had been banned, the principal could not sue for breach of contract if refused admission: *Said v Butt* (1920).

Student Activity 3

Summarise, in your own words, the rights and liabilities of an agent and consider how this concept of rights and liabilities may be relevant in a banking context.

10 Termination of agency

10.1 Agency can be terminated by:

- Act of the parties; or
- Operation of law.

Act of the parties

Mutual agreement

10.2 If both parties agree to terminate an agency, it is terminated.

Revocation by the principal

10.3 Revocation is where the principal withdraws the agent's authority to act on his behalf. If the agency has been created by a power of attorney, it cannot be revoked except in limited circumstances.

10.4 If the principal initially agreed not to revoke the agency, he can still revoke it but he may be liable for breach of contract to the agent.

10.5 If the agent has started to perform the agency and incurred liabilities for which he is entitled to reimbursement, the agency cannot be revoked: *Read v Anderson* (1884).

10.6 Any third parties dealing with the agent will not be affected by the revocation, unless they had specific or constructive notice of the revocation.

Renunciation by the agent

10.7 If the agent informs the principal that he no longer wishes to act for him the agency is terminated. However, the agent *may* be liable to the principal for breach of contract.

10.8 If the agency was created as an 'enduring power of attorney', and has been registered under the Enduring Powers of Attorney Act 1985 with the Court of Protection, the agency cannot be terminated (renounced), without the Court of Protection being given due notice.

Termination by operation of law

Fulfilment or frustration of purpose

10.9 If an agency is created for a specific purpose, then the successful completion of that purpose will end the agency. If the purpose cannot be fulfilled through no fault of either the principal or agent, then the agency is frustrated and will similarly terminate. For example, if the principal instructed his agent to purchase a specific item in an auction, specifying a maximum price to be paid, the agency would be terminated either if the agent purchased the item within the set price limit (fulfilment) or if the agent could not purchase the item because it was sold at a price above the limit set (frustration).

Illegality

10.10 If the agency becomes illegal it is immediately terminated. An example of this would be if the agent or principal were an enemy alien at the outbreak of war.

Death or mental incapacity of principal or agent

10.11 The death or mental incapacity of either principal or agent will normally terminate the agency. However, there are certain exceptions in connection with the Enduring Powers of Attorney Act 1985, and in connection with agency created by a power of attorney created as security.

Insolvency of the principal

10.12 The principal must have contractual capacity. An undischarged bankrupt or a company in liquidation does not have contractual capacity. In such a case the agency will be automatically terminated, even if the agent did not know of the circumstances. The exception is where a power of attorney has been given as security.

10.13 *Note*: the bankruptcy or liquidation of the agent does not automatically terminate the agency because the agent does not have to have contractual capacity. However, this may be grounds for the principal to revoke the agency.

Expiry of time

10.14 If an agency has been created to run for a specific period of time, e.g. whilst the principal is working abroad, it will terminate upon the expiry of the time period set.

11 Powers of attorney

Drawn under the Powers of Attorney Act 1971

11.1 A power of attorney is created by deed. The deed must be signed by the principal (donor) and witnessed.

11.2 Under s.1, Powers of Attorney Act 1971, the deed may be signed by another person if the principal is present and instructs this to be done, e.g. if the principal cannot read or write. In this situation there must be two witnesses to the deed.

11.3 A power of attorney can be either:

- Special; or
- General.

Special power of attorney

11.4 A special power of attorney is one which limits the agent to act in the way laid down in the deed, usually for a specific purpose.

General power of attorney

11.5 This creates a universal agent, i.e. one who can act on behalf of the principal in all matters without restriction, or with very little restriction.

11.6 A general power of attorney is often used if the donor (principal) is ill, or going abroad, or where a trustee or personal representative delegates his power.

Enduring Powers of Attorney Act 1985

11.7 This Act relates only to powers of attorney drawn up by individuals. If the deed states that the donor (principal) intends it to continue even if he subsequently becomes mentally incapable, and states that the donor has read or has had read to him and understood the contents, then the deed will be valid under the Enduring Powers of Attorney Act 1985. The donor must be mentally capable at the time the deed is executed. The attorney (agent) appointed under this deed must be either an adult or a trust company. There can be more than one attorney appointed (joint attorneys), but the attorney cannot be an undischarged bankrupt. (This differs from the usual situation where an agent can be an undischarged bankrupt.) A power of attorney drawn under the Enduring Powers of Attorney Act 1985 can give either special or general powers.

11.8 Whilst the donor remains mentally capable, the enduring power operates as an ordinary power of attorney, except that the agent cannot renounce his agency without giving written notice to his principal (donor).

11.9 When the donor becomes mentally incapable certain steps must be taken because the agent's power is suspended (not terminated). Full restoration of power will take place when these steps have been completed. The steps are:

- The agent must apply to the Court of Protection for registration of the deed, giving notice to the donor and any specified relatives.
- As soon as the application is made, the agent has a limited power to act so as to maintain the donor, e.g. to pay necessary bills such as medical expenses, heat and light. The agent can also act to prevent loss to the estate of the donor, e.g. for necessary repairs to property. The agent is also entitled to maintain himself; s.3(4) allows the agent to do what the donor might reasonably do to meet the agent needs, e.g. if the agent is the spouse of the donor, the agent will need to have access to money to enable them both to live on a day-to-day basis. The court may also authorise other action.
- When the court decides to register the power of attorney, the agent's powers are restored in full in accordance with the original deed.
- If the agent wishes to renounce the agency under a power of attorney he must give notice to the court.
- If for any reason the power is found to be invalid, or is revoked, the agent is protected. Any transaction with third parties will still be valid, unless the third party knew of the invalidity or revocation of the power of attorney: s.9.
- If a third party purchases the donor's property via the agent the purchase is valid provided that it takes place within 12 months of registration, or the third party makes a statutory declaration within three months of the purchase stating that he believed the agent had the power to act: s.9(4).

Student Activity 4

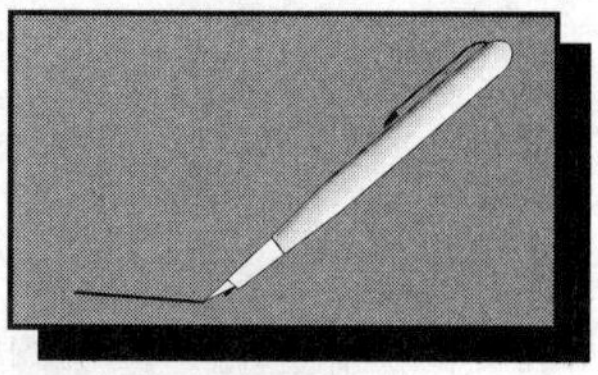

Do you have an example of a power of attorney in your branch. Under which Act is it drawn? How does the bank operate the account under this power of attorney?

Advantages of power of attorney

11.10 There are two main advantages to a power of attorney.

- First, if an agent is to have authority to act by deed, he must be appointed by deed. This would apply, for example, where the agent was to be involved on behalf of his principal in a legal conveyance of land (which must be executed by deed).
- Second, agency granted under a power of attorney cannot be revoked by the principal, nor can it be revoked by the death, mental incapacity, bankruptcy or liquidation of the principal, provided the agency is given to secure a proprietary interest or to secure the performance of an obligation owed to the donee (agent): s.4, Powers of Attorney Act 1971.

11.11 This second advantage is of particular interest to banks. If a bank has an equitable mortgage it may have taken this with a deed giving the bank a power of attorney to sell without recourse to the courts. The bank has the equitable mortgage as security against a loan, and this can be regarded as a 'proprietary' interest, or it may be regarded as an 'obligation' on the part of the customer to repay.

12 Banks as agents of customers

Student Activity 5

Consider the concept of agency as it applies to banks and list the ways in which a bank can act as the agent of a customer, then compare your list with the text which follows.

12.1 There are several ways in which a bank acts as an agent of a customer.

- *Collecting a customer's cheques.* The cheques are presented for payment to the drawee bank on behalf of the customer. The customer is normally, but not always, the payee of such cheques. The position of the collecting banker as agent is covered in Unit 11.
- *Obtaining foreign exchange and travellers' cheques* from overseas banks on behalf of its customers.
- Holding items in *safe custody*.
- *Stock and share transactions.* The bank approaches a stockbroker on behalf of its customer. (*Delegatus non potest delegare* does not apply here, because delegation to a stockbroker is essential for proper performance of the task.)

12.2 It is usual for the bank to share the commission on stock and share deals with the broker. The contract note issued by the broker, via the bank, to the customer will state that the commission is divisible, i.e. shared between the broker and the bank. This protects the bank against any claim that a secret profit has been made on the deal.

12.3 The other problem that may affect banks in relation to stock and share deals occurs when the bank itself not only carries out a stock or share deal for a customer, but also has knowledge of the company being dealt in, because that company is also a customer of the bank. This type of problem will usually arise when the bank not only deals in securities itself, but also has a separate department dealing with corporate finance. Information must not flow between the two parts of the bank, otherwise the bank could be gaining advantage and/or failing to maintain secrecy, about its principal's affairs. If such information were passed between departments, the bank could be guilty of insider dealing under the Company Securities (Insider Dealing) Act 1985. To prevent such information flows banks have 'erected' Chinese Walls (an invisible 'wall' through which information must not flow).

Banks and agency by estoppel

12.4 If a customer claims that the bank has acted in a manner that has caused him loss, or breached the rules of secrecy, then the bank may well be liable to the customer. However, if the customer by his words or deeds has caused the bank to believe that there was in fact an agency situation, then it will have agency by estoppel. For example:

- If a customer knows that his signature has been forged, but does not notify the bank, he cannot later deny the authenticity of the signature: *Greenwood v Martins Bank Ltd* (1932).
- If a customer regularly sends his wife into the bank to collect his statement, which is given to her in a sealed envelope addressed to the customer himself, and she opens the envelope containing the statement, the customer cannot then say that the bank has breached its duty of secrecy by releasing the statement. The bank would claim that it had released the statement to an agent of the customer who appeared to have the authority to collect it. Thus, by his conduct the customer has represented that his wife is acting as his agent.

13 Safe custody

13.1 Safe custody is a contract of 'bailment'. The customer is the bailor, i.e. the person who deposits the items for safe keeping, and the bank is the bailee. There is no obligation on the bank to accept items for safe custody under the implied terms of the banker-customer contract and the bank would reject bulky or undesirable items.

Gratuitous and paid bailees

13.2 When banks make a specific charge for safe custody, they are said to be paid bailees, and when no specific charge is made banks are gratuitous bailees. Legally a paid bailee is expected to exercise the best possible safeguards, whereas a gratuitous bailee is simply bound to take the same degree of care as would a reasonably prudent person with the same facilities at his command.

13.3 In practice the distinction is irrelevant because banks always keep safe custody items in the strong room and lay down strict key holding regulations. In other words banks always take the best possible safeguards with all safe custody items. In *Houghland v R R Low (Luxury Coaches) Ltd* (1962), it was held that the standard of care required by a bailee, whether paid or gratuitous, is the standard demanded by the circumstances of the particular case.

Liability for conversion of safe custody items

13.4 'Conversion' means dealing with someone's property so as to deprive him of possession of it. Good faith is no defence, conversion is a tort of strict liability, i.e. the actual act is enough, no mental element is required.

13.5 With safe custody, conversion can be committed in three main ways:

- Unauthorised release to someone other than the customer;
- Theft by a member of staff;
- Where the customer (bailor) is not the true owner of the item in safe custody

Unauthorised release to someone other than the customer

13.6 If the bank releases safe-custody items to an unauthorised person, it has no defence and is liable to the true owner for conversion.

13.7 If the signature of the true owner has been forged, the bank has no defence. The skill used in the forgery is irrelevant. Good faith and lack of negligence are no defence with forgery: *Langtry v Union Bank of London (1896).*

Theft by a member of staff

13.8 The practical position is that the bank would settle out of court to protect its good name.

13.9 In *Photo Production v Securicor* (1980), it was held an employer is not liable for the theft of safe-custody items by an employee other than one entrusted with the care of safe custody items. However, the bank, as employer, would have to prove that there had been no negligence, in other words the bank must prove that key holding regulations had been followed in order to be able to avoid liability for theft of safe custody items by bank employees.

Where the customer (bailor) is not the true owner of the item in safe custody

13.10 If the bank had already released the item to the bailor before it knew of the position, and before the true owner had taken steps to recover the item, there is no liability. All that would have happened would be that the return of the item to the bailor restored the *status quo.*

13.11 If the item is still in the bank's possession when the details of the true owner come to light, the bank must release the item to the true owner. If it is not clear who the true owner is, and if the two parties each claim the item, the bank will interplead. Interpleading means refusing to release the item to either party until either a court order is issued, or the two parties both agree and authorise the release of the item to one of them.

Liability when items in safe custody are damaged or destroyed

13.12 The level of care a bank must take in protecting items in safe custody is the same, whether the bank is a paid or gratuitous bailee.

Student Activity 6

Recently your branch strong room was flooded after a heavy storm and several of the boxes stored there were covered with water. An important customer tells you that a valuable stamp collection contained in his box has been ruined. He estimates the value to be £2,000 and tells you he will claim against the bank. What is the bank's position?

Summary

Now that you have studied this unit, you should be able to:

- **explain how agency is created;**
- **explain the difference between various types of agents;**
- **explain the rights and duties of principal and agent *inter se*;**
- **understand the effects of the doctrine of the undisclosed principal;**
- **describe the ways in which agency is terminated;**
- **understand the effects on agency of the Powers of Attorney Act 1971 and the Enduring Powers of Attorney Act 1985;**
- **explain the ways in which a bank acts as an agent for its customers.**

Self-assessment questions

Note: there may be more than one correct answer to the multi-choice questions in this unit.

1 An estate agent is a:

(a) General agent.

(b) Special agent.

(c) Universal agent.

(d) *Del credere* agent.

2 A principal is liable for the torts of his agent committed on the principal's business. Which case applies?

(a) *Port Swettenham.*

(b) *Lloyds v Grace Smith.*

(c) *Said v Butt.*

(d) *Langtry v Union Bank.*

3 A buys a brooch from T but does not disclose his agency. The transaction is within the authority given by P. Against whom does T have a valid claim should the transaction not be fulfilled?

(a) A only.

(b) P only

(c) P or A, provided P has not paid the consideration to A.

(d) P and A.

4 A customer's wife has collected his bank statement from the bank each week for many years. This is an example of:

(a) Agency of cohabitation.

(b) Agency of estoppel.

(c) Agency of necessity.

(d) Special agent.

5 Which of these automatically terminates an agency which has not been created by power of attorney?

(a) Death of the agent.

(b) Death of the principal.

(c) Bankruptcy of the agent.

(d) Bankruptcy of the principal.

(e) Insanity of the agent.

(f) Insanity of the principal.

6 A acts within his authority and makes a contract with T. However, unknown to A, P had suddenly died just before the time the contract was made. What is the position?

(a) T can sue P on the contract.

(b) T can sue only A for breach of warranty.

(c) T can sue P or A.

(d) T has no rights at all.

7 A acts outside his authority, but T thought that A was acting within the authority of P because of P's conduct.

(i) What type of agency is this?

(a) Cohabitation.

(b) Estoppel.

(c) Necessity.

(d) None of these.

(ii) Who is liable to T?

(a) A only.

(b) A and P.

(c) A or P.

(d) P only.

8 What is the term used to describe the release of safe-custody items to someone who is not entitled to them?

(a) Errata

(b) Commission.

(c) Degradation.

(d) Conversion.

9 A bank employee steals some valuable jewellery which had been held in safe custody. At law, in order to avoid liability to the customer, the bank would have to establish that:

(a) The employee was not one who was entrusted with safe-custody duties.

(b) The bank had followed its laid down safe-custody procedures, e.g. proper control of safe keys and safe-custody items.

(c) The jewellery belonged to the customer.

(d) That it was a gratuitous bailee.

10 Which case governs the answer(s) to Question 10?

(a) *McLaughlin v Gentles.*

(b) *Langtry v Union Bank.*

(c) *Port Swettenham.*

(d) *Photo-Production v Securicor.*

11 A valuable item in safe custody is damaged by a flood. The bank had taken all normal precautions. Which of the following statements is true?

(a) The bank is liable to compensate the customers.

(b) The bank is not liable.

12 You release an item from safe custody to a stranger who has forged your customer's signature with great skill. *Langtry v Union Bank* establishes that:

(a) The bank is not liable because the signature appeared genuine.

(b) The bank is not liable because it acted in good faith and checked the signature to see that it appeared correct.

(c) The bank is liable for conversion.

13 As regards safe custody:

(a) The bank must accept share certificates.

(b) The bank must accept small deed boxes.

(c) The bank must accept all items.

(d) The bank need accept only such items as it wishes.

14 The bank has granted an overdraft facility of £10,000 to Arthur, which was unsecured. The bank now learns that, unknown to it, Arthur had negotiated the borrowing on behalf of Percy, within the authority given by Percy. The bank wishes to call in the borrowing. Whom can it sue? The overdrawn account is in the name of Arthur.

15 How would your answer to Question 14 differ if Arthur's authority from Percy had been to negotiate an overdraft of £5,000? As before the bank was unaware of Percy's involvement when the overdraft was agreed. An overdraft of £10,000 exists in Arthur's name.

16 Peter wrote to Albert asking him to negotiate an overdraft of £20,000 with the bank on his (Peter's) behalf.

Later, before Albert visited the bank, Peter verbally told Albert that the facility he wanted was £15,000. Subsequently, Albert visited the bank and showed the letter to the branch manager. The bank agreed an overdraft of £20,000 in the name of Peter.

Who is liable to repay the bank?

17 What is the extent to which a wife is an agent of her husband as regards the incurring of indebtedness.

18 Advise the bank how it should deal with the following situations.

(a) Mrs Jones is in the habit of collecting her husband's statement from his bank every month. Recently, Mr and Mrs Jones separated, and Mr Jones now objects that this month's statement was handed to Mrs Jones without his authority.

(b) Mr Roger is authorised to sign on his wife's account. The bank learns that he has just been made bankrupt.

Further reading

- Milnes Holden, J — Chapter 11, *The Law and Practice of Banking*, Vol 1, 5th edition 1991, Pitman
- Penn, GA, Shea, AM and Arora, A — Chapter 15, *The Law Relating to Domestic Banking*, Vol 1, 1987, Sweet & Maxwell
- Raby, P — Chapter 6, *Law Relating to Banking Services*, 2nd edition 1992, Pitman

Unit 4

Individual and Joint Accounts

Objectives

After studying this unit, you should be able to:

- **explain the purpose of taking references before opening an account;**
- **state the characteristics of different types of individual customers, with special reference to borrowing;**
- **explain the purpose of mandates**
- **explain the effect of mental incompetence or death of a customer;**
- **state the procedure for closing accounts;**
- **understand and apply the rules of set-off.**

Student Activity 1

Before working through this unit, obtain a copy of the different mandate forms your bank uses and study them. Reread them after completing the unit. Having done so you will better understand why each clause in them is there.

1 Introduction

1.1 In Unit 1, we looked at the definition duties of a customer. In Units 4, 5 and 7 we look at the various types of customer, and in Units 6 and 8 we look at the effect of insolvency upon these customers.

2 References

2.1 When a bank opens accounts, it will not simply do so on the word of the person requesting an account. The bank will make certain enquiries to establish the honesty and creditworthiness of the customer. At one time it was normal banking practice to obtain two references on a potential customer from reputable referees, but nowadays it is more usual practice in the case of individual and joint accounts to conduct a credit reference agency search and to request satisfactory identification, e.g. a driving licence or passport.

2.2 Whilst this change in procedure could, in legal terms, lose the bank protection in the event of being sued for conversion in relation to cheques, the cost saving involved is considered to worth the additional risk.

2.3 Under the Code of Banking Practice banks and building societies are bound to satisfy themselves as to the identity of a person seeking to open an account, to assist in protecting customers, members of the public, and themselves against fraud.

Student Activity 2

Check your bank's practice on taking reference when opening an account. Compare your bank's procedures with those given above and make notes on what you consider to be the legal risks run by your bank in relation to its own procedures regarding references. When you have done this, compare your notes with the text below.

3 Individual accounts

3.1 The usual practice when opening an account for an individual is to obtain satisfactory identification and a credit reference search. If the bank is satisfied on these points, the customer will sign a signature card, which in some banks incorporates a mandate covering payments of cheques etc. In the past, normal procedure was to take two references, except in special circumstances such as when there was a personal introduction from an existing valued customer.

3.2 The danger run by not taking references relates to the bank being sued for conversion in relation to cheques. In *Marfani and Co Ltd v Midland Bank Ltd* (1968), Lord Justice Diplock said:

> What factors ought to be known to the banker, i.e. what enquiries he should make and what facts are sufficient to cause him reasonably to suspect that the customer is not the true owner, must depend upon *current banking practice* and change as that practice changes. Cases decided 30 years ago, when the use by the general public of banking facilities was much less widespread, may not be a reliable guide to what the duty of a careful banker, in relation to enquiries and as to facts which should give rise to suspicion, is today.

3.3 This statement would seem to uphold the current banking practice of taking positive identification, i.e. something signed by the customer, such as a driving licence, and a credit reference search. As the number of bank customers has shown a tremendous increase over the years, it could be argued that the old reference procedures are now just too cumbersome and that the current practice is reasonable in today's circumstances.

3.4 The bank will complete its usual account opening formalities, whether the account is a current account or a deposit account, since cheques can be passed through both these accounts.

3.5 If the individual wishes anyone else to sign on the account, he will complete the third-party signing authority on the mandate. This creates an agency whereby the third party is agent of the customer in the operation of his account. This agency may be restricted simply to signing cheques, or may be general, i.e. relating to all aspects of the account including overdrawing the account.

Minors

3.6 A minor is anyone under the age of 18: Family Law Reform Act 1969. A bank can quite safely open an account for a minor, provided the usual procedures are followed regarding enquiries. The problem arises for a bank who has a minor as a customer, when he or she wishes to borrow money.

3.7 Contracts (which include bank borrowing) cannot be enforced against minors except where they relate to 'necessaries' or contracts of employment which are substantially for the minor's benefit. What is a necessary item to one person is not necessary to another. For example, if a minor is appointed as a sales representative, but has to supply his own car, then a car is definitely a necessary item for him. However, whether a Porsche would be classed as a necessary in such circumstances would be rather doubtful!

3.8 If the bank lends to a minor, and the minor repudiates the debt, the bank can seek redress as follows:

- A court can order the minor to return any goods or property purchased with the funds to the bank, provided it is just and equitable to do so: s.3, Minors Contracts Act 1987.
- The bank can hope that when the minor attains his majority, i.e. 18, he will ratify the debt. This is possible under the s.1 of the 1987 Act which requires the debt to be ratified in full within a reasonable time of the minor attaining majority.

3.9 The most usual protection that a bank looks for when lending to a minor is to have the account guaranteed by a third party. Such guarantees cannot be invalidated solely because the borrower is a minor: s.2, Minors Contracts Act 1987.

Sole traders

3.10 A sole trader is a person who runs a business as its sole owner. He may employ people to help run the business, but for banking and other legal purposes he is the only owner. The account will be opened in the usual way, but the bank will designate it a business account for the purpose of charges.

3.11 As far as lending to sole traders is concerned, the bank will treat the security aspect as it would for any lending to an individual.

3.12 Many sole traders operate under a different name from their own, for example 'Acme Window Cleaning Service', owned by John Brown, is a sole trader. The law does not differentiate between the liabilities and assets of John Brown and the liabilities and assets of 'Acme Window Cleaning Service'. If the bank were to sue for repayment of borrowing on the account of 'Acme Window Cleaning Service', any court order which was issued would apply to Brown personally, and to his personal assets, as well as to the assets of the business.

3.13 Under the Business Names Act 1985, the names of all proprietors must be quoted on all business stationery. Banks will normally ask for headed notepaper if opening an account where the business name differed from the proprietor's name, although it is admittedly easy for anyone to prepare a false letterhead.

4 Joint accounts

4.1 A joint account is opened when two or more people request the bank to open an account in their names. When a joint account is opened, apart from the usual enquiries being made, a joint account mandate must always be signed. The joint account mandate will usually contain the following clauses:

- A statement that it is a *joint account* mandate.
- An *authority to the bank*, authorising the bank to honour all cheques and other orders or instructions authorising payment, provided they are signed by either/any one or two/both or all account holders, whether the account is in credit or overdrawn.
- An agreement that any liability incurred by the account holders will be their *joint and several* responsibility.

4.2 Mandates may also have additional clauses, such as instructions regarding the giving up of items held in safe custody, and the effect of death upon the account.

4.3 The mandate will contain the names and addresses of the account holders and their specimen signature. The bank must abide by the instructions given in the mandate. Most joint accounts, especially where the account holders are husband and wife, are operated on one signature. Thus, the bank must be particularly vigilant if the mandate has different signing instructions, otherwise it could debit items to the account without authority. This could result in the bank being liable for damages to the injured joint account holder: *Catlin v Cyprus Finance Corporation (London) Ltd* (1982).

4.4 However, in *B Liggett Ltd v Barclays Bank* (1928), it was held that the bank could benefit from the doctrine of subrogation if the unauthorised withdrawal had settled a legally enforceable debt on the part of the joint or partnership account. Thus, if a bank pays a cheque on one signature when the mandate requires two, the debit will be valid if the payee was someone definitely entitled to be paid from the joint account, because in such a situation the account holders are in no worse a financial situation than would otherwise have been the case, as the amount was due to the payee in any case. More generally, a prerequisite of an action for such a breach of mandate is that financial loss resulted – this will by no means always be the case.

4.5 Every party to a joint account must receive a separate copy of each statement under the Consumer Credit Act 1974. If they do not each wish to receive a statement, they must complete a dispensing notice, authorising the bank to send only one statement.

4.6 Any party to a joint account can stop a cheque issued by another party to the account.

Joint and several liability

4.7 When a joint account is opened, a mandate is always signed which gives joint and several liability. In the event of the bank having to sue for repayment, it can sue the customers jointly and severally, i.e. it has one right of action against the account holders together and a right of action against each of the account holders individually.

4.8 For example, if Jones and Smith have a joint account which is overdrawn £5,000, and the mandate signed when the account was opened gave joint and several liability, the bank could sue in the following combination for repayment:

- Jones and Smith;
- Jones;
- Smith.

4.9 The bank can sue all three combinations simultaneously if it wishes, although to save legal costs, they will first sue the combination most likely to repay the borrowing. If there is a shortfall, then the bank can proceed against the other party until all combinations have been exhausted, or until the bank has been repaid in full: Civil Liability (Contribution) Act 1978. The maximum amount the bank can recover (ignoring any possible legal fees), is the amount of the debt plus interest accrued.

4.10 The bank can, of course, also set off a credit balance on any of the account holders' sole accounts with the overdrawn joint account (see section 9).

Effect if joint and several liability is not assumed

4.11 If the bank mandate form does not have a joint and several liability clause in it (which is highly unlikely), or if the bank has failed to take a mandate at all, then the liability of the parties to the account will simply be joint.

4.12 Since the passing of the Civil Liability (Contribution) Act 1978, the only major difference between joint and several liability arises where one party to the account dies. In the event of death under joint liability the estate of the deceased is free from liability for an overdrawn joint account. The survivor inherits the debt. With joint and several liability the estate of the deceased person remains jointly and severally liable for the debt at date of death.

Notice of a dispute

4.13 If the bank becomes aware of a dispute between the parties to a joint account, even where the mandate authorises any one person to sign, care must be exercised. If a dispute exists one party may try to withdraw the full balance of the account, or both parties may try to do so at the same time. (This is quite possible if ATMs are used when the bank is not on real-time accounting.)

4.14 Even where notice is given informally, e.g. from a remark made by the customer to a member of staff, the bank must take action to ensure that all future withdrawals are authorised by all parties to the account as notice of a dispute cancels the mandate. If there are any conflicting claims on the bank in relation to a credit balance or items held in safe custody, the bank itself cannot decide in whom the balance vests. In extreme cases the bank may have to interplead. Interpleading involves the bank refusing to hand over the money or items and leaving it for the courts to give instructions as to the disposal of the balance or safe custody item.

Student Activity 3

Summarise in your own words what is meant by joint and several liability and the advantages to the bank over joint liability.

5 Trustees

Definition

5.1 A trust has been defined as:

> an equitable obligation imposing upon a person (who is called a trustee) the duty of dealing with property over which he has control (which is called trust property) for the benefit of persons (who are called the beneficiaries or *cestui que trust*) of whom he may himself be one, any one of whom may enforce the obligation. (Underhill)

Operation of the account

5.2 A trust is usually created by a trust deed and the bank will need to have sight of the trust deed when opening the account. The bank should examine the deed to establish how the bank account is to be run, and who is to sign on cheques and other authorities.

5.3 Unless otherwise authorised in the trust deed, or by s.25, Trustee Act 1925, all trustees must sign. Under s.25 of the Act, as amended by s.9, Powers of Attorney Act 1971, a trustee may by power of attorney delegate for a period not exceeding 12 months the execution or exercise of all or any of the trust's powers and discretions vested in him either solely or jointly with others. He cannot delegate to his only other co-trustee, unless that trustee is a trust corporation. The donor of a power of attorney drawn up for this purpose is liable for the acts or defaults of the donee, i.e. the agent appointed under the power of attorney.

5.4 If a power of attorney has been drawn up, the bank must have sight of it and act in accordance with its instructions. The bank must note particularly if there is a time limit specified. If there is no time limit, the bank can presume that the power will continue up to the maximum period of 12 months.

5.5 Apart from the exceptions quoted above, trustees cannot delegate their powers. However, this may cause them problems, especially if one of the trustees is too ill or elderly to carry out his duties. In such a case, the bank may be requested to allow only certain of the trustees to sign cheques and other instructions. In these circumstances, if the standing of the trustees warrants it, the bank may agree. The bank may ask the trustees to sign a certificate, say, every three months, stating that the entries shown in the bank statement are correct. If the trustees sign such a form, they cannot later deny any entries – they are estopped.

Borrowing on the account

5.6 If a trustee wishes to borrow, the bank must examine the trust deed to see whether this is allowed as there is no implied power to borrow; the power must be express, i.e. laid down in writing in the trust deed. If there are no powers to borrow in the trust deed, then s.16, Trustee Act 1925 – which covers borrowings for capital purposes – will come into play.

5.7 The most common occurrence of a trustee needing to borrow is when he is carrying on the business of a deceased person with the aim of selling it as a going concern or of winding it up. Any sale must be carried out as soon as is possible, and if there is any delay the bank will need to make enquiries. If the bank has lent money to the trustee for the purpose of carrying on the business, then the bank may be liable to the beneficiaries of the estate if the trustee has caused them to receive less than they would have done if he had sold as soon as he could: *Rowlandson and Others v National Westminster Bank Ltd* (1978).

Trusts not created by deed

5.8 There are occasions when trusts are not created by deed. If an account is opened styled 'John Doe re James Doe', the bank has actual (express) notice of a trust. If the account was styled 'John Doe – Police Account' it is also held to be express notice of a trust: *Re Goss.* The commonest form of trust is a trust created by a will, where on death, the deceased leaves instructions in his will for money to be held in trust for his beneficiaries.

5.9 If the bank has such accounts, it must treat them as trust accounts, and not allow the trustee to withdraw the money for his own purposes. If this happened, the bank would be liable for breach of the trust – as constructive trustees – provided it knew, or should have known of the breach (see Unit 1, section 4).

6 Mental incompetence

Sole accounts

6.1 Mental incapacity is governed by the Mental Health Act 1983. It is not for the bank to judge whether or not a customer has become mentally incompetent and therefore incapable of conducting his account. If the customer is admitted to a hospital or recognised nursing home on a certificate signed by two doctors, or if an application supported by two doctors is made to the local health authority asking for a guardian to be appointed, then the customer can be considered to be mentally incompetent.

6.2 In such a case, a receiver will be appointed by the Court of Protection to look after the affairs of the patient. When the bank is given notice of the receiver's appointment, it must inspect the receiver's authority, stop the patient's account, and open a new account in the name of the receiver. The receiver's authority terminates with the death or certified recovery of the patient.

6.3 If the account was already being operated under a power of attorney drawn under the Powers of Attorney Act 1971, the authority is automatically revoked on mentally incapacity. If the bank has reliable notice of mental incapacity as described above, there is a problem as regards operation of the account pending the formal appointment of a receiver. The patient may need access to the money in the account, but in theory there is no way of authorising any withdrawals until a receiver has been appointed.

5.4 In practice, the bank must ensure that any withdrawals in this interim period are for necessaries, such as medical bills, food, rent, etc. Provided this is the case, the bank can safely allow such withdrawals under the doctrine of subrogation: *B Liggett v Barclays Bank Ltd* (1928).

5.5 If the bank allows an overdraft to develop during the interim period between notice of mental incapacity and the appointment of a receiver, any interest or commission so incurred will be irrecoverable, since interest and commission are not necessaries: *Beavan, Davies, Banks and Co v Beavan* (1912).

5.6 Finally, if the patient subsequently recovers, he cannot claim a refund for withdrawals in connection with necessaries if such withdrawals were made after notice but without the authority of a receiver: *Scarth v National Provincial Bank Ltd* (1930).

5.7 If the bank returns any cheques presented after notice of mental incapacity, the answer of the cheque will be 'insufficient mandate'.

Joint account

5.8 When any party to a joint account becomes mentally incapable, the mandate is revoked and the account must be stopped. Application must then be made to the receiver appointed by the Court of Protection. Once a receiver has been appointed, he, along with the remaining joint account holders, can instruct the bank on how the account is to be run. This action applies whether the account is debit or credit.

5.9 Because of joint and several liability any debit balance on the joint account at the date of notice of mental incompetence of one party will be the responsibility of the estate of the mentally incompetent person and of the remaining parties.

Trustees

5.10 If a trustee becomes mentally incapable the account can continue to be operated by the remaining trustees. If the trustee who becomes mentally incapable is the only trustee, then the receiver appointed by the Court of Protection will act in accordance with the trust deed, unless the trust deed specifies alternative action in these circumstances.

7 Death of a customer

Sole account

7.1 Notice of death cancels the bank's mandate: s.75, Bills of Exchange Act 1882. The death certificate is taken as conclusive evidence of death.

7.2 On receipt of notice of death, the bank must stop the account and return cheques marked 'Drawer deceased', unless they are drawn under a cheque card in which case they must be paid. Any credit items can be placed either to the account or to a suspense account, awaiting receipt of the letter of administration or granting of probate. (Letters of administration are given when a person has died without making a will, probate is granted when a will has been made.)

7.3 Care needs to be exercised over credits that the bank knows cease to be payable upon death, e.g. pension or annuity payments. In these cases, credits must be kept on a separate account, and the bank must notify the remitter and/or the executor of the estate of the receipt of the credits.

7.4 No money, items in safe custody, or securities held can be released until the bank receives letters of administration or probate. These documents give the administrators or executors the right to administer the estate. In other words, the bank can accept instructions from validly appointed executors or administrators, and such instructions will give the bank a good discharge.

7.5 If the customer has made a will, the executors will need to have this in order to be granted probate. The problem arises if the will is in safe custody at the bank. The bank cannot release items in safe custody until it receives probate, and probate cannot be granted without the will. This creates a problem! Obviously there must be a solution to the problem, otherwise the estate could never be wound up. If the bank knows the executors personally to be reliable, or failing that, can obtain a satisfactory reference on them from a known, reputable solicitor acting on the executors' behalf, then the will can be released. Ideally, the will be released to the solicitor acting on behalf of the executors. The executors or solicitor must sign a receipt for the will, and the bank would be wise to photocopy the will before releasing it, in the event of an accident or dispute at a later date.

7.6 If the account is overdrawn at the time of death, the bank will advise the executors or administrators of the balance outstanding plus interest and charges accrued to the date of death. If the bank holds any security against the borrowing, this will also be notified to the executors or administrators. These officials then become responsible for ensuring that the bank is repaid from the proceeds of the estate.

Joint accounts

7.7 If one party to a joint account dies, the balance vests in the survivors under the doctrine of survivorship, i.e. the surviving party/ies to the account receive the balance of the account. If there is more than one survivor, the division of the balance is between themselves and is of no interest to the bank. On a normal joint account, the presumption is that the property is jointly owned, both legally and beneficially, so that the bank will obtain a good discharge from the survivor.

7.8 If there is an indication that the property at the bank is not jointly owned but is held in trust for the other party, then the legal title for the survivor is held in trust for the heirs of the deceased.

7.9 If any cheques drawn by the deceased are received they must be returned, marked 'Drawer deceased', unless they were drawn in conjunction with a cheque card. Cheques drawn by the other surviving account holders will be paid in the usual way. The only way in which cheques drawn by the deceased can be honoured is if the surviving party is prepared to authorise the bank to pay these cheques, either by countersigning the cheques, or by giving a general letter of authority to the bank.

7.10 If the account is overdrawn upon notice of death, the bank will not simply pass the balance on to the survivor, but will stop (or break) the account. This is to preserve the liability of the deceased's estate for the borrowing, and any cheques signed by the survivor will be debited to a new account or returned. If the account were allowed to continue unbroken, then the *Rule in Clayton's case* would operate against the bank. Briefly, this rule states that credit items paid into an unbroken account repay the debit items in strict chronological order (see Unit 5). The effect of *Clayton's case* is that the debit balance outstanding at the date of death could be effectively repaid by subsequent credits leaving the bank with no recourse against the deceased's estate, because the resultant debit balance consists of items debited after notice of the death of one party.

Trustees

7.11 Death of a trustee has the same effect as if he were to become mentally incapable. The account can continue to be operated by the surviving trustees s.18, Trustee Act 1925.

7.12 If it is the sole trustee who has died, then reference must be made to the trust deed. If no instructions are given there regarding death of the sole or last trustee, then the executor of the trustee may act, or may appoint new trustees. In the event of any difficulties, and as a last resort, the court can appoint new trustees s.41, Trustee Act 1925.

Student Activity 4

Summarise in writing the effect of death and mental incapacity on bank accounts. Consider how the procedures in your own bank might have arisen as a result of the legal principles which you have just studied..

8 Closing accounts

8.1 There will always be occasions when the bank no longer wishes to maintain a customer's account. If the account is in debit, the bank may wish to be repaid so that the relationship can be ended.

8.2 Even if the account is in credit, the bank may still wish to close the account of a troublesome customer. For example, if a customer habitually issues cheques when he does not have funds in the account and has not made any overdraft arrangements the bank may prefer to sever the relationship instead of continually returning cheques and writing letters to the customer.

Debit accounts

8.3 In the case of an overdrawn account it depends on the type of borrowing as to when the account can be closed. If the borrowing is an overdraft it is repayable on demand, unless there is a specific, written, agreement to the contrary, signed and held by the bank: *William and Glyn's Bank Ltd v Barnes* (1980). If the account is a loan account then demand for repayment cannot be made until the instalments are in arrears, or until there is a breach of one of the covenants of the loan agreement.

Credit accounts

8.4 A bank must give reasonable notice before closing an account in credit. The problem is what constitutes 'reasonable notice'. There is no legal definition, it differs according to the circumstances. In *Prosperity Ltd v Lloyds Bank Ltd* (1923), the bank gave Prosperity Ltd one month's notice to close their credit account. Prosperity Ltd sued the bank for breach of contract, and whilst the court agreed that the bank could close the account, it did not agree that one month's notice was sufficient in this case because Prosperity Ltd was in business and it would take longer than one month to make alternative banking arrangements. The bank lost the case.

8.5 In relation to *business customers*, the bank must be very careful if it wishes to close the account. The bank must consider what is likely to be a reasonable period of notice depending on the individual circumstances.

8.6 With a *private customer* the bank will probably be safe if it gives one month's notice. The Code of Banking Practice requires that banks do not close accounts without reasonable notice.

8.7 If the period of notice has expired and the customer is still issuing cheques, the bank has a problem. It could simply close the account, send the balance to the customer and dishonour any further cheques but it would have to pay those properly drawn in conjunction with a cheque card. In addition, the cheques may have been issued prior to expiry of notice and the payee may have delayed presentation.

8.8 The bank must ensure it does not issue any further cheque books and should endeavour to recover the cheque card and any unused cheques. It would be wise to time the notice to close when the customer has very few unused cheques left. If the customer continues to pay into the account after the period of notice, the credits should be placed to a suspense account and the balance sent to the customer.

9 Set off

9.1 Set off, or combination, or consolidation, is the right of the bank to set off one account against another of that same customer's accounts in order to establish the net debit or credit position.

9.2 In *National Westminster Bank Ltd v Halesowen Presswork and Assemblies Ltd* (1970), set off was described as 'an accounting situation in which the existence and amount of one party's liability to the other can only be ascertained by discovering the ultimate balance of their mutual dealings'. Following *Garnett v McKewan* (1872), confirmed in *Barclays Bank Ltd v Okenarhe* (1966), the accounts can be at different branches of the same bank, because the bank is a single legal entity.

9.3 There are three requirements that must be satisfied before a right of set off can be exercised, apart from any specific agreements to the contrary. These are set down in *Garnett v McKewan* (1872) as being:

- For certain sums;
- Between the same parties;
- In the same right.

Certain sums

9.4 Before two accounts can be set off, the bank must establish the amount of money in each account.

9.5 This is not a problem for a bank as precise figures can be quickly and accurately obtained. The only problem that could face the bank would be if it tried to set off a known sum of money against a contingent liability, i.e. a liability on the part of the customer that may have to be met (paid) at some future date. Not all contingent liabilities will become actual liabilities, for example if the bank's customer has guaranteed someone else's borrowing, he will only have to pay if the borrower defaults. If the bank wishes to set off accounts, it cannot do so against a contingent liability: *Jeffryes v Agra and Masterman's Bank* (1866). (The position is different in insolvency, see Units 6 and 8.)

Between the same parties

9.6 A bank can only set off accounts where the same person or people hold both accounts and in *Uttamchandi v Central Bank of India* (1989) it was held that a bank must have definite proof that accounts are between the same parties before it can combine accounts. In other words, the person who owes money on a debit account must be the same person to whom money is owed on a credit account.

9.7 The apparent exception to this rule relates to joint accounts. The bank's mandate makes each of the parties jointly and severally liable for any borrowing on the joint account, thus any credit balance on a sole account, where that sole account holder also is a party on a debit joint account, can be set off against the debit joint account. However, the reverse situation does not apply, i.e. a credit balance on a joint account cannot be offset against a debit balance on a sole account (unless there is a specific agreement to do so).

Example 1

Jones and Smith	Dr £1,500
Jones	Cr £1,000
Smith	Cr £ 500

The credit balances on Jones's private account and Smith's private account can be offset against the debit balance on the Jones and Smith joint account, because they are jointly and severally liable for the overdrawn balance.

Example 2

Sarah Smith	Dr £2,000
John and Sarah Smith	Cr £4,000

In this case, there is no automatic right of set off between the two accounts.

In the same right

9.8 Care must be taken when the credit account is in the name of one party where that party holds the funds in trust for someone else. If the bank has notice of this trust it cannot set off a credit balance on that account against a debit balance on another account held by the individual either in his own name or jointly with another.

9.9 Notice of the trust may be 'express', e.g. the account may be styled 'client account', or the notice of the trust may be constructive.

9.10 A constructive trust is one where the bank should have realised that the monies were held in trust. In *Barclays Bank Ltd v Quistclose Investments Ltd* (1970), for example, the bank knew that the monies held on a company's dividend account had been lent expressly to pay a dividend to preference shareholders. The purpose of the loan was frustrated when the company was put into liquidation, i.e. they could not pay the dividend because the company became insolvent. In the court's opinion, the fact that the bank knew of the circumstances behind the credit balance on the dividend account, meant that it had constructive notice of trust. This meant that the bank could not set off the credit balance on the dividend account against other debit balances held in the same name.

9.11 Apart from the bank having notice of trust, the bank can automatically exercise its rights of set off, unless it has specifically agreed not to combine the accounts, or if the debit account is a loan account which is not in arrears and not in breach of the loan agreement. (The position in bankruptcy or in liquidation is covered in Units 6 and 8.)

9.12 In *Re K* (1990) the courts held that the right of set off was simply an accounting exercise whereby the bank combined accounts to ascertain the true position between itself and its customer. As such, set off can be applied between debit and credit accounts in accordance with the usual principles, even if an order has been made under the Drug Trafficking Offences Act 1994 prohibiting the customer from disposing of or dealing with any assets, including the credit balances which the bank would wish to set off.

Student Activity 5

Your bank holds current accounts in the following names:

X Debit £50,000 (no security held)

Y Credit £30,000

You have repeatedly requested X to repay, but he has not complied. You suspect that Y is a mere nominee of X, and your assistant suggests that you combine the accounts.

Discuss the merits of this suggestion.

Summary

Now that you have studied this unit, you should be able to:

- **describe the following types of customers and the particular legal considerations which apply to each:**
  - **individuals**
  - **minors**
  - **sole traders**
  - **trustees;**
- **understand the purpose of mandates for the above types of customers;**
- **understand the legal implications of borrowing by such customers;**
- **understand the effect of mental incompetence on the accounts of the above types of customers;**
- **explain when a bank can close an account;**
- **explain the effect of a bank's right of set off.**

Self-assessment questions

1 What danger does a bank run by not taking references on a customer when opening an account?

2 Which case appears to uphold current banking practice of opening an account after taking positive identification and a credit reference search instead of references?

3 To what extent is bank borrowing by a customer during minority enforceable after majority?

4 What is meant by the doctrine of subrogation?

5 If your customer, Brian Jones, is a sole trader, trading under the name of Wizard Joinery, is there any difference between the assets and liabilities of Brian Jones and of Wizard Joinery?

6 What is meant by joint and several liability on a bank account?

7 Paul and Mary Brown have a joint account with you, with the signing instruction 'either to sign'. Mary Brown comes into your bank wanting to withdraw the full balance of the account and says 'My husband has gone off with another woman, so I don't see why he should have all our money.' What action would you take?

8 Alan Young and his wife Alice have a joint account at your bank. Today, Alice Young comes into the bank to stop a cheque issued by Alan Young, giving you all the details required, and signing the stop authority.

Next day the cheque appears in the clearing. Would you pay or return the cheque?

9 What action would you take if you received notice of death of your customer Fred Jones, who had a sole account with you? The account is in credit.

10 Would your answer to Question 9 differ if, instead, Fred Jones had a joint account with his wife at your branch?

11 Which case allows a bank to close a credit account upon giving 'reasonable notice'? What non-statutory authority applies in addition?

12 You have the following accounts in your books. Indicate whether the bank has an automatic right of set off by ticking the appropriate column. (Assume insolvency is not involved.)

	Right of set off applies	
	Yes (✓)	*No* (✓)
(a) A and B joint account credit, A private account overdrawn.		
(b) A and B joint account debit, A private account credit.		
(c) As for (b) but the private account is at a different branch.		
(d) As for (b) but the private account is at a different bank.		
(e) A current account credit and A loan account. (No bankruptcy or liquidation, or death or insanity involved and loan account instalments are up to date.)		
(f) A *Re Edgar* credit, A private account debit.		
(g) A *Re Edgar* debit, A private account credit.		
(h) A credit account, subject to an order under the Drug Trafficking Act, A debit account.		

Further reading

- Laidlaw, A and Roberts, G — Chapter 2, *Law Relating to Banking Services*, 2nd edition 1992, Bankers Books.
- Milnes Holden, J — Chapters 3 and 11, *The Law and Practice of Banking*, Vol 1, 5th edition 1991, Pitman
- Raby, P — Chapter 5, *Law Relating to Banking Services*, 2nd edition 1992, Pitman

Unit 5

Partnerships

Objectives

After studying this unit, you should be able to:

- **define a partnership, and types of partners;**
- **open a partnership account;**
- **list the rights and duties of partners;**
- **decide whether property is partnership property;**
- **state how a partnership is dissolved;**
- **explain the effect of retirement, death and mental incapacity on a partnership;**
- **explain and apply the rule in *Clayton's case.***

1 The nature of a partnership

Definition

1.1 Section 1(1) defines a partnership as a relationship which exists:

> ... between persons carrying on a business in common with a view of profit'.

1.2 All aspects of partnership are governed by the Partnership Act 1890. Although the rights of partners between themselves can be, and usually are, varied by agreement, the Act will apply in the absence of any such agreement.

Note: All statutory references are to the 1890 Act unless stated otherwise.

1.3 A 'business' is defined in s.45 as including every trade, occupation or profession. However, this description of 'a business' could also be extended to a limited company. Under s.1(2), companies are specifically excluded from the definition.

1.4 'In common' does not necessarily mean that if there is any agreement to share profits this automatically creates a partnership. In *Cox v Coulson* (1916) Coulson was a theatre manager who made an agreement with the manager of a travelling theatre company to present a play. Coulson provided the theatre, lighting and publicity whilst the actors and scenery were provided by the travelling theatre company's manager. There was an agreement to share the takings of the production. In the course of the performance Mrs Cox was accidentally shot by one of the actors. She sued Coulson for damages on the grounds that he was the partner of the travelling theatre company's manager, and thus liable for the actor's conduct.

1.5 The court did not agree, and said that the actor was solely employed by the travelling theatre company's manager. The sharing of the gross returns of the production did not in itself give rise to a partnership under s.2(2).

Numbers

1.6 With the exception of professional partnerships, e.g. stockbrokers, accountants and solicitors, the maximum number of partners is limited to 20: s.716(1), Companies Act 1985. The reason for this restriction is that larger partnerships should be encouraged to become limited companies. The exception of professional partnerships from the maximum of 20 members is because many professional bodies refuse to allow limited companies to be members of these professions.

Types

1.7 There are two types of partnership – trading and non-trading. A trading partnership is one where the main business is buying and selling: *Higgins v Beauchamp* (1914). Non-trading partnerships are partnerships such as solicitors, accountants, doctors and dentists.

Creating a partnership

1.8 A partnership can be created by implication from conduct, orally, or by articles of partnership, often by deed. There is no legal requirement for a partnership agreement to be in writing and the Partnership Act 1890 will cover all aspects. If the partners wish, a simple written agreement can be drawn up (articles of partnership), and signed by all partners.

1.9 A deed is the most formal way of creating a partnership. It will contain rules governing the conduct of the partnership. The Partnership Act 1890 lays down the rights and duties of partners amongst themselves but the deed of partnership can vary, omit or amend any of these provisions, except that there must always be at least one general partner in the partnership.

1.10 A partner can be a minor. However, a minor is not liable for debts incurred during his minority unless he chooses to ratify the debts in full and within a reasonable time of attaining his majority: s.3, Minors Contracts Act 1987.

Partnerships and limited companies

1.11 The basic difference between a partnership and a limited company is that a limited company is a separate legal entity from its owners – a corporation – which can be sued and put into liquidation with (usually) no effect on its members. A partnership is not legally separate form its members and the partners are fully liable for all activities of a partnership, unless they are limited partners.

2 Opening a partnership account

2.1 When a bank account is opened, the bank prefers not to see any partnership agreement since if it is seen by the bank the partnership's bank account must be conducted in accordance with its terms and the bank cannot rely on a partner's implied authority. Banks always conduct the account in accordance with the partnership mandate, which is based on the provisions of the Partnership Act 1890. Any items not covered in the mandate are decided in accordance with the Act.

2.2 Some banks have a separate mandate for partnership accounts, others have a multipurpose mandate covering all forms of joint, partnership and trust accounts.

Contents of the mandate

2.3 All partnership mandates incorporate a *joint and several liability* clause. A partnership is *not* a separate legal entity from the partners, and the partners are jointly and severally liable for the bank debts of the partnership.

2.4 The following are the other usual items and clauses found in a bank partnership mandate:

- The *signing authority*, stating how many of the partners must sign in all transactions with the bank. Examples from the wording of bank mandates regarding transactions are:
  - To make, draw, accept and endorse cheques, orders for payment, bills of exchange and promissory notes on behalf of our said partnership.
  - To sign orders for the withdrawal of all securities or other items lodged with you or moneys held on deposit or other account with you in the partnership name.
  - To instruct you with regard to any accounts or banking transactions of the partnership.
- Authority to debit the partnership account with all cheques and other payment instructions, whether the account is debit or credit. *Note*: this does not bind the bank to allowing the account to go overdrawn or further overdrawn. It simply confirms the partners' liability if the account is debit.
- The joint and several liability clause (see Unit 4, paragraphs 4.7–14).
- Specimen signatures of all partners.

2.5 If the partnership trades under a name other than the names of the partners, e.g. Acme Financial Services, then the names of each partner must be shown on all business stationery. The names of each of the partners must also be displayed prominently on the business premises: Business Names Act 1985. When opening the account, the bank will wish to see the letterheads to confirm the names of all the partners.

2.6 If the partnership trades in a name other than that of the partners, the bank must open the account in the name of the partnership, e.g. Acme Financial Services. If the bank opened the account only in the name of a partner, any debt owed to the bank could only be enforced against that partner and not against the partnership: *Alliance Bank Ltd v Kearsley* (1871).

2.7 If the bank does not know any of the partners it will make the usual enquiries upon them before opening the account. If one of the partners is known to the bank, then he is, in effect, introducing his co-partners, and this is sufficient for the bank.

Student Activity 1

Check your own bank's mandate form covering partnership accounts. Identify the clauses therein. Write down whether and why you consider it provides good protection to your bank.

3 Conduct of a partnership account

3.1 Once the mandate has been signed, the account will be run in accordance with its instructions.

3.2 Section 5 of the Act states that every general partner is the agent of the partnership and his co-partners. This means that any general partner has implied authority to draw cheques or to borrow money on behalf of a trading partnership. However, the bank always relies on the mandate since this express authority supersedes any implied powers under the Act.

3.3 Any partner can stop a cheque issued by the partnership even though he has not signed the cheque himself. This right applies to any joint account, however, and is not restricted to partnerships.

Collecting and paying cheques

3.4 Care must be taken by the bank when a partner issues a cheque drawn on the partnership that is payable to himself. The bank must check the mandate to ensure such cheques are authorised. If the bank mandate states that the partners of the partnership authorise the bank

> until we or any one of us give you notice to the contrary in writing, to honour any one of our signatures for all purposes on behalf of the said firm and we agree that we shall be jointly and severally liable for liability so created

then the bank is safe in paying such cheques. There will not necessarily be any hint of misconduct in such a transaction, after all, someone has to issue the salary or profit sharing cheques to the partners.

3.5 If cheques payable to the partnership are tendered for the credit of an individual partner's account, the bank must take special care (such as making enquiries as to why the individual wishes to pay the cheque into his own account) when collecting such cheques. There is a serious risk that the partner may be depriving the rightful owner (the partnership) of the cheque. If this were the case, the bank would be committing conversion and could not rely on s.4, Cheques Act 1957 for protection.

Professional partnership accounts

3.6 If the partnership is a professional practice, such as a firm of solicitors, then separate bank accounts must be kept for its clients' monies. These client accounts are trust accounts because the solicitor is holding the money in trust for his clients. The bank must take care that no breach of trust occurs in this situation, otherwise the bank may be liable as constructive trustee: *Lipkin Gorman v Karpnale Ltd and Another* (1986).

Borrowing by partnerships

3.7 General partners of a trading partnership have implied powers to borrow and pledge security in the name of the partnership. However, the bank will rely on the express instructions in the mandate when a partnership wishes to borrow and/or pledge security.

3.8 In a non-trading partnership, partners do not have an implied authority to borrow or pledge security, so the bank will simply rely on the mandate.

3.9 All types of partner have the right to inspect the firm's books or nominate an agent (such as an accountant) to do so: s.24.

4 Types of partner

Student Activity 2

In Unit 3 we covered the various types of agent.

1 Write down your description of a general agent and compare your description with that in Unit 3.

2 Consider what general agency means in the context of a partnership. Compare your suggestions with the text below.

General partner

4.1 A general partner is a general agent of the partnership for the purpose of the partnership business and while acting in the usual business of the partnership has authority to bind the firm: s.5.

4.2 A general partner:

- Takes an active part in the management of the firm.
- Is entitled to share in the profits of the firm either equally (s.24(1)) or on any other agreed basis laid down in the partnership agreement.
- Has implied authority to draw cheques and other instruments, to borrow and, in the case of a trading partnership, to pledge partnership property as security. The bank, however, will rely on the express authority in the mandate for all these areas.
- Will have to contribute capital to the partnership on a basis agreed between the partners in the partnership agreement.
- Is liable for the debts of the partnership jointly with his other partners: s.9 (except in the case of creditors with whom joint and several liability has been agreed).

Limited partner

4.3 A limited partner is one whose liability for partnership debts is limited to his capital contribution. A limited partner must register the limited partnership with the Registrar of Companies if he is not to be treated as a general partner. All limited partnerships must contain at least one general partner: Limited Partnership Act 1907.

4.4 A limited partner cannot take part in the day-to-day running of the partnership, or deal with outsiders. He can, however, advise the remaining partners. He will share in the profits of the partnership on the agreed basis, which is usually limited by his capital contribution.

Quasi or nominal partner

4.5 A quasi or nominal partner is one who has by his actions given the impression to creditors that he is a partner. This is known as 'holding out'. Any creditor who gave credit to the firm relying on the fact that he thought the quasi-partner was a genuine partner can sue the quasi-partner if the partnership defaults.

Sleeping partner

4.6 A sleeping partner is someone who has contributed capital to a partnership but who does not take part in the management of the firm. A sleeping partner shares in the profits and is liable for the firm's debts.

Salaried partner

4.7 A salaried partner is one whose name appears on the firm's notepaper and whose conduct makes it appear that he is a partner. However he receives a salary rather than a share of the profits. A salaried partner is usually a 'junior partner'.

4.8 The legal position is vague, but it appears that such a partner will be liable for the firm's debts, so long as the creditors are unaware that he is merely salaried: *Stekel v Ellice* (1973).

5 Partners as agents of the partnership

Student Activity 3

In Unit 3 we studied the rights, duties and liabilities of an agent. Reread the appropriate sections before studying this section.

5.1 The Partnership Act 1890 provides that every partner is a *general agent* of the partnership for the business of the partnership. Every partner has implied authority, therefore, to enter into binding contracts on behalf of the firm on matters connected with the firm's usual business, unless the deed or articles of partnership specify otherwise.

5.2 Examples of such contracts are:

- Buying goods usually employed in the business;
- Employing staff;
- Giving a valid receipt for payments made to the business;
- Drawing cheques.

5.3 A partner in a trading partnership (one whose business consists mainly of buying and selling) also has implied authority to:

- Draw, issue or accept bills of exchange in the firm's name;
- Borrow money in the firm's name;
- Pledge the firm's assets as security for the firm's borrowing.

5.4 Although the Partnership Act gives an individual partner implied power to bind the firm in relation to bills of exchange and borrowing, the bank would always in practice ensure that the instructions in its mandate were followed. With regard to pledging assets as security, in practice a bank would always insist on the completion of a charge form, signed by all partners, when the firm's assets are being given as security for the firm's borrowing. In practice, pledging is rare, being a throwback to the late 19th century, involving the physical deposit of the assets used as security with the lender.

5.5 If a partnership mandate states 'both to sign' or 'any two to sign' in relation to cheques, the bank must be careful when paying such cheques. If a cheque is not signed in accordance with the mandate, the bank will return the cheque marked 'another signature required'. Even though the cheque was issued for normal partnership business, the bank will rely on its mandate rather than the Partnership Act 1890.

Transactions outside the implied authority of a partner

5.6 Certain transactions cannot be carried out under the implied authority of a partner but must be authorised by all the partners in the firm, *or* all the partners of the firm must authorise one partner to carry out such transactions.

5.7 The transactions *outside* the implied authority of a partner are:

- The execution of deeds – an agent can only execute a deed if appointed by deed.
- The giving of guarantees – this is of particular importance to banks who require a partnership to give a guarantee to cover another customer's borrowing. The bank must either obtain the signatures of all partners to the guarantee *or* ensure that the individual partner giving the guarantee has been expressly authorised by all the other partners to give a guarantee.
- The authorisation of the use of the firm's name in any legal action, e.g. if the partnership is suing another person over a debt due to the partnership.
- The acceptance of property in settlement of the partnership's debts. A partner has implied authority only to accept money in settlement of partnership debts.
- The submission to arbitration of any disputes involving the firm.

Holding out

5.8 Section 14 states that if any individual by his words or deeds leads a third party to believe he is a partner and relying on this representation the third party extends credit to the firm, the individual will be treated as a partner and be liable for partnership debts incurred by his actions. He is thus holding himself out to be a partner This is also referred to as partnership by estoppel or a quasi-partnership.

5.9 Holding out can occur if the third party is told that the quasi-partner is a partner by another person who has either the partnership's authority or the quasi-partner's authority to do so: *Martyn v Gray* (1863). If it is the partnership that is holding him out to be a partner the partners would be estopped from denying this.

5.10 Holding out is of particular importance when dealing with retirement of a partner.

6 The rights and duties of a partner

Rights

6.1 Whilst the rights of a partner are laid down in the Partnership Act 1890, these can be varied by the articles of partnership, or by mutual agreement of all the partners.

6.2 The statutory rights are as follows, *unless modified by agreement*:

- That all general partners have the right to participate in the day-to-day management of the firm: s.24–35.
- That all partners (whichever type they are) must consent to the admission of a new partner.
- That a partner cannot be expelled from the partnership, even if all the other partners agree.
- That when a partner wishes to retire the partnership is dissolved.
- That the partnership books must be kept at the main office of the partnership and be freely available for inspection by all partners, or by the duly authorised agent of a partner: s.24(a).
- That all partners share the profits and losses of the partnership equally (unless they are limited partners in relation to losses).
- That no partner has any right to any interest on the capital he has contributed to the business except where the capital contributed is in excess of the amount he is due to subscribe. Interest is then paid on this extra capital at either an agreed rate or 5% p.a.
- That when a partner acting in the ordinary course of business or in preserving the assets of a partnership incurs any costs or suffers any loss he has the right to be indemnified by the other partners, the partners sharing such costs or losses equally.
- That a partner is the joint owner of partnership assets; on his death his share of the assets will pass to his estate.
- That a partner can assign his share of the partnership to another person. This includes both partnership assets and partnership profits. The assignment can be absolute, i.e. by sale or gift, or by mortgage.

  The assignee, i.e. person to whom the partner assigns his property or profits, does not become a partner and has no right to be involved in the day-to-day running of the firm unless all the other partners agree. The assignee does not become liable for any debts of the partnership.

Duties

6.3 The duties of a partner stem from his rights. They are to:

- To act in good faith. As a partner is an agent of the partnership, he must render accurate account of all monies received and spent and give full information on all partnership matters: s.28. Nor must he make a secret profit: s.29.

  In *Bentley v Craven* (1853) one of two partners was responsible for buying goods for the firm. Without informing his partner, he sold his own goods to the firm, making a large profit for himself. It was held that the partner had to account to the firm for the profit.
- Not make a secret profit or take a bribe.
- Account to the firm for all monies or benefits received.
- Contribute capital to the business.
- Share equally in the losses of the partnership unless there is any agreement to the contrary, such as arises with a limited partner.

7 Partnership property

7.1 Partnership property is property that is deemed to be owned jointly by all the partners. Property in this case refers to all assets of the partnership.

7.2 Partnership property consists of assets:

- Bought with partnership money: s.21.
- Brought into the partnership when the firm was originally formed: s.20(1).

7.3 Not all of the assets used by a partnership will necessarily belong to the partnership. An individual partner may have provided, say, the buildings from which the partnership operates. If this partner retains the title to the property it is his sole property not the partnership's.

7.4 Partnership land is not treated as real land, but as 'personality', i.e. personal property: s.22. A partner's own land is treated as 'realty'. Thus, on death, a bequest of 'my personal property' would include a share in partnership land. The value of the land is the specified portion of the proceeds which would be left after its notional sale and payment of the firm's debts.

8 Dissolution of a partnership

8.1 Subject to any agreement to the contrary between the partners, ss.32–38 provides that a partnership is dissolved either automatically or by court order.

Automatic dissolution

8.2 This is the result in the following situations.

- If entered into for a fixed period, by *expiration of the term*: *Abbott v Abbott* (1936).
- If entered into for a particular undertaking by *completion of that undertaking*.
- If entered into for an undefined time, by *notice* from any partner to the

Table 5.1: *Comparison of partnership property and property owned by an individual partner but used in the firm's business*

	Partnership Property		*Partner's own Property*
1	Must appear in the partnership's balance sheet and be used exclusively for the business.	1	Does not appear in the firm's balance sheet.
2	Any increase in value (e.g. rise in value of a factory) vests in the firm.	2	Any added value belongs to the partner only: *Robinson v Ashton* (1875).
3	Under the Insolvency Act 1986 partnership property must be used first of all towards meeting partnership liabilities in the bankruptcy of a partnership. Any surplus is then distributed to the partners.	3	The partner's own property is first of all used to meet his own debts if the partnership is made bankrupt. Bankruptcy of a partnership normally involves bankruptcy of the individual partners. However, under the Insolvent Partnerships Order 1986, partnership creditors can confine their rights in bankruptcy to the partnership assets. If partnership creditors elect to do this, then and only then, will the bankruptcy of the partnership have no effect on the property of individual partners.
4	On the death of a partner his estate will receive the agreed proportion of the value of the partnership property.	4	On death of the partner, the property vests in the estate of the partner: section 20.
5	On dissolution of the partnership the property is distributed amongst all the partners after paying off all partnership debts: s.39.	5	On dissolution of the partnership, the whole of the property reverts to the partner if the firm is solvent.

others of his intention to dissolve the partnership: s.26(1).

The partnership must be dissolved with effect from the date specified in the notice.

The right for one partner to dissolve a partnership at any time can only be revoked if so stated in the articles of partnership. This is a common clause in the partnership agreement because dissolution of the partnership would mean that each partner would have his capital repaid after the partnership debts had been settled. In order to prevent one partner from using dissolution as a method of obtaining his capital, the articles of partnership often exclude s.26(1). In such a case dissolution would have to be by mutual agreement: *Moss v Elphick* (1910).

- By *death or bankruptcy* of a partner. Bankruptcy of a partner does not necessarily involve the bankruptcy of a partnership, only its dissolution. In some cases, particularly professional partnerships, it is common for the articles of partnership to exclude death as being an automatic dissolution of the partnership.
- At the option of the others, if any partner allows his share of the partnership property to be *charged* for his personal debts: s.33.
- The partnership becoming *unlawful*, e.g. when one of the partners is a national of a country with which the UK is at war: s.34.
- *Frustration* of purpose.
- *Retirement* of a partner, although the articles of partnership may overrule this.

Dissolution by court order

8.3 Section 35 allows an application to the court to dissolve the partnership if a partner becomes incapable of carrying on through ill health or mental incapacity. In the event of mental incapacity, dissolution is not automatic. The application of dissolution in this situation is made to the Court of Protection under the Mental Health Act 1983.

8.4 The court may also grant a dissolution order if:

- A partner, other than the one applying for the petition is guilty of *conduct prejudicial to the firm's business*. In *Carmichael v Evans* (1904) a partner was convicted of the criminal offence of travelling on the railway without a ticket. The partnership agreement included the provision for dissolving the partnership if 'scandalous conduct detrimental to the partnership' occurred. The court agreed that the partnership should be dissolved.
- A partner *wilfully or persistently breaks the partnership agreement* in such a way as to destroy the fiduciary relationship, i.e. the relationship of trust between the partners.
- The business can *only be carried on at a loss*. A petition to wind up the partnership as an unregistered company may be granted under the Insolvency Act 1986 and the Insolvent Partnerships Order 1994.
- The court considers it is '*just and equitable*' for the partnership to be dissolved. This would be appropriate if the partners had reached deadlock over the way that the partnership was to be conducted, or if the majority of the partners were 'freezing out' another partner by refusing to co-operate with him. In both these cases it would usually be the majority of partners who refused to agree to the dissolution of the partnership and the minority who wished to dissolve the partnership.

Partners continuing authority

8.5 Once the partners have agreed to dissolve the partnership, or the court orders dissolution, the partners have authority to continue to contract on behalf of the firm in order either to wind up the firm, e.g. sale of assets, or to complete ongoing transactions. Thus, any transactions entered into at this stage must be solely for the purpose of winding up the partnership.

Distribution of assets at dissolution (excluding bankruptcy)

8.6 Unless varied by the partnership agreement, general partners contribute capital equally to the partnership and share equally in the profits and losses. When a partnership is dissolved the assets must first be used to pay off partnership debts in the following order (s.44(b)), repayment of:

- Debts and other obligations owed to third parties, e.g. bank borrowing and trade creditors.
- Loans made to the partnership by any partner. (This is money lent in excess of the minimum capital requirement.)
- Capital contributed by each partner. If capital was not contributed in equal shares, e.g. if a limited partner contributed less than the general partners, the capital is repaid in the proportion in which it was contributed.

  Note: capital in this case consists of money, not items such as technical expertise.
- Any surplus assets remaining are divided between the partners in the same proportion as they shared profits.

8.7 Provided that all outside debts and obligations are repaid, the partnership is not insolvent.

8.8 If there are losses arising after the outside creditors of the partnership have been repaid in full, then s.44(a) applies. This states that losses must be met in the following order:

- From the undrawn profits;
- From the firm's capital;
- By the partners individually in the proportions in which they shared profits.

9 Retirement of a partner

9.1 The partnership will automatically dissolve when a partner retires unless the articles of partnership state otherwise. It is quite common for the articles to allow the partnership to continue, and this is of particular importance both to the bank and to other creditors of the partnership.

Liability of a retired partner for future debts

9.2 To be freed from liability for debts incurred *after* his retirement, the partner needs to notify creditors of his retirement.

9.3 If they are *existing creditors*, he must give each of them specific notice of his retirement. If such creditors are not specifically notified of the retirement, they are entitled to continue to hold him liable for debts: s.36(1).

9.4 To be effective against future creditors, the retiring partner should give notice of his retirement in the *London Gazette.*

9.5 A retiring partner must be careful not to hold himself out to be a partner. If he does so, on the basis of estoppel he will be liable for debts incurred after his retirement with regard to creditors who thought he was still a partner. If his name still appears on letterheads or stationery he will only be liable via holding out if he *knowingly allowed* the continued use of his name. If the letterheads showing his name were used negligently or carelessly, he is not liable to holding out: *Tower Cabinet Co v Ingram* (1949).

9.6 A creditor cannot take advantage of a holding out situation by taking action against both the old partnership and the new partnership. He must decide which of the two forms of partnership he is going to sue, i.e. including or not including the retired partner, and cannot later change his mind: *Scarf v Jardine* (1882).

Liability of a retired partner for debts incurred at the time of retirement

9.7 Section 17(2) provides that a retiring partner remains liable for debts incurred up to the date of his retirement. However, it is possible under s.17(3) for the retiring partner to be released from liability by the process of novation.

9.8 Novation is an agreement to release the retiring partner from liability for old debts made between himself, the partnership's creditors and the partnership as newly constituted.

9.9 Ideally, the novation agreement should be express, i.e. in writing, however it may be implied from the course of dealings. In the case of implied novation it must be clear from the creditor's conduct that they have accepted the new firm as liable for the debts in the place of the old firm. The fact that creditors have simply continued to trade with the new firm is not sufficient evidence of implied agreement to novation.

9.10 If the bank agrees to novation, it must remember to obtain a new mandate signed by all the partners of the new firm.

Note: novation can also apply when a partner has died and the partnership as newly constituted takes over the debts of the old partnership which included the now deceased partner.

10 Death of a partner

10.1 Section 33 provides that a partnership is automatically terminated on the death of a partner unless the articles of partnership state otherwise.

10.2 If the partnership is to be dissolved the partners can only continue to contract in order to wind up the partnership. If the partnership is to continue, the bank will obtain a new mandate.

10.3 If the account is overdrawn the bank must break, or stop, the account to preserve the debit balance against the estate of the deceased partner. If the bank fails to break a debit account, the *Rule in Clayton's case* (1816) will operate against the bank (see section 12).

10.4 If cheques are presented signed by the deceased partner, the bank may either obtain the confirmation of the surviving partners to pay the cheques, or return them marked 'Drawer deceased'.

11 Mental incapacity of a partner

11.1 Mental incapacity does not automatically dissolve a partnership, but any of the other partners can apply to the Court of Protection to dissolve the partnership.

11.2 The bank should not pay any cheques signed by the mentally incapable partner without obtaining the consent of the remaining partners. If the account is overdrawn it should be broken to prevent the *Rule in Clayton's case* (1816) working against the bank.

11.3 If third parties are not aware of a partner's mental incapacity, he still has authority to bind the partnership. The remaining partners should consider whether to apply for an interim injunction to restrain him from acting, pending the court hearing to dissolve the partnership.

12 The rule in Clayton's case

12.1 The *Rule in Clayton's case* (1816) is of particular importance to banks and occurs in various parts of the syllabus. Appendix 1 gives a summary of all aspects of the effect of *Clayton's case.*

12.2 Essentially *Clayton's case* states that credits into the account are appropriated in chronological order to the debits paid out of the account.

Table 5.2 Example Andromeda and Daughters

Date	*Dr* £	*Cr* £	*Balance* £
Jan 1	300		Dr 300
Feb 1		500	Cr 200
Mar 1	400		Dr 200
May 1		700	Cr 500
Jun 1	600		Dr 100
July 1	200		Dr 300

12.3 Under *Clayton's case* the debit balance of £300 shown on the above account consists of the £200 debited on 1 July, and £100 being the amount remaining undischarged from the £600 debited on 1 June.

Practical application of *Clayton's case*

Notice of death, retirement or mental incapacity of a partner when the partnership account is overdrawn

12.4 In this case the bank should break the account, since if it fails to do so any credits paid in after notice of death, retirement or mental incapacity will discharge debit items incurred prior to the event, whilst any fresh debit items on the account will constitute new borrowing and the estate of the dead, mentally incapacitated or retired partner will not be liable for them.

Example

The bank has a partnership account ABC and allows unsecured overdraft facilities relying upon the ability of A, who is wealthy, to repay. The bank is notified of A's death on 1 October.

ABC

Date	*Debit* £	*Credit* £	*Balance* £
30 Sept	500		Dr 500
(Notice of A's death 1 Oct)			
2 Oct		600	Cr 100
7 Oct	600		Dr 500

12.5 In the above example the bank has allowed the account to continue unbroken with the result that the debit balance of £500 on 7 October is the liability of B and C only since the credit paid in on 2 October has discharged the debt incurred prior to A's death. Thus, A's estate is freed from liability.

12.6 The solution in this case would have been to break the account on notice of death. Thus, the account should appear as follows:

ABC (Old account)

Date	*Dr* £	*Cr* £	*Balance* £
30 Sept	500		Dr 500
1 Oct	Account ruled off		

ABC (B & C trading as) (New account)

Date	*Dr* £	*Cr* £	*Balance* £
2 Oct		600	Cr 600
7 Oct	600		Nil

12.7 The new account should be kept in credit, unless suitable arrangements can be made to justify an overdraft. The bank will enter into negotiations with A's personal representative, B and C, to arrange for repayment of the £500 on the old account.

Note: bankruptcy of a partnership is dealt with in Unit 6.

12.8 The same principles apply to notice of retirement or of mental incapacity of one of the parties to a partnership or joint account which is overdrawn.

Summary

Now that you have studied this unit, you should be able to:

- **define a partnership and types of partnership;**
- **describe how a partnership account is opened and conducted;**
- **explain the difference between different types of partner;**
- **explain the rules of agency as applied to partnerships;**
- **state the rights and duties of a partner;**
- **identify partnership property;**
- **explain how a partnership is dissolved and the distribution of partnership assets on dissolution;**
- **explain the effect of retirement, death and mental incapacity on a partnership;**
- **explain the liabilities of a retiring partner for debts incurred before and after retirement;**
- **understand the operation of the rule in *Clayton's case* in relation to partnerships.**

Self-assessment questions

1 A sleeping partner is a partner who:

(a) Takes part in management for a salary

(b) Contributes capital but has no personal liability for debts of the firm

(c) Contributes capital, is personally liable for partnership debts, but does not take part in management

(d) Has personal liability, but only to a limited extent?

2 The maximum number of partners as laid down by the Companies Act 1985 is:

(a) 7

(b) 20 in all cases

(c) 15

(d) 20 in all cases except for solicitors, accountants, stockbrokers and banks?

3 A partner as regards a partnership is a:

(a) General agent

(b) Special agent

(c) Universal agent

(d) *Del credere* agent?

4 E, F and G are partners. E retires. What must E do to avoid liability for subsequent partnership debts?

(a) Give notice in the *London Gazette.*

(b) Advise the retirement to all creditors who had dealings on or before his retirement.

(c) Both the above.

(d) Neither of the above.

5 A retiring partner is normally personally liable for partnership debts which existed at the date of his retirement. Which word describes a process which will free him from the liability?

(a) Ratification.

(b) Cancellation.

(c) Estoppel

(d) Novation.

6 What constitutes 'holding out' when a partner has retired?

(a) Use of the old firm's notepaper without the knowledge and agreement of the retiring partner.

(b) Use of the old firm's notepaper with the knowledge and agreement of the retiring partner.

(c) Both of the above.

7 A partner in a firm of accountants buys a gold ring on behalf of the partnership. If the partnership repudiates the contract:

(a) The third party can claim against the partner only.

(b) The third party can claim against the partnership.

8 ABC Ledger – *retirement of partner and death of partner*

Date	*Dr*	*Cr*	*Bal*
	£	£	£
Jan 1	300		Dr 300
5		200	Dr 100
7	100		Dr 200
8		100	Dr 100

The above is the copy of the ledger of A, B & C, a partnership.

(a) (i) To what extent is A liable for the partnership overdraft if he gave notice of his retirement from the partnership on 2 January?

(ii) What action should the bank have taken on receipt of the notice?

(b) (i) To what extent is B's estate liable if the bank received notice of his death on 6 January?

(ii) What action should the bank have taken on receipt of the notice?

9 While A, B, C and D are in partnership the following events occur.

(a) A accepts a bill of exchange in the firm's name.

(b) B opens a bank account saying that as he is the only partner resident in Extown, the account had better be in his name. This is done, and the account is subsequently allowed to become overdrawn.

(c) C seeks to introduce his son into the partnership.

(d) D is convicted of travelling on the London Underground without a ticket.

Explain the legal implications of each of these events so far as the other partners are concerned.

10 Hop, Skip and Jump are the only partners in a firm of accountants. The senior partner, Hop, has just reached the age of 60 and wishes to retire. He would like his son, who has recently obtained the appropriate professional qualification, to join the firm as a new partner at the same time.

How can these changes be effected, and what consequences would they have as regards the partnership liabilities of Hop and his son?

11 Tom and Jerry carried on business as a firm under the style of *The Glebeshire Meat Co* until December 1996. Then Tom retired and the partnership was dissolved, notice of dissolution duly appearing in the *London Gazette*. Thereafter, goods were ordered by Jerry on an old order form of the Glebeshire Meat Co (giving the names of Tom and Jerry as partners) from Dick, who had supplied goods for several years, and from Harry, a new supplier. As Jerry is now in financial difficulties, Dick and Harry wish to take action against Tom.

Consider the legal concepts which might be relevant and advise Dick and Harry of their legal position.

12 Pip, Squeak and Wilfred are partners in a firm which has an account with the Countryside Bank. Pip becomes of unsound mind. Discuss the legal position and the action the bank should take if the firm's account is:

(a) In credit.

(b) Overdrawn.

Further reading

- Laidlaw, A and Roberts, G — Chapter 2, *Law Relating to Banking Services*, 2nd edition 1992, Bankers Books.
- Milnes Holden, J — Chapter 11, *The Law and Practice of Banking*, Vol 1, 5th edition 1991, Pitman
- Raby, P — Chapter 7, *Law Relating to Banking Services*, 2nd edition 1992, Pitman

Unit 6

Individual Insolvency

Objectives

After studying this unit, you should be able to:

- **understand the reasoning which underpins bankruptcy procedures;**
- **appreciate the significance of the sequence in which the procedures take place;**
- **assess the effect of bankruptcy on the assets of a bankrupt individual or partnership;**
- **understand the significance of discharge of a bankrupt;**
- **appreciate the implications of bankruptcy for the operation of a bank account;**
- **understand the concept of different categories of creditors;**
- **appreciate the significance of the concepts of preferences and transactions at undervalue;**
- **understand the concept of voluntary arrangements or deeds of arrangements as an alternative to bankruptcy;**
- **understand the concept of proof and double proof.**

1 Introduction

1.1 A person or a partnership is generally insolvent when it cannot pay its debts. Any individual or group of creditors who is owed at least £750 unsecured can petition the court for the bankruptcy of the individual or partnership. They will first have made a statutory demand for repayment within three weeks, but repayment will not have been made.

1.2 Note 1 Registered companies are not made bankrupt, they go into liquidation.

2 Bankruptcy is governed by the Insolvency Act 1986 and Insolvency Rules 1986, to which all references are made in this unit unless otherwise stated.

2 Purpose of bankruptcy

2.1 The bankruptcy process exists to:

- Effect an orderly realisation of the debtor's assets so that creditors can receive a percentage (or possibly all) of their entitlement in accordance with the Act. Thus, the same class of creditors are all treated *para passu* (equally): s.328(3).

- Expose any malicious conduct on the part of the debtor so as to encourage a more honest standard of commercial behaviour.
- Enable the debtor to make a fresh start and to protect the debtor from harassment by his creditors.

3 Who may become bankrupt

3.1 Only *individuals* can be made bankrupt. Partnerships are 'wound up' under the Insolvent Partnerships Order 1994.

3.2 *Minors* can be made bankrupt, but only for debts in connection with necessaries, unpaid taxes or unsatisfied judgments in tort, i.e. a court case that has awarded damages against a minor for some wrongdoing.

3.3 The debtor must be present personally in *England or Wales* on the day the petition is presented.

3.4 *Aliens* may be made bankrupt provided they are domiciled in England or Wales now, or provided they have had a place of residence or carried on business in England or Wales at some time within the last three years: s.265.

3.5 Under the Mental Health Act 1983, a person who is *mentally incapable* can only be made bankrupt in respect of debts incurred before he became mentally incapable, and only if the Court of Protection consents.

3.6 A *deceased person* can only be made bankrupt if proceedings were commenced prior to his death. If on his death his liabilities exceed his assets, his estate will be administered in bankruptcy, i.e. under the Insolvency Rules 1986.

4 Sequence of events in bankruptcy

4.1 Either the debtor, or a creditor, or creditors jointly, or a supervisor of a voluntary arrangement or the official petitioner in the case of criminal bankruptcy, can present a petition to the court to have the debtor made bankrupt. The most common petitioners are the debtor himself and a creditor or creditors jointly. The petition will usually be based on the failure to repay under a statutory demand within three weeks.

Debtor's petition

4.2 The debtor presents a petition against himself claiming that he is unable to pay his debts: s.272. A statement of affairs must accompany the petition. This statement of affairs is a list of the debtor's assets and liabilities.

4.3 The court will then make a bankruptcy order provided the unsecured debts exceed £20,000 in total and provided there are sufficient assets to cover the cost of realisation. If the total of unsecured debts is below the 'small bankruptcy' level of £20,000, and the value of the assets above the minimum amount of £2,000, the court may appoint an insolvency practitioner to look at the feasibility of a voluntary arrangement or it may be requested by the debtor. This voluntary arrangement cannot be ordered if the debtor has been an undischarged bankrupt within the past five years, or has entered into an arrangement with his creditors. If the insolvency practitioner reports back to the court that a voluntary arrangement is feasible, then it will go ahead and the bankruptcy petition will not be granted. This method is called a 'court sponsored voluntary arrangement or 'summary administration'.

4.4 The official receiver will take over the assets of the debtor and repay the creditors. The exception is when a voluntary arrangement has been made. (The official receiver is a person authorised to act as such in relation to a bankruptcy or winding up. Official receivers are civil servants and officers of the court with insolvency jurisdiction.)

Creditor's petition

4.5 The creditor or creditors acting jointly must serve a statutory demand on the debtor to pay a sum owing. The amount must be at least £750, must be unsecured, and must represent actual money due either on demand or at a future date. A petition cannot be presented based on contingent debts, e.g. a person who guarantees a bank account, in other words he will only have to pay up if the person who owes the money to the bank defaults.

4.6 The creditor can then petition the court if the debtor has not paid or secured the statutory demand, i.e. given security for the debt, within three weeks.

4.7 An alternative ground is the failure of the debtor to meet a judgment debt in favour of the creditor. In such a case once a warrant has been served on the debtor by the bailiffs (who are court officials) and failure to pay or failure of the bailiffs to find assets of sufficient value to cover the debt will mean that the judgment debt has not been satisfied (paid).

4.8 The court, after considering whether the statutory demand is justified, will either grant a bankruptcy order or will dismiss the petition. Bankruptcy commences from the granting of the bankruptcy order.

4.9 The official receiver takes over the debtor's property.

Student Activity 1

Draw a diagram showing the process from the presentation of the petition to the granting of the bankruptcy order. Compare your diagram with Fig. 6.1 (para. 13.51).

Criminal bankruptcy

4.10 A person who has committed a crime and is tried in the Crown Court can, if loss or damage to the extent of £15,000 or more was caused, in addition to any sentence passed by the court, be made criminally bankrupt: Criminal Justice Act 1972. Similar provisions are also provided under the Criminal Courts Act 1973.

5 The bankruptcy order

5.1 The court will grant a bankruptcy order only if it is satisfied that:

- A debt payable at the time the petition is considered by the court, has neither been paid nor secured, i.e. security given to the creditor that could be realised to repay the debt.
- The debtor has no reasonable prospect of being able to pay the debt when it falls due.

5.2 The bankruptcy commences from the date of the bankruptcy order. The assets of the bankrupt are taken over by the official receiver who will look after the assets, i.e. ensure they remain intact and protected, for example, by paying any insurance premiums due, until a trustee in bankruptcy is appointed. The official receiver can claim any property that the trustee in bankruptcy can claim.

5.3 The official receiver can also dispose of any assets that are perishable or that would decrease in value if left until the appointment of a trustee. This protects the interests of the creditors who look to gain the maximum repayment from the estate of the bankrupt.

5.4 The bankrupt must prepare a 'statement of affairs', a statement of his assets and liabilities. This must be produced within 21 days of the date of the bankruptcy order.

5.5 The official receiver will conduct an investigation into the affairs and conduct of the bankrupt. If he has grounds to suspect that the bankrupt has acted fraudulently, is concealing assets, or that the bankrupt is merely being uncooperative, he can call for a public examination of the bankrupt. If creditors who are owed at least 50% of the debts due from the bankrupt request the official receiver to apply to the court for a public examination, then he must do so. A public examination is conducted in open court and the bankrupt is questioned as to his conduct and affairs.

5.6 The application for a public examination can be made at any time before the bankrupt is discharged.

5.7 Within 12 weeks of the granting of a bankruptcy order, the official receiver must call a creditors' meeting for the purpose of appointing a trustee in bankruptcy, or give notice that he does not intend to call a meeting. A creditor or creditors owed 25% or more of the total debts may, if they so wish, call a creditors' meeting. If no creditors' meeting is called then the official receiver acts as the trustee in bankruptcy: ss.292–94. If the bankruptcy is a criminal bankruptcy, there may not be a creditors' meeting, and the official receiver will act as trustee.

5.8 The trustee in bankruptcy must be an insolvency practitioner. The trustee's function is to sell the bankrupt's assets and to pay out to the creditors in the order of priority laid down by s.305(2).

5.9 An undischarged bankrupt has restricted contractual capacity. The Act imposes various restrictions upon the bankrupt as does the Company Directors Disqualification Act 1986. An undischarged bankrupt cannot:

- Act as a company director, liquidator, administrator, receiver or manager, or take part directly or indirectly in the management or formation of a company, unless authorised by the court: s.11, Company Directors Disqualification Act 1986. (Full details of limited companies and liquidation are found in Units 7 and 8.)
- Obtain credit, by either buying goods on hire purchase or borrowing money, unless he discloses the fact that he is an undischarged bankrupt to the creditor: s.360. The undisclosed bankrupt can, however, enter into small credit transactions of £250 or less without any restrictions.
- Engage in business, directly or via a nominee, unless he either does so under the name in which he went bankrupt, or he discloses this name to all parties with whom the business deals: s.360.
- Hold certain public offices such as a MP, local authority councillor or justice of the peace.

6 Duties and powers of the trustee in bankruptcy

6.1 The trustee's function is to get in, realise and distribute the estate in accordance with the Act, and in carrying out that function he is entitled (subject to the Act) to use his own discretion: s.305(2).

6.2 The general powers of the trustee are listed in s.315 and Schedule 5. He can exercise some powers without the sanction of the court or committee of creditors. Some have to have either the permission of the court or committee of creditors. (A committee of creditors may be appointed by the creditors' meeting if they so wish.) Any permission required from the court or the committee must be specific, not general.

6.3 If anyone deals with the trustee in good faith and for value, i.e. he pays for goods or services and does not receive them as a gift, then he does not need to establish whether or not the trustee has permission to deal with the items concerned.

6.4 If a trustee acts without permission, his acts can be ratified by the court, or by the committee provided he acted in an emergency and sought ratification swiftly.

6.5 If the trustee disposes of any property to an associate of the bankrupt or engages a solicitor to instigate legal proceedings on the bankrupt's behalf, or carries on the business of the bankrupt, he must have the permission of the committee of creditors (if one has been appointed): s.314(7).

6.6 The trustee can claim any interest or dividends due to the bankrupt and can issue receipts for monies taken.

6.7 The trustee can call a general meeting of all creditors at any time, and must do so if 10% or more in value of the creditors request such a meeting.

6.8 When the trustee feels that the administration of the estate is 'for practical purposes complete', he must call a final general meeting of creditors to receive the trustee's report of his administration. The creditors will then decide whether the bankrupt can be discharged: ss.331–32.

Bankruptcy offences

6.9 When a person is bankrupt he may, before he is discharged (or sometimes, even before bankruptcy commences), commit a variety of bankruptcy offences. These offences are listed in ss.350–62:

- Failure to disclose property or its disposal;
- Failure to hand over property to the trustee;
- Concealment, removal or failure to account for loss of any debt or property;
- Failure to deliver up books and records;
- Misinforming the trustee, or not telling him of false debts proved;
- Fraudulently disposing of his property or having done so within five years prior to the commencement of bankruptcy (see paragraphs 9.7–10 – transactions at an undervalue);
- Concealing property within two months before an unsatisfied judgment for payment is obtained against him;
- Absconding with property;
- Disposing of property obtained on credit and not paid for;
- Obtaining any form of credit exceeding £250 while being undischarged and not revealing the fact;
- Engaging in business in a different name, without disclosing the fact;
- Carrying on business without proper accounts;
- Gambling, if this contributed to his insolvency or to loss of property.

For these offences he may be fined or imprisoned.

7 Discharge of bankruptcy

7.1 Bankruptcy commences at the date of the bankruptcy order, and continues until the bankrupt is discharged. Discharge does not necessarily mean that the bankrupt has repaid his debts in full, because in most types of bankruptcy discharge is automatic after a set period of time. Discharge gives the bankrupt back his full contractual capacity and releases the bankrupt from all the debts he was subject to at commencement of the bankruptcy proceedings: s.382.

7.2 Discharge is covered by ss.278–80 and is obtained in the following ways.

- When the bankruptcy is a criminal bankruptcy, discharge is only obtained by court order, and cannot be requested by the bankrupt until five years from the date of the bankruptcy order.
- In the case of a bankrupt who has been an undischarged bankrupt at any time in the 15 years prior to the commencement of the current bankruptcy, the bankrupt must himself apply to the court for discharge after five years from the commencement of the current bankruptcy, i.e. five years from the date of the bankruptcy order.

- In other cases discharge is obtained automatically three years from the date of the bankruptcy order. However, if the official receiver considers that the bankrupt is not complying with his obligation, i.e. not making his best efforts to repay his creditors, then the official receiver can ask the court to suspend the running of the time period, so that discharge is not automatic.

Student Activity 2

Draw up a diagram showing the process from the granting of the bankruptcy order to the discharge of bankruptcy. Compare your diagram with Fig. 5.2 (para. 13.51).

8 Assets available to the trustee in bankruptcy

8.1 Not all assets of a bankrupt are available to the trustee in bankruptcy for repayment of creditors. The Act recognises that provision must be made for the bankrupt, spouse and any children, to provide them with the necessaries of life and not to leave them destitute. All distributable property of the bankrupt vests in the trustee in bankruptcy from the date of his appointment.

8.2 The items that are not classed a distributable property are defined in s.283(2) as:

- Tools, books, vehicles and other items of equipment as are necessary to the bankrupt to use personally by him in his employment, business or vocation;
- Such clothing, bedding, furniture, household equipment and provisions as are necessary for satisfying the basic domestic needs of the bankrupt and his family.

8.3 In the above cases the property may be claimed by the trustee if it appears that the realisable value of the whole or part exceeds the cost of a reasonably adequate replacement. If the trustee serves a notice claiming such property, usually within 42 days of first learning about the property, the property vests in him, and the trustee's title goes back to the date of the bankruptcy order. (The only exception is if a *bona fide* purchaser for value has purchased any of the property in the intervening period.) If the trustee claims such property, he must use funds in the estate of the bankrupt to purchase a reasonable replacement, and these funds are taken ahead of other creditors' claims.

8.4 Section 283(3) excludes property held in trust by the bankrupt for another person and s.269 excludes property that is subject to a prior charge by another person, e.g. a charge in favour of a bank or building society over that property.

After-acquired property

8.5 After-acquired property is property acquired by the bankrupt after bankruptcy has commenced but before he is discharged. Such property does not automatically vest in the trustee, but can be claimed by him by serving notice on the bankrupt within 42 days of discovering the existence of the property (unless such property would not vest in the trustee as described in above.

8.6 There is a slight problem relating to 'after-acquired property'. Section 307 is partly contradicted by ss.283–84. The problem arises because there is a delay between the making of the bankruptcy order, which appoints the trustee, and the date of the vesting order. Whilst bankruptcy commences at the date of the bankruptcy order, the general view is that s.307 should be interpreted as applying to the period *after* the vesting order.

Income payments order

8.7 Under s.310, the trustee can apply to the court for an order to pay any income to him for the benefit of the creditors. The court will only grant an income payments order if the bankrupt has an income in excess of what appears to the court to be necessary for meeting the reasonable domestic needs of himself and his family. The order may be made to the bankrupt or direct to the person paying the bankrupt to pay the money to the trustee.

The bankrupt's home

8.8 The bankrupt's home is liable to be sold by the trustee. Even if the house is in joint names or where the spouse has a right of occupation under the Matrimonial Homes Act 1983, the trustee could claim the house and sell it.

8.9 The trustee does not have an automatic right of sale, but he must apply to the court for an order to sell under s.30 of the Law of Property Act 1925. The court will consider the following aspects before making its decision, the:

- Degree to which the spouse contributed to the bankruptcy;
- Interests of the creditors;
- The needs and financial resources of the spouse;
- The needs of any children resident in the property;
- Any circumstances 'other than the needs of the bankrupt': s.336.

8.10 If the bankrupt has children under 18 who are still living at home, the bankrupt is unlikely to be evicted until 12 months have passed, because the trustee cannot evict unless the court grants permission. However, this does not mean that the trustee has no right over the house. The trustee can obtain a charging order over the property which means that when the property is eventually sold, the bankrupt's share of the sale proceeds will go to the creditors. This charging order remains in force even after the bankrupt has obtained his discharge, The charging order means that the purchaser of the property will pay the purchase price direct to the trustee who will distribute the proceeds amongst the creditors of the bankrupt.

Onerous property

8.11 Certain property of the bankrupt may provide the trustee with more problems than profit. If property is not saleable, or if it consists of rights under a contract that can only be completed at a loss, then the trustee can disclaim such property. This is because it would reduce the assets available to creditors (if it is something that could only be completed at a loss), or because it is so unsaleable that the bankrupt's estate could never benefit from it.

9 Transactions prior to bankruptcy

Petition to order

9.1 Under s.284(1), any dispositions of the debtor's property after the date of the bankruptcy petition are void. This means, in principle at least, that the trustee could claim back the property that had been sold or given away between the date of the petition and the date of the bankruptcy order. This could be unfair on third parties who had innocently taken such property, so the Act offers some protection.

9.2 If the debtor's property is disposed of between the dates of the bankruptcy petition and bankruptcy order, the court can ratify the disposal. Alternatively the debtor could ask the court to grant permission for the disposal of the property in advance.

9.3 If a third party received property before the bankruptcy order, but after the bankruptcy petition, he will be protected by s.284(4) provided he took the property:

- In good faith;
- For value
- Without notice of presentation of the bankruptcy petition.

9.4 The implication for banks in relation to payments into and out of an account are dealt with in paragraphs 13.16–25.

Preferences

9.5 A preference occurs when the debtor enters into a transaction that places one creditor in a better position than that creditor would otherwise have been in when the debtor subsequently becomes bankrupt. Under s.340 the trustee can apply to have the transaction set aside if he can establish that:

- The creditor was placed in a better position than would otherwise have been the case. The preference does not have to be a deliberate preferment of one creditor over another, simply that one creditor's position is better than it would otherwise have been.
- That the transaction took place within the relevant time. Relevant time runs from the date of the petition, i.e:
  - Six months for ordinary preferences for an ordinary creditor;
  - Two years for preferences given in favour of an associate. An associate is widely defined, and includes spouses, relative, partners (and their spouses or relatives), trustees who may benefit under a trust, and employees: s.435.
- That the debtor was insolvent at the time of the preference, or became insolvent as a result of the preference.
- That the debtor was influenced by a desire to prefer. (This is presumed where an associate is involved.)

9.6 A preference is voidable, i.e. it can be set aside.

Transactions at an undervalue

9.7 A transaction at an undervalue is defined by s.339 as one:

- In which the other party did not give any consideration, i.e. money or money's worth, to the bankrupt, e.g. the bankrupt had given the property away as a gift.
- Where the consideration given by the other party is significantly less than the value of the property, e.g. selling a house worth £150,000 for £100,000.
- In consideration of marriage.

9.8 To set aside the transaction it must be established that:

- The transaction took place within the relevant time, i.e. up to five years prior to the date of the bankruptcy petition; and
- The bankrupt was insolvent at the time of the transaction, unless the transaction took place within two years of the petition, in which case it is irrelevant whether or not the bankrupt was insolvent at the date of the transaction: s.341. If the transaction is in favour of an associate, then insolvency is presumed.

9.9 If the bankruptcy is a criminal bankruptcy then the relevant time period for a transaction at an undervalue or for a preference is the time period specified in the criminal bankruptcy order. No proof of insolvency is required in the case of criminal bankruptcy.

9.10 If the trustee can prove the transaction complies with these rules he can apply to the court for an order to recover the property.

Transactions defrauding creditors

9.11 These are similar to transactions at undervalue, but under ss.423–25 they involve a transaction made with the purpose of:

- Putting assets beyond the reach of a creditor;
- Prejudicing the interests of a creditor.

9.12 It is not the effect of the transaction alone which counts, but the purpose for which it is done. To rank as a 'transaction defrauding creditors' the transaction must be:

- At an undervalue;
- For one of the above specified purposes.

9.13 There are no time limits prior to bankruptcy with transactions defrauding creditors. The court can order the original position to be restored, i.e. effectively reversing the transaction.

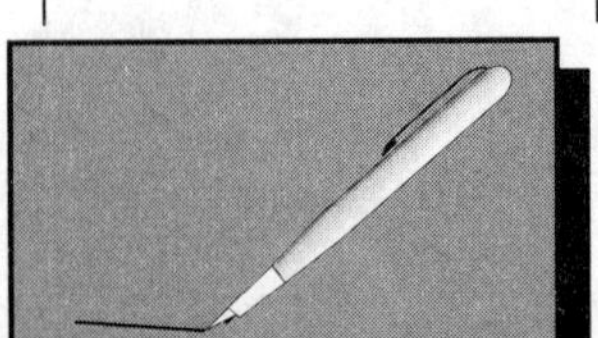

Student Activity 3

Summarise the differences between a preference, a transaction at an undervalue and a transaction defrauding creditors. Ask your branch manager for examples of any these that he is aware of involving customers of the branch.

10 Categories of creditor

10.1 There is a set order of repayment of creditors. Each class of creditor according to their position in the hierarchy of creditors must be paid off in full before the next category can receive any money. Each creditor within each class ranks *pari passu* (equally). Thus, if there is any shortfall in a category, the creditors in that category will receive a dividend. A dividend is calculated by dividing the sum owed to that category of creditor into the amount of money available. This will result in a dividend of X pence in the pound payable to each creditor in that category, e.g. a dividend of 10p in the pound would result in a creditor owed £5,000 receiving £500, and a creditor owed £200 receiving £20. All subsequent categories will receive no money.

10.2 The order of repayment is:

- Creditors with direct security, to the extent of the value of that security: s.328(6).
- Pre-preferential creditors: s.308.
- Costs of the bankruptcy: s.324(1) and 331(4).
- Preferential creditors: s.328(2).
- Unsecured creditors s.328(3).
- Any surplus then goes to pay interest for the period since bankruptcy commenced on the preferential or unsecured debts. Preferential and unsecured debts rank equally for this interest: s.328(4) and (5).
- Deferred creditors, i.e. the spouse of the bankrupt, married at the time bankruptcy commenced, who has lent the bankrupt money. The spouse is entitled to the debt plus interest: s.329.
- Any surplus is paid over to the bankrupt: s.330(5). Whilst it amy seem unlikely that there would ever be a surplus, the situation could arise if a person perversely refused to pay a particular creditor, despite having funds available. In that case, the only way forward may be for the creditor to instigate bankruptcy proceedings.

Creditors with direct security

10.3 Direct security exists when a lender has a right over an asset of the debtor. The creditor can sell the asset and use the proceeds to pay off the debt. Any surplus proceeds are paid over to the trustee in bankruptcy for the benefit of the unsecured creditors. If the proceeds of the asset are insufficient to pay off the lender in full, then the lender can prove as an unsecured creditor for the deficit.

10.4 The Act gives the holder of direct security four choices a regards proof in a bankruptcy:

- Rely on the security and do not prove at all. This is likely if the security value is well in excess of the borrowing but it is difficult to sell the asset which comprises the security. In such a case the bank would have adequate security and would ultimately intend to sell this security to repay the debt.
- Value the security and prove as an unsecured creditor for the shortfall. This is likely if the security value is less than the borrowing but the asset

is difficult to sell. The trustee has the right to take over the asset at the secured creditor's valuation.

- Sell the security, and prove as an unsecured creditor for any deficit, or pay over any surplus to the trustee. This is likely if the asset is easy to sell but is insufficient to cover the debt, or exceeds the debt. (This is the normal course of action taken by a bank.)
- Surrender the security for the benefit of the unsecured creditors in general and prove for the whole debt. This does not normally apply in practice unless the security is 'onerous property', e.g. a listed building which must be maintained to a certain standard, or a difficult lease (one which will cost more to keep up than it will realise). A creditor may adopt this course, however, in order to obtain maximum voting power at a subsequent meeting of all the creditors.

Pre-preferential creditors

10.5 Pre-preferential creditors include the funeral expenses of a bankrupt who died after the bankruptcy proceedings commenced. Also, if the trustee sold assets that would not normally be available to him and replaced them with items that performed the same function but that were cheaper, the cost is a pre-preferential creditor.

Preferential creditors

10.6 These are set out in Schedule 6 as:

- Any deductions for income tax during the 12 months prior to the bankruptcy order, if these deductions have not been paid over to the Inland Revenue. The same applies to deductions for National Insurance.
- Any unpaid VAT for six months prior to the bankruptcy order.
- Social security contributions due in the 12 months prior to the bankruptcy order.
- Contributions to an occupational pension scheme which should have been paid over by the bankrupt employer to the pension scheme.
- Unpaid wages or salaries subject to a:
  - maximum period of four months prior to bankruptcy order; *and*
  - maximum amount of £800 per employee.
- Any money lent to pay the qualifying wages ranks as a preferential debt. A lender in such circumstances is taking over the rights of the person who received the wages. This is an example of subrogation.

10.7 Between themselves the preferential creditors rank *para passu*. If there is insufficient cash to pay them all off in full, each preferential creditor obtains the same dividend in the pound.

10.8 The preferential creditors must be paid off in full before the unsecured creditors receive any money.

Unsecured creditors

10.9 These are creditors (apart from deferred creditors) who do not have any form of security, or who do not rank as preferential creditors, or who hold direct security which when realised is insufficient to cover the debt, or where part of the claim is preferential and part is not, e.g. wages in excess of the four-month/£800 per employee limit.

10.10 Between themselves the unsecured creditors rank *para passu.*

Third party security

10.11 Third party security can be by way of guarantee, or can apply when the lender has rights over an asset of a third party which can be used to pay off the debtor's borrowing.

10.12 As regards proof in bankruptcy, third party security is ignored. The asset belongs to someone other than the debtor and is completely outside the control of the trustee in bankruptcy: *Re Sass* (1896) (see section 11).

Student Activity 4

1 You bank has an account in a sole name which is unsecured and overdrawn. What danger does the bank run if a bankruptcy petition is presented in connection with unpaid VAT.

2 Study the order of repayment of creditors. Do you consider it fair that those who might seem not to need protection are classed as preferential creditors? Do you think that there is a case for changing the composition of the various classes of creditor?

Conclusion

10.13 Not all of the above categories of creditor will appear in every bankruptcy. In the case of an individual, many of the items under preferential creditors will not apply. Items such as VAT and wages will only apply in the case of a sole trader or partnership bankruptcy.

11 Proof in bankruptcy

11.1 Proof in bankruptcy means that a creditor of a bankrupt must usually submit a formal proof to the trustee in bankruptcy. The claim will show how much is claimed as a secured, preferential or unsecured creditor. The trustee may require formal documentation in support of the claim. A letter from the bankrupt to the creditor acknowledging the debt may be admissible as a formal document, but that would be at the trustee's discretion.

Double proof

11.2 There may be occasions where two creditors try to claim for the same debt. Under *Re Fenton* (1931) two persons cannot claim for the same debt. Obviously this would be inequitable (unfair) to the other creditors. The usual occasion for this to happen is when a bank has lent money against the security of a guarantee from a third party.

11.3 If the bank is owed money by the bankrupt, it will prove in the bankruptcy for the sum owing. It can also claim from the guarantor for any shortfall. This would result in the guarantor wishing to claim in the bankruptcy for the same debt as the bank. There are various clauses in the guarantee form covering this situation, and for the purposes of this unit, the effect of these clauses is that:

- The bank can claim for the full debt in the estate of the bankrupt.
- Any shortfall is claimed from the guarantor.
- If the guarantor pays the amount due under the guarantee, the bank can place this sum to a suspense account if the amount is less than the customer's total indebtedness. The bank can then prove for the whole debt. The bank will receive a dividend in the pound from the trustee in bankruptcy, and then and only then will the bank use the guarantee monies to meet the shortfall: *Ulster Bank v Lambe* (1966).
- If the guarantor pays the amount of his liability to the bank, the guarantor cannot then claim in the bankruptcy, unless the whole of the customer's debt is repaid: *Re Sass* (1896). This is under the 'whole debt' clause. Whilst a guarantee usually limits the amount payable by the guarantor to a specific monetary amount, if the guarantor pays off the *whole amount* owing to the bank, only then can he prove in the bankruptcy. In such cases the bank will credit the monies to the bankrupt's account and will then cease to need to claim in the bankruptcy.

Statute barred debts

11.4 These are debts that cannot be accepted as proof in bankruptcy because by statute they cannot be enforced.

- Under the Limitation Act 1980, any debt becomes statute barred six years after demand for repayment has been made. This period is extended where there is a subsequent acknowledgement within the six years: s.6, Limitation Act 1980.
- Gambling debts are classed as illegal, they cannot be enforced at law and therefore cannot be admitted as proof in bankruptcy.

12 Bankruptcy and partnerships

12.1 *Note*: For individuals and sole traders, the correct term is 'bankruptcy', for partnerships the correct term is 'winding up'.

Bankruptcy of an individual partner

12.2 This does not mean that the partnership becomes bankrupt. Many partnerships adopt articles which state that the partnership can continue, the bankrupt must resign, and a new partner or the existing partners can buy out the stake of the bankrupt. In this case, the new partners must account to the bankrupt's trustee in bankruptcy for the sum paid to 'buy him out'.

12.3 If partnership articles do not exist, or if they do not cover this aspect, the firm will be dissolved and the solvent partners must account to the trustee in bankruptcy for the bankrupt's share of the partnership.

12.4 If any cheques are presented which have been signed by the bankrupt partner, the bank should get them confirmed by one of the solvent partners.

Winding up of a partnership

12.5 Normally the winding up of a partnership will mean the bankruptcy of all the individual partners. A partnership cannot be wound up voluntarily by the partners: s.221(4).

12.6 However, under the Insolvent Partnerships Order 1994, the partnership creditors can specifically opt to sue the partnership alone and not the individual partners. This will occur when none of the partners has any private assets of any value.

12.7 The grounds for a petition are as described in paragraphs 4.5–9, with the addition of the ground of the partnership liabilities exceeding its assets: s.244.

12.8 If the creditors decide to make both the partners and the partnership bankrupt, the position is:

- Under the Insolvent Partnerships Order 1994, partnership property is first used to pay the expenses of winding up the partnership.
- Partnership assets are then used to meet partnership liabilities.
- The individual partners' assets are used to meet their personal liabilities. Any surplus proceeds from an individual partner will be added to the partnership assets and will be distributed to partnership creditors.

Student Activity 5

The partnership of Tom, Dick and Harry has recently been wound up. The final position is that the firm's assets amount to £25,000 and its debts to £50,000. Tom's private assets total £20,000 and his private debts total £15,000. Dick has private assets of £14,000 and debts of £14,000. Harry has private assets of £18,000 and private debts of £24,000. All creditors involved are unsecured creditors.

Calculate the amount received by the creditors of Tom, Dick, Harry and the partnership and then compare your figures with ours.

13 Bankruptcy of a customer

13.1 Up to now we have looked at the various aspects of bankruptcy in general terms. We now look at the effect upon the bank of the bankruptcy of a customer, and then consider the action the bank can take to minimise its losses.

Practical effect on the bank of the various stages in bankruptcy

Presentation of a petition

13.2 If a debtor is subsequently adjudged bankrupt, all transactions between the date of the petition and the date of the bankruptcy order will be void, unless approved by the court.

13.3 Since the withdrawal from the bank account is a 'transaction', there could be problems for the bank. However, s.284 protects all such transactions where the bank has acted in good faith and without notice of the presentation of a petition. Thus, the bank will be protected as regards all transactions prior to a bankruptcy order, provided it had no notice of a petition.

13.4 As soon as the bank learns of a petition, it must stop any withdrawals from the account. The customer must be advised that withdrawals can only be allowed if he can obtain a court order under s.284(1). Safe custody items cannot be released without a court order.

13.5 The decision in *Re Grays Inn Construction Ltd* (1980) seemed to indicate that courts would be reluctant to retrospectively validate any transaction between the date of the presentation of a petition and the winding up order (which is the equivalent in a company insolvency to a bankruptcy order in an individual bankruptcy). However , a later decision in *Re Barncrown Ltd* (1994) has cast some doubt on the *Grays Inn* reasoning. In practice, banks will continue to stop the bank account once there is notice of a petition, but may try and rely on the *Barncrown* decision if payments are made inadvertently and are challenged by the trustee in bankruptcy.

13.6 If the customer pays in any money and is unsecured and overdrawn it would be better to credit such sums to a suspense account. These items could be claimed by the trustee in bankruptcy and the bank could prove for too low a figure in the bankruptcy if the money had been credited to the customer's account; alternatively the trustee in bankruptcy could claim the amount credited as it is a disposition of the debtor's property in favour of the bank.

13.7 If the customer's account is in credit, any sums paid in can be credited direct to the account, but of course no withdrawals can be allowed.

13.8 On notice of a petition:

- No withdrawals must be made unless sanctioned by the court under s.284(1). Return cheques marked 'refer to drawer'. If items were debited they would be a disposition of the debtor's property and would be void.
- All payments can go into the account direct if the account is in credit.
- All credits must go to a suspense account if the account is overdrawn.
- Advise the customer of the position.
- If the petition is dismissed then the account can operate normally as regards legal requirements.

On notice of the bankruptcy order

13.9 The bank should stop the account, if not already stopped. If the account is in credit, the bank must pay over the balance to the official receiver or trustee in bankruptcy. If the account is overdrawn, the bank will claim any unsecured borrowing from the trustee in bankruptcy and receive a dividend in the pound.

13.10 Any withdrawals not authorised by the official receiver or trustee after notice of the bankruptcy order will be void and the bank must refund such amounts to the official receiver or trustee in bankruptcy. Safe-custody items cannot be released without the consent of the official receiver/trustee in bankruptcy.

13.11 Any withdrawals from an overdrawn account on or after the date of the bankruptcy order will however be valid under s.284(5) provided the bank:

- Did not have notice of the bankruptcy order; and
- Cannot reasonably recover the money from the person who received the proceeds of the withdrawal, e.g. the payee of a cheque drawn by the bankrupt.

13.12 If the bankruptcy petition is advertised in the *London Gazette* ('Gazetted'), then this is taken as notice to the world of the petition. If the bank overlooks this notice, that means that any withdrawals or dispositions of money on other property are void unless validated by the court: s.284.

13.13 *Note*: it is the bankruptcy order *not* the bankruptcy petition that is *always* Gazetted. The petition may or may not be Gazetted so care needs to be taken if the petition is Gazetted or otherwise advertised, as it would render disposition void.

13.14 However, if the withdrawals were made from a credit account, s.284(5) does not offer any protection. The only remedy the bank might be able to obtain is if the court will agree to ratify the payments retrospectively.

13.15 In practice, such problems are unlikely to occur, as the official receiver will contact the bank as soon as the bankruptcy order has been granted, provided he knows of the existence of the bank accounts.

Action to take with various types of account

Sole accounts

13.16 If the bank receives notice of a petition or bankruptcy order it must stop the account and take the action as detailed in above.

Joint accounts

13.17 The bank must stop the account and release the balance only on the joint authority of the trustee and the solvent party. The same applies to safe-custody items.

13.18 Any cheques presented on the joint account should be returned marked 'Joint account party ... involved in bankruptcy proceedings', if signed by the solvent party. Cheques signed by the bankrupt can be returned 'Refer to drawer'.

13.19 Likewise safe-custody items can only be released on the joint authority of the trustee and the solvent party.

Trust accounts

13.20 Such accounts are not affected by the bankruptcy of the trustee. However, the bank should examine the trust deed to see if the matter is covered there.

13.21 If the trust deed is silent, the bankrupt can continue as a trustee, but the bank must be vigilant for misuse of the funds.

Company directors

13.22 An undischarged bankrupt cannot be a director of a limited company, unless the court has granted approval.

13.23 If the bank holds the account of the relevant limited company, the only action required is to obtain a new mandate. Any cheques signed by the bankrupt director before the bankruptcy order must be confirmed by the other directors. Do *not* stop the company's account or return any cheques because of the bankruptcy of the director. A company is a separate legal entity from its directors, thus bankruptcy of a director has no effect upon the company's operation unless the minimum number of directors falls below that stipulated in the articles or Companies Act 1985.

Partnerships

13.24 On notice of a petition or bankruptcy order, the bank will:

- Stop the partnership account in all cases.
- Normally the bank will also stop the accounts of the individual partners. If the order is drawn up under the Insolvent Partnerships Order 1994, it only applies to the partnership account and the individual accounts of the partners are not affected, because such an order only involves the winding up of the partnership and not the bankruptcy of the individual partners. Therefore check the bankruptcy order to see if the Insolvent Partnerships Order 1994 applies. If it does, do not stop individual partners' accounts. If it does not apply then stop the accounts of the individual partners as well as the partnership account.

13.25 Where joint and several liability is held (which will be the case provided a bank mandate has been used when opening the account), this means that each partner is both jointly and individually liable for the partnership borrowing. Thus, on winding up of a partnership a bank can claim in both the partnership's winding up and in the bankruptcy of any or all individual partners for the amount owed by the partnership (subject to not receiving more than 100p in the pound).

Opening an account for an undischarged bankrupt

When the bank was unaware of the bankruptcy

13.26 If the bank opens an account for an undischarged bankrupt, even though it is unaware of the fact, the money paid into such an account would be classed as 'after-acquired property'. As after acquired property the trustee in bankruptcy can serve notice on the bank to pay over all such monies: s.307.

13.27 This would cause a problem for the bank if it had allowed withdrawals from the account, as the trustee can claim back money from the date of the bankruptcy order. However s.307(4) protects the bank provided it opened the account without knowledge of the bankruptcy and it acted in good faith. Provided these requirements have been fulfilled, the bank will not have to refund any money. The only exception would be if the credit balance consisted of money which was subject to an income payments order. In this case a refund would have to be made by the bank to the trustee.

When the bank was aware of the bankruptcy

13.28 In such a case the bank would be liable to refund all monies to the trustee in bankruptcy.

When the bank opens an account and subsequently discovers the customer is an undischarged bankrupt

13.29 If the bank opens an account, and then subsequently discovers that the customer is an undischarged bankrupt, it must:

- Stop the account and advise the customer. If possible phone head office and get them to do an immediate search in the Bankruptcy Register.
- Give notice to the trustee in bankruptcy, or to the Department of Trade if the trustee is not known. Use registered post.
- Follow the instructions received from the trustee. He may either claim the balance or indicate he is not interested.
- If there is no response from the trustee, the bank would seem safe to operate the account after the period of 42 days has expired, (this period being the time allowed to the trustee to claim after-acquired property). This is why the bank will use registered post, so that it can prove that the information was sent to the trustee in accordance with this time limit.

Cheques drawn under a cheque guarantee card

13.30 If a bankruptcy order is made, bankruptcy commences from the date of the order. However, the bank will have a problem if the customer has issued cheques in conjunction with a cheque card and if these are presented for payment after the bankruptcy order was made. The payee is entitled to payment, because the bank has guaranteed payment.

13.31 Under s.284(5), a bank can pay cheques to the debit of a bankrupt's account, after the bankruptcy order, provided the:

- Bank did not have notice of the order (not applicable here), and
- Money cannot be recovered from the person to whom it was paid (this does apply).

13.32 There are no decided cases but the bank would argue that the cheque, backed by the guarantee card, had been 'effectively paid' at the time of its issue. It would also argue that the money cannot be recovered from the payee.

13.33 The practical solution is to debit the customer's account, as the cheque must be paid anyway, and then try and convince the trustee of the bank's case, via the proof claim form.

Banks and preferences

13.34 There are various situations in which a bank may be exposed to the danger of a preference:

- If the customer repays his loan or overdraft, the bank may be held to be preferred.
- A customer repays his borrowing and then asks for the release of a guarantee or third party security held by the bank. This may constitute a preference of the bank if the customer's repayment had resulted in the

bank being put in a better position than other creditors in a subsequent bankruptcy commencing within the relevant time limits. The payment into the bank account could be reclaimed as a preference by the trustee and yet the bank would have given up its guarantee or third party security.

The reason for the 'early repayment' is obviously that the customer sensed impending bankruptcy and preferred the bank in order to protect the guarantor or person depositing the third party security.

- Security given by the customer to secure his borrowing (direct security) may be a preference.

13.35 If the trustee in bankruptcy can prove that any of these situations was a preference, he can claim the money or take over the direct security from the bank.

Repayment of loan or overdraft

13.36 This could present the bank with a problem if the bank had not put pressure on the customer to repay. The trustee may claim that the repayment was a preference, and thus repayment must be made to the trustee.

13.37 However, in *Re M C Bacon Ltd* (1989), the decision was that provision of financial facilities to a company in financial difficulties, and the taking of security by the bank to secure the lending, was not a preference if done under proper commercial considerations. *Bacon* held that the transaction would not be set aside as a voidable preference unless the company positively wished to improve the creditor's position in the event of its own insolvent liquidation. The bank had given the company the ultimatum of providing security or else the bank would call in the borrowing. This was held as sufficient reason to give the security.

13.38 Whilst *Bacon* concerned the liquidation of a company, and not bankruptcy, these principles will also apply to bankruptcy.

Release of third-party security

13.39 If an account has been guaranteed by a third party, and if the borrowing is repaid, then the bank may be requested to release the security. Care needs to be taken here. The customer may be trying to 'prefer' the guarantor by having the guarantee released by the bank. However as the money owing has been repaid to the bank, it is the bank who may have to repay to the trustee in the event of a preference as, at law, it is the bank that has been preferred.

13.40 If the guarantee is given by an unconnected person, i.e. not an associate of the customer, the bank is only at risk for six months. If the guarantee was given by an associate, e.g. spouse or relative, then the relevant period is two years, prior to the date of the presentation of the petition.

13.41 The bank is also protected by s.342(2) if it receives payment from the bankrupt:

- In good faith;
- For value;
- Without notice of bankruptcy proceedings or that the transaction was a preference.

13.42 If the above section applies, the bank will not have to make repayment to the trustee.

13.43 If the bank did have to repay credits received after releasing the guarantee, the court could order the restoration of the guarantee: s.342(1). This remedy could prove very helpful to the bank so long as the guarantor remained good for his liability.

13.44 In practice, the bank will not release the security for the six-month or two-year period from the date of request. There is a clause in the guarantee form which allows the bank to retain the guarantee undischarged for the relevant period of time.

13.45 The bank would need to be careful if an overdrawn account suddenly went into credit, and request was made to release the guarantee held as security. If the account went into credit suddenly, and especially if withdrawals had not been made, there may be a chance that the customer was trying to 'prefer' the guarantor. In such a case the bank would decline to release the guarantee for the relevant period of either six months or two years.

13.46 It would appear from *Re M C Bacon*, that if the bank had put pressure on the customer to repay, then the payment of money to the bank would not be classed as a preference.

13.47 Similar considerations apply when the bank holds third-party security other than by way of guarantee, for instance when a relative of the customer deposits his (the relative's) shares as security.

Security given by the customer to secure his borrowing

13.48 If the customer has given his own assets as security to the bank for his borrowing, it is unlikely that this security would be classed as a preference if bankruptcy occurred within six months. If the only way in which the bank would lend, or continue to lend money, was against security, then the granting of this security would not be a preference: *Re M C Bacon Ltd* (1989).

Student Activity 6

Horace is married with three children under 16 years of age. He lives in a modest terraced house in London which he occupies on a short lease. He has a small business which has got into difficulties, and he is overdrawn at his bank. The bank sees little prospect of success for him, and is reviewing its position.

A creditor brings a bankruptcy petition against Horace on 1 May. This is advertised in the *London Gazette* on 3 May. On 5 May the following transactions take place on the account: a payment in of £3,000, followed by a payment out of £2,000 to Charles.

On 6 May the bank discovers the existence of the petition. Horace owes £15,000 to his various creditors, including the bank.

Consider the following.

1 The payment in of £3,000 is recorded by the bank as reducing the overdraft by that sum. Is this correct?

2 The payment out of £2,000 is recorded by the bank as increasing the overdraft by that sum. Is this correct?

Set off

(Recap on set off in Unit 3, section 9 before you read on.)

13.49 Statutory set off is covered by s.323. The main provisions are that:

- There must have been credits and debits between the customer (debtor) and the bank (creditor) prior to bankruptcy.
- Any credit balances held must be set off against any debit balances held before the bank can prove in bankruptcy.
- Debts incurred after bankruptcy cannot be offset against credit balances once the bank knows of the bankruptcy. Debts incurred after bankruptcy cannot be claimed in bankruptcy.

13.50 Any prior agreement not to set off such balances is revoked upon bankruptcy: *National Westminster Bank Ltd v Halesowen Presswork and Assemblies Ltd* (1972).

14 Voluntary arrangements

Voluntary arrangements

14.1 As an *alternative* to bankruptcy a person may make a voluntary arrangement to be administered by a insolvency practitioner ('nominee'): s.253. The insolvency practitioner is either authorised as such by a recognised professional

Figure 6.1 Diagrammatic representation of the bankruptcy process

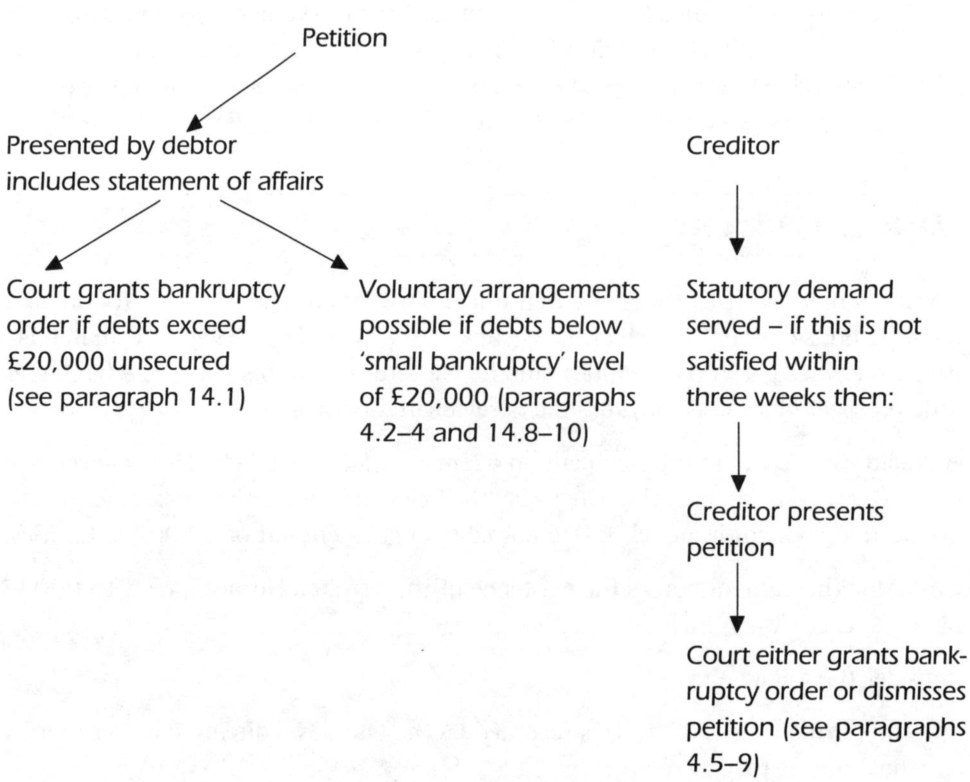

Figure 6.2 On granting of the bankruptcy order

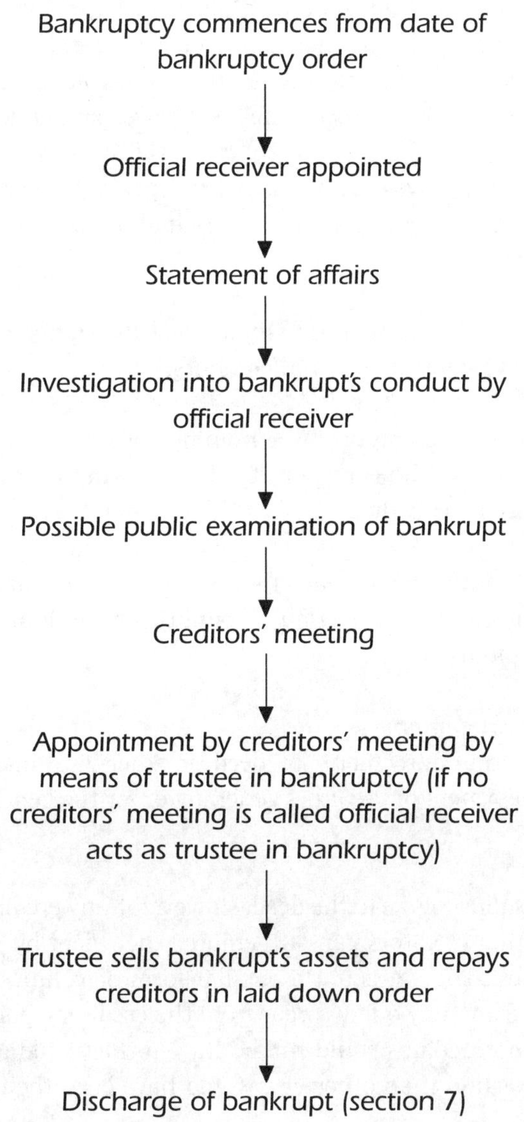

body, e.g. Insolvency Practitioners Association, or the 'relevant authority' set up by the Secretary of State. Most insolvency practitioners are accountants who are authorised by the accountancy bodies.

14.2 An interim order may be made upon application to the court; this normally ceases to have effect after 14 days, although this period can be extended by the court upon application for extension. During this time no bankruptcy proceedings or any other proceedings whatsoever can be effected. Before the period ends the nominee provides a document setting out details of the scheme or composition put forward by the debtor together with a statement of affairs. The court will only grant a voluntary arrangement if it is satisfied that:

- The debtor intends to make a proposal to the creditors for the repayment of the debts;
- He has not made a similar application within the past 12 months;
- He is not already bankrupt or in a position to present a petition himself.

14.3 If the nominee decides that the creditors should consider the proposals, the interim order will be extended and the meeting of creditors may approve the proposal with or without modification. If at least 75% of the creditors in value vote in favour, the arrangement will be passed. If more than 50% of the creditors in value (excluding secured creditors) vote against it, the proposals will fail and bankruptcy proceedings will be recommended by the court.

14.4 If the creditors approve the voluntary arrangement, the court will be advised and the scheme will bind everybody who had notice of it and was entitled to vote at the meeting.

14.5 Any voluntary arrangement must not affect the rights of a secured creditor and must provide for preferential creditors.

14.6 Once the proposal is approved the nominee or his replacement is known as the 'supervisor' and he is responsible for ensuring that the arrangement is carried through correctly.

14.7 A voluntary arrangement means that the debtor is *not* made a bankrupt. This means he has not got the 'stigma' of bankruptcy on him. It is also a cheaper process to administer.

Deeds of arrangement

14.8 This includes any agreement (by deed or otherwise) made by an insolvent debtor for the benefit of creditors generally or for the benefit of three or more creditors.

14.9 The creditors must agree to the deed. However if any creditor(s) did not agree, these dissenting creditors can still enforce their debt by presenting a bankruptcy petition. Thus, it is not a popular form of voluntary arrangement in practice there are only a few a year from the creditors' point of view because bankruptcy proceedings could still be started that could leave them in a less favourable position than otherwise would have been the case.

14.10 For the deed of arrangement to be valid:

- It must be registered with the Department of Trade within seven days of it being executed. It must also be properly stamped.
- A majority in number and value must assent (agree) to the deed of arrangement within 21 days of registration.
- Within 28 days of registration a statutory declaration is filed confirming that the agreements, have been obtained.
- Within a further seven days the trustee must give security, unless the creditors dispense with this requirement. If the trustee fails to give security, or dispensation for this is not obtained from the creditors, the court may declare the deed void, or appoint a new trustee.

Summary

Now that you studied this unit, you should be able to:

- **understand and describe the sequence of events in bankruptcy;**
- **understand the consequences of a bankruptcy order;**
- **explain when a bankrupt is discharged from his bankruptcy;**
- **identify assets available to the trustee in bankruptcy;**
- **identify transactions that may take place prior to bankruptcy but which may subsequently be overruled by the trustee in bankruptcy;**
- **describe the various categories of creditor;**
- **explain the meaning of 'proof' and 'double proof' in bankruptcy;**
- **describe the effect of bankruptcy on partnerships;**
- **understand the effect of the bankruptcy of a customer on the operation of the bank account;**
- **explain the problems of releasing security in the event of subsequent bankruptcy.**

Self-assessment questions

1 A partnership becomes bankrupt. Who has first call on the following items?

(a) Partnership property

(i) The partnership creditors.

(ii) The partners' own individual creditors.

(b) A partner's own property which is used in the firm's business

(i) The partnership creditors.

(ii) The partner's own individual creditors.

2 E, F and G are partners and the partnership becomes bankrupt. There are no assets in the partnership name and F and G have no personal assets. E has £10,000. To whom is the £10,000 distributed?

(a) To the personal creditors of all the partners.

(b) To the personal creditors of E with any surplus retained by E.

(c) To the partnership creditors.

(d) To the personal creditors of E with any surplus being available for partnership creditors.

3 A bank holds a joint account in the names of A and B with a credit balance of £700. You have been notified of a bankruptcy order against A.

Today a cheque for £500 signed by B is presented. The mandate is either to sign. What do you do?

(a) Pay the cheque.

(b) Return the cheque 'Refer to drawer'.

(c) Return the cheque 'Joint account, party A involved in bankruptcy proceedings'.

4 You have the account of a company, and you receive notice of a bankruptcy petition against one of the directors. Is the director's authority to sign cheques determined:

(a) Immediately?

(b) From the date of the bankruptcy order, if made?

(c) From the date of the vesting order?

5 X has authority on the bank's standard 'per pro' mandate to sign cheques on behalf of Y.

A bankruptcy petition has been made against X, and a cheque is presented in the clearing, signed by X on Y's account. There are adequate funds.

What action do you take?

(a) None, apart from checking that there seems nothing suspicious about the cheque.

(b) Return the cheque 'Refer to drawer'.

(c) Return the cheque 'Mandate inoperative'.

(d) See if Y is prepared to cancel the mandate but pay the cheque.

6 Assume the facts as in Question 5, except that you now have notice of a bankruptcy order against X.

What action do you take? The choices as in Question 6.

7 A bankruptcy order is made against B. Can you release safe-custody items to B?

(a) Yes.

(b) No.

8 What is the name of the procedure by which a trustee in bankruptcy is allowed to take over the bankrupt's assets and sell them?

(a) Bankruptcy order.

(b) Statement of Affairs.

(c) Vesting Order.

9 Which of the following are preferential creditors under Schedule 6?

(a) Rates.

(b) Electricity.

(c) VAT for six months.

(d) Wages: maximum £800 per person, maximum four months prior to bankruptcy.

(e) Deductions of tax and NI for one year which have been paid over to the relevant authorities.

10 Which of the following could be liable for bankruptcy proceedings?

(a) Minors for any debts.

(b) Minors, but only for necessaries or unpaid taxes.

(c) Individuals.

(d) Partnerships.

(e) Limited Companies.

(f) Aliens who are domiciled in the UK or who have been so domiciled within the last three years.

11 What is the minimum unsecured amount on which a statutory demand can be based?

(a) £50

(b) £250

(c) £750

(d) £1,750

12 A creditor can bring a bankruptcy petition to court if the debtor has not paid or secured a statutory demand within:

(a) Three days.

(b) Three weeks.

(c) Three months.

(d) Three years.

13 At what stage does bankruptcy officially commence?

(a) The making of a statutory demand.

(b) The presentation of a petition.

(c) The making of a bankruptcy order.

(d) The issue of a 'statement of affairs'.

(e) The appointment of a trustee.

(f) The date of the vesting order.

14 What action will a bank take on notice of the service of a statutory demand on its customer? Assume his balance is in credit.

(a) No action at all.

(b) Stop the account and advise the customer.

(c) Return any cheques drawn by the customer marked 'Refer to drawer'.

(d) Advise the customer that no withdrawals can be allowed, unless he has a court order under s.284.

15 Your bank has paid a cheque after the date of the presentation of a bankruptcy petition but before notice of it. What is the bank's position?

(a) It is fully protected under s.284.

(b) The bank must refund the money if a bankruptcy order is subsequently made.

16 You have the account of a company and you learn of the presentation of a bankruptcy petition against one of the directors. What action do you take as regards the company's account?

(a) No action at all.

(b) Stop the company's account.

(c) Obtain a new mandate, omitting the director mentioned above.

(d) Have all cheques signed by this director confirmed by the other directors.

17 You learn of a bankruptcy order against one of the directors of a limited company. What action do you take as regards the limited company?

(a) No action at all.

(b) Stop the limited company's account.

(c) Obtain a new mandate, omitting the director mentioned above.

18 All bankrupts, apart from a few exceptions, qualify for automatic discharge after:

(a) 10 years.

(b) Five years.

(c) Three years.

19 Apart from automatic discharge, which types of bankrupt have to wait for a different period before obtaining a discharge? How long is the period in each case, and how do they obtain their discharge?

20 For some two years John Smith has maintained an entirely satisfactory credit account at your branch. He is also a director, with James Harris, of a small private limited company banking with you. A competitor of theirs, who also banks with you, tells you that Smith was made bankrupt some two years ago and has never obtained his discharge.

How would you confirm this information and what action would you take if it proved to be true?

Further reading

- Laidlaw, A and Roberts, G — Chapter 10, *Law Relating to Banking* Services, 2nd edition 1992, Bankers Books
- Penn, GA, Shea, AM and Arora, A — Chapter 28, *The Law Relating to Domestic Banking*, Vol 1, 1987, Sweet & Maxwell
- Raby, P — Chapter 9, *Law Relating to Banking Services*, 2nd edition 1992, Pitman

Unit 7

Limited Companies

Objectives

After studying this unit, you should be able to:

- **understand the nature of a limited company and how a limited company is formed;**
- **appreciate the relationship between the company and its directors;**
- **understand the remaining significance of the *ultra vires*;**
- **understand how various legal concepts affect the operation of the bank account of a company.**

1 What is a limited company?

1.1 A limited company is first and foremost a business organisation which has a separate legal entity from its owners (members): *Salomon v Salomon and Co Ltd* (1897). The owners (or members) of a limited company are its ordinary shareholders. The day-to-day running of the company is undertaken by the directors, who are appointed by the shareholders. A limited company can be sued, punished by a fine and be put into liquidation without any legal consequences upon its owners (except in the case of liquidation, see Unit 7).

1.2 Companies are governed primarily by statute law, specifically the Companies Act 1985 and the Companies Act 1989. All references are to the 1985 Act unless stated otherwise.

2 Public and private companies

2.1 The Companies Act 1985 defines a *public company* as a company:

- Limited by shares.
- Stated to be a public company in its memorandum of association.
- With a minimum of two shareholders.
- Whose name ends its name with 'Plc' or 'Public Ltd Co' (or its Welsh equivalent for companies whose registered office is in Wales).
- With a minimum authorised and issued share capital of £50,000.
- Correctly registered or re-registered as a public company.

2.2 Under s.1(4), Companies Act 1985, all other companies are private companies. If a company name ends with 'Ltd', 'Co Ltd or 'Limited' it will be taken to be a private limited company. The minimum number of shareholders in a private company is one: Companies (Single Member Private Limited Companies) Regulations 1992.

2.3 The accounts of both private and public companies must be filed at Companies House, where they are freely available to anyone to inspect, although private companies need file only a modified balance sheet.

Differences between a private and a public company

2.4 The main differences are that a private company:

- Cannot offer its shares or debentures to the public, whereas a public company can.
- Is not subject to the £50,000 minimum capital rule. It only needs two shares in its capital, i.e. a minimum issued share capital of £2.
- Will have the word 'Limited' or 'Ltd' after its name.
- Can have a minimum of one director, provided the sole director is not also the secretary. A public company must have a minimum of two directors.
- May in its articles restrict the transfer of its shares, but it need not do so. A public company cannot restrict the transferability of its shares. When a small limited company is first incorporated, the proprietors (those who are acting as both shareholders and directors) may wish to ensure that control cannot subsequently pass to outsiders through the sale of the shares. This restriction on transfer is often included in the articles so that control remains with the original proprietors. For major public companies which are listed on a stock exchange, such an article, as well as being contrary to the Companies Act, would be incompatible with the need to have swift and simple procedures for the purchase and sale of the shares.

Other types of company

2.5 Whilst not very common, there are two other forms of company:

- Companies limited by guarantee; and
- Unlimited companies.

Companies limited by guarantee

2.6 These are companies that do not have any share capital subscribed by their members. Instead the members guarantee to contribute a set sum in the event of the company going into liquidation. This sum is usually a nominal £1 per member. Companies limited by guarantee do not have any owners in the sense of public or private companies limited by share, and are usually non-profit making, education or charitable organisations. This type of company's name will usually end in 'Incorporated' or 'Inc'.

Unlimited companies

2.7 These are companies which do not have any limit to the liability of their members for the debts of the company in the event of liquidation. They are usually involved in the service industry rather than trade. One notable example of an unlimited company is Coutts and Co – one of the smaller clearing banks.

Student Activity 1

You have already studied partnerships. Before reading further, draw up a rough table comparing the benefits and drawbacks of partnerships and companies. When you have done this, compare your table with the text below. It would then be useful to construct a second, fuller table and keep it in your study folder.

Advantages and disadvantages of companies and partnerships

Advantages of a partnership

2.8 These are that:

- *Formation costs* are cheaper. A partnership can be formed or created by word of mouth or by implication. Articles of partnership can be drawn up, but they are not essential.
- *Privacy*: no balance sheets have to be filed, whereas all limited companies have to file copies of accounts at Companies House, although private companies can file a modified form of balance sheet.
- All partners can, unless the articles state otherwise, share in *management*, whereas it is the directors who are in day-to-day control of a limited company. Ownership is divorced from control with a limited company be it private or public.

Advantages of a limited company

2.9 These are that:

- There is no limit on the *maximum number of members* (shareholders) unless in the case of a private company its articles of association stipulate a limit. A partnership is limited to 20 partners, apart from certain professional partnerships.
- A limited company has *perpetual succession*, whereas, subject to its articles, a partnership is dissolved on the death of a partner.
- Provided the shares are fully paid, a shareholder has no *personal liability* for the debts of the company, unless it is an unlimited company, whereas a partner (except a limited partner) is personally liable for the partnership's debts.
- A shareholder can easily *transfer shares* in a quoted company and can usually find a buyer for all of private company shares. It is much more difficult to negotiate a sale of the interests in a partnership.
- A limited company is a *separate legal entity* from its members and the company can be sued, fined or put into liquidation with no effect (usually) on its members. Partners are fully liable for all aspects of the partnership.

3 Incorporation

3.1 A company is formed by a legal process under the Companies Act 1985, requiring various steps to be completed prior to it attaining legal existence. The first steps are common to both public and private companies.

- The memorandum of association and articles of association must be drawn up.
- The memorandum of association and articles of association must be filed with the Registrar of Companies. The Registrar must also be satisfied that all the Companies Act requirements have been met. The company must also file a statement detailing the first directors and secretary of the company, and also a statutory declaration that all the legal requirements have been complied with.
- If the Registrar is satisfied, he will issue the certificate of incorporation. This is conclusive evidence of the legal status of the company and states whether it is a public or private company. The certificate of incorporation also is proof that the company has been registered.

  At this stage a private company can commence trading, however, a public company must make the declaration described below after receiving its certificate of incorporation.
- A director or secretary of a public company must make a statutory declaration that the £50,000 minimum share capital has been raised. The Registrar will then issue the public company with a trading certificate (also called a 'certificate to commence business'). The public company cannot commence trading before receiving the trading certificate, otherwise it will commit an offence under the Companies Act 1985.

3.2 Whether it is a public or a private company, the date of its creation is the date of issue of the certificate of incorporation.

3.3 If a public company commences trading after receiving the certificate of incorporation, but before receiving the trading certificate, any transaction entered into will not be void. If the company fails to meet such obligations within 21 days of being asked to do so in writing, then the directors of the company become personally liable for any losses suffered by the other party to the transaction.

3.4 If the company, whether public or private, enters into any transaction prior to receipt of the certificate of incorporation, the transaction is not binding on the company and under s.35 the directors will be personally liable upon any such transaction, unless otherwise agreed.

4 Memorandum and articles of association

4.1 The memorandum of association regulates the external activities of the company. The articles of association regulate the internal activities.

Student Activity 2

Examine the memorandum and articles of association of one of your limited company customers and see how it expresses the clauses stated below.

Memorandum of association

4.2 The memorandum of association is a statement of the constitution and powers of the company. There are six main clauses in the memorandum:

- The name of the company followed by the word 'Limited' or 'Public Limited Company' (or by their Welsh equivalent).
- A statement as to whether the registered office is in England, Wales or Scotland. (This is important in order to establish whether English or Scottish law applies to the company.)
- The objects clause which show what a company is allowed to do. This clause must state both the *powers* and the *objects* of the company.
- A statement that the liability of the members (shareholders) is limited to the amount unpaid, if any, on their shares. Thus, a shareholder only has personal liability with partly paid shares.
- A statement as to the details of share capital (authorised capital).
- The association clause, which gives details of the original shareholders.

Name of the company

4.3 'Limited' or 'Public Limited Company' identifies which of the two major types of company you are dealing with. If the company is limited by guarantee then, under s.30 the name need not contain 'Limited' or 'Public Limited Company'.

4.4 The Registrar of Companies can refuse to register a company name under s.26, as follows:

- A company cannot chose any name it wishes. The registered name must not be the same or similar to that of an existing company. For example, a company cannot set up as 'Harrodds' as the Registrar would consider it too close to the famous Knightsbridge store 'Harrods'.
- The name must not use words indicating any link with the government.
- It should also avoid words such as 'English' or 'International' unless its business is in these areas.
- Great care must be taken over the use of the word 'bank' in a company name. A bank is recognised as such under the Banking Act 1987. Only such a recognised organisation can use the title 'bank' in its name. Any breach of this rule is a criminal offence.
- The name must not be offensive.

4.5 If a company wishes to trade under a name other than its own registered name, then the registered name must be disclosed on all stationery and be displayed prominently at the place of business: Business Names Act 1985.

4.6 The company name must also appear on the outside of every office or place where business is carried out, in legible form: s.348.

Registered office

4.7 A company must state the address, to the extent of stating 'England', 'Wales' or 'Scotland', of its registered office. If this is in England or Wales then the company is subject to English law. If it is domiciled elsewhere, e.g. Scotland, then it is subject to the company law as laid down in that country. The domicile is the country in which the company is registered.

Note: remember that Scottish law is different from English law, so always point this fact out clearly and never refer to UK law!

4.8 The registered office is the place where certain documents or registers must be kept, and where writs may be served on the company.

Objects clause

4.9 The objects clause states the business objectives and the powers of the company. The Companies Act 1989 made a major change in the effect of the objects clause on the powers of a company. Under the 1989 Act, where the company's object is to carry on business as a *general commercial company*, the company has the power to carry on any trade or business whatsoever and do all things conducive to that trade or business: s.110(3)(a). If the objects clause is not stated in theses terms, then the company will need to consider the effect of the abolition of the *ultra vires* rule as described in section 5. A company can also change its objects clause as explained below.

Liability of members

4.10 The members of the company are the shareholders. If the company were to go into liquidation, then the maximum amount they would lose would be the amount they originally invested in the company (not the value of the shares, as this is only a paper figure).

4.11 The only time the ordinary shareholder may have to pay out more money is if the shares are partly paid. Partly paid means that when the shares were purchased from the company only part of the share price was required to be paid, and the remainder was due at a later date. If the company goes into liquidation, the shareholder remains liable for the unpaid amount to the liquidator of the company. This liability also remains for a period of up to 12 months after the shares have been sold. If the purchaser fails to pay the balance due to the liquidator, then the liquidator can come back to the previous owner for the amount due. This is one reason why banks exercise extra care when taking a legal charge over partly paid shares.

4.12 Thus, the liability of the members is limited (not that of the company itself). However, all the shareholders in a private limited company can vote to make the company into an unlimited company, thus meaning the shareholder will have unlimited liability for its debts.

Details of share capital

4.13 By law a company must have ordinary share capital (except companies limited by guarantee). A company can if it wishes have other forms of capital (see section 6). The memorandum of association will state the amount of the authorised share capital of the company, e.g. the share capital of the company is £1,500,000 divided into 6,000,000 shares of 25p each.

4.14 The company does not have to issue all the authorised share capital when it is formed, so a company's balance sheet may show a different, lower, figure for issued share capital from the figure for authorised share capital.

The association clause

4.15 This clause simply gives historical information, i.e. the names of the original shareholders (members) of the company and the number of shares they originally held.

Changing the memorandum of association

4.16 At some time, the company may feel that its memorandum of association is restricting its activates, or circumstances force a change upon the company that requires the memorandum of association to be amended. If, and how, the clauses detailed above can be changed is dealt with below on a clause-by-clause basis.

Name of the company

4.17 This can be changed by means of a special resolution of the ordinary shareholders passed by a 75% majority of the votes cast at a general meeting of the company. The votes cast may be by people actually present and entitled to vote, or by proxy. A proxy vote occurs where a shareholder cannot attend the meeting in person but nominates another person, who will be present, to vote on his behalf. It is simply 75% of the votes cast at the meeting, not 75% of the voting share capital, that carries the resolution.

4.18 The other time that a company will change its name is if the Department of Trade insists on a change because it considers the existing name to be undesirable or misleading. This change does not require the consent of the shareholders.

4.19 The new name must be registered with the Registrar of Companies and a certificate of change of name (and in the case of a public company, a new trading certificate) will be issued.

4.20 The company name may change, but the old company debts are still due from the company trading under its new name. Legally, it is still the same company, it is simply trading under a different name.

Registered office

4.21 The address of the company consists of two parts: the address of the company, i.e. road, town and county, and the domicile of the company, i.e. the country in which it is registered. The company can physically relocate its registered office anywhere it wishes, provided it does not change its domicile. The domicile of the company cannot be changed.

4.22 The change of address is simply notified to the Registrar of Companies.

Objects clause

4.23 A company may by special resolution alter its memorandum with respect to the statement of the company's objects: s.110, Companies Act 1989. A special resolution is passed at a general meeting and requires 75% of the votes cast to be passed.

4.24 However, 15% or more of shareholders, by number of shares held, can object to any change within 21 days of the resolution being passed: s.5. The objection must be lodged with the court, which will decide either to confirm the alteration to the objects clause, modify it, or cancel it. If the court cancels the alteration to the objects clause, then the company cannot operate under that specific clause. If no objection is received within the 21 days period the change cannot later be challenged: s.6(4).

4.25 The objects clause can thus enable a company which was originally set up with the purpose of manufacturing silk purses to become a retailer of sow's ears, provided the special resolution is passed at a general meeting of the company, and no objections are lodged within the 21-day period by 15% or more of the shareholders.

4.26 A company can, if it wishes, adopt a new objects clause which gives it very wide powers. Under s.110(3)(a), Companies Act 1989 the memorandum of association may state that the object of a company is to carry on business as a 'general commercial company'. This enables the company to carry on any type of trade or business without having to change the objects clause if it wishes to change to another trade or business area. This clause gives the company the power to do all such things that are incidental or conclusive to the carrying on of any trade or business by it.

4.27 The objects clause also covers the powers of the company as well as the business objectives of the company. The powers of the company may include its power to borrow money and/or give security. This is not necessarily expressly stated, but a trading company has implied authority to borrow or give security. However, the powers of the company should only be exercised in support of its stated business objectives. This could lead to the company trying to exercise powers that are beyond the powers of the company (*ultra vires*). The powers of the company are changed in the way described in this section.

Liability of members

4.28 Whether the liability of the members of the company can be changed depends upon whether it is a public or private limited company.

4.29 A public company cannot change the liability of its members. The liability remains limited to their shareholding or any amount unpaid if the shares are partly paid: s.74, Insolvency Act 1986. This extends for a period of up to 12 months after the shares have been sold.

4.30 A private company can alter the liability of its members. Under s.49, if all the members agree to change their liability to unlimited and lodge that agreement with the Registrar of Companies, the company will be re-registered as an unlimited company. This is unlikely to be common occurrence in practice.

Details of share capital

4.31 The authorised share capital of the company is set down in the memorandum of association, and can be altered by means of a special or an ordinary resolution passed at a general meeting.

4.32 In order to reduce a company's share capital, a special resolution must be passed. This requires 75% of votes cast. Some quoted companies have taken this step by buying back some of their shares from the stock market.

4.33 This action also requires that the articles of association authorise the reduction, and that the court gives approval for the reduction in share capital (see section 12).

4.34 An ordinary resolution is passed if it attains a simple majority of the votes cast at the meeting. An ordinary resolution is used to alter the share capital by:

- Increasing the authorised share capital;
- Increasing the issued share capital;
- Consolidating the share capital;
- A share split.

4.35 *Increasing the authorised share capital* may be desired if the company wishes to raise money but does not have sufficient unissued shares available to do so. Such an operation is called a rights issue and the shares are initially offered to existing shareholders in proportion to their existing shareholding.

Note: there are other methods of raising capital via an ordinary share issue, but they are outside this syllabus.

4.36 *Increasing the issued share capital* can be done when the company has not issued all the authorised share capital. The increase can be to raise money for the company – a rights issue, or a simple bookkeeping exercise – a capitalisation issue.

4.37 *Consolidation of the share capital* alters the nominal value of the shares but has no effect on their capital value. The nominal value of a share is quoted in its title, e.g. 25p. A company may decide to consolidate the shares into £1 nominal shares, thus four shares of 25p nominal value become one share of £1 nominal value. This exercise has no effect on the balance sheet or market value of the company.

4.38 The reverse of a consolidation is a *share split* whereby, for example, shares that had a nominal value of 50p are split into shares of 25p nominal value. Again there is no effect on the balance sheet or market value of the company.

4.39 The Registrar of Companies must be notified of any changes in the capital of the company.

The association clause

4.40 As this is a historical fact, the association clause cannot be altered.

Articles of association

4.41 The articles of association govern the powers of the directors of the company in all their dealings. The directors are responsible for the day-to-day running of the company, and are elected by the ordinary shareholders in accordance with the rules laid down in the articles of association, i.e. at the company's annual general meeting (AGM).

4.42 The articles also cover the issue and transfer of shares, the rights of the shareholders, the conduct of meetings, appointment and retirement of directors, disqualification and removal of directors, the accounts and the winding up of the company.

4.43 Many companies do not bother drawing up their own set of articles of association, but adopt a model set of articles – Table A of the Companies Act. There have been various Companies Acts and, for example, a company incorporated in 1950 would be adopting Table A of the Companies Act 1948, whilst a company incorporated in 1989 would adopt Table A, Companies Act 1985. (Companies Act 1989 did not include a model set of articles, i.e. a Table A.) A company's articles of association must be registered with the Registrar of Companies. If no articles of association are registered, then Table A will apply. A company can also, if it wishes, adopt Table A, but make modification to any part of it as it wishes and register this as its articles of association.

4.44 The original articles of association must be approved and signed by each of the members named in the association clause of the memorandum of association and these signatures must also be witnessed.

Changing the articles of association

4.45 Any part of the articles of association can be amended by the passing of a special resolution by a 75% majority of votes cast at a general meeting: s.9. Any alteration must be consistent with the memorandum of association. It must not amount to a fraud on a minority of members, and must not increase the liability of a member to the company in any way, without that member's consent.

5 The Companies Act 1989 and the ultra vires rule

5.1 The memorandum of association, in its objects clause, lays down the business objectives and powers of the company. The articles of association lay down, amongst other things, the powers of the directors. In both the memorandum and articles of association, there will be limits on the powers of both the company and directors, and in the memorandum of association there will be a limit on the business objectives of the company, unless they have adopted the objects clause under: s.110(3)(a), Companies Act 1989 (the 'general commercial company' object).

5.2 If either the company or the directors act outside of the limitations laid down they are said to be acting *ultra vires*, i.e. beyond their powers. Prior to the Companies Act 1989 any acts of the company or the directors could have been void if they were *ultra vires.*

5.3 The 1989 Act changed the law on acts which are *ultra vires* the company's memorandum of association. Acts that are *ultra vires* the company's articles of association are also affected by the change in the Companies Act 1989.

Ultra vires and the memorandum of association and the articles of association

5.4 Section 108, Companies Act 1989 substituted a new s.35 into the Companies Act 1985. Section 35(1) states that:

> The validity of an act done by a company shall not be called into question on the ground of lack of capacity by reason of anything in the company's memorandum.

5.5 Section 35B states that:

> A party to a transaction with a company is not bound to enquire as to whether it is permitted by the company's memorandum or as to any limitation on the powers of the board of directors to bind the company or authorise others to do so.

This covers both the memorandum and articles of association.

5.6 The effect of s.35 is that anyone dealing with the company does not need to enquire whether there is any limitation on the company as laid down in its memorandum of association. This is of particular relevance to banks, who previously needed to examine the objects clause in the memorandum of association to establish whether the purpose for which a company wished to borrow was allowed by the memorandum. This action was of vital importance to banks because any borrowing by the company that was *ultra vires* the memorandum was void and therefore unenforceable).

5.7 With the 1989 change, the need for the bank to examine the objects clause of the memorandum of association is removed. Thus, borrowing by a limited company will be valid, provided there is a *bona fide* commercial justification for the borrowing. As a bank will always exercise great care in assessing any lending proposition, it will automatically consider whether there is commercial justification.

5.8 However, the bank will not be able to enforce borrowing or a guarantee by the company if the purpose is prohibited by ss.151–58; a company is not allowed to give financial assistance by way of gift, guarantee, security or loan to assist a third party to purchase the company's own shares.

Note: there are a limited number of exceptions (see section 11).

5.9 Under s.35(3), Companies Act 1985:

> It remains the duty of the directors to observe any limitations on their powers flowing from the company's memorandum; and action by the directors which but for subsection 1 would be beyond the company's capacity, may only be ratified by the company by special resolution.
>
> A resolution ratifying such action shall not affect any liability incurred by the directors or any other person; relief from any such liability must be agreed separately by special resolution.

5.10 Section 35A(1) states:

> In favour of a person dealing with a company in good faith, the power of the board of directors to bind the company, or authorise others to do so, shall be deemed to be free of any limitation under the company's constitution.

5.11 The effect of the s.35A is that the directors can still enter into an act which is *ultra vires* the articles of association. In such a case, the directors could be personally liable for such transactions. The only way that they could avoid liability is if the members of the company pass a special resolution at a general meeting to that effect.

5.12 A person who deals with a company in good faith is free from any limitation under the company's constitution even if the person knows that the act is beyond the powers of the directors. Under the Act, this is not regarded as acting in bad faith. Unless anything can be proved to the contrary, a person is presumed to have acted in good faith. Under s.35B a person is not obliged to enquire whether there is any limitation on the powers of the directors to bind the company.

5.13 Any member of the company does have the right to bring proceedings to restrain the doing of an act which is beyond the powers of the directors. Thus, the *ultra vires* rule is abolished for external purposes, but retained for internal purposes.

Invalidity of certain transactions involving directors

5.14 Section 322A(1) applies when a company enters into a transaction to which the parties include a:

- Director of the company; or
- Person connected with such a director or a company with whom such a director is associated.

5.15 In addition, the board of directors, in connection with the transaction, will have exceeded any limitations on their powers.

5.16 As a result of such action, under s.322A(2) the transaction is voidable, i.e. can be avoided, but is not automatically avoided, at the insistence of the company. Whether or not the transaction is avoided, the directors who authorised the transaction are liable to:

- Account to the company for any gain which has been made either directly or indirectly; and
- Indemnify the company for any loss or damage resulting from the transaction: s.322A(3).

5.17 Any third party who has rights against the company from a voidable transaction is protected provided he 'acquired *bona fide* for value and without actual notice of the directors exceeding their powers': s.322A(5).

5.18 A voidable transaction can be ratified by the company in general meeting, by ordinary or special resolution or otherwise as the case may require: s.322A(5).

6 The capital of a company

6.1 Every company by law must have ordinary share capital. It can also raise capital by issuing other forms of capital. These are the most common forms of capital, and variations occur which are outside this syllabus.

Company loan stocks

6.2 These are fixed interest securities issued by a private or public company which usually carry a fixed redemption rate. They fall into three broad categories:

- Debentures;
- Unsecured loan stocks;
- Convertible loan stocks.

6.3 There are a few other types such as subordinated loan stocks, but these are not too common. A subordinated loan stock ranks after unsecured creditors but before shareholders in liquidation.

Debentures

6.4 A debenture is an acknowledgement of debt by a company. The debenture can be unsecured but it is usually secured by a fixed or floating charge on the assets of the company. If the charge is a fixed charge, then in liquidation the loan stock holders will rank first. If it is a floating charge, they rank after preferential creditors.

Unsecured loan stocks

6.5 These rank with the unsecured creditors in liquidation. They are more risky than a debenture issued by the same company. However, an unsecured loan stock issued by a 'blue-chip' company such as ICI is safer than a debenture issued by a small company, simply because ICI is unlikely to go into liquidation.

Convertible loan stocks

6.6 These are loan stocks (usually unsecured) that carry the right for the holder to exchange the loan stock for a preset number of ordinary shares at or between set future dates. Until conversion, they receive the fixed rate of interest. On conversion, they become ordinary shares and receive dividends. If the holder decides not to convert, then once the final conversion date is passed they become conventional loan stocks.

6.7 All loan stock holders receive interest on their holdings, which is a charge against company profits. Failure to pay interest due could result in the company going into liquidation or receivership.

Preference shares

6.8 Preference shares form part of the share capital of a company and rank after all creditors but before ordinary shareholders in the event of liquidation.

6.9 There are various types of preference share, but all receive a *fixed* rate of dividend which is shown in the title of the stock. The preference dividend is paid after loan stocks interest but before the ordinary share dividend is paid.

6.10 The main types of preference share are:

- *Cumulative*: where any unpaid dividends are carried forward and must be paid before any ordinary share dividends are paid.
- *Non-cumulative*: where a dividend unpaid is lost forever.
- *Participating*: where, on top of the fixed dividend, an extra dividend is paid if profits, or ordinary share dividends exceed a preset figure.
- *Redeemable*: some preference shares carry a date on which they will be repaid.
- *Convertible*: where they can be converted into ordinary shares at a preset date and number.

6.11 A preference share can have several of these features, and they will be reflected in the title of the stock (except for non-cumulative).

Ordinary shares

6.12 Ordinary shares are also known as equity capital. Section 744 defines equity shares capital as:

> ... in relation to a company, its issued share capital excluding any part of that capital, which neither as respects dividends nor as respects capital, carries any right to participate beyond a specified amount in distribution.

6.13 Thus, ordinary shareholders receive the right to participate in profits either by way of retained profit and/or dividend. Dividends are paid out each half year (usually) and are paid net of basic rate tax.

6.14 Dividends are paid out of profits available to ordinary shareholders (also called distributable profits). Some profit can be retained in the company for future developments and some is paid out by way of ordinary dividend. The decision as to the amount of the ordinary dividend paid out of distributable profits is made by the directors. This decision is agreed by the shareholders at the next AGM.

Redeemable preference shares and redeemable ordinary shares

6.15 Under the 1985 Act such shares can be issued provided:

- The articles of association allow it;
- There are also some irredeemable ones.

6.16 Such shares can only be redeemed from profits or from the proceeds of a fresh issue of shares. However, a private company can redeem the shares from capital, provided the directors issue a statement saying that the company will remain a going concern for the next 12 months despite the redemption. This statement must be approved by the auditors and by a special resolution passed at a general meeting.

7 Opening and closing a company bank account

Opening a company bank account

7.1 When opening an account for a limited company, the bank will use the purpose-designed mandate. Standard clauses:

- State that the bank was appointed the company's bankers at a meeting held on the date specified in the mandate.
- Request the bank to pay all cheques, bills of exchange, promissory notes, acceptances, negotiable instruments and other orders drawn.
- Requests the bank to pay such items even if the account becomes overdrawn or further overdrawn. However, it also states that the bank has the right to refuse payment of such items if it increases or creates an overdraft.
- Deal with the delivery and disposal of any safe custody or security items.
- Incorporate a signing authority.
- Contain instructions on where and to whom all correspondence is to be sent.
- Certify that the clauses in the mandate are a true copy of the minutes of

the meeting appointing them as bankers. This is signed by the chairman and secretary.

- The mandate also includes specimen signatures of all signatories to the account.

7.2 The mandate acknowledges receipt of a copy of the memorandum and articles of association (for retention by the bank), the certificate of incorporation (for inspection and return), and in the case of a public company the certificate to commence trading (for inspection and return).

Note: it could be argued that (new) s.35 has ended the need for a bank to ask for the memorandum and articles of association.

Student Activity 3

Examine your bank's company mandate form and its clauses. Underline the clauses on the mandate which correspond to those above.

Closing a company account

Note: reread Unit 4, section 8; this section simply recaps the main points.

7.3 A company account can be closed by the bank. If the account is overdrawn the procedure depends on the form of borrowing:

- An overdraft is repayable on demand: *Williams & Glyn's Bank Ltd v Barnes* (1980).
- If the account is a loan account, repayment cannot be demanded unless the:
  - instalments are in arrears; or
  - company has breached one of the covenants in the loan agreement form.

7.4 If the account is in credit, the bank must give reasonable notice to close the account: *Prosperity Ltd v Lloyds Bank Ltd* (1923). However, there is no definition of 'reasonable notice', and a limited company may need several months' notice to find new bankers and rearrange all its business accordingly.

8 Set off

8.1 The bank only has an automatic right of set off if it can satisfy the requirements as laid down in *Garnett v McKewan* (1872) (reread Unit 4, section 9).

8.2 To recap, the amounts must be:

- For certain sums;
- Between the same parties;
- In the same right.

8.3 Note that in the situation of a group of companies, which may well have consolidated accounts, there is no automatic right of set off between the parent and any of the subsidiaries nor for that matter is there any automatic right of set off between the different subsidiaries. There can of course be a right of set off if there is a specific agreement to that effect, for example a guarantee arrangement.

9 The rights and liabilities of directors and their relationship with the company

9.1 A director is appointed by an ordinary resolution of the shareholders at a general meeting. He is one of the board of directors, and it is the board's responsibility to run the company on a day-to-day basis. A director is an agent of the company. An agent does not normally incur liability for acts carried out on behalf of his principal but in certain circumstances this does occur. Likewise, the agent has certain rights against his principal.

Rights of a director

9.2 The director has the same rights as described in Unit 3, section 6, particularly to be compensated for any loss or expenses incurred properly on behalf of the company and to be paid provided he has fulfilled his duties.

9.3 A director also has the right to participate in the running of the company. If he is wrongly excluded, then under s.122, Insolvency Act 1986 he can petition the court to have the company compulsorily wound up. The court will grant the petition if it judges it to be 'fair and equitable' to do so. This type of action is rarely used, and is generally' used by small private companies where the management has become deadlocked, or a director is 'frozen out'.

Liabilities of a director

9.4 Apart from the usual liabilities of an agent (see Unit 3, section 7), there are certain other situations in which a director may become personally liable, some in connection with agency and some in connection with other matters:

- Pre-incorporation contracts;
- Guarantees;
- Bills of exchange;
- Minimum membership;
- An unlimited company;
- Contravention of s.151;
- *Ultra vires* acts;
- the Company Directors Disqualification Act 1986;
- Insolvency Act 1986.

9.5 *Pre-incorporation contracts* – a limited company does not legally exist before the certificate of incorporation is issued. If a director or the directors enter into contracts prior to incorporation on behalf of the company then they would be personally liable upon them. A director could only avoid liability if he had disclaimed personal liability at the time of signing the contract. The company cannot, after it has been incorporated, ratify the contract: *Kelner v Baxter* (1866), because a contract cannot be ratified when the principal (the company) did not exist at the time the contract was made. The company can only be bound by the contract if it enters into a *new* contract once the company has been formed (see also Unit 3, paragraphs 3.12–15).

9.6 If the director signs a bill of exchange, cheque or other order to obtain money or goods, and the full registered name of the company does not appear, then he will be personally liable s.349(4), Companies Act 1985 and *Maxform SpA v B Mariani and Goodville Ltd* (1979).

9.7 Note that in this context:

- If the 'Ltd' is omitted, the director will be personally liable: *British Airways Board v Parish* (1979).
- If a bank incorrectly prints the company name on the cheques, then the signatories may be personally liable but the bank may be liable to compensate the signatories in such a situation: *Hendon v Adelman* (1973).
- 'Limited' can be abbreviated to 'Ltd' wherever a company's name is required to be shown, and the director will not be personally liable: s.27(4)(a).
- 'Company' can be abbreviated to 'Co' wherever a company's name is required to be shown, and the director will not be personally liable: *Banque de L'Indochine et de Suez SA v Euroseas Group Finance Co Ltd* (1981).
- If a bill of exchange is drawn with the wrong name, i.e. the company's name is incorrect, due to the error of the drawer (this is not the company who signs the bill), then the director is not personally liable on the bill. This is because the error was not caused by the company, but by the other party to the bill, who is thereby estopped from claiming due to the fact that it was he who made the mistake: *Durham Fancy Goods Ltd v Michael Jackson (Fancy Goods) Ltd* (1968).
- If a director fails to indicate his capacity when signing a bill of exchange, he will not incur personal liability provided the cheque clearly and accurately states the name and account number of the company: *Bondina Ltd v Rollaway Shower Blinds Ltd* (1986)

9.8 If the number of the company's *membership falls below two* and the company carries on business for more than six months after, the remaining member is jointly and severally liable with the company for debts incurred thereafter: s.24.

9.9 If the company is an *unlimited company*, the director, if he is a member of the company (which is usual) will be liable for the debts of the company.

9.10 If a director acts in contravention of s.151 – *covering financial assistance given by companies* – he will be liable for debts thus incurred: *Wallersteiner v Moir* (1974).

9.11 If a director acts *ultra vires* the articles of association, and the act is not ratified by special resolution, he will be personally liable.

9.12 If a director is *disqualified from being a director* under the Company Directors Disqualification Act 1986 he will be personally liable.

9.13 If the company goes into *liquidation*, the directors can be made personally liable for debts under the wrongful and fraudulent trading provisions of the Insolvency Act 1986.

9.14 If a director personally *guarantees* the limited company's account, he is liable up to the amount of his guarantee for the indebtedness of the company but note that his liability is entirely personal and not based on his position as a director as such.

Relationship of director to the company

As agents

9.15 Directors are agents of the company and as such they have certain powers vested in them by the articles of association. These constitute actual authority. Directors also have ostensible authority. Ostensible authority arises from s.35. This protects third parties who do not have specific knowledge of any limitations on a director's power, provided they acted in good faith. Any director can bind the company unless specifically excluded from doing so by the articles of association. Thus, to a third party all directors have ostensible authority to bind the company. This will be binding on the company provided the third party does not know of the limitation.

9.16 Even if the articles of association clearly indicate some limitation in the director's authority, under s.711A(1) a third party is not affected by the clause. The exclusion of deemed notice states that a person should not be deemed to have notice of any matter merely because of its being disclosed in a document kept by the Registrar of Companies (and thus in the public domain and available for inspection) or being made available by the company for inspection. However, s.711A(2) also states that this does not affect the question of whether a person is affected by notice of any matter by reason of a failure to make any enquiries as *ought reasonably to be made.*

9.17 There may be circumstances when a third party could not rely on the abolition of deemed notice under s.711A(2), and in such cases the third party could be protected by *Royal British Bank v Turquand* (1856) (more commonly called the Rule in *Turquand's* case). Under this judgment a third party is not obliged to enquire whether the company is observing its own rules as laid down in the memorandum and articles of association. The third party can assume that the company is abiding by these rules, and thus gain full protection in the event that the transaction is *ultra vires* the directors.

Interested directors

9.18 If a director (or more than one director) has an interest in a resolution being passed, he must declare that interest prior to voting taking places: s.317. Whether or not the director can then vote will be decided by the articles of association. If the articles allow the interested director to vote, then a certified copy of the board's resolution will record the disclosed interest. If the articles forbid the interested director to vote, the resolution must be passed by a quorum of independent directors, or failing this being possible, by a general meeting. (A quorum is the minimum number of directors that must be present at a meeting to make the proceedings valid. The number constituting a quorum will be specified in the articles of association.)

10 Disqualification of directors

10.1 If a director proves unfit to hold office, then he can be statutorily barred from being a director under the Company Directors Disqualification Act 1986. Under this Act the court can make a disqualification order against a director if he has either:

- Been a director of an insolvent company, including where wrongful or fraudulent trading is proved; or
- Been convicted of an indictable offence in connection with a company, e.g. insider dealing under the Company Securities (Insider Dealing) Act 1985; or
- Persistently failed to comply with obligations under the companies acts, e.g. persistent failure to file the company's annual accounts with the Registrar of Companies.

10.2 If a disqualified director continues to act as a director he is committing a criminal offence under s.13, Company Directors Disqualification Act 1986. He is also liable jointly and severally with the company for any debts incurred if the company has knowingly allowed him to act as a director whilst disqualified: s.14, Company Directors Disqualification Act 1986. The director is also personally liable for any debts incurred by the company under this section.

10.3 A register of disqualification orders is maintained at Companies House. The period of disqualification will last for a minimum of two years to a maximum of 15 years, depending upon the judgment of the court. Over the 10-year period to 1996, 3,000 directors were disqualified and in the first quarter of 1996, the number disqualified was 200, twice the number for the corresponding period in 1995.

Student Activity 4

The provisions of the Act seem to provide some protection against unscrupulous directors but how effective a deterrent do you think this is in practice? Look in the index of articles on directors and disqualification in a publication such as the *Financial Times* and then consider whether the deterrent is valid.

10.4 The other two types of person disqualified from holding directorships are:

- An undischarged bankrupt: s.11, Company Directors Disqualification Act 1986. An undischarged bankrupt cannot be a director, nor can he be involved in the formation, promotion or management of a company.
- In the case of a public company, the maximum age for a director is 70, unless the articles stipulate to the contrary: s.293, Companies Act 1985.

11 The giving of financial assistance by companies

11.1 This comes under two separate headings:

- Financial assistance to enable the purchase of its own shares; and
- Financial assistance to directors and connected persons.

Assistance to purchase own shares

11.2 Sections 151–58 generally prohibit the provision of financial assistance by a company, either directly or indirectly or by gift, to enable an individual to purchase its own shares. Direct assistance is by way of money or loan, indirect assistance by way of guaranteeing or giving security against the borrowing of the individual.

11.3 There are various exceptions laid down in ss.151–58 that enable companies to give financial assistance under certain circumstances. Under s.153(1), which relates solely to public companies, financial assistance for share purchase is valid where 'the company's purpose in giving the assistance is not solely to assist share purchase, or where assistance is part of some larger purposes of the company'; the assistance must also be given 'in good faith in the best interests of the company'. In *Arab Bank Plc v Mercantile Holdings Ltd and Anor* (1993), it was held that the prohibition does not extend to as subsidiary which has been incorporated outside the UK and gives such assistance for the purchase of shares in its English parent company.

11.4 The definition of 'larger purpose' is somewhat vague, and in *Brady and Another v Brady and Another* (1988), the House of Lords decided that a narrow concept must be given to this definition. However, this narrow concept has not been specifically defined, and is not found in the Companies Act 1989.

11.5 An example of a larger purpose could be if a company made a takeover bid for another company. The target company (the one being bid for) could agree to guarantee a loan to the bidder in order to enable the bidder to purchase the target's shares. If the agreement to guarantee the loan were just a 'gentleman's agreement' (albeit in writing), e.g. a written confirmation of intent which would not constitute a binding contract, then the financial assistance would be a criminal offence subject to a maximum penalty of two years' imprisonment plus a fine. However, if the target company were part of a group of companies, and if the group would benefit from the bidder becoming part of the group, then the guarantee from the group would be valid as it would benefit the 'larger purpose' of the group.

11.6 There are certain other occasions laid down in s.153 where financial assistance to purchase the company's share are valid:

- When lending money is the company's ordinary business. Thus a bank can lend its customers money to enable them to purchase the bank's shares.
- When financial assistance is given to employees to enable them to purchase the company's shares under an employee share scheme. Financial assistance can be either money lent to the employee by the company, or the guaranteeing of a loan by a lender to the employee. The shares acquired by the employee under the employee share scheme must be fully paid: s.153(4)(b).

11.7 The rules apply to both public and private companies. However, for *public* companies giving assistance as described in the latter instance above the assistance must not have the effect of reducing the company's net assets, or the assistance must be given out of distributable profits. If these rules are broken then the assistance is a criminal offence.

11.8 For a *private company*, there is an additional proviso for financial assistance to be in any circumstances and for any purpose provided that:

- The net assets of the company are not reduced by such assistance, unless the assistance is provided from distributable profits.
- The assistance is approved by means of a special resolution passed at a general meeting. The assistance cannot be given within four weeks of the date of the resolution unless *all* members eligible to vote at a general meeting were in favour. (A special resolution only needs 75% of votes cast at a general meeting to be passed.)
- The directors must make a statutory declaration of solvency, i.e. that the company could pay all its debts due within 12 months if it were to be wound up. The assistance must be given within eight weeks of the statutory declaration. The statutory declaration must be accompanied by an auditor's report confirming the declaration.
- The company lodges with the Registrar of Companies within 15 days:
  - a copy of the special resolution;
  - the statutory declaration of solvency;
  - the auditor's report.

11.9 Holders of 10% of the nominal value of the issued share capital can apply to the court within 28 days for the special resolution to be cancelled.

11.10 For a private company, a common occurrence of needing to provide financial assistance to purchase its shares will arise when a new director is appointed and there is a requirement in the articles of association that a director must have a 'qualification holding' – a minimum number of shares needed to be a director. Either the company will lend the director the money, or the bank will lend against a guarantee by the company. If the bank has lent to the director, against the company's guarantee, the guarantee will be enforceable provided the above conditions have been met.

Financial assistance to directors and connected persons

11.11 A connected person is a person connected to the director: the director's partner or spouse; directors' families; companies with which the director is associated (if he controls over 20% of the voting power); the trustee of a trust whose beneficiaries include the director. 'Director' includes a shadow director.

11.12 Under s.330, financial assistance to directors and connected persons is prohibited whether it is by way of a loan or by a guarantee or other security. The loan can be a 'quasi-loan', i.e. a transaction that does not appear to be a loan, but which is one in effect. For example, a company charge card where the company settles the bill and is later reimbursed by the director is a quasi-loan because the company is lending the director money which is later repaid by the director.

11.13 Sections 332–38 provide certain exceptions:

- For a public company or member of a group of public companies, a 'quasi-loan' can be made for a short term providing the maximum amount does not exceed £5,000: s.332.

- Any company can make small loans to directors up to a maximum amount of £5,000: s.334.
- Money lending companies can make loans or quasi-loans up to £100,000 to a director: s.338. The loan must be made in the ordinary course of business and on terms no more favourable than would be offered for similar facilities to unconnected persons. A bank can lend to its directors on the same terms as to its employees, i.e. at preferential rates. A bank, however, is not subject to a maximum amount of loan as are other money lending organisations.
- A company is allowed to make loans or quasi-loans to other companies in the group of which it is a member, or to guarantee or give security for the borrowing or quasi-borrowing of the other companies in the group: s.333.
- Any company can give a director financial assistance to enable him to carry out his duties as a director properly, provided that prior approval has been granted at a general meeting and that all details were disclosed at that meeting.

11.14 If a bank lends for any of the purposes specified above as being an 'exception' under ss.332–58, then the lending will be enforceable. If the lending is not for one of these exceptions it will be unenforceable against the company.

11.15 Similar considerations apply to the validity of a guarantee given by a limited company to secure the borrowing of a director.

Student Activity 5

Summarise, perhaps in the form of a table, the circumstances in which a company can give financial assistance. Differentiate between public companies and private companies. Compare your answer with section 11 above.

12 A company purchasing its own shares

12.1 If a company has issued shares, whether redeemable or not, it can buy these shares back, provided the articles of association allow it to do so: s.162. If the articles do not so allow, then the company must have a special resolution passed at a general meeting to amend the articles accordingly. A company can only purchase its own shares provided that some of the shares remaining are irredeemable. A company cannot have share capital consisting solely of redeemable shares as it would eventually cease to have any share capital.

On-market purchase

12.2 Shares can be purchased via the stock market if the company is a quoted company. This is called an 'on-market' purchase. Under s.166, the company must follow the following procedure:

- An ordinary resolution must be passed at a general meeting authorising the purchase.
- The authorisation must specify the maximum number of shares to be purchased and the maximum and minimum price to be paid.

- Authorisation is only valid for 18 months unless it is renewed.
- A copy of the resolution must be filed with the Registrar of Companies within 15 days.

Off-market purchase

12.3 If the company is unquoted it can only purchase off-market. It must comply with s.164, which requires that:

- A special resolution must be passed prior to the purchase.
- The shares that are to be purchased cannot have a vote on the special resolution, otherwise the resolution is void.
- If it is a public company, the resolution must have a fixed expiry date, not exceeding 18 months from the passing of the special resolution.

12.4 A public quoted company can chose to purchase either on or off the market. Any purchase must be reported to the Registrar of Companies within 28 days of the purchase shares being delivered to the company.

Summary

Now that you have studied this unit, you should be able to:

- **define a limited company;**
- **differentiate between private and public limited companies;**
- **differentiate between a limited company and a partnership;**
- **describe how a limited company is incorporated;**
- **outline the contents of a company's memorandum and articles of association and how they can be amended;**
- **understand the effect of the Companies Act 1989 on the *ultra vires* rule;**
- **outline the various types of capital contributed to a company;**
- **explain how a company bank account is opened and closed;**
- **explain a bank's rights of set off in relation to company accounts;**
- **describe the rights and liabilities of directors and their relationship with the company;**
- **show how directors can be disqualified;**
- **understand the effect of a company giving financial assistance both for the purchase of its shares and to directors and connected persons;**
- **understand when a company can purchase its own shares.**

Self-assessment questions

1 Which of the following is a creditor of a limited company?

(a) Ordinary shareholder.

(b) Preference shareholder.

(c) Debenture holder.

(d) Unsecured loan stock holder.

2 To which type of business organisation might the concept of *ultra vires* apply?

(a) Limited companies.

(b) Partnerships.

(c) Sole traders.

(d) All of the above.

3 What factors govern the dividend of a limited company?

(a) Gross profit.

(b) Distributable profits, subject to directors' approval.

(c) A dividend must be paid or the company could go into liquidation.

(d) All the distributable profits are paid out as dividends.

4 Which type of preference share may qualify for an 'extra' dividend over and above the fixed amount?

(a) Cumulative.

(b) Convertible.

(c) Participating.

(d) Redeemable.

5 Which of the following requirements does not relate to a public company?

(a) It must be limited by shares.

(b) The minimum share capital is £50,000.

(c) It must have a minimum of two shareholders.

(d) The minimum authorised and issued share capital is £50,000.

6 When can a public limited company commence trading?

(a) When it has filed its memorandum and articles of association with the Registrar of Companies.

(b) When it receives its certificate of incorporation.

(c) When it receives its trading certificate.

(d) When the directors have made a statutory declaration that the minimum shareholding requirement has been met.

7 Which of the following clauses is not found in the memorandum of association?

(a) The directors' borrowing powers clause.

(b) The objects clause.

(c) The association clause.

(d) The name of the company.

8 A special resolution requires:

(a) Seventy-five per cent of all shareholders to vote in favour in order for it to be passed.

(b) Seventy-five per cent of all votes cast in favour in order for it to be passed.

(c) To be passed at an extraordinary general meeting.

(d) Fifty-one per cent of all votes cast in favour in order for it to be passed.

9 Which of the following classes of capital must a company have?

(a) Redeemable ordinary shares.

(b) Ordinary shares.

(c) Preference shares.

(d) Debentures.

10 Which case lays down the bank's right of set off between accounts?

(a) *Garnett v McKewan.*

(b) *Maxform SpA v B Mariani and Goodville Ltd.*

(c) *Selangor United Rubber Estates v Craddock.*

(d) *Re Lundie Bros Ltd.*

11 Which of the above cases in Question 10 covers the right of a director to petition a court to have a company compulsorily wound up if he is wrongly excluded from his right to participate in the running of the company?

12 Which case states that a director will be personally liable on a bill of exchange or cheque if the word 'limited' or 'ltd' is omitted?

(a) *Kelner v Baxter.*

(b) *British Airways Board v Parish.*

(c) *Durham Fancy Goods Ltd v Michael Jackson (Fancy Goods) Ltd.*

(d) *Bondina Ltd v Rollaway Shower Blinds Ltd.*

13 Which of the above cases in Question 12 states that a contract made before a company is incorporated cannot be ratified after incorporation?

14 Outline how the six main clauses in the memorandum of association can be changed, if in fact they can be changed.

15 How is a new director appointed, and what special requirement may apply in relation to a director's shareholding?

16 John Brown is a builder who has had an account in his own name for many years. The average balance is £2,000 credit. He tells you that he is about to make his business into a limited company, John Brown Limited. He expects the formalities to be completed in about five weeks and promises to bring in the memorandum and articles as soon as they are available.

Meanwhile, he wishes to open an account in the name of John Brown Limited. No borrowing is expected in the foreseeable future. How would you deal with the request?

Further reading

- Milnes Holden, J — Chapter 11, *The Law and Practice of Banking*, Vol 1, 5th edition 1991, Pitman
- Laidlaw, A and Roberts, G — Chapter 2, *Law Relating to Banking* Services, 2nd edition 1992, Bankers Books
- Raby, P — Chapter 8, *Law Relating to Banking Services*, 2nd edition 1992, Pitman
- Swinson, C — Chapter 8, *A Guide to the Companies Act 1989*, Butterworths, 1990

Unit 8

Company Insolvency

> ### Objectives
>
> **After studying this unit, you should be able to:**
>
> - **appreciate the differences between compulsory and voluntary winding up;**
> - **understand the role of the liquidator;**
> - **appreciate the significance of the different priorities of creditors;**
> - **understand the concepts of wrongful and fraudulent trading, transactions at an undervalue, preferences and shadow directors;**
> - **appreciate the implications of the various legal principles on insolvency as regards the operation of company bank accounts;**
> - **understand why wages accounts should be operated in certain circumstances.**

1 Introduction

1.1 A limited company is a separate legal entity from its members: *Salomon v Salomon and Co Ltd* (1897). In order for a company to cease to exist (whether a public or private company), it has to be wound up – a process that is also called liquidation. A company does not have to be insolvent, i.e. unable to pay its debts, for it to go into liquidation. Liquidation is also the process used to wind up a solvent company. The company's assets are realised and creditors are paid off. Once the process of liquidation is completed, the company ceases legally to exist.

1.2 All references in this unit are to the Insolvency Act 1986 unless stated otherwise.

1.3 *Note*: administration orders and receivership are dealt with in Unit 17.

2 Winding up a company

2.1 Winding up can be:

- Voluntary; or
- Compulsory.

2.2 Voluntary winding is much more common than compulsory winding, which is a more expensive and slower process.

Voluntary winding up

2.3 Voluntary winding up can be by way of members' voluntary winding up or creditors' voluntary winding up. Both forms of voluntary winding up begin with a special or an extraordinary resolution passed by the members of the company, except where the articles are invoked (see below) when an ordinary resolution is passed.

2.4 A special resolution will be used most commonly in a members' voluntary winding up, and requires 75% of the votes cast at a general meeting. An extraordinary resolution is most commonly used in a creditors' voluntary winding up, is passed at an extraordinary general meeting, and requires 75% of the votes cast.

2.5 Under s.84, the grounds for voluntary liquidation are where the:

- Articles of association impose some condition (either as to time, or otherwise) upon which the existence of the company depends, and the time having expired or the event occurred, a general meeting passes an ordinary resolution for winding up.
- Company resolves by special resolution (requiring 21 days' notice) that it be wound up voluntarily.
- Company resolves by extraordinary resolution (requiring 14 days' notice) that it cannot by reason of its liabilities continue its business, and that it is advisable to wind up.

2.6 The first of these is rarely seen, but an investment trust is sometimes set up with the articles stating that it will be wound up on or between set future dates. Apart from this specific type of company, the articles rarely state a set time or purpose for existence.

2.7 With the last of these grounds – the passing of an extraordinary resolution – the company's position will be hopeless and creditors will be pressing, thus winding up in this way saves some time. Notice of the resolution must appear in the *London Gazette*: s.85. If it is not published in the *London Gazette* the directors will be liable to a fine.

2.8 The resolution has the following effect:

- Winding up commences from the time of passing of the resolution: s.86.
- After commencement of winding up, the company will cease to carry on business, *except* in so far as is necessary to complete the winding up. Corporate status and powers remain until the company is dissolved at the end of the winding up process: s.87.
- Any transfer of shares or alteration of status of the members is void unless approved by the liquidator: s.88.
- The directors' power to dispose of property ceases on the passing of the resolution and appointment of the liquidator. The directors' ostensible authority ceases on the *gazetting* of the resolution.

Members' voluntary winding up

2.9 A members' voluntary winding up is possible when the company is able to meet its debts in full within 12 months, i.e. it is solvent. The directors make a statutory declaration of solvency stating that the company will be able to pay all debts in full, plus any interest on those debts, within 12 months. A recent statement of the company's assets and liabilities must be included in the declaration. The declaration must be made within the five weeks prior to the passing of the resolution. The statutory declaration must be presented to the Registrar of Companies within 15 days of the special resolution being passed. If the company debts are not paid in full with any interest due within the 12-month period, the directors are liable to a fine or imprisonment unless they can show that the declaration was made based on reasonable grounds: s.89.

2.10 Once the declaration of solvency has been made, a liquidator (who must be an insolvency practitioner) is appointed to wind up the company's affairs and distribute the assets in the set order of priority.

2.11 If the liquidator believes that despite the declaration of solvency, the company is not able to pay its debts and interest on the debts within the 12-month period, he will call a meeting of creditors. From the date of that meeting the winding up ceases to be a members' voluntary winding up, and continues as a creditors' voluntary winding up.

Creditors' voluntary winding up

2.12 A creditors' voluntary winding up commences with the passing of an extraordinary resolution. Within 14 days of the resolution being passed, a meeting of creditors must be called to consider the resolution. The notice of the meeting must be advertised in the *London Gazette* and in the papers local to the area the company operated in.

2.13 The directors must preside at this meeting. The company meeting and the creditors' meeting must appoint the liquidator, and if there is a disagreement over who should be appointed liquidator, the creditors' meeting takes precedence. In a creditors' voluntary winding up, the liquidator appointed by the shareholders can only exercise restricted powers, pending approval of his appointment by a creditors' meeting.

2.14 The restricted powers are to:

- Dispose of perishable goods or other goods which will rapidly diminish in value unless sold quickly;
- Protect the assets, e.g. insure them;
- Take under his control all the assets (but not to sell them except as above).

2.15 The creditors' meeting and the company may appoint a committee which may sanction the continuance, in whole or part, of the directors' powers: s.103.

2.16 The liquidator needs the sanction of the committee or of the court to exercise certain of his powers, however he is free to deal with the disposal of property unless he disposes of it to a person connected with the company. In such cases he must give notice to the committee and gain its sanction: s.167(2).

2.17 The committee is appointed to represent the whole body of creditors, thus making it easier for the liquidator to wind up the company.

Dissolution

2.18 In both types of voluntary winding up a liquidator is appointed. Once the winding up is complete, the liquidator presents a full account of what has occurred to meetings of the company and creditors. This is then sent to the Registrar of Companies, who registers the account and other returns. The company is then dissolved in three months, unless a court defers the date: ss.106 and 201.

Differences between a members' and a creditors' voluntary winding up

2.19 In a members' voluntary winding up, the directors make a *statutory declaration of solvency* that the company will be able to pay its debts in full, including interest within 12 months. The declaration must be made within the five weeks prior to the passing of the resolution, and must be registered with the Registrar of Companies within 15 days of the passing of the resolution.

2.20 In a creditors' voluntary winding up, the directors do not issue a declaration of solvency.

2.21 In a members' voluntary liquidation, the shareholders can *appoint a liquidator*. In a creditors' voluntary winding up the liquidator initially appointed by the shareholders must have his appointment approved by a majority of the creditors at a creditors' meeting to be held within 14 days of the resolution. If the creditors' meeting does not agree with the choice of the members, the creditors' choice of liquidator prevails.

2.22 In a members' voluntary winding up the liquidator can *deal with the assets* from the date of the resolution. However, the liquidator has a duty to call a creditors' meeting if he forms the opinion that the company will not be able to pay its debts in full. The creditors' meeting can vote to change the liquidator if it wishes. The liquidation then continues as a creditors' voluntary liquidation.

Compulsory winding up

2.23 Compulsory winding up occurs when a petition is presented to the court and the court orders a company to be wound up. The most common reason for a company to be wound up is that it is insolvent, but there are also two other reasons:

- The Secretary of State may apply for a company to be wound up s.124A(1). This will occur when it appears to the Secretary of State that it is in the public's interest following the publication of an inspectors' report or on obtaining information from the company. This petition can also be based on investigations under the Financial Services Act 1986, Companies Acts 1985 and 1989, and Criminal Justice Act 1993. The court will grant the petition if it thinks it is 'just and equitable' to wind up the company.
- Under the Banking Act 1987 the Bank of England may petition for a bank to be wound up.

2.24 Insolvency petitions can be presented under s.122. The main provisions are if the:

- Company so resolves, by *special resolution*, to be wound up by the court.
- Company *fails to commence business within one year of incorporation*, or suspends its business for one year.
- *Number of members falls below two*, except in a case of private company.
- Court is of the opinion that it is *just and equitable* to wind up the company. This petition could be presented by a director who has been frozen out of management, or if the management of the company has become deadlocked.
- Company is *unable to pay its debts.*

Inability to pay its debts

2.25 This is by far the most common ground for winding up and is defined by s.123 as follows:

- If a creditor who is owed a minimum of £750 unsecured has made a *statutory demand* to the company at its registered office, and has not been paid within three weeks or given security for the sum to the satisfaction of the creditors. The debt must be undisputed and in *Re A Company* (1990) it was held that a statutory demand for payment of a debt sent through the post and actually delivered to the company's registered office was validly served for the purposes of s.123.
- If the court believes the company *cannot meet its debts as they fall due*. The fact that a company's assets exceed its liabilities does not prove that the company is solvent, if the company cannot pay its debts as they fall due. If the assets are very illiquid, and thus not easily saleable, then the courts may grant the petition to wind up the company. If, however, the assets are easily saleable and are sufficient to pay all immediate liabilities in full, the petition will be refused.
- If the court believes that the company's *assets are less than its liabilities* (including prospective and contingent liabilities).

  The asset test is very wide. From time to time it may affect many companies whose assets are less than the liabilities, especially as it is unclear whether contingent assets could be set off against contingent liabilities. With the growth of derivatives, this issue could assume major importance in a decision as to whether winding up petition should be granted. However, the court has discretion to dismiss a petition or to make an administration order. It is usually assumed that it is market value, as opposed to book values, which will influence the court's decision under the asset test.
- If the company has failed to fulfil the terms of a previous court order to pay a creditor (called 'unsatisfied execution of a judgement creditor').

Who can petition?

2.26 Under s.124(1) petition can be presented by the:

- Company;
- Directors – in *Re Instrumentation Electrical Services Ltd* (1988) a petition presented by two out of three directors had no standing. This case establishes that the directors must petition together or expressly appoint one to act on behalf of the others. However, this would be seen by some as a restrictive interpretation of s.124(1), since it can effectively prevent a

director who wishes to avoid, say, wrongful trading from doing so unless the other directors agree.

- Any creditor(s) including contingent or prospective creditors, i.e. creditors not yet due to be paid but who, at some future date, may be due to be paid;
- One or more contributories; or by the
- Secretary of State under s.124A or the Bank of England under the Banking Act 1987.

2.27 *Note*: s.79 defines a contributory as a person who is liable to contribute to the assets of the company in the case of winding up. Contributories nowadays are most commonly holders of partly paid shares. Holders are liable to the amount unpaid on the shares, and remain liable for up to 12 months after the shares have been sold: s.74.

After the petition is presented – compulsory winding up

2.28 After the petition has been presented, but before the winding up order has been made, the court may appoint a provisional liquidator: s.135. This freezes the position of the company, and takes away the directors' power to dispose of the assets. It is often done at the time of filing the petition, by an application to a judge in chambers, where the creditor has grounds to fear misappropriation of the assets by the director(s).

2.29 Under s.126, any creditor or contributory can apply to have a stay of action of any proceedings against the company, i.e. the proceedings or action are stopped for a period of time.

2.30 Under s.125, the court can:

- Grant the petition;
- Dismiss the petition;
- Adjourn the hearing either without any special conditions being specified or subject to some conditions being observed;
- Make any other order it sees fit.

2.31 In reaching a decision the court will take into account the wishes of the majority of creditors and contributories. It can order a meeting of creditors and contributories to determine the wishes of the majority: s.195.

On granting of the winding up order – compulsory winding up

2.32 Winding up (liquidation) commences from the time of presentation of the petition, or if there was a prior resolution for a voluntary winding up, from the passing of that resolution: s.129. This means that there is a period of time between the petition and the granting of the winding up order. This 'backdating' of the commencement of liquidation has implications for the bank that are discussed in section 8.

2.33 After liquidation has commenced, the company's assets are disposed of by the liquidator, the company ceases to carry on business except as is necessary to wind up the company (unless the liquidator intends to sell it as a 'going concern'), the powers of the directors cease, and employees are made redundant.

2.34 If any assets are disposed of between the date of petition and granting of the winding up order the disposals are void, unless the court consents to the disposition at the time, or subsequently: s.127.

Final meeting of creditors and dissolution – compulsory winding up

2.35 If the liquidator considers that for all practical purposes liquidation is complete, he will call a general meeting of creditors. If they receive his report they can then choose to release him: s.174.

2.36 The Registrar of Companies is informed of the decision of the creditors' meeting that the winding up is complete. He will register the notice of completion of winding up, and three months later the company is dissolved, unless the Secretary of State defers the date: s.205.

Student Activity 1

One aim of the Insolvency Act 1986 is to expose any malicious conduct on the part of the debtor in order to encourage a more honest standard of commercial behaviour.

Consider to what extent this aim has been fulfilled by the Act. Discuss this with an experienced banker who has been involved with 'recovery' work.

3 The role of the liquidator

3.1 The liquidator's functions are to secure that the assets of the company are got in, realised and distributed to the company's creditors and, if there is a surplus, to the person entitled to it: s.143. He is appointed by the meeting of creditors. He does not have power to perform any other act without further permission. The court or committee of creditors can control his powers.

3.2 He is responsible for calling a general meeting of creditors in order to establish their wishes. He must also call a meeting of creditors if meetings direct him to, or if 10% in value of the creditors require him to do so. If he feels that the committee of creditors, or any other persons, are obstructing his duties, he can apply to the court for directions and powers.

3.3 If any person feels that the liquidator has not acted in that person's best interest, he can apply to the court under s.168(5). The court will either confirm, reverse or modify the act or decision made.

3.4 3.5 In a voluntary winding up the liquidator takes over the powers of the company, in a compulsory winding up the liquidator has the powers granted by the court or the committee. In either case the court cannot interfere with the day-to-day administration, nor question the liquidator's good faith, nor hold him liable for any error of judgement: *Leon v York-O-Matic* (1986). However, this does not mean that the liquidator does not owe some duty of care to the company. He is effectively a trustee of the assets of the company, thus owes some of duties of an agent to the company.

3.5 Under s.168(4), a liquidator may use his own discretion in managing and distributing the company's business assets. Any person aggrieved by the liquidator's acts or decisions may apply to the court, which may confirm, reverse or modify the act complained of: s.168(5). A liquidator may apply to the court for direction if he is in doubt as his powers or duties. So long as the liquidator follows the court's directions he will be protected from any personal liability.

4 The order of repayment in liquidation

4.1 The order of priority of repayment is:

- *Creditors secured by fixed charges.* With valid fixed charges, creditors can use the sale proceeds to pay off the debts. Any surplus must be paid over to the liquidator to augment the funds available to him. If there is a shortfall after the sale proceeds have been utilised, then the creditor will prove unsecured for the deficit.
- *Liquidator's expenses.* In the case of a voluntary winding up, the expenses of winding up are payable in priority to all other claims (except secured creditors): s.115. In a compulsory winding up, the court has discretion to order payment of expenses in whatever priority it wishes: s.156.
- *Preferential creditors.* These are specified in s.386 and Schedule 6 as:
  - Wages or salaries up to a maximum of £800 per employee for four months;
  - Advances or loans made to pay qualifying preferential wages or salaries (see section 9 for full details of wages account loans);
  - Deductions in respect of Income Tax and National Insurance during the 12 months prior to liquidation that have not been paid over to the relevant authorities;
  - VAT for six months prior to liquidation;
  - Social security contributions due in the 12 months prior to liquidation;
  - Contributions to occupational pensions schemes that should have been made by the company.

  All preferential creditors rank *pari passu.*
- *Holders of floating charges* – subject to various conditions (see Unit 17).
- Unsecured creditors. Includes any part of a secured or preferential claim that cannot rank as such due to the monetary limits set by the Act, e.g. the limit set on wages as a preferential debt.
- Interest on debts since *the date of liquidation.* Called deferred debt.
- *Members of the company.* If there is money left for this class of 'creditor', then the company was not insolvent. (Strictly speaking members of the company are not creditors, but owners of the company.) The division at this stage depends on the articles of association, which may specify an order of repayment amongst the different classes of shareholder.

Student Activity 2

1 Consider why a bank manager should be worried if one of his company customers has a large unsecured overdraft and the bank has just dishonoured a cheque for VAT?

2 Y Ltd has just gone into compulsory liquidation, and claims against the company amount to:

- £7,000 owing to the Z Bank and secured by a floating charge (on all assets) created seven months ago;
- £5,000 lent by a director, X, for the payment of wages at the rate of £1,000 per month for the last five months;
- £14,000 owing to trade creditors;
- £2,000 deducted and due in respect of Income Tax for the last 12 months;
- £300 estimated to be the liquidation expenses.

(a) Set out the order of priority for the payment of these claims.

(b) Explain with reasons whether there would be any change in the order if instead of being a floating charge, the charge taken by the bank seven months ago had been a legal charge on the company's premises?

5 Directors: wrongful trading and fraudulent trading

Wrongful trading

5.1 Under s.214 a director can be personally liable for a company's debts if he allows the company to trade when there is no reasonable prospect of the debts being paid.

5.2 Wrongful trading is committed where the:

- Company has gone into insolvent liquidation (specified as being when the company's assets are insufficient to pay its debts, liabilities and expenses of liquidation: s.214(6); and the
- Defendant at some time before liquidation commenced 'knew or ought to have concluded that there was no reasonable prospect that the company would avoid going into insolvent liquidation'; and where
- At the relevant time (when he should have so concluded) the person was a director of the company.

5.3 If a director realises that a company has no reasonable chance of avoiding insolvent liquidation and he took 'every step' he 'ought to have taken' to minimise the potential loss to creditors, then he will not be liable for wrongful trading.

5.4 There is no definition of 'every step' he 'ought to have taken', as it will vary from person to person. The court would in each case take into account how a reasonably diligent person would have acted, taking into account the level of skill, knowledge and experience that may reasonably be expected of a person carrying out the role of the director in that specific company.

5.5 In *Re Produce Marketing Consortium Ltd* (1989) the decision confirmed that each case of wrongful trading will be examined on its own merits. It clarified the level of skill required by directors, in that a higher level of skill, knowledge and experience would be expected from the directors of a public company than from the directors of a small private company.

5.6 In *Fairmont Tours (Yorkshire) Ltd* (1989), the directors were held liable under s.214 wrongful trading because they knew when they signed the annual accounts that there was no reasonable prospect that the company could avoid going into insolvent liquidation, yet they allowed the company to continue trading.

5.7 This potential personal liability applies to 'shadow directors' (someone on whose instructions the directors are accustomed to act) and non-executive directors (see section 7).

Fraudulent trading

5.8 If a company goes into insolvent liquidation, and it appears that a director or some other person was a 'knowing party' to carrying on the company's business with intent to defraud creditors, or for any other fraudulent purpose, the court may order him to be personally liable for some or all of the company's debts: s.213. If any person who was a 'knowing party' to the carrying on of company business in this manner was also a creditor of the company, then any claim he had as a creditor would be offset against the contribution due from him to the liquidator. The court could also order that he rank behind all other creditors in liquidation.

Student Activity 3

You will recall that the decision in *Re Instrumental Electrical Services Ltd* resulted in the rejection of a winding up petition on the grounds that it was presented on the authority of one director only. Why might the director who petitioned feel concerned if his reason for presenting the petition was to avoid what he thought could only be a larger and larger loss to creditors if trading continued? On what grounds might he feel that the attempt to present the petition would help him in the event of a future insolvent liquidation. *(Paragraphs 2.26 and 5.3)*

The differences between wrongful trading and fraudulent trading

5.9 These are that:

- The risk of personal liability for wrongful trading only applies to directors, whereas the risk with fraudulent trading can apply to anyone who caused a company to incur further liabilities when they had no reasonable belief that these liabilities could be met.
- In wrongful trading, the directors have acted honestly but recklessly. In fraudulent trading the purpose has been to defraud creditors.
- If a court rules that a director is liable in connection with wrongful or fraudulent trading, then he may be disqualified as a director under the Company Directors Disqualification Act 1986.
- Essentially, what is required to prove wrongful trading is to show that the

director knew, or ought to have known, that the company was insolvent, and that he failed to take action to minimise losses to creditors.

6 Transactions at an undervalue and preferences

6.1 The principle behind transactions at an undervalue and preferences is the same in both individual and corporate insolvency, except in relation to 'relevant time'. Recap by re-reading Unit 6, paragraphs 9.5–13.

Transactions at an undervalue

6.2 A transaction at an undervalue occurs when a company makes a gift or enters into a transaction where it receives no consideration, or considerably less consideration than the true value of the asset transferred: s.238.

6.3 With a company no claim can be made if the company entered into the transaction in good faith and for the purpose of carrying on its business if at the time the transaction was entered into there were reasonable grounds to believe that the transaction would benefit the company: s.238(5) (see Unit 17).

6.4 In *Aveling Barford Ltd v Perion Ltd* (1989) a property was sold in 1987 by Aveling Barford to Perion for £350,000 and sold about six months later by Perion for £1,560,000. Both Aveling Barford and Perion were effectively owned by the same person. Aveling Barford Ltd went into liquidation. The liquidator brought an action claiming that the transaction was in substance an unauthorised distribution of capital which was fraudulently depriving creditors of assets. The court agreed and the purchaser (Perion Ltd) had to account for the amount including the profit on the subsequent resale of the property because this was a transaction at an undervalue.

6.5 In *Re M C Bacon* (1989) the giving of security was held not to be a transaction at undervalue. The ownership of the assets has not changed, the company had merely appropriated the assets to meet liabilities due. Thus, the company's assets had not been depleted and thus the transaction could not be set aside by the liquidator under s.238.

Preferences

6.6 A preference occurs when a debtor enters into a transaction that places a creditor in a better position than he would otherwise have been in when the company subsequently goes into liquidation, within the relevant time: s.239.

6.7 If the person receiving the preference was connected with the company, then a preference is presumed unless the contrary is proved: s.239(6). A person connected with a company is a director, shadow director or an associate of these or an associate of the company: s.249. An associate includes a director or employee of the company or another company if it is controlled by the same person, or controlled by an associate of the person controlling the company giving the preference: s.435.

Relevant time

6.8 For a company the relevant time starts from the commencement of winding up or the date of a petition for an administration order (see Unit 17).

Transactions before commencement of winding up are affected thus:

- Transaction at an undervalue – two years;
- Preferences – six months;
- Preferences to connected persons – two years.

6.9 If the company was able to pay its debts at the time of any of the above transactions, then the transactions are not affected. It is only if the company was unable to pay its debts at the time of the transaction, or as a result of carrying out the transaction, that the court can invalidate the transaction.

6.10 The court, once it has established that it is a transaction at an undervalue or a preference may make a variety of orders under s.241. It may require the:

- Re-transfer of the property or its proceeds;
- Property to be vested in the company;
- Release or discharge of any security given by the debtor company; or require
- Payments to be made to the debtor by the recipient of the transactions;
- That anyone who had guaranteed or secured the company's account, and whose security was released because of the transaction, be put under such new or revived obligations as the court feels fit (see Unit 17).

7 Shadow directors

7.1 A shadow director is 'a person in accordance with whose directions or instructions a company is accustomed to act': s.251. A parent company may be classed as a shadow director if it has acted in accordance with this section. Professional advisors are excluded. A shadow director can be personally liable for the debts of an insolvent company if wrongful trading is proved: s.214(7).

The problem for banks prior to *Re M C Bacon*

7.2 Many bankers were worried that a bank or its business advisory service could be construed as a 'shadow director', and that the bank could find itself liable for company debts in liquidation if wrongful trading could be proved along with 'shadow directorship'.

7.3 If a bank could be proved to be a shadow director, and if it could be proved that the bank, as shadow director, had known or ought to have known that continued trading would result in subsequent liquidation (with a larger deficiency than would have occurred had trading ceased earlier) then the bank would have been liable to make good the extra deficiency.

7.4 What was unclear prior to the Bacon case was whether a bank came under the heading of a 'professional advisor'. A bank's business advisory arm was almost certainly a 'professional advisor' as it charges a fee for its services. The situation was less clear over the position of a branch manager or his superiors. As they were not specifically remunerated for their advisory services, there was uncertainty over whether or not they were 'professional advisors'.

The result of *Bacon*

7.5 The claims regarding shadow directorship were abandoned by the liquidator, therefore no claim was made against the bank regarding wrongful trading.

7.6 In *Bacon*, the company had been in financial difficulties and the bank had insisted that its own investigating accountant team should investigate. The team had reported back that the company was 'virtually insolvent', but could survive if certain steps were taken. The bank therefore agreed to renew the £250,000 overdraft facility, but only on condition that a mortgage debenture was granted.

7.7 The fact that the liquidator abandoned the case means banks are less likely to be classed as 'shadow directors'. However, the branch manager still needs to take care that he and his staff do not get involved in directing the day-to-day running of their customers' affairs, and every case is decided on it own facts.

8 The effect of liquidation on the bank account

8.1 If any of the company's assets are sold, shares transferred or any alteration is made to the status of members in the period between the petition and the winding up, these transactions will be void unless the court rules to the contrary: s.127. This presents a danger to the bank if it allows any withdrawals from the bank account, releases any security held or items held in safe custody during this period.

8.2 If the bank has allowed withdrawals from a credit account, by either cash; cheques, standing orders, direct debits or any other form of debit, the bank could have to refund such monies to the liquidator. If the account is overdrawn, any credits paid in will have to be refunded to the liquidator. If the account is overdrawn any debits after the date of the petition will not be eligible for proof in the liquidation. The effect is that the bank account stands at the balance it was showing on the date of the petition.

8.3 The winding up petition is published in the *London Gazette*, and this is taken as being notice to the world that winding up may follow. Even if the bank did not see the notice of a winding up petition, that is no defence and the bank remains liable to make a refund, as detailed above, to the liquidator.

8.4 In *Re Gray's Inn Construction Co Ltd* (1980) the liquidator claimed that payments into and out of the overdrawn account were 'dispositions' of the company's property. The court agreed that both the payments in (to an overdrawn account) and payments out were invalid and must be refunded to the liquidator. The reasoning behind this decision was that payments out would be placing the recipient creditor in a better position than he would otherwise have been in, compared with the other creditors. Payments into the overdrawn account would have put the bank in a better position than it would otherwise have been in because the overdrawn balance was less. Thus the bank will obtain a court order to operate the account as soon as the petition is *Gazetted*, or, as is more usual, it will stop the account. Whilst *Re Barncrown Ltd* (1994) cast some doubts on the decision in *Re Grays Inn*, and whilst such payments can be validated at the court's discretion, the bank will prefer to play safe and stop the account in this situation.

Action upon notice of a winding up petition – compulsory winding up

8.5 On notice of a winding up petition a bank should not allow any withdrawals unless the directors can obtain court approval under s.127. Any cheques presented should be returned marked 'notice of winding up petition received'.

Effect on bank when it receives notice of a resolution for a voluntary winding up

8.6 If the account is *overdrawn*, stop the account and prove for the debt, or take the normal actions of a secured creditor if secured.

8.7 If the account is *in credit*:

- *Members' winding up* – the mandate is cancelled and the liquidator takes over from the date of the resolution.
- *Creditors' winding up* – the mandate is cancelled, and the liquidator takes over. The bank must scrutinise all withdrawals, pending the approval of the appointment by the creditors' meeting.

The bank's right of set off

8.8 Recap set off in Unit 4, section 9, in relation to s.323 (bankruptcy).

8.9 Except in the case of trust monies and wages accounts, the bank must set off any credit balances held against any overdrawn accounts in the same name and prove for the balance in liquidation. This is the case even if prior to liquidation the bank had agreed with its customer not to set off accounts. On liquidation the bank can automatically set off the accounts: *National Westminster Bank Ltd v Halesowen Presswork and Assemblies Ltd* (1970). Rule 4.9, IR 1986 gives statutory backing to this right of set off.

When a company has money on an account held for a specific purpose

8.10 When a bank has opened an account which is used, say, to hold deposits from the company's customers for work done, or goods ordered, then if the bank knows of the purpose of the account, the bank effectively has notice of trust. Where the facts are such that the bank should have known, then the bank would have constructive notice of a trust. Each case will turn on its own facts as to whether constructive notice applies.

8.11 If the company then goes into liquidation the bank cannot set off the credit balance on the trust account against the overdrawn balance held, nor can the liquidator claim the trust monies: *Barclays Bank Ltd v Quistclose Investments Ltd* (1970) (where the money was paid into a separate account to meet a dividend payment). In *Re Kayford* (1975) the liquidator could not claim the trust monies held but had to account for them to the beneficiaries of the trust. In *Re EVTR Ltd, Gilbert and Another v Barber* (1987) a loan was made to the company for a specific purpose, but that purpose failed. In such a situation the money is held on a resulting trust for the lender and is not available to the liquidator.

Banks and preferences

8.12 If the liquidator can prove that a transaction was a preference (see **7.5.2**) then the court declare the transaction void. There are several situations in which a bank could be exposed to the danger of a preference, particularly:

- If the company repaid its borrowing in full, the bank may be held to be preferred. However if the bank had put pressure on to the company to repay, or to provide security for the loan it would not be a preference: *Re M C Bacon Ltd* (1989).
- If the company repaid its borrowing then requested the release of security given by a third party this could amount to a preference if the company went into liquidation within the 'relevant time': *Re R M Kushler Ltd* (1943). The bank may have to refund the money paid in to the liquidator: s.241(2). However the court could order the reinstatement of the security: s.241(2). (See Unit 17.)

The bank and transactions at an undervalue

8.13 There is no danger here to the bank provided that the company entered into the transaction in good faith and for the purpose of carrying on its business if at the time of the transaction there were reasonable grounds for believing that the transaction would benefit the company: s.238(5). The liquidator would have to prove that the above was not the situation before the bank could be liable.

9 Wages accounts

Why banks operate wages accounts

9.1 Wages unpaid, up to a maximum of £800 per employee, or for a maximum period of four months prior to the liquidation (whichever comes first), rank as preferential debts, both in the case of companies and partnerships and sole traders. The bank or any other lender can rank as a preferential creditor for money lent for the purpose of paying such wages: s.386.

9.2 Therefore the bank operates a wages account for a limited company when it feels that there is a danger of it going into liquidation and that the bank lacks adequate security. In the event of liquidation the bank can rank as preferential creditor for such advances.

Student Activity 4

Does your branch operate a wages account for any of your customers'? If so, see how the entries are monitored and compare this with the text below.

How should the wages account be opened and operated?

9.3 Cheques drawn on the wages account should be payable to 'wages'.

9.4 The directors should submit a list naming the employees and the amount to be paid to each. The bank should analyse the balance of the wages account each week to ensure that the balance is made up only of qualifying items, i.e. maximum of £800 per employee, maximum period four months back.

9.5 After the first four months of operation of the wages account, or when the £800 limit has been reached, credit the wages account with the first amount which was originally debited there and debit the current account.

9.6 If there was a limit marked on the current account prior to opening the wages account, amend the computer records to ensure that the limit applies to the net position on both accounts.

9.7 There is little point in allowing the overall borrowing of the company to increase once a wages account is opened.

Is it legally necessary to open a wages account to rank as a preferential creditor for advances for wages?

9.8 No: *Re Rampgill Mill Ltd* (1967); but if the bank does not open a wages account it suffers the following problems in the event of liquidation:

- It may be difficult to prove beyond all doubt what part of the company's borrowing was for qualifying wages advances.
- If the current account is active, the rule in *Clayton's case* could ensure that the debit balance consists of items debited later than the four month qualifying period.

Example of effect on the bank by not operating a wages account

9.9 *Example. X Ltd Current A/c.* The company went into liquidation on 1 May.

Date	*Debits (£)*	*Credits (£)*	*Balance (£)*
			Dr 50,000
Jan	20,000	20,000	Dr 50,000
Feb	30,000	25,000	Dr 55,000
March	10,000	12,000	Dr 53,000
April	15,000	18,000	Dr 50,000

9.10 Under the rule in *Clayton's case* the debit balance is made up of the following debits:

	£	
April	15,000	
March	10,000	
Feb	25,000	out of the 30,000 debited
	50,000	

9.11 Therefore part of the £20,000 could have been advanced for wages in January and could have qualified as preferential, but under the rule in *Clayton's case* the money advanced in January has been repaid by the credits paid in.

Is a wages account necessary when the bank holds security?

9.12 If the bank has a *fixed charge* which is certain to cover the maximum overdraft, there is little point in operating a wages account because a fixed chargeholder ranks prior to all other creditors.

9.13 If there is doubt as to whether the bank would obtain sufficient from its fixed charge, the bank could benefit by operating a wages account. The bank could claim as a preferential creditor for qualifying wages and use the proceeds of its security to clear the rest of the overdraft. The secured creditor position will not reduce the bank's preferential claim: *Re William Hall (Contractors) Ltd* (1967).

9.14 If the bank has only a *floating charge*, the wages account should be opened. Preferential creditors rank before a floating charge.

Wages accounts, partnerships and sole traders

9.15 Money lent to pay qualifying wages ranks as a preferential debt, irrespective of whether the borrower is a company, partnership or sole trader.

Practical example of the use of wages accounts

9.16 The example here is given to aid your understanding of the effects of operating and not operating wages accounts.

X Ltd went into liquidation on 31 March last and the details are:

	£		£
Preferential creditors	20,000	Freehold factory	90,000
Trade creditors	90,000	Plant	5,000
		Stock	40,000
Bank	140,000	Debtors	20,000

A summary of the bank account since last November is:

		Debits	*Credits*	*Balance*
1990		£	£	£
November 1				50,000 Dr
November		110,000	90,000	70,000 Dr
December		130,000	120,000	80,000 Dr
1991				
January		140,000	120,000	100,000 Dr
February		174,000	130,000	144,000 Dr
March	1		5,000	139,000 Dr
	4 Wages	11,000		150,000 Dr
	11 Wages	10,000		160,000 Dr
	18 Wages	10,000		170,000 Dr
	19	81,000	150,000	101,000 Dr
	25 Wages	10,000		111,000 Dr
	26	29,000		140,000 Dr

Note: wages of £30,000 in November, £30,000 in December, £30,000 in January and £29,000 in February are included in the summary.

There is no security for the borrowing and your assistant comments that the bank's loss would have been much smaller if a wages account had been opened last November. What does he mean?

Calculate whether there would have been any advantage to the bank if it had adopted your assistant's suggestion.

Note: ignore all costs and charges. Assume that the wages of each employee do not exceed the maximum permitted in making a preferential claim and that the assets realise the figure estimated by the liquidator.

Suggested solution

9.17 Unpaid wages or salaries in a liquidation are preferential creditors up to £800 per employee or a maximum time period of four months prior to the liquidation, whichever comes first.

Under the Insolvency Act 1986 banks lending to companies (*and* partnerships/sole traders) rank as preferential creditors for money lent to pay wages. The wages paid must come within the limit set above.

9.18 *Position without a wages account*

Under *Clayton's case* the balance of £140,000 consists of the last £140,000 of debit turnover, i.e. from 11 March.

Wages which qualify are wages cheques between 11 March and 26 March, i.e. £30,000, leaving the bank with £110,000 as an unsecured creditor.

Position is as follows:

Cash from assets		155,000
Less preferential creditors		50,000
Available to meet unsecured creditors		£105,000

Total unsecured creditors are £200,000

Therefore, dividend in £ is 105 = 52.5p in £200

Therefore, bank receives	preferential	30,000
	unsecured	57,570
		£87,750

Therefore, net loss £52,250

9.19 *Position with a wages account*

Bank's preferential claim would not have been affected by *Clayton's case.* The bank's claim in the liquidation would have been:

Preferential calculated December £30,000 + January £30,000 + February £29,000 + March £41,000 = £130,000

Preferential (30 + 30 + 29 + 41)	£130
Unsecured	£10
	£140

Liquidation would have been:

Cash from assets	£155
Less preferential creditors	£150
For unsecured creditors	5

Dividend is $\frac{£5}{100}$ = 5p in £ for unsecured.

Therefore the bank receives	130,000	preferential
+5p in £ unsecured	500	
	£135,500	

Net loss only £9,500

Set off and preferential claims

9.20 If the bank wishes to claim as a preferential creditor for certain of its advances to the company, most commonly in the case of a wages account, then the decision in *Re Unit 2 Windows Ltd* (1985) will reduce the value of its claim. If the bank holds another account of the company which is in credit and a further account which is overdrawn, and this account ranks as an unsecured creditor, the bank would prefer to set off the credit balance against the non-preferential debt, and claim in the liquidation for the full amount of the preferential debt and the smaller amount of the unsecured creditor. This would increase the chances of the bank minimising its loss.

9.21 However *Re Unit 2 Windows Ltd* (1985) held that a credit balance should be off set against preferential and non-preferential debts on a pro rata basis.

Student Activity 5

A bank holds an account of Andromeda Ltd which has gone into liquidation. The balances are as follows:

No 1 account	£4,000 credit
No 2 account (loan)	£10,000 debit
Wages account	£5,000 debit

The bank has no security at all.

1 Imagine that the bank was not constrained by the Re Unit 2 *Windows* and set out the proof which the bank would wish to make to the liquidator.

2 Set out the proof which the liquidator would insist on bearing in mind the decision in *Re Unit 2 Windows.*

9.29 *Re Unit 2 Windows Ltd* (1985) only applies if there are three or more accounts, one at least of which is credit, the remaining two or more being debit.

9.30 Thus:

- Current account credit
  Loan account debit
  Wages account debit

Re Unit 2 Windows applies.

- Current account credit
  Wages account debit

  Re Unit 2 Windows does not apply; the accounts are simply set off.

- Current account credit
  No 2 account credit
  Wages account debit

  Re Unit 2 Windows does not apply; the two credit balances are set off against the debit balance.

Summary

Now that you have studied this unit, you should be able to:

- **understand what is meant by liquidation;**
- **outline the process of winding up a company;**
- **describe the role of the liquidator;**
- **understand the order of repayment in liquidation;**
- **appreciate the consequences of wrongful and fraudulent trading;**
- **describe transactions at an undervalue and preferences;**
- **describe shadow directors and their liability;**
- **describe the effect of liquidation on bank accounts of companies;**
- **explain the use of wages accounts by banks.**

Self-assessment questions

1 Your company customer has a credit balance of £10,000, and in today's clearing there is a cheque for £3,000 which is properly drawn and not stopped. You receive notice of a winding up petition. What action do you take?

(a) Pay the cheque.

(b) Return the cheque without any reference to the directors, with the answer 'Refer to drawer'.

(c) Tell the directors that the cheque will be paid only if they can obtain a court order under s.127 by close of business. Otherwise it will be returned.

(d) Return the cheque without any reference to the directors, with the answer 'Orders not to pay'.

2 When does compulsory winding up begin?

(a) From the date of the winding up order.

(b) From the date of the presentation of a petition.

(c) From the date of the passing of a special resolution.

(d) From the date the liquidator accepts his appointment.

3 Which of the following are preferential creditors under the Insolvency Act 1986?

(a) Rates.

(b) Unpaid wages up to £800 incurred within four months of liquidation.

(c) Corporation tax.

(d) Twelve months' VAT.

4 With which of the following winding up situations is the company stating that it is solvent?

(a) Creditors' voluntary winding up.

(b) Members' voluntary winding up.

(c) Compulsory winding up.

5 In what circumstances could a director be personally liable for debts of his company?

(a) If he acts in contravention of a disqualification order under the Company Directors Disqualification Act 1986.

(b) If he is guilty of wrongful trading or fraudulent trading (ss.213–14).

(c) If the director personally guarantees the company account.

(d) All of the above.

(e) None of the above.

6 Why does a bank open a wages account?

(a) To rank as a preferential creditor for money lent for qualifying wages.

(b) For ease of proof.

(c) To avoid the effect of *Clayton's case* which can reduce the bank's preferential claim.

(d) To benefit from the judgment in *Re Unit 2 Windows Ltd.*

7 Your customer, Evans & Co plc, is an engineering company borrowing up to £1 million unsecured from you on current account. It has incurred losses in the last two years and sought extra facilities of £100,000 last month to pay an interim dividend to its preference shareholders, but this request was declined. Accordingly, the company raised the money from a merchant bank and placed these funds in a separate account at your branch. However, before the dividend cheques could be drawn, a winding up petition was presented to the court and a compulsory liquidation followed. The balances in your books on the day when the winding up was made were as follows.

Current account:	£950,000 debit
Dividend account:	£100,000 credit
Tax account:	£38,000 credit

Explain, with reasons, what your claim would be in the liquidation.

8 Your customer, X Ltd has a credit balance of £20,000. Today the bank receives notice of a winding up petition and it stops the customer's account.

(a) Why has the account been stopped when there is a credit balance?

(b) What must the directors do to enable the bank to carry on operating the account?

9 The most frequently used ground for the compulsory winding up of a

company by the court is that the company is unable to pay its debts. Explain what is meant by inability to pay debts. Could it apply to a company whose assets considerably exceed its liabilities?

10 Extra Ltd has had a winding up petition granted and the company is now in liquidation. Extra Ltd's liability comprises:

(a) Trade creditors;

(b) One year's business rates;

(c) A bank overdraft fully secured by a mortgage over the premises;

(d) Value added tax for the last six months;

(e) A loan from one of the directors;

(f) The workmen's wages for the past fortnight.

State the order of priority of payment of these claims.

What difference would it make if the bank overdraft were unsecured but the bank could show that half of the debt had been incurred by the company cashing cheques to pay his workmen's wages last month?

11 The directors of Z Ltd are advised by the company's auditors that there is no possibility of the company trading at a profit in the foreseeable future and no reasonable prospect of its paying its debts. What are the legal implications?

12 Your customer, X Ltd, has an unsecured overdraft facility of £50,000. One month ago you received a cheque for £60,000 from a finance company with a covering letter which stated that the funds were advanced for the sole purpose of purchasing a computerised machine.

The balance on the account on receipt of the letter was debit £20,000, and since that date the only transaction has been the £60,000 credit.

You learn today of the following facts:

(a) Notice of a winding up petition appears in today's *London Gazette.*

(b) The vendor of the computerised machine never delivered it, and no payment was made. The contract has been cancelled.

(c) The finance company claim £60,000 from you.

How will the bank act in this situation? Ignore interest. Today's ledger balance is £40,000 credit.

Further reading

- Penn, GA, Shea, AM and Arora, A — Chapter 28, *The Law Relating to Domestic Banking*, Vol 1, 1987, Sweet & Maxwell
- Raby, P — Chapter 9, *Law Relating to Banking Services*, 2nd edition 1992, Pitman

Unit 9

Cheques and Principles of Negotiability

Objectives

After studying this unit, you should be able to:

- **define a cheque;**
- **appreciate the importance of the Cheques Act 1992;**
- **understand the roles of the collecting bank, drawee bank and paying bank;**
- **appreciate the significance of endorsement;**
- **understand the drawer's liability on a cheque;**
- **differentiate between negotiability and assignability;**
- **understand the terms holder, holder for value and holder in due course;**
- **appreciate the significance of forged endorsements;**
- **understand the legal position when the payee becomes a holder in due course;**
- **differentiate between cheques, banker's drafts, dividend and interest warrants.**

1 Introduction: Cheques Act 1992

1.1 The Cheques Act 1992 has in many ways created two types of cheque, those printed in the traditional way with the words 'or order' after the payee's name and those that have the words 'account payee' or 'account payee only' printed on their face.

1.2 Under s.1, Cheques Act 1992 crossed cheques marked 'account payee' or 'account payee only' are not transferable and are valid only between the drawer and payee and, where appropriate, the drawer and the drawee bank. Such non-cheques are *not* negotiable instruments, whereas the traditional 'or order' cheques are. The concepts of holder in due course or holder for value *cannot apply* to non-transferable cheques.

1.3 As both forms of cheque currently exist, this unit must describe the legal position for both 'or order' and non-transferable cheques. The non-transferable cheque will increasingly become the norm.

2 What is a cheque?

Student Activity 1

Before reading further, write down your definition of a cheque, then compare this with the definition given below. You will probably do this from a functional perspective, rather than adopt legal terminology, this is fine – you can then compare functional use with legal terminology

2.1 The definition can be found in ss.3 and 73. A simplified definition from these combined sections is that:

> A cheque is an unconditional order, in writing, addressed by one person to a bank, signed by the person giving it, requiring the bank to whom it is addressed to pay on demand a sum certain in money to or to the order of a specified person, or to bearer.

2.2 The short definition of a cheque is:

> A bill of exchange, drawn on a banker, payable on demand.

2.3 The drawer is the drawee bank's customer who orders his bank to pay a certain sum of money to the payee, or to the payee's order. The payee will normally pay the cheque in for credit to his bank account at the collecting bank.

2.4 The cheque is presented through the clearing to the appropriate branch of the drawee bank. If the cheque is paid, the drawee bank then becomes the paying bank, and it debits its customer's (the drawer's) account. In cases where the payee banks at the same bank and branch as the drawer, the one bank fulfils the roles of both paying and collecting bank. The clearing system does not apply in such cases.

2.5 Because the cheque is a particular type of bill of exchange, the Bills of Exchange Act 1882 applies in so far as it is appropriate to cheques. In addition, the Cheques Act 1957 and the Cheques Act 1992 apply to cheques. All references are to the Bills of Exchange Act 1882 unless stated otherwise.

Student Activity 2

Clearly, the law relating to cheques is based on an old statute, amended piecemeal by two later statutes. Consider the implications of this. How have times changed? What specific issues is the 1882 Act unlikely to be able cope with? Jot down your thoughts, keep them with this unit and consider them again when you have finished the Units 9–12.

Negotiation of cheques made out in favour of the payee or order

2.6 In most cases, the payee will pay the cheque in for the credit of his bank account. Alternatively, but relatively unusually, the cheque may be negotiated to a third party. The full implications of negotiation are covered in section 7, but you need to know the basic definition now.

2.7 Under s.31, negotiation is defined as the transfer of a cheque from one person to another in such a way as to constitute the transferee the holder. A holder is the possessor of a bearer cheque, or the payee or endorsee of an order cheque.

2.8 A bearer cheque can be negotiated by simple delivery, whereas an order cheque must be negotiated by endorsement and delivery. Coupled with physical delivery, there must be the intention on the part of the transferor to transfer the rights embodied in the instrument.

2.9 A cheque is payable to bearer when it explicitly says 'pay bearer', or when the last or only endorsement is an 'endorsement in blank' (see below), or when the payee is a fictitious or nonexistent person: s.7.

2.10 In *Clutton v Attenborough* (1897) it was held that a cheque made payable to a fictitious or nonexistent person would still be considered as being payable to bearer, although the drawer believed that he had made the cheque payable to a real person. In the case a clerk tricked his employer into making out cheques in favour of a nonexistent payee for work supposedly done. The clerk then obtained possession of the cheques, forged the endorsement of the nonexistent payee, and negotiated them to third parties for value. It was held that even though there may be an actual person with the same name as the one used for the payee, the payee was fictitious since:

- There was no one of that name known to the drawer;
- The name of the payee had been provided by a person who wished to defraud the drawer.

2.11 Care must be taken to distinguish between this from *Vinden v Hughes* (1905) where the circumstances were similar but where the employee used a name of an actual customer of his employer. It was held that the payee could not be regarded as fictitious or nonexistent here because the drawer intended certain identifiable persons to be payees, believing, wrongly, that money was owed to them.

2.12 In addition, cheques drawn in favour of impersonal payees such as 'cash' or 'wages' are not cheques at all but merely mandates: *Orbit Mining and Trading Co v Westminster Bank* (1963). A pay 'cash or order' document means no more than that if the amount of the instrument is paid to the person intended to receive it, the drawer cannot claim that money from the bank.

2.13 Finally, under the Cheques Act 1992, cheques crossed 'account payee only' or 'account payee' are not negotiable, being valid only between the parties thereto.

3 Endorsements of cheques when the cheque is made out in favour of the payee or order

Endorsement in blank

Front of cheque	Pay X or order A	Back of cheque	X

3.1 The endorsement consists of the payee's signature only. No endorsee is specified. This makes the cheque payable to bearer. In this example, the transferee of X could transfer the cheque by simple delivery.

3.2 When the payee's name has been misspelt, the payee must endorse by spelling his name in the way it is shown on the face of the cheque. The payee could then add his correct signature in addition, if he thinks it fit.

Special endorsement

3.3 The endorser signs and specifies an endorsee. The cheque then becomes payable to the endorsee or his order:

Front of cheque	Pay X or order A	Back of cheque	Pay Z or order X

3.4 If Z, the endorsee, wishes to negotiate the cheque, he must endorse it before transferring it to someone else. The endorsement of Z could be either a special endorsement or an endorsement in blank. Section 34 defines the terms 'special endorsement' and 'endorsement in blank'.

Restrictive endorsement

3.5 Restrictive endorsements restrict further negotiation. A typical example of this would be if X had written 'pay Z only' above his signature as endorser.

3.6 With such an endorsement, the endorsee has the right to receive payment and to sue any party whom the endorser could have sued. However, the endorsee under a restrictive endorsement has no power to transfer his rights to a subsequent endorsee so long as the restrictive endorsement categorically forbids this.

3.7 Some restrictive endorsements are not worded quite as restrictively as one which uses the word 'only'. The following are examples.

Front of cheque	Pay X or order A	Back of cheque	Pay Z for the account of Y X

Front of cheque	Pay X or order A	Back of cheque	Pay X or order for collection X

3.8 Where a restrictive endorsement can authorise further transfer, as in the above examples, any endorsee subsequent to Z takes the cheque subject to the same restrictions as Z. Hence in practice such cheques are unlikely to be transferred by the endorsee who in the above examples is Z.

Conditional endorsement

3.9 When an endorser adds a condition to his endorsement, the fulfilment or otherwise of the condition is irrelevant: s.33.

Liability of endorser

3.10 Under s.55, the endorser warrants, i.e. contractually promises, that the cheque will be paid on presentation. The endorser is also precluded (estopped/prevented) from denying the genuineness of the drawer's signature and of any prior endorsements to a holder in due course. (For now we can consider that a holder in due course is a subsequent transferee who is entitled to payment, see section 8 for details.) Hence, an endorser in effect is liable to a subsequent holder of a cheque if it is dishonoured.

Transferor by delivery

3.11 When a cheque has been endorsed in blank, it becomes a bearer cheque. Hence any subsequent holder need not endorse if he wishes to transfer title of the cheque.

3.12 Section 58 defines the term 'transferor by delivery'.

Front of cheque	Pay P or order A	Back of cheque	P

3.13 If P endorses in blank and transfers the cheque to Z, Z could validly transfer the cheque to T without the need for further endorsement.

3.14 In such circumstances, Z is a transferor by delivery and, provided T gave value, Z warrants to T that:

- The cheque is genuine and not a forgery;
- Z has the right to transfer it;
- Z was unaware at the time of transfer of anything which would make the cheque valueless.

3.15 Whilst Z cannot be directly liable in the event of nonpayment (unless the cheque is a forgery), he would still be liable in damages to T for breach of any of the warranties specified above. Only persons who have endorsed the cheque or signed it as drawer, are liable purely for nonpayment.

3.16 If the cheque is genuine and it is subsequently dishonoured, a transferor by delivery will only be liable if he knew at the time of transfer that the cheque was valueless.

3.17 *Note*: for cheques crossed 'account payee' or 'account payee only' endorsements will be irrelevant since such cheques are valid only between the parties thereto.

Student Activity 3

Summarise the types of endorsement that can be found on a cheque and describe the effect of each of these types of endorsement. How is the position changed if the cheque has been crossed 'account payee only'? One way to do this would be to annotate diagrams of cheques bearing the endorsements involved. We realise that this is pretty basic knowledge but, believe us, pretty basic mistakes are made in examinations!

4 The liability of a drawer on a cheque

4.1 Under s.55 the drawer warrants that the cheque will paid on presentation. If a cheque has been dishonoured, the drawer is legally obliged to compensate the payee or any endorser who has been obliged to compensate the cheque's holder. If the cheque has been crossed 'account payee only' then the drawer's liability will be restricted to the original payee.

4.2 The drawer also warrants that the payee exists and that the payee has capacity to endorse. This warranty applies as between the drawer and a holder in due course. This explains why cheques which are made out in favour of fictitious or nonexistent payees can be treated as payable to bearer when the payee's endorsement has been forged (see *Clutton v Attenborough* (1897) in paragraph 2.10). Hence, such cheques are perfectly valid and a person to whom they have been negotiated can become a holder in due course, provided s.29 has been complied with and provided there is no 'account payee' crossing.

4.3 However, when the drawer knew the payee and intended that payment be made to that person, lack of endorsement or forged endorsement would destroy the negotiability of the cheque and would free the drawer from any liability on it if the cheque were to be subsequently dishonoured *Vinden v Hughes* (1905).

5 The liability of an agent who signs on the drawer's behalf

5.1 When someone signs a cheque on the drawer's behalf as agent, then that person will not be personally liable in the event of dishonour, *provided* it is clear that the person signs purely in the capacity of agent. Hence, the words '*per pro*' or 'for and on behalf of' absolve an agent from personal liability: s.26. However, the Act also states that the mere addition to the signature of the word 'agent' or similar without the name of the principal, will not protect the agent from personal liability.

5.2 Furthermore, *Bondina Ltd v Rollaway Shower Blinds Ltd* (1986) states that an agent will not normally be personally liable on a dishonoured company cheque, even if the words '*per pro*' or 'for and on behalf' of are omitted, provided the cheque is on the standard printed form which clearly identifies the company's account.

5.3 Section 349, Companies Act 1985 requires a company to have its correct name stated legibly on all its cheques. Any breach of this requirement can result in a fine for the company or for any officer who signs such cheques. Any officer who signs such cheques will be liable to the holder of the cheque unless it is paid by the company.

5.4 Relevant cases which concern the personal liability of an agent who signs on behalf of a drawer are:

- *Banque de L'Indochine et de Suez SA v Euroseas Group Finance Co Ltd* (1981) – it is acceptable to use 'Co' instead of 'Company', and no personal liability can arise from this.
- *British Airways Board v Parish* (1979) – the omission of 'Ltd' from the company's name is enough to establish personal liability.
- *Hendon v Adelman* (1973) – the bank printed the name on the company's cheque as 'L R Agencies Ltd', whereas the correct title was 'L & R Agencies Ltd'. It was held that the omission of '&' was sufficient to establish personal liability on the part of signing officers, but that the bank may be liable in negligence to compensate such signatories.
- *Maxform SpA v B Mariani and Goodville Ltd* (1979) – the use of the company's trading name is insufficient to enable the signatories to avoid personal liability.

6 The essential features of negotiability of order cheques

6.1 The best-known examples of negotiable instruments are cheques, bills of exchange and promissory notes (bank notes are promissory notes). Bills of Exchange and promissory notes are not in this syllabus.

6.2 To be classed as negotiable, an instrument must possess the following characteristics:

- Title must pass by delivery, or by endorsement and delivery.
- The transferee must not be required to give notice of the transfer to any prior parties.
- The transferee can acquire a good title, even if his transferor had a defective title to the instrument.

  To acquire such a title, the transferee must have acted in *good faith* and *valuable consideration* must have been given for the instrument. In such cases, the transferee will be a holder in due course or a holder for value, the former taking the instrument free of any defence, counterclaim or set off between the person liable on the instrument and any prior parties.

  Under s.27, valuable consideration is any:

  - Consideration sufficient to support a simple contract;
  - Antecedent debt or liability.
- The transferee can sue in his own name if the negotiable instrument is dishonoured at maturity.

Note 1 If a negotiable instrument requires the endorsement of the transferor prior to being transferred, the transferee *cannot obtain a good title if that endorsement is forged*: s.24. If the endorsement is irregular, e.g. a signature which does not correspond *exactly* with the name of the transferor, the transferee will obtain no better title than his transferor: *Arab Bank v Ross* (1952).

2 If the instrument is crossed 'not negotiable', then it is not a negotiable instrument and the transferee acquires no better title than his transferor.

3 Under the Cheques Act 1992 cheques crossed 'account payee only' or 'account payee' cannot be negotiable instruments. Such cheques are valid only between the parties thereto.

7 Negotiability and assignability compared

7.1 An assignable instrument is an instrument the rights to which can be transferred (assigned) by the holder to a third party. The best known examples of assignment are assignment of monies due under a contract, or assignment of monies due under a life policy.

7.2 Here the person to whom payment will be due may assign his rights to third parties and the positions regarding assignability and negotiability differ as follows:

Negotiability	*Assignability*
1 Transfer by delivery or by endorsement and delivery.	1 The transfer must be evidenced in writing and there is sometimes a particular form of wording required.
2 There is no need to give notice of transfer to any prior parties.	2 It is necessary to notify the person liable on the instrument. If full legal rights are to be acquired, written notice is essential. (The differences between legal and equitable rights are set out in Unit 13.) Where notice is not given, the assignee has only an equitable assignment.
3 The transferee can sue in his own name.	3 The assignee can only sue in his own name if he has a legal assignment. Otherwise the assignee must ask the transferor (assignor) to join in the court action.
4 The transferee of a negotiable instrument under certain defined circumstances can acquire a good title even though the transferor had a defective title. Thus, the transferee in these	4 The assignee takes the instrument subject to set off, counterclaim and any other equities. The normal rule of *nemo dat quod non habet* applies.

circumstances will not be affected by any counterclaim, set off, or other equitable rights between the transferor and the person ultimately liable on the instrument. This reverses the usual law of *nemo dat quod non habet* – nobody can give a good title if his own title is defective.

Note: when a negotiable instrument is transferred to a person who obtains the full benefits of negotiability, the instrument is said to be 'negotiated'. If the transferee merely obtains whatever title his transferor had, the instrument is said to be 'transferred'. 'Account payee only' cheques are effectively not negotiable instruments, being valid only between the parties thereto.

8 Holder, holder for value and holder in due course of cheques made out to the payee or order

8.1 A *holder* is the possessor of a bearer cheque, or the payee or endorsee of an order cheque: s.2.

8.2 A *holder for value* is defined by s.27(2) as the holder of a cheque for which value has at sometime been given, although that value need not have been given by the present holder personally.

8.3 A *holder in due course* is defined by s.29 as a holder who has taken a cheque:

- Complete and regular on the face of it;
- Before it was overdue;
- Without notice of previous dishonour (if applicable);
- In good faith;
- For value;
- Without notice of any defect in the transferor's title.

Note: when someone is in possession of a cheque which bears a forged endorsement, that person is not a holder at all, merely a 'wrongful possessor'. This is because by s.24 a forged signature on a cheque is 'wholly inoperative'. Thus, if the possessor cannot be a holder, *a fortiori*, the possessor cannot be a holder in due course. This provision in s.24 is something you must always remember and apply when you are faced with a situation involving a forged signature on a cheque (or other bill of exchange).

Notes on the requirements of a holder in due course

Complete

8.4 If any material detail is missing, a cheque is said to be an inchoate instrument. Typical examples would be cheques which were undated, or in which the amount had not been inserted.

8.5 Under s.20, the person in possession may complete the missing details and may then have a valid claim against all prior parties, provided the details inserted conform to the authority given, and provided the details are completed within reasonable time. An example of acting within the authority given would arise when a cheque had been issued in the past to settle an invoice, and the drawer had not completed the date or amount in words. In this case, it would be considered that the payee had acted in conformity with the provisions of s.20, if he inserted the amount claimed in the invoice in words and filled in the date on receipt of the cheque.

8.6 However, s.20 goes on to say that a subsequent holder in due course of an inchoate instrument which has been completed by a prior holder can enforce the cheque against all parties as if it had been completed in reasonable time and in accordance with proper authority.

Pay B or order X	Pay B or order One Hundred pounds £100.00 X

If B completes the amount in accordance with X's authority, and if the amount is inserted within a reasonable time, then B could claim against X if the cheque were dishonoured. However, if the amount that X had intended to pay was only £50, then B could still claim against X if the cheque were dishonoured, but B's claim would be subject to a counterclaim from X for £50.

8.7 Continuing this example, if B endorses as follows, and if Z fulfils all the criteria of a holder in due course, then Z can claim £100 from either X or B if the cheque is dishonoured.

Pay Z or order B

Z, as holder in due course, takes the cheque free from any prior equities.

Note: in *Wilson and Meeson v Pickering* (1946) it was held that the drawer of an inchoate instrument which has been wrongfully completed may deny payment to the holder or recover payment where it has already been made if the cheque has been crossed 'not negotiable'.

Regular on the face of it

8.8 Likewise, if the cheque is an order cheque, it must purport to be endorsed. The absence of endorsement would mean that the cheque was not 'regular' and the holder of such a cheque cannot be a holder in due course. If the endorsement was irregular, the holder cannot be holder in due course: *Arab Bank v Ross* (1952).

8.9 The need for regularity of endorsement was explained by Lord Denning as:

> A bill of exchange is like currency. It should be above suspicion. Completeness and regularity must be determined by looking only at the bill itself. Both sides

must be in apparent order and an irregularity in the endorsement will deprive a subsequent holder of the rights of a holder in due course.

Before it was overdue

8.10 A cheque is overdue when it has been in circulation for an unreasonable length of time. What is 'unreasonable' depends on the facts and there is no statutory definition of the meaning of 'unreasonable', though in practice six months is taken as a maximum. However, Laidlaw and Roberts tentatively suggest that a cheque would become overdue well before the six month period which banks apply to stale cheques. Their reasoning is presumably that the financial position of a drawer can change very quickly nowadays and the longer the time the cheque has been in circulation, the more the possibility that some fraud could arise.

Without notice of previous dishonour

8.11 If the drawee bank refuses to pay a cheque, it writes the reason (e.g. 'Refer to drawer') in red ink on the face of the cheque. This wording constitutes notice to any subsequent holder that the cheque has already been dishonoured.

In good faith

8.12 In s.90, 'good faith' is defined as something done honestly, even if negligently. Once again, what constitutes 'good faith' depends on the facts of the case.

For value

8.13 The holder must give valuable consideration in exchange for the cheque.

8.14 Section 27 defines valuable consideration as:

- Any consideration sufficient to support a simple contract; or
- Any antecedent debt or liability.

8.15 If you have completed the Banking Certificate, try to recall the rules of consideration in contract law. Then think of an example of a situation whereby a potential holder in due course could give valuable consideration for a cheque. If you have not studied the subject, you should study the recommended preliminary reading before formulating an example.

8.16 Having thought about this matter, you might think of a person, H, who completes some house decorating for P. The amount agreed is £500 which is a reasonable fee in the circumstances. If P is the payee of a cheque for £500, P could hand over the cheque, duly endorsed in blank , to H. In this case, assuming the cheque were an order cheque, H would have fulfilled the 'valuable consideration' requirement in connection with being a holder in due course.

Without notice of any defect in the transferor's title

8.17 If the holder knows that his transferor has a defective title, or if the holder deliberately ignores facts which a reasonable person would have construed as a warning of a defect of title, then that person cannot be a holder in due course.

8.18 *Note*: a holder in due course has full rights to payment of the cheque, and those rights are not affected in any way by prior equities or counterclaims.

Example: difference between holder in due course and holder for value where the cheque is made out to the payee or order

Holder in due course

Pay B or order

A

8.19 A gives the cheque to B, B endorses it in blank and hands it to C. C endorses it in blank and hands it to D. In each case the transfer is to settle a debt.

... B

... C

8.20 If X steals the cheque from D and persuades a publican to cash it, the publican (P) is a holder in due course, provided P took the cheque in accordance with the conditions of s.29. P is entitled to be paid. If A stops the cheque, P will be able to claim from A, or B, or C (or X for what it is worth), and P's claim will not be affected by any prior equities or counterclaims.

Holder for value

8.21 If, in the above example, P were to give the cheque to Q as a gift, Q would be a holder for value. If the cheque were unpaid, Q's rights on the cheque would be as follows:

- A holder for value who has not given value personally cannot claim from his immediate transferor, the party who 'gave' him the cheque.
- A holder for value can claim against all parties prior to the immediate transferor, provided his immediate transferor had a good title. Thus, any claim by a holder for value is subject to prior equities.

Thus Q could claim from A, B, C or X, provided P had a good title.

8.22 The definition of a holder for value is given in s.27.

8.23 Where value has at any time been given on a bill, a holder who has not himself given value is deemed to be a holder for value.

8.24 The holder for value acquires full rights on the bill against all parties apart from the person who 'gave' him the bill, provided the immediate transferor had a good title.

8.25 Under s.29(3), a holder for value who derives title to a cheque through a holder in due course, and who is not himself a party to any fraud or illegality affecting it, has all the rights of a holder in due course as regards parties prior to the immediate transferor who 'gave' him the cheque.

9 The position of the holder of a cheque where there are both forged and genuine endorsements

9.1 Consider the following example.

Pay P or order £100 D	P's endorsement is forged X's endorsement is genuine

9.2 Suppose A steals the cheque from P and gives it to X for value. X then endorses the cheque in blank and gives it to B in settlement of a debt.

- If the cheque is paid by the drawee bank, B must refund to P, the true owner, when the facts come to light. B cannot be a holder in due course under a forged endorsement. However, B can claim from anyone who has endorsed the cheque, or anyone who has transferred the cheque after a genuine endorsement.

  Hence B must refund £100 to P, but can claim reimbursement from X whose only rights are against the thief, if he can be found and if he has any funds.
- If the cheque is dishonoured by the drawee bank, e.g. if D stops it, B has no rights against D or P, but can claim against X. X's only reimbursement will be from the thief, A.

10 The position of the payee as a holder in due course

10.1 In *Jones Ltd v Waring and Gillow* (1926) it was held that the original payee of a cheque cannot be a holder in due course because the cheque has been issued to him as opposed to having been negotiated to him. Thus, if the original payee does not negotiate the cheque to anyone else, then he has the right to sue the drawer if the cheque is dishonoured. However, the payee's claim on the dishonoured cheque will be subject to any counterclaim which the drawer may have against the payee.

10.2 However, under *Jade International Steel Stahl and Eisen Gmb Hand Co, K G v Robert Nicholas (Steels) Ltd* (1978) the original payee can become a holder in due course if he negotiates an 'or order' cheque and that cheque is subsequently negotiated back to him.

10.3 For example, If X issues a cheque to B or order and B negotiates the cheque to C, then C negotiates it to D and D negotiates it back to B, then B can become a holder in due course provided he fulfils all the criteria. If the cheque is then dishonoured, B can sue all prior parties and, being a holder in due course, B can claim free from any prior equities. If the cheque had been crossed 'account payee' or 'account payee only' the original payee's rights would have been against the drawer only.

10.4 However, if B had simply paid the cheque straight into his bank account as soon as it had been originally issued, then B could not have been a holder in due course. In such a case, any claim by B, in the event of dishonour, would be subject to any counterclaim from the drawer of the cheque.

10.5 *Note*: remember that cheques crossed 'account payee' or 'account payee only' are not transferable, and the concepts of negotiability and holder in due course/holder for value do not apply to them. Thus, in practice there is nowadays much less likelihood of a cheque being negotiated back to the original payee as in happened in Jade International.

Student Activity 4

1 Assess the legal implications of a forged endorsement for a person wishing to claim as a holder in due course or as a holder for value.

2 Consider how the Cheques Act 1992 has affected the position of someone who wishes to claim as a holder in due course.

11 Other payment orders

11.1 This section will briefly describe instruments which perform functions similar to cheques.

Bankers' drafts

11.2 Banker's drafts used in domestic UK transactions are similar to cheques except that the drawer is usually a branch of a bank and the drawee is the head office of the same bank. Thus, a banker's draft is not a cheque, since the drawer and drawee are the same person. However, by s.5, the holder of such an instrument has the right to treat it as a negotiable instrument. Hence banker's drafts may be regarded as negotiable instruments.

11.3 Bank drafts cannot be made payable to bearer, as this would amount to the issue of bank notes.

11.4 In international trade, drafts are drawn by one bank on another, and such drafts are in fact the same as cheques, being drawn by one person on another.

11.5 *Midland Bank plc v Brown Shipley & Co* (1992) held that where a bank has confirmed to the payee of a bank draft that the draft is in order, then it is estopped from denying the validity of such a draft at a later date. In this case the draft had been issued against instructions which did not conform to the mandate.

Dividend and interest warrants

11.6 Such warrants are nowadays often drawn in the form of cheques. Where they do not take the form of cheques, there are special rules to protect the paying and collecting banker. These rules are covered in subsequent units.

Summary

Now that you have studied this unit, you should be able to:

- **define a cheque**
- **explain the roles of the collecting bank and paying bank;**
- **understand the effects of various types of endorsements on cheques;**
- **understand the implications of the Cheques Act 1992;**
- **know the extent of a drawer's liability on a cheque;**
- **appreciate the essential features of negotiability;**
- **compare negotiability with assignability;**
- **differentiate between a holder, a holder for value, and a holder in due course;**
- **understand the effect of forged endorsements on the rights of those in possession of cheques;**
- **know the position regarding the original payee as holder in due course;**
- **differentiate between cheques, banker's drafts, dividend and interest warrants.**

Self-assessment questions

1 A cheque is made payable to 'bearer' and negotiated. What are the rights of a holder if the cheque bears a forged endorsement? Assume that the cheque is *not* crossed 'account payee only'.

(a) The holder cannot be a holder in due course because of the forged endorsement.

(b) The forged endorsement does not in itself prevent the holder from being a holder in due course.

(c) The holder can only be a holder for value.

(d) Forged endorsements free the drawer from liability.

2 A cheque made out to order is endorsed as follows by the payee 'Pay Y or Order provided Y delivers goods to me'. Subsequently Y negotiates the cheque to Z, having endorsed it in blank. Y does not fulfil the condition.

Referring only to the conditional endorsement, consider the position of Z, who is unaware of the nondelivery of goods by Y and who has no means of knowing whether the condition has been fulfilled. Consider which of the following statements is correct.

(a) Z could have been a holder in due course but only if Y had delivered the goods.

(b) Z can be a holder in due course and the fulfilment or non fulfilment of the condition is irrelevant.

3 Which instruments enable the transferee to obtain a better title than his transferor, provided certain conditions such as good faith and the giving of value are fulfilled?

(a) Cheques made out to the payee or order.

(b) Assignable instruments.

(c) Cheques crossed 'account payee only'.

(d) Cheques crossed 'Not negotiable'.

4 X issues a cheque made payable to P or order, who endorses it. P then negotiates the cheque to D in settlement of a debt. The cheque is then presented by D's bank and is paid by the drawee bank.

It then transpires that P had no right to any payment from X, but had tricked him into issuing the cheque. X wishes to claim reimbursement from D, since P has disappeared.

What are X's rights, assuming D had no knowledge of P's trickery when the cheque was negotiated and that good faith applied?

(a) D must reimburse X.

(b) X has no claim against D provided D has fulfilled the normal criteria of a holder in due course.

(c) C has no claim against D in any circumstances.

5 Consider the facts in Question 4, but assume that X had placed a 'stop' on the cheque. What are D's rights?

(a) D can only claim from P (for what worth?).

(b) D can claim from X or P, and D's claim is not affected by the position between X and P.

(c) D can claim reimbursement from the drawee bank.

(d) D can claim from the collecting bank.

6 Suppose the cheque in Question 4 had been crossed 'account payee'. How would this affect D's title?

(a) D has no rights against X.

(b) D can be a holder in due course even if P had no title to the cheque.

(c) D can be a holder in due course because P's endorsement was genuine.

(d) D could be a holder in due course so along as he had given P full value for the cheque.

7 D is the payee of a cheque, crossed 'account payee only', which is stolen from him by X. Later, X forged D's endorsement and then gives the cheque to Y in exchange for goods. What is Y?

(a) Holder in due course.

(b) Holder.

(c) Holder for value.

(d) Wrongful possessor.

Further reading

- Milnes Holden, J — Chapters 4 and 5, *The Law and Practice of Banking*, Vol 1, 5th edition 1991, Pitman
- Laidlaw, A and Roberts, G — Chapter 5, *Law Relating to Banking* Services, 2nd edition 1992, Bankers Books
- Raby, P — Chapter 10, *Law Relating to Banking Services*, 2nd edition 1992, Pitman

Unit 10

The Paying Bank

Objectives

On completion of this unit, you should be able to:

- **understand what is meant by completion of payment of cheques;**
- **appreciate the duties of a paying bank regarding its customer's cheques;**
- **list the situations when the bank's duty to pay cheques is terminated;**
- **assess the position when a drawer's signature has been forged;**
- **understand the bank's position in the case of wrongful dishonour;**
- **appreciate the bank's position if it pays a cheque in breach of mandate;**
- **understand the position in connection with encashment of open cheques;**
- **understand the implications of the clearing system for the paying banker;**
- **assess the possible courses of action when a bank has paid a stopped cheque by mistake.**

Note: All references in this unit are to the Bills of Exchange Act 1882 unless stated otherwise.

1 Completion of payment of cheques

1.1 From Unit 8 you will recall that the drawee bank is the bank and branch where the drawer has his account. The cheque will be presented to the drawee bank who will become the paying bank if the cheque is honoured on presentation.

1.2 Payment is not made finally to the payee until the expiration of time within which the drawee bank/branch may dishonour the cheque. Hence, as regards cheques, completion of payment will differ depending on the method used to present the cheque.

Cheques presented through the general clearing

'Normal' rules

1.3 On day one, the cheque is paid in at the collecting bank; on day two the cheque is processed at the clearing house; on day three the cheque is presented to the account holding branch of the drawee bank.

1.4 Under the clearing house rules, the drawee bank/branch must return any dishonoured cheque to the collecting bank by first-class post on the same day as it was presented, i.e. on day three. Hence, the drawer may 'stop' a cheque and have the 'stop' accepted by the drawee bank at any time up to the close of business on day three of the cheque clearing cycle.

'Late returns' procedure under clearing house rules

1.5 When a bank has inadvertently paid a cheque on day three, then it may return the cheque on day four. If the amount of the cheque exceeds £500, then the drawee bank/branch must telephone the collecting bank before 12 o'clock on day four with the details.

1.6 Examples of what comes within 'inadvertence' are:

- A stop authority was overlooked and the cheque was not returned on day three.
- The drawer withdrew cash from his account on day three, and as a result there were insufficient funds to meet the cheque, whereas the account holding branch thought that there were sufficient funds available to cover the cheque on day three.
- The account holding branch had overlooked notice of death or a bankruptcy order which had been notified to it on or before day three.
- The account had been closed on day three and the amount of the cheque had been overlooked in calculating the balance paid out.

Note 1 The bank cannot use the late returns procedure when the reason for nonpayment is that there is a technical irregularity, e.g. 'postdated' or 'words and figures differ'.

2 If a customer sends a 'stop authority' which reaches the account holding branch on day four, i.e. the day after the cheque has been presented, then the account holding branch must not use the late returns procedure. Basically, the late returns procedure applies only when the cheque was 'paid' because of inadvertence on day three.

Telephone enquiries by the collecting bank

1.7 Sometimes a collecting bank may telephone on behalf of the person whose account has been credited to ask for the fate of the cheque. If there are adequate funds, no stop authority, and the cheque is technically in order, the drawee bank should confirm to the collecting bank that the cheque is paid. This telephone call will be made on the same day as the cheque itself has been presented for payment.

1.8 Once this has been done, payment is completed, and the paying bank cannot subsequently change its mind and return the cheque. This applies even if the drawer communicates a stop instruction which is received by the drawee bank/branch before close of business on the same day, but after completion of the telephone call to the collecting bank.

Open cheques cashed at the counter of the drawee bank/branch

1.9 Payment is completed when the cash is handed over to the presenter of the cheque.

1.10 In *Chambers v Miller* (1862), a bank cashed a cheque on presentation, but immediately afterwards discovered that the drawer, its customer, had insufficient funds. The recipient had not left the bank and still had the cash. It was held that payment was irrevocable and that innocent third parties should not be made to make restitution. The mistake lay between the bank and its own customer.

Position when the payee presents the cheque and asks for its fate

1.11 In *Ringham v Hackett* (1980), a payee presented a cheque at the counter of the drawee bank, along with a credit transfer slip, and asked if the cheque was paid. It was held that the bank had a duty to provide an answer and that if the answer was 'yes', payment was irrevocably completed at that time.

2 The duties of a paying bank regarding its customers' cheques

2.1 A bank must pay its customers' cheques provided they are properly drawn, signed in accordance with the mandate and backed by adequate funds.

2.2 When a cheque has been issued in conjunction with a cheque guarantee card, the bank has an additional duty: it must honour the cheque provided the conditions of the cheque guarantee card have been met. This additional duty is a duty to the *payee* which arises because of the general guarantee the bank has given in connection with cheque guarantee cards.

2.3 The duties of a bank towards the payee of a cheque drawn in conjunction with a cheque card were discussed in *First Sport Ltd v Barclays* (1992). The bank had issued a cheque guarantee card to its customer and the card and cheque book were stolen. The fraudster used the card to persuade First Sport to accept a stolen cheque in exchange for goods. The fraudster forged the drawer's signature and the vendor had no reason to doubt that the transaction was a genuine one. The forged signature resembled that of the authorised signatory.

2.4 It was held that on the construction of the wording of the cheque guarantee card a retailer who in good faith accepted the cheque in conjunction with the card could insist that the cheque be honoured, even against a forged drawer's signature.

2.5 It is likely that banks will amend the wording on their cheque guarantee cards to indicate that cheques will be honoured only against a genuine drawer's signature, for otherwise they could continue to find themselves having to honour cheques for which there is no authority to obtain reimbursement from the drawer.

Student Activity 1

Look at the wording on your own bank's cheque guarantee card. Do you think the wording would overcome the problem of liability on forged signatures as discussed above? Write a few paragraphs explaining your view.

2.6 Normally, i.e. in the absence of any special arrangement, such as a cheque guarantee card, there is no responsibility on the part of the bank as regards the payee, since the bank's contractual duties in connection with cheques are solely with its customer, the drawer.

3 When should a bank not pay its customers' cheques?

Student Activity 2

List as many situations as you can think of where you either (a) know and (b) think that the bank should not pay a cheque. Explain the reason(s) in each case. When you have done this, compare your list with the text below.

3.1 The situations in which a bank is not required to honour its customers' cheques are:

- Notice of the *death* of its customer.
- When payment has been *countermanded.*
- Notice of *mental incapacity* of the customer.
- Notice, actual or constructive, that the cheque has been issued for an *illegal purpose.*
- On the *bankruptcy or liquidation* of the drawer.
- On receipt of a *garnishee order* or of an *injunction.*
- Where the drawer becomes an *enemy alien.*
- Notice of a *defect in the title* of the presenter.
- When the cheque is *not in proper form.*

3.2 On *notice of the death of its customer* the bank's authority ends: s.75. Cheques paid after death of the drawer, but prior to notice of death can be validly debited to the deceased's account. Notice can be 'actual', e.g. in the form of a letter or phone call from a near relative of the deceased, or it can be 'constructive', e.g. from a newspaper article. Cheques should be returned, marked 'Drawer deceased', once the bank has had notice of death.

3.3 Section 75 also states that the bank's duty to pay its customers' cheques is terminated by *countermand of payment. Curtice v London, City and Midland Bank* (1908) established that the actual notice must be received at the account holding branch. In *Curtice* the customer had sent a countermand by telegram which had been delivered into the bank's letter box because the bank was closed. The court held that delivery of the telegram into the letter box was not constructive notice, even though the bank would have discovered the countermand in time had it emptied the letter box on a daily basis.

What transpired after the 'stopped' cheque had been paid was that the plaintiff drew a cheque on the bank for the whole of his balance (including the amount represented by the 'stopped cheque'. When this cheque was dishonoured , the bank was sued in debt. Whilst the court ruled that constructive notice did not apply, the court held that the bank may be liable in damages, but the measure of damages may not necessarily be the same as the amount of the debt.

3.4 Receipt of a countermand notice by another branch of the drawee bank is not effective notice. In *London Provincial and South Western Bank Ltd v Buszard* (1918) it was held that if the countermand is given to another branch, then that branch should communicate the stop to the account holding branch. However, if the cheque is paid in the interim, there is no liability on the paying bank.

3.5 Any stop authority must be unambiguous. If the stop instructions are unclear, the bank will be protected if it acts in good faith. The most important detail is the cheque number: *Westminster Bank v Hilton* (1926). Where there is a joint account, any party to the account can authorise a 'stop', even if that party is not the person who has signed the cheque, unless the mandate itself specifically contradicts this.

3.6 As with death, it is receipt of *notice of mental incapacity*, as opposed to the actual date of mental incapacity, which determines the duty to pay.

3.7 Notice, actual or constructive, that the cheque has been *issued for an illegal purpose.* (See *Lipkin Gorman* and *Selangor United Rubber* in Unit 1.)

3.8 On the bankruptcy or liquidation of the drawer, the bank's authority terminates. (See Units 5 and 7 for a more detailed discussion.) Similarly, on receipt of a garnishee order or of an injunction whereby a court order 'freezes' the customer's funds with a bank.

3.9 The bank's authority is also terminated when the drawer is a national of another country and war has been declared against that country and when the bank has notice that there is a defect in the title of the presenter of a cheque.

3.10 Finally, when the cheque is not in proper form, i.e. there is a technical irregularity, for example the words and figures differ, the bank's authority is terminated. Strictly speaking, when the words and figures differ, the bank could pay according to the words, relying on s.9(2). In practice the cheque would normally be returned as an ambiguous order with the answer 'words and figures differ'. In the case of a postdated cheque, this must be dishonoured as there is no authority to pay it.

4 Forged or unauthorised drawer's signature

4.1 Under s.24, a *forged signature is wholly inoperative* on a cheque (or bill of exchange). Hence, if the bank pays a cheque with a forged drawer's signature, it will have paid without authority and must refund the money to its customer. The only protection for the bank is if the doctrine of estoppel applies.

4.2 Note how the case of *First Sport v Barclays* applies to cheques issued in conjunction with a cheque card.

Student Activity 3

Think back to Unit 1. Which case illustrates the bank's obligation to refund the amount of any cheque paid on a forged drawer's signature? Which case illustrates estoppel? Check you answers.

4.3 Section 24 also states that an *unauthorised signature on a cheque is wholly inoperative*. The most common example of an unauthorised signature occurs when an agent signs cheques at variance with the customer's mandate to the bank.

4.4 In this case of an unauthorised drawer's signature, the only defences which the bank can plead are:

- *Ostensible authority*. To plead ostensible authority, the bank must have had no notice of any restriction on the agent's actual authority to sign on behalf of the drawer. In practice, this defence is unlikely to be available to the bank.
- *Ratification*. The customer may ratify if he wishes and, if so, the bank will be protected from any future claim.
- *Estoppel*. Estoppel occurs when the customer has, by his actions, made it seem that the agent was authorised when in fact he was not. Negligence on the part of the customer in supervising the agent would not amount to estoppel: *Tai Hing Cotton Mill Ltd v Liu Chong Hing Bank* (1985).

5 Wrongful dishonour of a cheque

5.1 Apart from special arrangements, such as cheque guarantee cards, or credit open facilities, a bank has no responsibility to the payee of a cheque if it wrongfully dishonours that cheque.

5.2 However, wrongful dishonour can render a bank liable to the drawer on two counts:

- Breach of contract;
- Libel.

Breach of contract

5.3 If the bank dishonours a cheque which is properly drawn, not countermanded and sufficient funds or overdraft facilities exists, it will be liable to the drawer for breach of contract. The amount of damages payable will be the court's assessment of the financial damage actually suffered, e.g. loss of credit facilities for a business: *National Westminster v Oceancrest* (1985).

5.4 When the customer is a private customer, it would be difficult to prove that the wrongful dishonour had resulted in significant financial loss and nominal damages only would be payable unless he could prove special circumstances of which the bank was aware when the account was opened.

Libel

5.5 In *Jayson v Midland Bank* (1968), the words 'Refer to drawer' on a wrongfully dishonoured cheque were held to be libellous in that they lowered the reputation of the drawer in the eyes of right thinking people. The amount of damages awarded for libel would depend on the amount of publicity attracted by the dishonour and on the amount of the cheque (the lower the amount of the cheque, the greater the damage to reputation). If the bank takes immediate steps to apologise and to tell the payee the true facts once the error comes to light, then the damages for libel will be lessened. In practice, a bank would almost certainly wish to settle out of court in connection with a libel claim.

6 Breach of signing authority in the mandate

6.1 Consider the following.

ABC is a partnership. A cheque is drawn payable to Brown. The mandate calls for two signatures, but only one partner, A, signs. The cheque is paid.

6.2 There are two possibilities. If Brown has a commercial debt owed by the partnership, then the bank is protected under *B Liggett v Barclays* (1928). By subrogation, the bank can step into the shoes of a satisfied creditor if the bank has paid that creditor and is therefore entitled to debit the account.

6.3 If Brown is a personal creditor of A, then the other partners have a right to claim for the loss caused by payment of the cheque: *Catlin v Cyprus Finance Corporation (London) Ltd* (1983). Whilst the other partners would have a right of action against Brown, in practice they would normally claim against the bank unless Brown settled with them very quickly.

7 Encashment of open cheques at the counters of the drawee bank

7.1 Under s.60, Bills of Exchange Act 1882 and under s.1, 1957, the bank obtains a good discharge if it pays any cheque:

- In good faith; and
- In the ordinary course of business.

7.2 An additional duty in respect of encashment of open cheques is for the bank to see that the cheque *purports* to be endorsed by the payee: *Committee of London Clearing Banks* (1957). Thus, provided there are no suspicious circumstances and the endorsement purports to be correct, the bank may pay the cheque, i.e. cash it, provided:

- It is not stopped;
- The drawer's signature is valid.

Failure to cash the cheque could damage the customer's credit.

7.3 Consider the following situation. Brown draws a cheque payable to Mr Jones or order. It is properly drawn, there are adequate funds and the cheque is not stopped. It bears the apparent endorsement of F Jones on the back.

7.4 If someone purporting to be Jones presents the above open cheque to the drawee bank and branch and asks for £100 in cash, the drawee bank can cash the cheque if the cheque already purports to be endorsed by Jones and provided that there are no suspicious circumstances (see below).

7.5 If the cheque is not so endorsed, then the bank can simply ask the presenter to endorse. If the presenter signs on the back of the cheque in the name of Jones, then no further action is required by the bank and the cheque can be cashed in the absence of any suspicious circumstances.

7.6 Naturally, if there are any suspicious circumstances, for instance if the presenter of the cheque had been a woman when the payee was named as Mr Jones, then the bank should not pay without the drawer's specific authority and without correct endorsement.

7.7 In *Auchteroni v Midland Bank* (1928) it was held that payment of large sums over the counter was not in itself outside the ordinary course of business, so long as there were no other suspicious circumstances.

8 Payment of cheques presented via the clearing system

8.1 If a cheque is properly drawn, not stopped, and correctly signed by the drawer, the paying bank will be protected from any liability if it pays the cheque to the holder, provided the presenter is the person entitled to the money: s.59.

8.2 The problem arises, of course, when the presenter is someone who is not entitled to the money. If the cheque bears a forged or unauthorised endorsement, a paying bank is protected by:

- Section 60, Bills of Exchange Act 1882, provided it pays:
  - in good faith; and
  - in the ordinary course of business.
- Section 1, Cheques Act 1957 provided it complies with the two requirements above, where the cheque is unendorsed or irregularly endorsed.
- An additional protection is provided by s.80, Bills of Exchange Act 1882 in that a paying bank is protected if it pays a *crossed* cheque:
  - in good faith;
  - without negligence;
  - in accordance with the crossing.

  Section 2, Cheques Act 1992 extends this protection to cheques which are not transferable because they have been crossed 'account payee' or 'account payee only'.

3.3 *Note*: when a paying bank pays 'analogous instruments' such as bank drafts or payment orders, its statutory protection is s.1, Cheques Act 1957, or s.19, Stamp Act 1853. These statutes protect the paying bank if it pays an analogous instrument with a forged or irregular endorsement. Once again the bank must pay in good faith and in the ordinary course of business.

3.4 Legal opinion is divided as to whether the words 'in the ordinary course of business' in s.60, Bills of Exchange Act and s.1, Cheques Act amount to the same as 'without negligence'.

3.5 In *Carpenters' Company v British Mutual Banking Co* (1937) it was held that 'negligence does not necessarily preclude the protection of s.60'. However, the judges were split, so it apparent that a fine line exists between these two phrases.

3.6 In *Baines v National Provincial* (1927) a cheque was paid five minutes after closing time. The drawer had issued the cheque shortly before close of business in the belief that the payee would not be able to obtain clearance that day. However, the cheque had been paid in at a nearby sub-branch and had been paid at the main office when the clerk returned. The next morning the customer 'stopped payment' and claimed the amount of the cheque from his bank. The court held that payment was in the ordinary course of business and that banks must be allowed a reasonable time in which to complete their business.

9 Rights of the customer and bank when the bank pays a stopped cheque by mistake?

9.1 The *customer* can insist on being refunded by the bank because the bank paid the cheque without authority.

9.2 If the *bank* refunds the money and the cheque was for goods the bank can claim the goods and sell them on the basis that the customer cannot have both goods and the refund. Once again, the doctrine of subrogation applies, since it is the bank's own money which has paid for the goods. This situation comes within the general description of subrogation found in *Orakpo v Manson Investments* (1978): 'It is a convenient way of describing the transfer of rights from one person to another without assignment or assent ... which takes place by operation of law.'

9.3 Otherwise the bank can claim from the payee on the basis that the cheque was paid by mistake, i.e. the payment was not one authorised under the customer's mandate; the payment was caused by mistake of fact, not mistake of law.

9.4 In *Barclays v W J Simms Son and Cooke (Southern) and Sowman* (1979) it was held that the bank could recover from the payee unless he had altered his position on the basis that he thought the cheque had been paid. (However, the bank could not recover from the person whose account is credited if the cheque had been negotiated to him and he was a holder in due course. This applies only with 'order' cheques.)

9.5 Therefore, the bank will be able to recover where it is the payee whose account has been credited and the payee has not altered his position relying on the fact that the cheque had been paid.

9.6 Whether the payee has altered his position depends on the facts of the case. If the payee had delayed release of goods until he thought the cheque had been paid, then he would have 'altered his position'. If the goods had been released as soon as the cheque had been issued, then the payee would not have altered his position.

10 Position when a customer telephones to stop payment of a cheque

10.1 You should:

- Confirm that the cheque has not been issued under a cheque card, as it cannot be stopped in these circumstances, and ensure it has not already been paid.
- Ask the customer for written confirmation.
- If the cheque is presented for payment before written confirmation is received, return it 'Payment stopped, drawer's written confirmation awaited'. If the bank does not proceed thus, it will have to refund the amount to the customer even though the written confirmation has not been received.

10.2 If someone purporting to be the payee of a cheque telephones to ask the drawee bank to stop payment because the cheque has been stolen, then that bank has a possible dilemma. The obvious course of action is to contact the drawer at once and follow his instructions. However, if the drawer cannot be contacted, and if the cheque is in the meantime presented for payment, what should be done?

10.3 If the drawee bank pays the cheque, it will lose the protection of s.1, Cheques Act 1957 and s.60, Bills of Exchange Act 1882. Payment would not be made in the ordinary course of business. Thus, the cheque must be dishonoured with an answer which will not damage the drawer's reputation. One possible answer is 'Payment stopped, written confirmation awaited'.

11 Truncation

11.1 Today, it is a simple matter for a collecting bank to initiate credit entries to its own customer's account and debit entries onto the drawer's account at the drawee bank without the need to physically present the cheque to the drawee bank. This process is known as truncation.

11.2 Before looking at the legal issues, it is useful to consider the benefits of truncation. Briefly these are:

- Removal of the need to physically move paper around the country as in the traditional clearing system;
- Speedy settlement;
- Avoiding the danger of loss of any dishonoured cheques which would be returned by post to the person paying in;
- Harnessing modern technology to achieve cost savings and swifter settlement.

11.3 Modern technology is capable of reducing physical movement of paper and achieving the above benefits in a number of money transfer systems, e.g. electronic bills of lading could replace paper bills of lading in international payments such as documentary credits and collections, but there are legal issues to be resolved . Basically, as is frequently the case, technology develops at a much faster pace than the relevant law.

Legal issues in truncation

11.4 An old case, *Hare v Henty* (1861), gives the collecting bank a duty to collect a cheque by the method normally employed as expeditiously as possible. This involves physical presentation of the cheque at the paying bank's bank and branch. Presumably this technical problem could be overcome by asking customers to complete an authority waiving this duty .

11.5 Under long-established banking practice, a paying bank is under an obligation to pay cheques only on physical presentation. Technically, payment when the actual cheque was at another bank would amount to a breach of this duty and the customer's authority would be required.

11.6 Section 45 provides that 'a bill must be duly presented for payment'. However, s.59 would appear to support the fact that payment of truncated cheques would not, in itself, amount to contravention of the need to pay bills 'in due course' as such payment is shown as 'payment made at or after maturity of the cheque, to the holder thereof in good faith and without notice that his title to the bill is defective'.

11.7 The protection of s.60 requires that payment be in the ordinary course of business. Thus, until truncation becomes normal banking practice, a paying bank will not be allowed to rely on s.60 in the case of a truncated cheque when there is a forged or unauthorised endorsement on the cheque.

11.8 Section 80 would appear to protect a paying bank which pays a truncated cheque in good faith and without negligence, provided payment is made to another bank, so long as truncation was a well-established system.

11.9 Although existing law may give adequate protection to banks using truncation procedures, and any breaches of law may be technical only, it is possible that courts may hold that the introduction of truncation without prior consent of customers could deprive both paying and collecting banks of their statutory protection. Legislation may be necessary to cover the situation, just as the 1992 Cheques Act was required to cover nontransferable cheques.

Student Activity 4

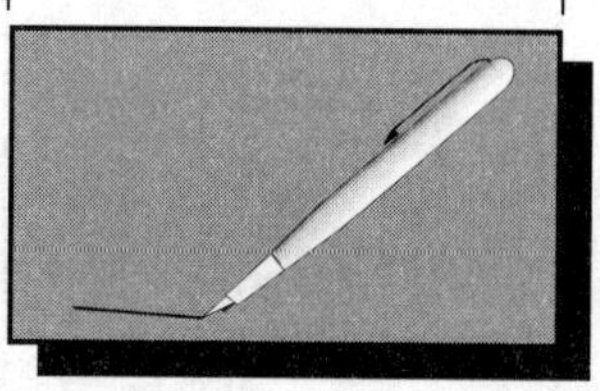

Ascertain the extent of the use of truncation by your bank. Is it used in connection with cheques paid in for collection at other branches of your bank? Write a few paragraphs explaining your bank's policy and procedures. (Keep abreast of technological developments generally and consider whether they pose legal problems.)

Summary

Now that you have studied this unit, you should be able to:

- **explain when the process of paying a cheque has been completed;**
- **state the duties of a paying bank in relation to its customers' cheques;**
- **understand which events lead to a termination of a paying bank's duty to pay its customers' cheques;**
- **state the effect of paying a cheque when the drawer's signature is forged or unauthorised;**
- **understand the implications for the paying bank of wrongly dishonouring a cheque;**
- **explain what occurs when a breach of mandate is committed by a customer;**
- **describe the legal procedures and protection for encashing an open cheque;**
- **describe how the payment of a cheque presented via the clearing system is made, and the legal protection available to the paying bank;**
- **understand what is meant by a stopped cheque, the events that take place in stopping a cheque, and the effect of paying a stopped cheque by mistake.**

Self-assessment questions

1

XYZ Bank

Pay Jones or order £100

Brown

Brown owes Jones £100. Jones pays in the cheque at ABC bank and it is paid.

(i) What is Brown?

(a) Drawer.

(b) Payee.

(c) Endorser.

(d) Holder in due course.

(ii) What is XYZ Bank?

(a) Collecting bank.

(b) Paying bank.

(c) Lending bank.

(d) Collecting and paying bank.

2 Study the cheque above. Assume that Jones endorsed the cheque and gave it to Smith in exchange for goods, and that there were no suspicious circumstances.

(i) What is Smith?

(a) Holder.

(b) Holder for value.

(c) Holder in due course.

(d) None of these.

(ii) What is Smith if Jones had acquired the cheque by fraud, but Jones had genuinely endorsed it?

(a) Holder.

(b) Holder for value.

(c) Holder in due course.

(d) None of these.

(iii) What is Smith if the cheque is crossed 'Account payee only' and Jones had acquired the cheque by fraud?

(a) Holder.

(b) Holder for value.

(c) Holder in due course.

(d) None of these.

(iv) What is Smith if X had stolen the cheque from Jones and had forged Jones' endorsement? Smith gave value to X for the cheque.

(a) Holder.

(b) Holder for value.

(c) Holder in due.

(d) Wrongful possessor.

3 Which statutes protect a paying bank?

(a) Section 4, Cheques Act 1957.

(b) Section 1, Cheques Act 1957.

(c) Section 60, Bills of Exchange Act 1882.

(d) Section 29, Bills of Exchange Act 1882.

4 *Cheque* *Bank Giro Credit*

Cheque	
XYZ Bank	
Pay Jones only	£100
Account payee	Brown

Bank Giro Credit
ABC Bank
Credit Jones
£100

You work for XYZ Bank and Brown has a current account with you, balance £10,000 credit. There are no stops.

Jones asks if the cheque is paid. What do you do?

(a) Refuse to answer because the cheque is crossed 'account payee'.

(b) Confirm that the cheque is paid.

(c) Ask Jones to come back at 3.30 pm.

(d) Ask Jones to endorse the cheque and then pay it.

5 Which case governs the answer to Question 4?

(a) *Tai Hing Cotton Mill.*

(b) *Greenwood v Martins Bank.*

(c) *Ringham v Hackett.*

(d) *MacMillan & Arthur.*

6 What does 'not negotiable' mean when applied to cheques?

(a) The cheque cannot be transferred.

(b) The cheque can only be paid in to the credit of the payee's account.

(c) The transferee acquires no better title than the transferor.

(d) Nobody is liable on the cheque.

7 What action does a paying bank take when a cheque crossed 'account payee' is presented in the clearing?

(a) None.

(b) Return the cheque.

(c) Make enquiries of the collecting bank.

(d) Make enquiries of the customer.

Further reading

- Laidlaw, A and Roberts, G — Chapters 5 and 6, *Law Relating to Banking Services*, 2nd edition 1992, Bankers Books.
- Milnes Holden, J — Chapter 7, *The Law and Practice of Banking*, Vol 1, 5th edition 1991, Pitman
- Raby, P — Chapter 10, *Law Relating to Banking Services*, 2nd edition 1992, Pitman
- Penn, G, Shea, AM and Arora, A — Chapters 6–8, *The Law Relating to Domestic Banking*, 1987, Sweet & Maxwell

Unit 11

The Collecting Bank

Objectives

After studying this unit, you should be able to:

- **understand the legal position when a collecting bank acts as agent;**
- **understand the concept of conversion as applied to collecting banks;**
- **appreciate the legal position of a collecting bank when it is also a holder in due course or a holder for value.**

All references in this unit are to the Bills of Exchange Act 1882 unless stated otherwise.

1 The role of the collecting bank

1.1 When the holder pays in a cheque for the credit of his bank account, the bank and branch which the holder uses is known as the collecting bank. Normally, the collecting bank will stamp a counterfoil which is retained by the holder as a receipt for the cheque. The collecting bank will then present the cheque to the drawee bank for payment.

Presentation through the clearing system

1.2 When the cheque is drawn on another bank, or on another branch, and when the holder issues no special instructions, then the cheque will be presented via the clearing system. Normally, the cheque will be presented at the relevant branch of the drawee bank after two working days. Thus, a cheque which has been paid in on Monday, will be presented at the drawee bank on Wednesday. The holder's bank account will be credited on the Monday but the collecting bank retains the right to debit the account back, should the cheque be dishonoured.

1.3 The drawee bank will then decide by close of business whether to pay the cheque. If the cheque is paid, the drawer's account will be debited, if the cheque is dishonoured, the amount of the cheque will be debited back under advice. The holder's bank account will normally be debited back with the amount of any dishonoured cheque on the fourth working day.

1.4 To follow our previous example, a cheque paid in on Monday will be presented for payment on Wednesday. If payment is refused, the holder's bank account will be debited back on the Thursday.

1.5 There is a 'late returns' procedure in operation, and you should refer back to Unit 9, section 1 which covers completion of payment under 'normal' circumstances and under the 'late returns' procedure, if you are in any doubt about the rules.

Special presentations

1.6 Sometimes the holder will ask the collecting bank to 'specially present' a cheque. If the branch of the drawee bank is located nearby, the collecting bank may, for a fee, arrange for a member of staff to take the cheque and ask for a banker's payment.

1.7 If the drawee bank is satisfied with the cheque, it will issue a payment. The benefit for the holder is that he knows that payment is guaranteed.

1.8 When the drawee bank/branch is not local, the cheque can be sent direct by first-class post. The collecting bank can then phone on the following day to see if the drawee bank will agree to pay the cheque. Once again, the verbal agreement to pay is binding on the drawee bank.

Where the cheque is drawn on the collecting bank/branch

XYZ Bank North Town	
Pay Payee	or order
	Drawer

1.9 If the payee of the above cheque banked at XYZ Bank, North Town, he may well pay the cheque in at the same branch and bank on which the cheque is drawn.

1.10 Here, XYZ Bank, North Town would be acting as both collecting and paying bank. In *Carpenters' Company v British Mutual Banking Co Ltd* (1938), it was held that where the same bank branch fulfils both functions it must fulfil the duties of the paying bank as regards the drawer, and the duties of the collecting bank as regards the holder.

1.11 Reference has already been made in Unit 9 to *Ringham v Hackett* (1980) in which it was held that a holder is entitled to an answer if he specifically asks for the fate of a cheque paid in by him over the counter of the drawee bank.

Student Activity 1

List the duties which you (a) know and (b) consider a bank owes as agent of the holder of a cheque when the bank is collecting a cheque? Note down what you think is the reasoning behind each of these and then compare what you have written with the text in section 2 below..

2 The duty of the collecting bank as agent

2.1 A collecting bank acts as the agent of the holder of the cheque. As with any agency, the bank's duties are to perform his task with professional competence.

2.2 When cheques are presented through the clearing system, the collecting bank's duty to the holder is discharged only when the cheque is physically delivered to the relevant branch of the drawee bank for a decision on whether or not it should be paid: *Barclays Bank plc and Others v Bank of England* (1985). Hence, if a cheque is lost, the responsibility will remain with the collecting bank, unless the cheque went missing only after it reached the bank/branch on which it was drawn.

2.3 The other main duty which the collecting bank owes to his principal is to notify him immediately if the cheque has been dishonoured. Failure to do so could mean:

- The holder would lose the right to sue any prior parties to the cheques other than the drawer. If the holder wishes to sue any endorser, that endorser must be notified of dishonour and s.49 requires the notice to be given within a reasonable time of dishonour. 'Reasonable' would normally be deemed to be a communication sent within one working day of dishonour. (Obviously, this problem cannot arise if the cheque has been crossed 'account payee' or 'account payee only'.)
- The holder may lose the opportunity to take quick action against the drawer if the holder is unaware of the dishonour. Although the holder's legal rights against the drawer will remain unchanged, delay in notifying the holder could damage the holder's practical chances of rectifying matters *vis-a-vis* the drawer.

2.4 Failure properly to undertake the duties of agent will render the collecting bank liable for damages for breach of contract. The amount of the damages will be the financial damage actually deemed by the court to have been suffered by the holder of the cheque.

3 Collecting bank as a holder in due course of 'order' cheques

3.1 Under s.29, a holder in due course is a holder who has taken a cheque:

- Completed and regular on the face of it;
- Before it was overdue;
- Without notice of any previous dishonour;
- In good faith;
- For value;
- Without notice of any defect in the transferor's title.

3.2 For a collecting bank to qualify as a holder in due course it must, *inter alia*, give value. The giving of value in these circumstances can arise from one of the following:

- Specifically allowing the holder to withdraw cash against an uncleared cheque.
- Accepting a cheque in specific reduction of an overdraft or loan.
- Paying cheques drawn by the holder, before the cheque which the holder has paid in has been cleared;
- When the bank cashes a cheque for the holder and then sends that cheque to the drawee bank for payment.

3.3 Relevant cases to support the above are:

- *A L Underwood v Bank of Liverpool* (1924), where the bank was unable to set itself up as a holder for value because the bank's paying in slips had a pre-printed warning which said that the bank had the right to refuse withdrawals until the customer had sufficient cleared funds. Thus, the bank cannot claim to have given value if it expressly or by implication tells a customer that he cannot draw against uncleared effects. Hence, the collecting bank will be on safe ground as regards the giving of value if it has specifically allowed the customer to draw against uncleared effects.
- *M'Lean v Clydesdale Banking Co* (1883), where it was held that a bank had not given value by simply crediting a cheque to an overdrawn account in the *ordinary course of business*. Hence, to give value, the bank must specifically accept the cheque in reduction of an overdraft, for example, by having threatened legal action and then calling off the action because the customer paid in a cheque to the account.
- *Westminster Bank v Zang* (1966), where it was held that the collecting bank must retain possession of the dishonoured cheque, otherwise it will lose its right of lien and therefore its ability to recover from the drawer. (Liens are covered in Unit 12.)

3.4 Finally, the position about endorsements and the collecting bank is covered by s.2, Cheques Act 1957 which provides that:

> A banker who gives value for, or has a lien on, a cheque payable to order, which the holder delivers to him for collection without endorsing it, has such (if any) rights as he would have had if, upon delivery, the holder had endorsed in blank.

Thus, a collecting bank is not affected if the person from whom he received the cheque has failed to endorse it, provided that person is the payee or endorsee.

Example of the collecting bank as holder in due course of 'order' cheques

3.5 Suppose ABC Bank has a customer, Mr A Jones, who pays in the following cheque on Monday when his balance is nil.

XYZ Bank	
Pay A Jones	or order
	£800
	B Smith

3.6 Suppose in addition, ABC Bank specifically allows Jones to withdraw £800 in cash on Monday, because the drawer of the cheque is known to be a wealthy businessman. Jones's bank ledger will appear as follows:

A Jones

Date	*Detail*	*Dr*	*Cr*	*Balance*
		£	*£*	*£*
Monday	Balance			Nil
Monday	Cheque		800	800 Cr
Monday	Cash	800		Nil

If the cheque is subsequently returned by XYZ Bank, what are ABC Bank's rights?

The collecting bank's rights

3.7 ABC Bank could debit Mr Jones's account, but what happens if Jones has no money to repay the overdraft of £800? In such a case, the ABC Bank may wish to preserve its rights against the drawer, Smith.

3.8 Provided ABC Bank can comply s.29, which it apparently can, then it is a holder in due course. The absence of Jones's endorsement is immaterial to this claim: s.2, Cheques Act 1957.

3.9 Thus, ABC Bank will debit the cheque to a suspense account and claim reimbursement from both Smith and Jones. Prompt notification is recommended, although in theory there is no need immediately to notify the drawer: s.50.

3.10 ABC Bank would have a valid claim for £800 from Jones, and could also claim £800 from Smith, provided it was a holder in due course. Naturally, the bank's total claim would be restricted to £800 in all.

4 Conversion and the collecting bank

4.1 Normally the collecting bank will not be a holder in due course. Collecting banks do not usually allow customers to draw against uncleared effects, nor are cheques usually accepted in specific reduction of an overdraft. In the majority of transactions, a collecting bank will present a cheque for payment and the customer will not draw against the cheque until it has been cleared. In these circumstances, the collecting bank will act as agent for its customer, and the only risk it runs is that of *conversion.*

4.2 In the Torts (Interference with Goods) Act 1977 conversion was defined as 'an unauthorised act which deprives another person of his property'. Thus, if the person whose account has been credited is not entitled to the proceeds of the cheque, then the true owner of the cheque can sue him for conversion. However, the true owner will normally sue the collecting bank in its capacity as agent of the wrongdoer. The true owner will claim the amount of the cheque since this will be the value of the property which has been misappropriated.

The statutory protection of a collecting bank

4.3 In the absence of statutory protection in connection with conversion, the cheque clearing system could grind to a halt. In practice, it is virtually impossible for a collecting bank to be able to assess whether every cheque paid in over the counter is the property of the presenter. The time involved in making enquiries would be simply too much. Thus, some form of statutory protection is required to balance the commercial imperative to process the cheque clearing efficiently with the need to protect the true owner of any cheque from being deprived of the proceeds without any redress against a negligent collecting bank.

4.4 In order to be protected, the collecting bank will need to be able to show that it acted in accordance with s.4, Cheques Act 1957, which protects a collecting bank provided it collects the cheque:

- In good faith;
- For a customer;
- Without negligence.

4.5 Note that the protection of s.4 extends to 'analogous instruments' such as dividend and interest warrants, and bank drafts, and it also applies to cheques which are technically nontransferable (s.3, Cheques Act 1992). Section 4 does not apply to postal orders, but the bank may be protected by s.21, Post Office Act 1953.

In good faith

4.6 Good faith is defined by s.90 as something which is done honestly, whether it is done negligently or not.

For a customer

4.7 In Unit 1 we considered the definition of a customer, which can be wider than the traditional definition of 'someone who has an account of some sort with a bank'.

4.8 However, in the context of s.4, the word, customer, must mean someone who has opened a bank account with the collecting bank, and the cheque must have been credited to that account. The length of time the account has been opened is immaterial, provided there are no other suspicious circumstances.

Without negligence

4.9 In *Commissioners of Taxation v English, Scottish and Australian Banks* (1920) it was said that 'the test of negligence is whether the transaction of paying in any given cheque, coupled with antecedent and present circumstances, was so out of the ordinary course of business that it ought to have aroused doubts in the banker's mind and caused him to make enquiry'. In addition, the bank must not only make enquiries when there are unusual circumstances, but the answers received must appear satisfactory in the light of the circumstances surrounding the transaction and bearing in mind the customer's conduct generally.

4.10 Collecting banks generally fail the 'without negligence' test in one of four broad areas:

- Failure to properly complete account opening formalities.
- Failure to enquire when there is a fiduciary relationship between the customer and the drawer, or the customer and the payee.
- Failure to enquire and receive a satisfactory answer when there are suspicious or unusual circumstances;
- Collecting a cheque crossed 'account payee only' for a third party.

Relevant cases on the 'without negligence' test

Failure properly to complete account opening formalities

4.11 Until the 1980s, when opening accounts banks had always insisted upon personal introductions from existing customers or written references from persons considered fit to act as referees. In *Ladbroke v Todd* (1914) it was held that failure to take up references and follow them up by asking for a reference on an unknown referee meant that the bank had acted negligently and was thus deprived of the statutory protection of s.82, Bills of Exchange Act 1882 (replaced by the very similar provision in s.4, Cheques Act 1957). In a similar vein, *Hampstead Guardians v Barclays Bank Ltd* (1923) held that the bank must ensure that the named referee was suitable if it wished to pass the 'without negligence' test for the purposes of the then s.82.

4.12 Nowadays, references have been to some extent superseded when opening personal accounts. The normal procedure is to identify the new customer and then to search at a credit reference agency to ensure there is nothing untoward on file. There have been no decided cases to show whether these new procedures would pass the 'without negligence' test for s.4, but in *Marfani v Midland Bank Ltd* (1968), it was accepted that the current practice of careful bankers was unlikely to be negligent. Under the Code of Banking Practice banks undertake to satisfy themselves as to the identity of new customers when the account is opened.

Failure to enquire when there is a fiduciary relationship between the customer and the drawer or the customer and payee

4.13 *Cheques drawn by the employer.* In *Lloyds Bank Ltd v E B Savory and Co* (1933) a bank was sued for conversion when two employees had stolen cheques drawn on their employer's accounts payable to various creditors of the employer. It was held that the nature of the fiduciary relationship between the employer and the bank's customer should have put the collecting bank on enquiry. In this case, the bank opened an account for a married woman but failed to note the name of her husband's employers. However, as a result of the Sex Discrimination Act 1975, many banks have ceased to make enquiries about the employers of the spouse when opening an account in the sole name of a married man or in the sole name of a married woman. In *Orbit Mining and Trading Co Ltd v Westminster Bank* (1962), it was held that where, subsequent to opening the account, a customer had changed his employment without notifying the bank, then the collecting bank could not be expected to know of the fiduciary relationship between the customer and his new employers.

4.14 *Other cases involving fiduciary relationships.* In *Marquis of Bute v Barclays Bank Ltd* (1954) the bank collected a cheque payable to its customer 'D McGraw or order, for Marquis of Bute'. (The cheque had been handed to McGraw in his capacity as agent for the Marquis of Bute, who was the true owner of the cheque.) It was held that the collecting bank had committed conversion and could not rely on s.4. The words 'for the account of Marquis of Bute' should have put the bank on enquiry.

4.15 In *Morison v London County & Westminster Bank* (1914), the bank collected the following cheque without enquiry for the personal account of the agent.

Pay Agent	or order
pp Principal	
__________	(agent's signature)

It was held that failure to make enquiries, rendered the collecting bank liable for conversion because it should have noticed the fiduciary relationship between the drawer and payee.

Failure to enquire and receive satisfactory answers when there are suspicious or unusual circumstances

4.16 Each case must turn on its own facts, but the basic test is whether the circumstances were so unusual as to warrant enquiry, and whether the response was sufficiently plausible as to be acceptable to a prudent banker. The following cases are useful guidelines.

4.17 *Cheques payable to a company.* A company is a separate legal entity and cheques payable to the company should not be collected for other accounts: *A L Underwood v Bank of Liverpool* (1924). Failure to comply will mean that the collecting bank will fail the 'without negligence' test. The exception here is when companies are all part of a group and cheques payable to one member of the group are credited to the account of another group member. Normal practice here is to take authorities, backed by indemnities, from all group members.

4.18 *Cheques payable to a partnership.* Similar considerations to *Underwood* apply to cheques payable to partnerships. Such cheques should not be collected for other accounts: *Baker v Barclays Bank* (1955). In this particular case, the amount of damages payable by the bank was reduced pro rata because the partners shared profits and losses equally, and the proceeds of the cheque have been misappropriated by one partner.

4.19 *Collection other than for the account of the payee.* Banks should only collect cheques for an account other than the payee when the:

- Cheque purports to have been endorsed by the payee;
- Explanation from the customer is such as would satisfy a reasonably prudent banker: *Bevan v National Bank* (1906).

Section 3, Cheques Act 1992

4.20 Cheques which are crossed 'account payee' or 'not transferable' can still be collected for a third party account. Provided the third party for whom the cheque has been collected is the person entitled to the proceeds of that cheque, then the collecting bank has no liability.

4.21 If it subsequently turns out that the third party was not entitled to the cheque, then the collecting bank will still be able to cite s.4, Cheques Act 1957 in defence against the tort of conversion. However, the bank is most unlikely to pass the 'without negligence' test when the cheque is one that is classed as nontransferable by the 1992 Act.

5 Other means of reducing liability for conversion

Contributory negligence

5.1 When the true owner has by his own actions contributed to the fraud, the damages payable by the collecting bank will be reduced to the extent of such contribution: s.47, Banking Act 1979.

5.2 If the collecting bank can rely on s.4, he will not need to rely on the doctrine of contributory negligence. However, if s.4 does not apply, then the doctrine of contributory negligence may mitigate the damages. In *Lumsden & Co v London Trustee Savings Bank* (1971) the plaintiffs' damages were reduced by 10% because their own carelessness had contributed to the fraud. However, as this is the only reported case in connection with s.4, so the plea would not seem to be widely used in practice.

Collecting bank as a holder in due course

5.3 If the collecting bank cannot rely on s.4, an alternative defence is to claim to be a holder in due course (in the case of order cheques).

Ex turpi causa non oritur actio

5.4 This may be translated as 'out of an immoral situation an action does not arise.' In *Thackwell v Barclays* (1986), the collecting bank could not rely on s.4, but the 'true owner's' claim arose indirectly out of a criminal act. Hence the court refused to allow a claim against the bank to succeed.

5.5 When a collecting bank is guilty of conversion, the bank has the right to be reimbursed by debiting its customer's account: *Hichens, Harrison, Woolston & Co v Jackson & Sons* (1943). An agent is entitled to be indemnified against losses incurred in the reasonable performance of his duties. However, in practice, the bank's customer will probably be a 'man of straw' who has already withdrawn all the funds in his account. Hence the remedy will be of academic interest only.

Student Activity 2

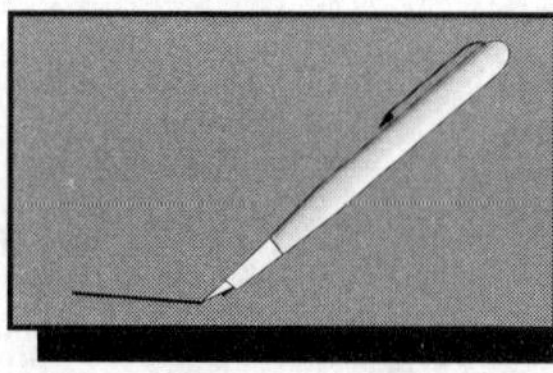

Summarise the provisions of s.4, Cheques Act 1957. Briefly explain what the collecting bank must do to gain its protection.

6 The effect of 'not negotiable' and 'account payee only' crossings

6.1 As far as a collecting bank is concerned, 'not negotiable' crossings are irrelevant. The only time a collecting bank need concern itself with 'not negotiable' is if it wishes to set itself up as a holder in due course.

6.2 'Account payee only' now has statutory meaning, and the collecting bank must make careful enquiries before collecting such a cheque for a third party.

7 Exam technique

7.1 If a question refers to the position of a collecting bank, it will almost certainly cover one of two aspects:

- Conversion;
- Collecting bank as holder for value or holder in due course.

Question concerns collecting bank

↙ ↘

The cheque has been paid.	The cheque has been dishonoured
↓	↓
The question will concern conversion.	Conversion cannot apply. The question must concern a holder in due course.
↓	↓
Can s.4 be relied upon? If 'yes' no problem. Care with 'account payee only' cheques.	Can the bank rely on s.29, Bills of Exchange Act? Consider s.2, Cheques Act.
↓	↓
If s.4 cannot be relied upon, can the bank rely upon holder in due course, contributory negligence, *ex turpi causa, non oritur actio*, or the right of indemnity against the customer?	Is the cheque an 'order' cheque, or is it crossed 'account payee' in which case the concept of holder in due course or holder for value cannot apply?

7.2 There may be some exceptions to the above, but these will be obvious. They will normally concern the duty of a collecting bank towards its customer, and will concern *Barclays v Bank of England* (1985), or the failure of the collecting bank to notify its customer of dishonour.

Summary

Now that you have studied this unit, you should be able to:

- **understand the role of the collecting bank and its duties as agent;**
- **appreciate the situations in which the collecting bank can be a holder in due course;**
- **know the situations in which being a holder in due course will benefit a collecting bank;**
- **understand the relevance of the tort of conversion in collecting cheques and the protection available to the collecting bank.**

Self-assessment questions

1 Which statute protects a collecting bank if it is sued for conversion?

(a) Section 1, Cheques Act 1957.

(b) Section 2, Cheques Act 1957.

(c) Section 4, Cheques Act 1957.

(d) Section 60, Bills of Exchange Act 1882.

2 You collect a cheque payable to a partnership for the private account of a partner.

For what are you liable if the transaction was fraudulent?

(a) Nothing.

(b) Nothing, provided you made enquiries and received a reasonable answer.

(c) Negligence.

(d) Conversion.

3 Can a bank collect a cheque crossed 'Account payee only' for someone other than the payee? Assume the customer is perfectly respectable.

(a) No, because it is legally prohibited from doing so.

(b) Yes, provided it is certain that the customer has a good title.

4 Note the facts in Question 3. What would be the position if the cheque were crossed 'Not negotiable'?

(a) It can be collected in the same way as any other cheque.

(b) The bank is legally prohibited from collecting the cheque.

5 The bank opens an account and takes the normal precautions. It collects a cheque for the customer and allows him to draw the full amount (at once). The cheque is subsequently dishonoured. There are no other transactions on the account. The cheque is crossed 'account payee only'. What is the bank's position?

(a) The bank has committed conversion.

(b) The bank is a holder in due course.

(c) The bank is liable for negligence.

(d) The bank can sue either the customer or the drawer.

(e) The bank cannot claim from the drawer, but could claim from its customer.

6 The doctrine of contributory negligence helps a bank in what circumstances?

(a) A paying bank whose customer's signature was forged.

(b) A collecting bank which cannot claim the protection of s.4, Cheques Act.

7 Which items are covered by s.4, Cheques Act?

(a) Dividend warrants.

(b) Postal orders.

(c) Cheques with an 'R' on them.

(d) Conditional orders.

(e) Cheques crossed 'account payee only'.

Further reading

- Laidlaw, A and Roberts, G — Chapter 5, *Law Relating to Banking Services*, 2nd edition 1992, Bankers Books.
- Milnes Holden, J — Chapter 6, *The Law and Practice of Banking*, Vol 1, 5th edition 1991, Pitman
- Penn, G, Shea, AM Arora, A — Chapter 9, *The Law Relating to Domestic Banking*, Vol 1, 1987, Sweet & Maxwell
- Raby, P — Chapter 10, *Law Relating to Banking Services*, 2nd edition 1992, Pitman

Unit 12

Money Transmission Services

Objectives

After studying this unit, you should be able to:

- **explain the operation of credit transfers, standing orders and direct debits;**
- **understand possible defects in the title of the payees of credit transfers and direct debits;**
- **appreciate the importance of the Code of Banking Practice in this context;**
- **understand the operation EFTPOS and the legal issues which it raises.**

1 Introduction

1.1 Although the cheque is currently the most frequently used method of payment in the UK, the use of alternative money transmission mechanisms is becoming more and more common.

1.2 In this unit each means of payment will be briefly described and the legal implications considered. You will see that the legal principles in many cases are very similar, whichever means of money transmission is being examined.

2 Credit transfer

The credit transfer system

2.1 A credit transfer involves the transfer of funds, initiated by the payer, within the same bank or between two banks.

2.2 When the transfer is within the same bank branch, the payer provides written details of the account to be credited, and either hands over cash or an authority to debit his own bank account. The bank will effect the transfer during the course of the day and the payee's account will be credited that day.

2.3 When the transfer takes place between different banks, the clearing system is used. The timescale for crediting the payee's account is as follows.

- *Day one*: The payer provides written details of the payee's account, together with an authority to debit his own account (or cash). At the end of the day the credit transfer slip is sent to the Clearing House.

- *Day two*: Each bank agrees the credit totals at the Clearing House.
- *Day three*: The banks complete final settlement and the payee's account is credited.

Completion of payment

Accounts at the same bank and the clearing system is not used

2.4 In *Gibson v Minet* (1791) it was held that payment was complete and irrevocable as soon as both the payer's and payee's accounts had been debited/ credited.

2.5 In *Momm and Ors v Barclays Bank International* (1976) it was held that payment was complete when the bank had decided to accept the instructions to credit the payee's account and had set the computer processes in motion. It is immaterial whether the payee has been advised of the transfer.

2.6 In *Momm* the bank transferred funds from one account to another at the same branch in accordance with the payer's instructions. Next morning it was discovered that the payer's account had become overdrawn as a result of the transfer. The bank then reversed the entries to recredit the payer's account. It was held that the reversal was invalid, because the mistake lay between the bank and the payer and not between the bank and the payee.

2.7 Similar reasoning applied in *Chambers v Miller* (1862) when a bank cashed a cheque on presentation, but immediately afterwards discovered that the drawer, its customer, had no funds. The recipient had not left the bank and still had the money. It was held that payment was irrevocable and that innocent third parties should not suffer for a mistake made between the bank and its own customer.

When the clearing system is used

2.8 There is no direct authority as to when payment is irrevocable, but it is considered that when the Clearing House is used, payment is completed when the net amount to be paid by one bank to another is agreed between them. Prior to that time, the collecting bank can return wrongly delivered forms, and the paying bank can request the return of wrongly delivered forms.

2.9 As technology advances, scope for simultaneous electronic debiting and crediting will grow. You will have noticed that the cases cited above are old, in some cases very old. There is the constant problem of the law not keeping pace with technology (see also 'Truncation' in Unit 10, section 11.

Student Activity 1

Why is it important to establish the time at which payment is completed for a credit transfer? Write down your answer and then read on.

Defects in payee's title

2.10 The transaction cannot be reversed once payment is completed. If the payer wishes to obtain reimbursement of the transfer, for whatever reason, he will have to take action via the courts. Prior to completion of payment, the *transaction itself* could be reversed.

Forged or unauthorised instruction from the payer

2.11 Under s.24, Bills of Exchange Act 1882, and in accordance with *Tai Hing* (1985), the payer's bank has no authority to debit the payer's account if his signature on the authority to debit his account is forged or unauthorised. For example, a signature would be unauthorised when the payer had provided a mandate for his bank to accept the authority of an agent to make credit transfers up to a specified limit and the limit has been exceeded. *(Note:* the position would be reversed if the bank could establish estoppel: *Greenwood v Martins Bank* (1933).

2.12 The paying bank must reimburse its customer and can then claim from the forger/unauthorised agent in deceit or for breach of warranty of authority: *Orr v Union Bank of Scotland* (1854).

2.13 If the payment, despite being unauthorised, was in respect of genuine obligations of the customer, the paying bank could rely on subrogation and would have a defence: *B Liggett (Liverpool) Ltd v Barclays Bank Ltd* (1928).

2.14 In *National Westminster Bank v Barclays Bank International Ltd* (1975) it was held that provided the *collecting* bank did not know about the fraud, the payer or his bank could recover from the collecting bank only such amounts as had not been paid out to the payee or on the payee's instructions.

2.15 If all else fails, the bank can claim from the payee *Barclays Bank Ltd v WJ Simms Son and Cooke (Southern) Ltd* (1980) (see Unit 10, section 9).

Credit transfer made by mistake of fact

2.16 This could arise in two situations:

- The payer may sign a credit transfer form by *mistake*, believing it to be an entirely different document. In such cases the payer could plead *non est factum*, in other words, that he was completely mistaken as to the nature of the transaction.

  In *Saunders v Anglia Building Society* (1970) it was held that in the absence of misrepresentation, literate persons of sound mind who sign documents which they broadly understand are bound by such contracts. In contrast, *Lloyds v Waterhouse* (1990) illustrates the principle that if an illiterate person is misled by the explanation of the other party, then the transaction is voidable.
- The payer may have made the transfer in the belief that he was under an *obligation to pay*, when this was not in fact the case.

Student Activity 2

You are a payer who has initiated a credit transfer under mistake of fact. Whom would you wish to sue for recovery of money? Write down your answer and read on.

Position under mistake of fact

Paying bank

2.17 The paying bank incurs no liability unless it knew or ought to have known of the mistake. It is simply carrying out its customer's mandate.

Collecting bank

2.18 It is considered (see Penn, Shea and Arora, Chapter 18) that s.4(1) and (2), Cheques Act 1957 would probably apply in connection with credit transfers. Thus, if the collecting bank acts for a customer, in good faith and without negligence, there will be no liability to the payer. (See also *National Westminster Bank v Barclays Bank International* above.)

The payer

2.19 The payer will be able to claim from the payee in accordance with the principles set out in *Barclays Bank Ltd v WJ Simms Son and Cooke (Southern) Ltd* (see Unit 10, section 9).

3 Standing orders

3.1 A standing order arises when the payer instructs his bank to make credit transfers of set amounts at regular intervals to the bank account of a payee. Thus, a standing order is a form of credit transfer, but with additional legal complications.

- *Whitehead v National Westminster Bank* (1982) held that the bank's duty to pay standing orders relates simply to complying with the payment of each standing order instalment on its due date. If there are insufficient monies in the payer's account on the due date, then the bank is not under any obligation to check on subsequent days to see if there are sufficient funds to pay that overdue instalment.
- There is no privity of contract between the payer's bank and the payee. Thus, the bank must not accept any instruction from the payee to amend or cancel a standing order.
- The normal duty of secrecy applies, so the bank must not disclose the reason for non-payment of a standing order if asked to do so by the payee: *Tournier v National Provincial (1924).*

4 Direct debits

Operation

4.1 The payer completes an authority instructing his bank to allow his account to be debited in connection with payments originated by the payee.

4.2 Only a limited class of payees may originate direct debits, usually major companies or public authorities. As a condition of being allowed to join the system, a payee must complete a general indemnity in favour of all the London and Scottish clearing banks. This promises to reimburse these banks against all claims, actions or damages which might arise because of any direct debit which may have been initiated by that payee.

4.3 You do not require a detailed knowledge of the operation of the direct debit system, but a general understanding is necessary so that the legal implications can be understood. Many payees use a computerised system linked to BACS (Bankers' Automated Clearing System) whilst others use paper-based systems.

BACS system

4.4 The payee or the payee's bank acting on his behalf, delivers to BACS a computer-based list of all the names, bank account details and amounts due from the payers. BACS then arranges for the individual payer's bank account to be debited and for the payee's bank account to be credited with the total amalgamated amount for the day. The debits and credits are passed through the respective bank accounts on the same day.

Paper-based systems

4.5 The payee sends a direct debit voucher containing details of the debt, including the payer's and the payee's bank account details, to the London head office of the payer's bank. Arrangements are then made for the respective accounts to be debited and credited two working days later. The practical effect is that the debit and credit will take effect on the same day.

4.6 The payer's bank may refuse to accept a direct debit if there are insufficient funds or if the payer has revoked his authority to pay. In such cases the payer's bank claims reimbursement from the payee's bank through the mechanics of the clearing process, and ultimately the payee's account will be debited back.

4.7 The payer's bank must give a reason for dishonour of the direct debits, and the typical answers to be seen are:

- Refer to payer (lack of funds);
- No mandate (no authority held to pay);
- Payer deceased (equivalent to drawer deceased with a cheque);
- Mandate cancelled (the payer has stopped payment).

Credit transfers and direct debits: operational differences

4.8 The main operational differences are that:

- The direct debit is initiated by the payee.
- The payer must have a bank account for direct debits, whereas payers who do not have bank accounts can use cash to initiate credit transfers.
- With direct debits, only payees who are approved of by the London and Scottish clearing banks may join the scheme, and such payees must sign the general indemnity in favour of those banks.

Completion of payment

4.9 The payer's bank may dishonour a direct debit on the *day of presentation*. In addition, a 'late returns' process has been agreed by the banks for any items debited inadvertently to the payer's account. Such items can be returned on the business day after presentation, and if the amount is £500 or over, the payer's bank must telephone the payee's bank by 12 noon on the day in question. The system operates in a similar way as the late returns procedure for cheques.

4.10 It follows that payment will be completed on the day the respective bank accounts are debited and credited, unless the payer's bank dishonours the debit. Hence, as between the payee and payer, payment will be *irrevocable at close of business on the day the direct debit has been presented at the payer's bank.*

The only exception will arise if there is scope for the 'late returns' process to be used.

Defects in the payee's title

Student Activity 3

What additional protection applies with direct debits (as opposed to standing orders) as regards the payee bank, when it pays against a forged/unauthorised payer's authority? Write down your answer and read on.

Payer's signature on the authority is forged or unauthorised

4.11 The payer will have the right to claim immediate reimbursement from his bank, and the payer's bank will have a right of action against the forger for deceit or breach of warranty. However, the major practical difference from a credit transfer is that the payer's bank will be able to claim reimbursement from the payee because of the general indemnity that the payee will have signed. A claim under the indemnity will be a much quicker and simpler process to enforce than an action for deceit or breach of warranty taken via the courts.

Payment made under mistake of fact

4.12 The principles are similar to those already described for credit transfers. The main difference is that if either the payee or collecting bank had to refund the payer, the banks could automatically claim reimbursement from the payee under the terms of the general indemnity.

5 Code of Banking Practice applied to plastic cards

Scope of the Code

5.1 The Code of Banking Practice applies to card issuers with respect to their personal customers. The Code defines a card as a general term for any plastic card which may be used to pay for goods and services or to withdraw cash. Cards which store value, i.e. pre-payment cards, are excluded from this definition.

5.2 Common examples are:

- *Credit card.* A card which allows customers to buy on credit and to obtain cash advances. Customers receive regular statements and may pay the balance in part, usually subject to a certain minimum, or in full. Interest is payable on outstanding balances.
- *Charge card.* Similar to a credit card, it enables customers to pay for purchases, and in some cases to obtain cash advances. When the monthly statement is received the balance must be paid in full.
- *Debit card.* A card, operating as a substitute for a cheque, that can be used to obtain cash or make a payment at a point of sale. The customer's account is subsequently debited for such a transaction is two working days in the same way as the cheque clearing operation.
- *Budget card.* Similar to a credit card but customers agree to pay a fixed amount into their card account each month.

- *Cash card.* A card used to obtain cash and other services from an ATM (automated teller machine/cash machine).

Note that the rights and obligations of cardholders under the Consumer Credit Act 1974 vary depending on which type of card is involved (see Unit 19).

Student Activity 4

Why is the Code of Banking Practice important when it is a purely voluntary code? Write down your answer and refer to Unit 1 to check your understanding.

Lost cards

5.3 The code provides that card issuers:

- Will inform customers that they must tell their card issuers as soon as reasonably practicable after they find that:
  - their card has been lost or stolen;
  - someone else knows their PIN.
- Will tell customers, and will remind them at regular intervals on their statement or by other means, of the place and the telephone number where they can give the details of a lost or stolen card at any time of the day or night. Card issuers will arrange for that telephone number to be included in British Telecom phone books.
- Will act on telephone notification but may ask customers also to confirm in writing any details given by telephone.
- On request, will inform customers whether or not they accept notification of loss or theft of a card from card notification organisations.
- On being advised of a loss, theft or possible misuse of a card or that the PIN has become known to someone else, will take action to prevent further use of the card.

Liability for losses

5.4 Under the Code:

- Card issuers will bear the full losses incurred:
  - in the event of misuse when the card has not been received by the customer
  - for all transactions not authorised by the customer after the card issuer has been told that the card has been lost or stolen or that someone else knows or may know the PIN (subject to fraud or gross negligence by the customer)
  - if faults have occurred in the machines, or other systems used, which cause customers to suffer direct loss unless the fault was obvious or advised by a message or notice on display.
- Card issuers' liability will be limited to those amounts wrongly charged to customers' accounts and any interest on those amounts.
- Customers' liability for transactions not authorised by them will be limited to a maximum of £50 in the event of misuse before the card issuer has been notified that a card has been lost or stolen or that someone else knows the PIN (subject to fraud or gross negligence by the customer).

- Customers will be held liable for all losses if they have acted fraudulently. They may be held liable for all losses if they have acted with gross negligence.
- In cases of disputed transactions the burden of proving fraud or gross negligence or that a card has been received by a customer will lie with the card issuer. In such cases card issuers will expect customers to cooperate with them in their investigations.
- Card issuers will provide customers with a written record on their statement of account of all payments and withdrawals made.
- Card issuers will inform customers that they should tell them as soon as reasonably practicable if they receive a statement of account that includes an item which seems to be wrong.

5.5 *Gross negligence* as referred to above may apply if any of the conditions set out below had not been complied with. Cardholders should:

- Not allow anyone else to use their card and PIN;
- Take reasonable steps to keep the card safe and the PIN secret at all times;
- Never write the PIN on the card or on anything usually kept with it;
- Never write down the PIN without making a reasonable attempt to disguise it;
- Destroy any PIN advice promptly on receipt.

5.6 Failure to observe the above may amount to gross negligence and make the cardholder liable for losses.

5.7 As you should recall from Unit 1, the code is not law nor legally binding. 'Gross negligence' is not a 'legal' term in civil law and therefore the 'non-legal' status of the Code is all the more apparent in this particular respect. The examples given in the Code, if tested at law, may be held to amount to 'negligence' only and therefore be outside the terms of the Code. It would seem unlikely that the Code will ever be 'tested' on the exact meaning of 'gross negligence', although there are some cardholders who do write their PIN on their cards!

6 Position of the card issuer

Card issuer's duty to honour transactions

6.1 A bank which issues a debit card will have an implied duty to honour all transactions properly initiated by the customer for amounts which are within the credit balance or agreed overdraft facility. This duty may also be expressly stated in the debit card agreement. If a card transaction is wrongly refused, the position will be analogous to wrongful dishonour of a cheque. The bank will be liable for:

- Breach of contractual duty to pay;
- Libel.

6.2 For breach of contractual duty the amount of damages would be the court's assessment of the actual financial loss suffered *(National Westminster v Oceancrest)*. In the case of a private customer, nominal damages only would apply unless there were special circumstances.

6.3 If libel can be proved (see Unit 10), the amount of damages would depend on the amount of adverse publicity attracted to the customer. If the bank were to take immediate steps to apologise to the customer and the would-be beneficiary, then liability should be nominal.

6.4 The Code of Banking Practice states that card issuers will bear the full losses incurred if faults have occurred on machines or systems which cause the customer to suffer direct loss unless the fault was obvious or advised by a message or notice.

In the event of liquidation of the card issuer

6.5 *Re Charge Card Services Ltd* (1987) held that in the event of liquidation of the company operating a charge card scheme, the:

- Retailer has no right of recourse against the cardholders, as payment in this way is unconditional, but may be entitled to a restitutionary claim for the value of the goods;
- Retailer will be an unsecured creditor of the charge card company, and will not have a lien over sums paid by the cardholder to the charge card company;
- Cardholder will still be liable to meet all card debts due to the charge card company in connection with purchases made with the card from retailers.

7 ATMs

Failure to deliver cash

7.1 Most bank cash card agreements have clauses excluding liability if the machine fails to deliver the cash. Whilst such clauses would have to be 'reasonable' under the Unfair Contract Terms Act 1977, it is probable that the courts would not hold the ATMs to be a 'guaranteed' service. Thus, banks would not be liable for ATM failures provided they had followed their normal procedures and so long as a 'reasonable' exclusion clause applied. If the problem had been caused by the bank's carelessness, the cardholder would be able to submit a claim via the Banking Ombudsman. Note: the Code of Banking Practice also applies, see above. If the customer, for whatever reason, preferred to do so, he could, of course, simply claim from the bank at law.

Disputed withdrawal

7.2 The Code of Banking Practice, s.20.5 states that in the event of a disputed transactions, the burden of proving fault or gross negligence, or that a card has been received by a customer, will lie with the card issuer. In such cases, card issuers will expect customers to co-operate with them in their investigations (see paragraph 5.4).

8 EFTPOS

8.1 This stands for electronic funds transfer at point of sale.

8.2 This method of payment is still not generally in use although there are experimental users of EFTPOS in various parts of the UK. Essentially, EFTPOS payment involves the seller, after identifying the buyer, taking the buyer's card and 'swiping' it through a machine. The buyer will then input into the machine his own PIN and the bank accounts of the seller and buyer will be credited and debited simultaneously.

8.3 At present the period which elapses between debiting an crediting can be 24–48 hours, although the ultimate aim is to have the transactions settled across bank accounts immediately after entry of the PIN into the machine.

8.4 As authorisation under EFTPOS is by a PIN, rather than by a signature, legal complexities could arise. Currently, the leading case is *Charge Card* (see above). Although this case dealt with a conventional signature-based card debit authority, commentators generally agree that, by analogy, it would also apply to EFTPOS.

9 Conclusion

9.1 Some commentators consider that existing case and statute law can be applied to the legal problems which may arise under money transmission systems such as ATMs and EFTPOS. However, as yet there are no decided cases. Whilst the preceding remarks on cases such as *MacMillan and Arthur* and *Barclays Bank v Simms* can be taken as a general indication of what may influence the legal position, no definite answers can be given until cases are decided or statutory rules enacted.

9.2 Thus, the Code of Banking Practice will have a major influence on claims by personal customers, even though it is a non-statutory code.

Summary

Now that you have studied this unit, you should be able to:

- **explain how credit transfer system operates and know when payment is complete;**
- **appreciate the legal position when the payee's title to a credit transfer is defective;**
- **know the special conditions which apply to standing orders;**
- **explain how the direct debit system operates and when payment is completed;**
- **appreciate the legal position when the payee's title to a direct debit is defective;**
- **understand the importance of the Code of Banking Practice;**
- **know how EFTPOS operates and appreciate the legal issues it raises;**
- **understand how ATMs operate and appreciate the legal implications.**

Self-assessment questions

1 Your customer has given a standing order to make mortgage payments on the 18th of each month. On Monday 18th your bank withheld the payment because of insufficient funds. On Tuesday 19th, sufficient cash is paid in to cover the transfer but the customer made no reference to the standing order. Later in the month, cheques were presented which exhausted the balance once more. This has occurred for several months and, as instalments are in arrears, the mortgagee now threatens to repossess the property.

For what is your bank liable:

(a) Negligence.

(b) Wrongful dishonour.

(c) Nothing.

(d) Wrongful payment of cheques.

2 The beneficiary of a standing order asks the payer's bank to advise him of the reason for non-receipt of last month's instalment. What reply would you give and why?

3 A customer who is the payer of a direct debit phones his bank at 3.15 pm to stop all further payments. A payment, which between the customer and the originator is genuinely due, is to be debited electronically on that day.

What action should the payer's bank take?

4 The payer's bank has paid a direct debit which is for a greater sum than the mandate authorises. What is the position?

5 Why is a bank in a stronger legal position if it has paid a direct debit under a forged authority than if it has paid a standing order against a forged payer's signature?

6 In the following circumstances, what is the maximum amount for which a cardholder can be held liable in the event of misuse before the card issuer has been notified that a card has been lost or stolen?

(a) In the absence of customer fraud or gross negligence.

(b) In the event of customer fraud or gross negligence.

7 Your bank receives an instruction from X to transfer £500 to Y who banks at the same bank and branch. Next morning, X telephones to stop the transfer.

What is the bank's position, assuming Y has not been advised?

8 Your customer was stranded in a small town because he was unable to obtain cash from an ATM to pay his rail fare. Consequently, he failed to keep an important appointment. The ATM failed because of a power cut.

What is the bank's position?

9 Give examples of what might amount to gross negligence on the part of a cardholder, in accordance with the Code of Banking Practice.

Further reading

- Penn, GA, Shea, AM and Arora, A — Chapter 18, *The Law Relating to Domestic Banking*, Vol 1, 1987, Sweet & Maxwell
- Raby, P — Chapter 11–12, *Law Relating to Banking Services*, 2nd edition 1992, Pitman

Unit 13

Introduction to Securities

Objectives

- **After having studied this unit, you should be able to:**
- **understand the basic purpose of security to a lending banker;**
- **appreciate the distinction between legal and equitable mortgages, and between direct and third party security;**
- **appreciate the significance of the Code of Banking Practice on bank securities procedures;**
- **explain the meaning and effect of the main clauses in a direct charge form;**
- **know what is meant by a bankers' lien.**

1 Introduction

1.1 This unit aims to provide you with a basic background to securities, the terms used, differences between direct and third party security, and the effect of clauses found in bank's direct charge forms.

1.2 The taking of specific types of security, i.e. stocks and shares, life policies, land and guarantees, is covered in Units 14–16 and the giving of security by limited companies is covered in Unit 17.

2 What is meant by security?

2.1 The best-known form of security occurs where a lender advances money for house purchase and the advance is secured by a mortgage over the house. A mortgage is a charge over the house, so that if the borrower defaults on his repayment obligations, then the lender may be able to sell the house, if necessary, to recoup the borrowing. Thus, in simple, non-legal terms, security means that the bank has a right over an asset which can be realised to meet the customer's obligations if all else fails.

2.2 Banks take security for many types of borrowing, and hopefully, they will never have to realise the security in order to repay the borrowing. However, the bank needs to ensure that it has completed the requisite procedures accurately so that in the event of the security having to be realised this can be done with the minimum of problems.

Direct compared to third party security

2.3 Direct security exists when the asset charged is owned by the borrowing customer. Third party, or collateral security, exists when the asset charged belongs to someone other than the borrowing customer, or where the bank's right to recover is against a third person such as a guarantor. With direct security, any charge form is signed by the owner of the asset, who is also the borrowing customer. With third party security, the charge form or written memorandum will be signed by the owner of the asset.

2.4 When the owner of the asset which is charged as security is also a party to the borrowing joint account or partnership account, then the bank has a choice of procedures. For example, Jack Stamp wishes to mortgage his shares as security for the borrowing on the account of Jack and Jill Stamp.

2.5 The bank's choices are to:

- Let Jack Stamp sign a direct or first party charge form. This form will contain a clause which states that the security will cover all borrowing or liabilities on any account whatsoever. The security will be valid as regards the joint account borrowing, since Jack will be personally liable for this under the usual joint and several liability clauses in the mandate.

  This method would be particularly useful if Jack was borrowing on his personal account as well as on the joint account, since both borrowings would be covered. Jack must be made aware of this at the time he signs the charge form.

- Let Jack sign a third party security form which states that the security is lodged to cover all borrowing on the joint account of Jack and Jill Stamp.

  This procedure precludes the bank from using the security to cover any borrowings on Jack's personal account, but it does show beyond all doubt that the security covers the joint account.

Why banks invariably require a charge form to be completed

2.6 A charge form is the form that is signed by the person or persons depositing the security. The charge form contains various clauses which will be binding upon the depositor of the security. Once the charge form has been signed, the bank has certain rights to deal with the security deposited. Those rights are discussed in Units 14–17 where the different types of security are covered. The main clauses to be found in a direct security charge form are covered in section 3 below, and the main clauses to be found in a third party charge form are covered in Unit 16.

2.7 Banks invariably have charge forms signed when they take security, since this provides certainty of intention of the depositor and enables the bank to take advantage of the various clauses included in the charge form.

A bank's duties to private individuals giving third party security

2.8 Under the Code of Banking Practice banks and building societies will advise private individuals proposing to give them a guarantee or other security for another person's liabilities:

- That by giving the guarantee or third party security he or she might become liable instead of or as well as that other person;

- Whether the guarantee or third party security will be unlimited as to amount or, if this is not the case, what the limit of the liability will be;
- That he or she should seek independent legal advice before entering into the guarantee or third party security.

2.9 Guarantees and other third party security documentation will contain clear and prominent notice to the above effect.

3 Legal and equitable mortgages

Creation of legal and equitable mortgages

3.1 Under the Law of Property Act 1925, a legal mortgage can only be created in one of two ways:

- By a charge by deed expressed to be by way of a legal mortgage; or
- In the case of land, by the granting of a lease of the land for a term absolute in years, subject to proviso that the lease ceases upon repayment of the loan.

3.2 Apart from over land, an equitable mortgage can be created whenever documents of title such as shares or life policies are deposited with the bank with the intention that they be held as security. There is no legal requirement for memorandum of deposit (contract) to be signed, although taking a signed memorandum is standard bank practice. An equitable mortgage of *land*, however, cannot be created by simply depositing documents of title with the intention of creating an equitable mortgage, the contract must be *in writing and signed by all parties*: Law of Property (Miscellaneous Provisions) Act 1989. (Land as security is fully covered in Unit 15.)

3.3 When the security is third party security, simple deposit of the security is insufficient to create an equitable mortgage. There must be some written evidence, signed by the third party, before any valid equitable mortgage can exist: Statute of Frauds Act 1677, s.4.

3.4 The above guidelines hold good for registered shares and life policies except where the borrowing comes within the terms of the Consumer Credit Act 1974. As a general rule any borrowing by non-corporate customers of up to £15,000 comes within the regulations of this Act. In such cases the Consumer Credit Act 1974 has very specific requirements as to the documentation required to create security (see Unit 19). For the purposes of this unit, we shall assume that the Consumer Credit Act 1974 does not apply to the examples shown.

Remedies of a legal mortgagee

3.5 A legal mortgage gives the mortgagee (the lender/bank), the right to sell the asset given as security in order to repay the borrowing if the borrower is in default. Provided the bank had no knowledge of any equitable interests in the security that existed at the time the item was charged to the bank, then its legal security will normally rank ahead of such interests. The only time when a pre-existing equitable charge will take precedence over a bank's subsequent legal charge is if the charge has been registered at the relevant place, e.g. Companies House if the borrower is a limited company, and the bank fails to make the requisite searches (see Units 14–17).

3.6 The bank can exercise its power of sale over the security given but under s.103, Law of Property Act 1925, this power cannot be exercised until the following steps have been taken:

- Notice requiring repayment of the money owed has to have been served on the mortgagee, and he has failed to repay the money after the expiration of three months from service of the notice; or
- Interest is in arrears and unpaid for two months after becoming due;
- The mortgagor (the borrower) has broken some provision in the mortgage deed other than the covenant for repayment of the mortgage money and interest.

3.7 In practice, the bank avoids the problems that can occur due to the time periods laid down in s.103 by specifically excluding its operation in the bank's form of legal mortgage.

Rights of legal and equitable mortgagees compared

3.8 Generally speaking the rights of an equitable mortgagee are not as effective as those of a legal mortgagee because:

- Unless the mortgagor complies with the bank's request to sell the property charged as security, a *court order* will be required before an equitable mortgagee can realise the asset to recover the borrowing. The court has the power to grant such an order under ss.90 and 91, Law of Property Act 1925. It is possible, of course, that the owner will agree to co-operate with the bank, but if this is not the case then the bank will face the time, trouble and expense of obtaining a court order. A legal mortgagee does not require a court order to exercise his power of sale.
- An equitable mortgagee is *subject to prior equities* even if the mortgagee was completely unaware of them. For example, Jones owes the bank £25,000 and has given the bank an equitable mortgage dated 1 January 1995 over his shares which have a value of £35,000. Unknown to the bank Jones had previously borrowed from a finance company, and had given them an equitable mortgage dated 1 January 1990. If the finance company is owed £20,000, and if the bank decides to realise the shares, the proceeds will be split as follows (assuming the bank has now become aware of the earlier mortgage and ignoring interest and charges).

	£
Sale proceeds of shares	35,000
Finance company prior equitable mortgage	20,000
Proceeds remaining for the bank	15,000

This leaves the bank with a shortfall of £10,000 because it ranks behind the first equitable mortgage. As you can see from the above example this could result in financial loss for the bank if it had to realise its security to repay the borrowing.

However, if the bank's mortgage had been a legal mortgage, and if the bank had been unaware of the prior equitable mortgage on the date its charge was created (January 1990), then the proceeds would now be split:

	£
Sale proceeds of shares	35,000
Bank's legal mortgage takes priority	25,000
Proceeds remaining for finance company	10,000

In this case, the finance company would be left with a shortfall of £10,000.

3.9 *Note:* it is not always the case that an equitable mortgagee loses priority to a legal mortgage that is created subsequently. In certain cases relating to land and life policies, a prior equitable mortgage will take priority over a subsequently created legal mortgage if the second lender has not carried out the correct search procedures, or taken note of the fact that the borrower has not produced the life policy, land certificate or deeds. (These are dealt with in Unit 14 and Unit 15).)

4 Main clauses in direct security charge forms

Student Activity 1

Obtain a copy of your bank's direct charge form and compare the clauses with the ones given below.

4.1 In practice banks' normal procedure is to have a charge form completed whenever security is taken. This unit will explain the main clauses which appear in all direct charge forms. Note that special clauses relating to particular assets will be covered in the relevant units on land, shares and life policies. Clauses which relate solely to third party securities are covered in Unit 16 which relates to guarantees.

All monies clause

4.2 This clause describes the nature of the liabilities secured by the charge form and attempts to cover all likely banking situations. A typical example of an all monies clause could be worded thus:

> THE Customer hereby covenants with the Bank that the Customer will on demand:
>
> (i) pay to the Bank the balance from time to time unpaid of all monies now due or hereafter to become due to the Bank by the Customer or by one or more of the persons who together are herein called 'the Customer' and
>
> (ii) discharge all liabilities now owing or hereafter to become owing to the Bank by the Customer or by one or more of the persons who together are herein called 'the Customer' actual and/or contingent and in each case whether the same shall be due or owing alone or jointly with any other person or persons or by any firm in which the Customer may be a partner on overdraft or otherwise and whether as principal or surety including commission and other usual banker's charges and interest thereon both before and after any demand made or judgement obtained at the rate or respective rates in force for

the time being for monies owing to the Bank by the Customer from the respective times at which such monies shall have become due until payment together with all costs and expenses which may be incurred by the Bank in obtaining payment hereof such interest to be computed and compounded according to the usual mode of the Bank from time to time.

(iii) SECTION 93 of the Law of Property Act 1925 shall not apply to this security and the Customer shall not be entitled to redeem this security without at the same time redeeming every or any existing or future mortgage for the time being held by the Bank on other property and/or policies now or at any time hereafter belonging to the Customer or to redeem any other such mortgages without at the same time redeeming this security.

4.3 The effect of these clauses is that the security covers all monies owing on *any account whatsoever* by the customer at whatever time. The words 'contingent liabilities' can mean any payments which a bank may have to make because of bonds or guarantees entered into on behalf of the customer. For example, if the bank is called upon to pay under a performance bond given on behalf of a customer in connection with one of the customer's contracts, the bank could use the security to reimburse itself if the customer will not pay: *Re Rudd & Son Ltd re Fosters and Rudd Ltd* (1986).

4.4 Coupled with the 'all monies' clause is a clause which specifically excludes s.93, Law of Property Act 1925. The Law of Property Act 1925 does not simply apply to land. 'Property' in the context of this Act is any asset that the customer owns which is given as security. This means that s.93 governs not only land as security but also the giving of the two other most common forms of security stocks and shares and life policies.

4.5 If s.93, Law of Property Act 1925 were not excluded, and the borrowing was secured by mortgages over several properties, then the borrower could make a partial repayment of the borrowing and insist upon the bank releasing one of the properties to him. If the properties securing the borrowing were not all equally marketable, then releasing such a property could leave the bank with the less marketable properties. This would cause problems if the bank had to exercise its power of sale to repay the borrowing.

4.6 However, this exclusion of s.93, is not a legal necessity provided that the bank's charge form has an 'all monies' clause in it. The 'all monies' clause gives the bank the right to retain all security until all borrowing is repaid. The s.93 exclusion clause is inserted into the 'all monies' clause simply to clarify and emphasise the point. The effect of this clause is to ensure that the bank can retain the security until all monies owing have been repaid.

Continuing security

4.7 A typical clause would read:

This security shall be a continuing security and shall extend to cover the ultimate balance due from the Customer to the Bank notwithstanding there may have been from time to time a balance to the credit of the Customer on any account between the Customer and the Bank or any other matter or thing whatsoever.

4.8 The effect of this clause is to prevent *Clayton's case* (1816) from working against the bank if the borrowing is on overdraft.

4.9 For example, consider the effect of *Clayton's case* if there had been no continuing security clause and direct security had been taken on 1 January 1995 to cover an existing overdrawn balance. Assume that the summarised ledger on 1 May 1991 is:

Date		*Dr*	*Cr*	*Bal*
		£	£	£
31.12.94	Balance	22,000		22,000 Dr
3.1.95	Withdrawn	10,000		32,000 Dr
10.2.915	Deposited		18,000	14,000 Dr
1.5.95	Withdrawn	5,000		19,000 Dr

In the absence of the continuing security clause, the bank's security would have been valid on 1 May 1995 only to the extent of £4,000, i.e. the remaining amount of the overdrawn balance of £22,000 on 31.12.94.

The £19,000 balance on 1 May, under *Clayton's case*, is made up of:

	£
Debited 1 May	5,000
Debited 3 January	10,000
Borrowing at 1.1.91 not yet repaid	4,000
	19,000

Fortunately for the bank, the continuing security clause will nullify *Clayton's case* and the security will therefore be valid for the full £19,000.

Repayment on demand

4.10 A typical clause could read:

(i) The Monies owing upon this security shall be deemed to have become due within the meaning of s.101 of the Law of Property Act 1925 immediately on demand for payment being made by the Bank.

(ii) A demand for payment or any other demand or notice under this deed may be made or given by any person duly authorised by the Bank by letter addressed to the person intended to receive the same or to his personal representative and left at or sent by post to his or their usual or last known address or in the case of a limited company its registered office or at its place of business last known to the Bank and if so sent by post shall whether or not the letter was posted and in proving such service by post it shall be sufficient to prove that the envelope containing the notice was properly addressed and stamped and delivered in to the custody of a Post Office and any notice to be given to the Bank may be sent by post to the registered office of the Bank or to the branch of the Bank at which the account of the Customer is kept.

4.11 Section 101, Law of Property Act 1925 states that every mortgage made by deed gives the mortgagee the power to sell the mortgaged property. However, as you have seen, s.103, unless excluded, qualifies this power. Thus, the purpose of this clause is to give the bank the right of repayment on demand and exclude delay under s.103.

4.12 An additional clause to be found on some banks' mortgage forms *specifically* excludes s.103, by stating that the bank can exercise its remedies one month after repayment has become due.

> The Bank shall become entitled to exercise the power of sale conferred on mortgages by statute in case all monies hereby secured shall not be completely discharged within one month after such monies shall have become or shall be deemed to have become due and the restrictions contained in s.103 of the Law of Property Act 1925 shall not apply to this security.

Additional security clause

4.13 A typical example could read:

> ... the security shall be in addition and without prejudice to any other security or remedy now or at any time held by the Bank including (without prejudice to the generality of the foregoing) any charge deposit, guarantee, indemnity, lien, set off, or other form of security whatsoever.

4.14 The security covered by this particular charge form is clearly stated to be in addition to any other security. Thus, this charge continues to be valid irrespective of whether new security is subsequently taken or existing security is released.

Conclusive evidence clause

4.15 A typical example could read:

> ANY admission or acknowledgement in writing by the Customer or by any person authorised by the Customer of the amount of the indebtedness of the Customer to the Bank and any statement of account sent by the Bank to the Customer showing the indebtedness of the Customer to the Bank on any one or more accounts or generally and not questioned by the Customer within fourteen days shall be binding and conclusive on and against the Customer in all proceedings and Courts of Law whether in England or elsewhere.

4.16 The object of this clause is to prevent any dispute as to the amount of debt. The clause was held to be valid in *Bache and Co (London) Ltd v Banque Venes et Commerciale de Paris* (1973). However, nowadays, the bank would have to act reasonably or else the Unfair Contract Terms Act 1977 could invalidate such a clause.

Successor clause

4.17 Any successor to the bank's title will take over the bank's rights to the security. Thus, if the bank is taken over by another bank, the new bank will take over the old bank's rights to the security.

Study aid

4.18 Remember the mnemonic ACRACS for the clauses in a bank security form:

- **A** ll monies
- **C** ontinuing security
- **R** epayment on demand
- **A** dditional security
- **C** onclusive evidence
- **S** uccessor.

5 Lien

5.1 A lien is the right to retain possession of the property of another in lieu of payment from that person.

Particular and general liens

5.2 A *particular lien is* limited to monies owed in a particular transaction under which a person has possession of another's goods, e.g. the right of a garage to retain possession of a repaired car until payment is made for the repairs by the owner. With a particular lien, there is no right to sell the items held.

5.3 A *general lien* covers all monies due from the owner of the property, and is not restricted to money owed for the particular transaction under which the creditor has possession of the goods. Banks, factors and solicitors are entitled to general lien, and this allows them to sell the items held to recover the money lent in the event of default.

Banker's lien

5.4 Under *Brandao v Barrett* (1846) a banker's lien is a general lien on all securities deposited with them as bankers by a customer, unless there is an express or implied contract to the contrary. Banker's lien usually applies when the bank acts as an agent for a customer, and the customer owes the bank money. The money owed need not be in connection with the particular transaction under which the bank holds the customer's property.

5.5 Examples of banker's lien are:

- When a bank *collects a cheques for a customer* and the cheque is dishonoured, the collecting bank may retain the cheque and use it in connection a claim against the drawer. This applies only in certain circumstances which are set out in Unit 11.
- When the bank collects documentary bills of exchange it has a lien over the documents such as the bills of lading. This gives the bank a right to use the goods to clear the borrowing.

5.6 Banker's lien does *not* apply to goods or items left in safe custody, because there is an implied or express agreement to return the goods to the customer on demand: *Brandao v Barrett* (1846).

Banker's lien as a form of security

5.7 Banker's lien arises from *operation of law* in certain circumstances, and it is *not* the result of agreement between banker and customer. Hence a banker's lien is *a form of non-consensual security.* A mortgage or charge arises by specific agreement between banker and customer.

5.8 A banker's lien will take priority over charges taken subsequent to the lien.

Banker's lien and contingent liabilities

5.9 Banker's lien does not apply unless the customer actually owes money. Therefore, a contingent liability cannot give the bank a lien over the customer's property: *Jeffryes v Agra and Masterman's Bank* (1866). (A contingent liability is one which will only have to be paid if a certain event occurs. In the case of a bank guarantee the event is the nonpayment of the debt incurred by the principal debtor to the bank. If the principal debtor refuses or cannot repay the debt, the guarantor will have to pay the debt.)

5.10 Thus, if a customer G has guaranteed the account of another customer X for £500, this will be a mere contingent liability on the part of G and banker's lien cannot apply.

5.11 If the bank were to make formal demand under the terms of the guarantee, and then debited G's account, then the liability of G would be actual, and banker's lien would apply.

Summary

Now that you have studied this unit, you should be able to:

- **describe what is meant by security;**
- **differentiate between a legal and an equitable mortgage;**
- **differentiate between direct and third party security;**
- **appreciate the requirements for advice under the Code of Banking Practice;**
- **describe the main clauses in a bank charge form and understand their relevance;**
- **explain the effect of banker's lien in relation to security.**

Self-assessment questions

1 The bank holds an account in the name of Roy Jones and it is offered as security shares registered in the name of Mrs Jones. Who will be required to sign the bank's charge form?

2 You have an account in the name of Mr and Mrs Smith and you are offered shares in the name of Mrs Smith as security. Who will be required to sign the bank's charge form and which type of form (direct or third party) could be used?

3 Briefly indicate two disadvantages of equitable as opposed to legal mortgages.

4 A customer asks for an overdraft of £20,000 and offers to hand over a share certificate registered in his name as security. He refuses, however, to sign anything. If the bank accepts the shares as security, will it have a valid mortgage? If so state the type of mortgage and name a relevant case.

5 Name the main clauses to be found in all direct security forms where the borrowing is outside the terms of the Consumer Credit Act 1974.

Further reading

There are no specific further reading references for this unit. The references for the following three units encompass reading for this unit.

Unit 14

Shares and Life Policies as Security

Objectives

On completion of this unit, you should be able to:

- **differentiate between company shares, loan stocks and debentures;**
- **understand the procedures for taking legal and equitable mortgages over stocks and shares;**
- **evaluate the relative merits of legal and equitable mortgages of stocks and shares;**
- **understand the implications of bonus and rights issues when a bank holds shares as security;**
- **appreciate the significance of the main clauses in the charge forms for stocks and shares;**
- **understand the nature of life policies, and the importance of insurable interest, *uberrimae fidei*, suicide, trust policies, and age admitted for lenders who take life policies as security;**
- **understand the procedures for taking a legal mortgage of a life policy;**
- **evaluate the merits of life policies as security for a lending banker;**
- **compare and contrast the benefits of legal mortgages as opposed to equitable mortgages;**
- **understand the significance of clauses in the life policy charge form;**
- **understand the rights of a lender secured by a life policy;**
- **appreciate the various ways in which life policies can be realised.**

1 Ordinary registered shares

Registered shares

1.1 The company which issues the shares keeps a register of the names of the shareholders. A change of ownership of shares is made by lodging the share certificate and a signed stock transfer form with the company. The company's register is then updated and a new certificate is issued to the new owner, with the new owner's name on it.

1.2 Dividends are paid by the company to the shareholder, or to his bank account if a dividend mandate is held.

1.3 Most shares issued by UK companies are registered. Under s.186, Companies Act 1985 a certificate is *prima facie* evidence of title to the shares.

1.4 We noted in Unit 9 that the advance of modern technology (truncation) has resulted in the need for serious consideration of the legal issues. In connection with stocks and shares, the relevant technological advance is CREST. In effect CREST will mean the potential disappearance of the need for paper share certificates, and the beneficial ownership of shares could be recorded electronically in a centrally maintained register. It is difficult to judge what the practical impacts of CREST will be, but shareholders will still have the right to insist on having a paper share certificate as the evidence of ownership.

1.5 Note that bearer bonds, shares registered in good marking names, national savings securities and unit trusts are not included in this syllabus.

Student Activity 1

When you read the *Financial Times*, *Economist* or other relevant publications, make a point of looking out for articles on the progress of CREST. See if any of the articles cover the implications of CREST in connection with shares as security.

Preference shares, loan stocks and debentures offered as security

1.6 A company can have various sources of long-term funds. It must have ordinary share capital. In addition it can also issue preference shares, loan stocks (either secured or unsecured) and debenture stocks.

1.7 As far as the bank is concerned, when accepting any of these preference shares or stocks as security from the registered owner, the procedure will be the same as for registered shares.

1.8 Similar principles apply when a bank is offered British Government Stocks, known as 'gilts', as security. Gilts are loan stocks issued by the British Government.

2 Quoted and unquoted stocks and shares

2.1 Quoted stocks and shares are stocks and shares in publics companies which are listed on the Stock Exchange. The prices of such stocks and shares are published daily. The stocks and shares can easily be sold at the current market price. Unquoted stocks and shares are not listed on the Stock Exchange.

2.2 Unquoted stocks and shares are difficult to value, and the company's articles of association must be examined as many private companies' articles restrict the sale of shares and prohibit the shares from being held as security for a loan. This prohibition most commonly applies to shares, because shares carry voting rights. The bank will need to check the company's articles of association if offered unquoted stocks as security to see if this prohibition applies to them.

2.3 A private or unquoted company may in its articles of association have a 'first and paramount lien' over its shares. This means that the shares could be forfeited if the shareholder owed money to the company on some other account. (For example a landlord may own shares in a brewery, and may owe money to the brewery for deliveries of beer. The brewery could, if necessary, cancel the shares as a set off against the money owing for the beer.)

2.4 A public quoted company is prohibited under the rules of the Stock Exchange from having a lien over its shares.

3 Taking a mortgage over registered stocks and shares

Equitable mortgage

3.1 With direct security, strictly at law all that is necessary is for the certificate to be deposited with the bank with the intention that it shall be held as security.

3.2 However, normal procedure is for the owner to sign a memorandum of deposit. In addition, some banks ask the owner to sign an undated stock transfer form in favour of the bank as transferee. The bank retains these documents and the stock or share certificate. (Many banks have nominee companies and in such cases the transferee is shown as the bank nominee company.)

3.3 The advantage of having a signed, undated transfer form is that the bank can sell the stocks and shares without the need for a court order even though its mortgage is only equitable. The bank will lodge its share certificate and signed stock transfer form with the registrar of the company whose shares are held as security. This will convert the equitable mortgage into a legal one. The bank can then sell without a court order if there is any breach of the conditions of the lending agreement.

3.4 However, should there be any prior equitable interest, the bank's equitable mortgage would be subject to prior equities, e.g. when the registered owner of the shares is a trustee who holds the shares in trust for a beneficiary. The beneficiary has an equitable interest.

Legal mortgage

3.5 The owner signs a memorandum of deposit and a stock transfer form in favour of the bank. The bank sends the certificate and stock transfer form to the company, who send a new certificate to the bank showing the bank as the registered owner.

3.6 Any other method of charge over registered stocks and shares gives only an equitable mortgage.

Notice of lien by a bank with an equitable mortgage

3.7 Banks give notice of lien on a standard form to the company when they have an equitable mortgage over private or unquoted shares.

3.8 The reasons are:

- Although any money owed by the shareholder to the company before the notice of lien takes priority over the bank's lending, any money advanced by the company to the shareholder after receipt of notice of lien will rank behind the bank's mortgage. No new rights of lien after notice will be effective against the bank: *Bradford Banking Co Ltd v Henry Briggs* (1866).

- The company may make an unofficial note of the bank's mortgage and refuse to issue a duplicate certificate to the shareholder without the bank's consent.

3.9 There is no point in giving notice of lien when the bank has a legal mortgage, as the shares are in the bank's name anyway. Likewise, with quoted public companies, notice of lien is not worthwhile because the company cannot have a first and paramount lien and is prohibited from accepting any notice of interest.

3.10 *Note*: An alternative to notice of lien is to obtain a 'stop order' on the company. This requires the company to give notice to the bank of any dealings proposed in the shares.

Bank's own shares offered as security

3.11 These can be taken as security. If the banks' shares are fully paid and quoted, the position regarding the security will be the same as with any other shares. If the bank's shares are partly paid or unquoted, the bank will have an additional alternative remedy. If its articles give it a first and paramount lien it may cancel the shares on the borrower's default.

4 Legal/equitable mortgages of registered securities compared

Advantages of a legal mortgage

4.1 These are as follows.

- The bank at all times retains complete control over its security. All bonus issues and rights accruing due to registered shares automatically become the property of the bank and all the necessary documents relating to these issues will automatically be sent to the bank.
- Provided that at the time the legal mortgage was created the bank had no knowledge of any prior equitable rights, the legal title of the bank takes priority.

Student Activity 2

Recall Unit 6 and the position of the holders of partly paid shares in liquidation. Consider whether a bank would be better off with a legal mortgage or an equitable one in this situation and then read on.

Disadvantages of a legal mortgage

4.2 These are as that:

- The procedure is time consuming.
- Where a legal mortgage is taken over partly paid stocks and shares the bank will be liable to meet any calls made on those stocks and shares,

should the company go into liquidation. This liability will remain for up to 12 months after the stocks and shares are transferred out of the bank/ nominee company's name if the subsequent shareholder fails to pay calls that may be made. This does not apply with an equitable mortgage.

- If the transfer form were forged the bank's mortgage would be invalid. This also applies to equitable mortgages. The moral is always to be sure that you know the identity of the depositor and always ensure that the name(s) on the stock or share certificate agree with those of the depositors who sign the charge form.

  In *Sheffield Corporation v Barclay* (1905), for example, the bank wished to obtain a legal mortgage over some of the corporation's stock. A stock certificate and a transfer in favour of the bank's nominee were lodged with the corporation but the signature of one transferor was forged. It was held that the corporation had to reimburse the owner whose signature had been forged with a new holding of stock and the bank had to reimburse the corporation for breach of implied warranty that the signatures on the transfer were genuine.
- If the depositor is a director of the company whose shares are being charged, the shares may represent that director's qualification holding (qualification holdings only relate to ordinary shares) and if a legal mortgage is taken he will have to resign from the board since the shares will no longer be registered in his name. This does not apply with an equitable mortgage. (Many companies insist in their articles of association that all directors own a minimum number of shares known as a qualification holding.)

Advantages of an equitable mortgage supported by a signed, undated stock transfer in favour of the bank

4.3 Such an equitable mortgage:

- Is quick and easy to process, with no expenses involved.
- Involves no risk of liability with partly-paid stocks and shares.
- Does not deprive a director of his qualification holding.
- Allows the bank to take a full legal mortgage without the cooperation of the depositor if at any stage it needs to. In fact this method is often described as a halfway house method, since all the bank has to do to obtain full legal title is to date the stock transfer form and forward it to the company along with the certificate. Alternatively, some banks rely on an attorney clause in the memorandum of deposit and do not take a signed but otherwise incomplete stock transfer form.

  A bank cannot, however, complete a legal mortgage if it has become aware of a prior equitable interest which preceded the date of its own equitable mortgage: *Coleman v London County and Westminster Bank Ltd* (1916).

Disadvantages of an equitable mortgage supported by signed undated transfer form

4.4 These are that.

- It is subject to prior equities. If the bank uses this method to charge stocks and shares, and at a later date has notice of another equitable charge created before its own, it is too late to proceed to create a full legal mortgage by registering the shares in its own name.

- A private unquoted company may have a lien over its shares although the bank can protect itself to some extent by giving notice of lien.
- The depositor may obtain a duplicate stock or share certificate from the issuing company. If these shares are then sold the certificate held by the bank could be considered valueless.

  If the bank suspects that the owner of registered stocks and shares held on equitable mortgage could be about to try to obtain a duplicate certificate, the bank could file a sworn affidavit at the court and request a 'stop order'. If the court agrees, the stop order can be served on the company, and the company must then give the bank eight days' notice of any attempt by the registered holder to transfer the shares.

  In practice most companies require an indemnity from a reputable financial services organisation before they will issue a duplicate share certificate. Hence duplicate certificates are not easy to obtain.
- A bonus rights issue applies to ordinary shares. Bonus and rights issue documents are sent direct to the owner of the shares, whereas these documents are sent directly to the bank (the owner of the shares) if the bank has a legal mortgage.

5 Bonus and rights issues

Bonus issues

5.1 A bonus issue of shares is a free issue of shares, on a *pro rata* basis, to existing ordinary shareholders. A bonus issue is also called a 'scrip issue' or a 'capitalisation issue'. It does not raise any capital for a company, but is a bookkeeping exercise which increases the number of shares issued without affecting the value of the individual's shareholding.

Effect on a bank's security

5.2 If the bank has a legal mortgage, bonus issues will automatically be registered in the bank's name, and thus the bank's security remains intact. However, with the normal type of security, i.e. memorandum of deposit and signed undated transfer form, the bonus shares would be sent direct to the depositor. Although the bank's memorandum of deposit stipulates that the depositor will forward all bonus issues to the bank, it is still essential to take steps to obtain any bonus certificates if the bank's security valuation is to remain unimpaired. If the bonus shares are sent to the depositor, and he sells them, there is little in practice that the bank can do. The value of the certificates lodged with the bank will have fallen.

5.3 Although it may be possible to call in the borrowing as a covenant of the memorandum has been breached, or sue the depositor for breach of warranty, it is much better if the bank can retain its security with the valuation unimpaired.

Rights issues

5.4 A rights issue is a sale of new shares by a company to existing ordinary shareholders in proportion to their existing shareholding at a favourable price. Because the shareholder has the right to purchase the rights, this type of issue will have an effect on the bank if it holds such shares as security.

5.5 If the bank has a legal mortgage, then the rights issue will come to the bank. If the bank is unwilling to lend the customer any more money to enable him to take up the rights, two courses of action are available to the bank:

- Sell the rights and use the proceeds to reduce the borrowing. The customer will still own the same number of shares as before, but the price will have fallen. This reduces the value of the bank's security.
- Sell enough of the rights to enable it to take up the remainder at no extra cost. Ignoring dealing costs, this will mean that the value of the security remains the same.

5.6 If the bank has an equitable mortgage, then it relies upon the customer to ensure that the new shares are deposited with the bank. (This is the same as for a bonus issue.) If the customer fails to deposit the rights issue shares, then it may be possible to call in the borrowing as a covenant of the memorandum of deposit has been breached. Alternatively the bank could sue the customer for breach of warranty.

6 Clauses in a standard bank memorandum of deposit

Student Activity 3

Obtain a copy of your bank's memorandum of deposit covering stocks and shares, and compare the clauses with those discussed here.

6.1 The standard bank memorandum of deposit contains the usual clauses referred to in Unit 13 under the acronym 'ACRACS':

- All monies.
- Continuing security.
- Repayment on demand.
- Additional security.
- Conclusive evidence.
- Succession.

6.2 In addition the major clauses included for stocks and shares cover:

- Bonus and rights issues.
- The bank's rights to exercise its power of sale.
- The depositor's agreement to provide a signed undated transfer or other relevant document if the bank does not already hold them.
- The bank's right to execute stock transfer forms and other documents on behalf of the customer if he will not do so.
- The bank's right to close off the old account and open a new account to be kept in credit if the bank so wishes if it becomes aware of any second mortgages or other rights over the shares.

  By taking such action, the bank will prevent the rule in *Clayton's case* (1816) from operating against it. The danger would have been that any new borrowing after notice would have been deemed to have lost priority to the second mortgage. However, the clause is carefully worded so that the bank will retain its priority in any event, even if it fails to break the old account. The efficacy of such a clause was upheld in *Westminster Bank v Cond* (1940).

- The bank disclaims all voting rights to the shares until it makes demand. This enables the bank to avoid the need to disclose its holding of a company's shares when the shares are registered in the name of the bank's nominee company and the amount so registered exceeds the statutory maximum. There is, however, a potential danger that the bank could be classed as a parent company.

7 The nature of life policies

7.1 The main types of life policy which are of interest to bankers are endowment policies, whole life policies and term policies. Under an *endowment policy*, the insurance company agrees to pay a set minimum sum known as the capital value (which may be increased by bonuses) on a certain future date, or on the death of the life assured, whichever comes first. In return the policy holder must pay regular premiums which are agreed at the outset. Prior to the maturity date, the policy may acquire a surrender value, depending on how long it has been in existence.

7.2 *Whole life policies* are policies where the insurance company pays out only on the death of the life assured. *Term life policies* are an agreement by the insurance company to pay out a lump sum if the life assured dies before a stipulated date. If the life assured survives the term, no payment is made by the insurance company. Term life policies are often used as security for fixed period loans, such as house purchase mortgages.

7.3 A *mortgage protection policy* is a special type of term life policy where the amount of cover reduces to match the reducing loan.

7.4 *Note*: some policies, usually whole life policies, are known as 'industrial policies' where the premiums are collected by agents in person and the owner has a premium receipt book. These policies usually contain a clause prohibiting any mortgage or assignment.

Insurable interest

7.5 There are three parties to a life policy:

- Proposer;
- Beneficiary;
- Life assured.

7.6 One person can fulfil all three roles, e.g. X can take out a policy on his life for his own benefit. Alternatively the three parties could be different e.g. X could take out a policy on his wife's life for the benefit of his children.

7.7 A person who takes out a policy on his own life, or on that of his spouse, is presumed to have an insurable interest. In all other cases the proposer must have a 'monetary' or insurable interest in the life assured. Examples of valid insurable interest are creditor in debtor to the amount of the debt, guarantor in principal debtor to the extent of the guarantee, employer in key employees, dependent child in parent.

7.8 The insurable interest must exist at the time the policy was taken out, and if it did not do so the policy is void: Life Assurance Act 1774. However, a policy is not invalidated if the insurable interest subsequently ceases.

7.9 Once a company has arranged a life policy, and has accepted notice of the bank's mortgage, it will rarely in practice attempt to lapse the policy as far as the bank's security is concerned. Thus, banks do not concern themselves with insurable interest when taking a mortgage of a life policy.

Uberrimae Fidei

7.10 An insurance contract is a contract *uberrimae fidei* – a contract of the utmost good faith. Hence, when taking out a life policy, the proposer has a duty to bring to the attention of the insurance company any material facts which affect the insurance. This duty not only refers to answering questions on the proposal form truthfully, but also to bringing any other relevant facts to the attention of the insurance company even when questions are not asked: *Woolcott v Sun Alliance and London Insurance Ltd* (1978).

7.11 Failure to disclose all relevant facts at the time the policy was taken out will render it voidable at the option of the insurance company. Contracts of insurance are excluded from the scope of the Unfair Contract Terms Act 1977 so the *uberrimae fidei* duty cannot be mitigated by the normal duty of reasonableness.

7.12 In practice, however, many insurance companies adopt a similar stance to that for insurable interest. If the bank in good faith takes such a policy as security, and if the insurance company has accepted the bank's notice, then the policy will be honoured to the extent of the bank's reliance on it as security.

Suicide

7.13 Most life policies contain clauses covering the suicide of the life assured. If there are no clauses covering the matter, and the life assured was sane at the time, the insurance company could avoid the policy because he deliberately brought about the event on which payment was being claimed *Beresford v Royal Insurance Co Ltd* (1938). However, if the assured committed suicide whilst the balance of his mind was temporarily disturbed, the insurance company must pay out: *Moore v Woolsley* (1854).

7.14 Most life policies expressly permit an assignee for value (which is what the bank becomes when it takes a mortgage or a charge over the policy) to claim to the extent of his interest should the life assured commit suicide. Thus, in practice, the bank need concern itself only with establishing the inclusion of the operative clause in the policy when taking a mortgage over it.

Trust policies

7.15 Care must be taken when a policy states that it has been effected under the Married Women's Property Act 1882. Such policies are proposed by a husband on his own life in favour of his wife and children, or by a wife on her own life in favour of her husband and children. Such wording creates a trust in favour of the beneficiary.

7.16 If the bank is to take such a policy as security it must ensure that:

- The beneficiary is named with some certainty; a description such as 'my wife' could cause problems if the husband subsequently divorced and remarried.
- Any children are aged 18 or over, otherwise no effective charge can be taken.
- Independent legal advice is offered when the circumstances require it (see Unit 16).
- All beneficiaries as well as the trustee join in the assignment.

Age admitted

7.17 The age of the life assured at the time he takes out a life policy determines the premiums and benefits. The younger the life assured the better the terms. Before paying out on a life policy the insurance company will require proof that the age stated by the proposer at the time the policy was taken out was correct. If it turns out that the proposer had understated his age, then the benefits payable will be reduced.

7.18 If the policy says 'age admitted' the insurance company is confirming that the age stated was correct. If the policy does not state 'age admitted', you should obtain the life assured's birth certificate, send it to the insurance company who will send back an 'age admitted' slip. Banks usually do this when taking a mortgage of a life policy, however certain insurance companies have special arrangements with banks in respect of policies issued before 1968. In such cases the bank need not concern itself if the policy does not state 'age admitted'.

8 Taking a legal assignment over a life policy

8.1 A mortgage of a life policy is taken by an assignment of the right to the policy proceeds from the beneficiary.

Basic procedure

8.2 Complete the following procedure.

- Ensure the policy is issued by a *UK insurance company*, or alternatively is issued by the London office of a sound overseas company,.
- Examine the policy for *onerous conditions*. It is essential to obtain and retain the policy, otherwise lack of the policy indicates it could be charged elsewhere.
- Request the insurance company to give the *surrender value* of the policy, unless the policy itself lays down a formula for calculating a surrender value.
- The charge form must be signed by the beneficiary. (Care must be taken with trust policies, since the trustee and all beneficiaries must join in the charge form.) In addition the signature of the mortgagor/assignor must be witnessed.

- For the bank to obtain a *legal mortgage* of the policy it must follow the Policies of Assurance Act 1867. This Act requires that:
  - the assignment is in writing
  - written notice is given to the insurance company together with any required fee, and that
  - the insurance company acknowledges receipt.

  If these formalities are not observed the bank will only have an equitable mortgage.
- Check that age is admitted. If not, send the assured's birth certificate to the company.
- Obtain up-to-date premium receipt, and diarise to ensure future premiums are paid. If possible, have premiums paid by standing order or direct debit.

Reasons for giving written notice to the insurance company

8.3 There are two:

- If the bank did not do so, under the Policies of Assurance Act 1867 it will have only an equitable mortgage, since this notice is a prerequisite for a legal mortgage.
- The standard form of notice will ask the insurance company whether there are any prior charges. If the insurance company confirms there are none, the bank's mortgage will take priority, provided the bank retains possession of the policy itself. However, under *Newman v Newman* (1885) a second assignee cannot obtain priority over an earlier assignee if the second assignee knows of the earlier assignment.

Duplicate life policy is offered as security

8.4 In *Spencer v Clarke* (1878) it was held that non-production of the policy, or production of a duplicate life policy constituted constructive notice that the policy was charged elsewhere. If the policy has been charged elsewhere, the prior charge which will take priority over a bank's subsequent legal charge even if he has not notified the insurance company. It is *possession* of the policy that gives priority, not notice to the insurance company.

Conflict of laws

8.5 When a bank takes a mortgage over a life policy which has been issued outside England and Wales, the assignment should contain a clause stating that it is governed by English law. This applies to policies issued by companies domiciled in Scotland since Scottish law is different.

9 Advantages and disadvantages of life policies as security

Advantages

9.1 These are that.

- The procedure for taking the security is relatively simple compared with, say, land.
- Life policies are easy to value, since insurance companies will always quote a surrender value.

- If the bank has a legal mortgage it can quickly and easily surrender the policy, should this prove necessary.
- The value of the policy normally increases with payment of future premiums.

Disadvantages

9.2 These are that.

- If the customer cannot afford future premiums, the bank has authority given in the charge form to debit the customer's account.

  However the amount by which the overdraft is increased by payment of the premium may well be more than the increase in the surrender value. If the bank does not ensure payment of future premiums, the policy could well lapse, depending on the terms relating to the issue of that particular policy.
- It is possible that the insurance company could refuse to honour the policy because the assured has not fulfilled the conditions, e.g. the policy may forbid the assured to take part in dangerous sports. If the assured does so, the policy could be declared void by the insurance company.

  However, should this arise, most insurance companies will not penalise a legal mortgagee who used the policy as security for a loan.

10 Legal/equitable mortgages of life policies compared

Disadvantages of an equitable mortgage

10.1 These are that:

- An equitable mortgage is subject to prior equities. If the policy had already been mortgaged elsewhere.
- The insurance company is not obliged to accept notice of an equitable mortgage.
- The beneficiary, or his personal representative if the beneficiary has died, must authorise the insurance company to pay the proceeds to the bank. If the beneficiary refuses to comply, the bank's mortgage is still valid, but the bank will have to obtain a court order authorising the insurance company to pay.

Advantages of a legal mortgage

10.2 These are that:

- Provided the bank retains possession of the policy and receives confirmation from the insurance company that it knows of no other mortgages, the bank's legal mortgage will take priority.
- The insurance company is bound to acknowledge receipt of notice of a legal mortgage.
- The bank can surrender the policy or claim the proceeds at maturity or death without any need for the agreement of the beneficiary.

11 Usual clauses in an assignment of a life policy

Student Activity 4

Obtain a copy of your bank's charge form covering life policies and mark the ACRACS clauses and the other clauses shown.

11.1 In addition to the usual clauses found in the standard bank memorandum of deposit for all types of security, the standard legal assignment of a life policy contains other important clauses.

Reassignment

11.2 The bank undertakes to reassign the policy to the customer, at his expense at any time the customer so instructs, provided all indebtedness has been repaid.

Obligations of the customer

11.3 The customer must pay all future premiums and must not take part in any activities which are forbidden by the policy. The purpose of this clause is to ensure that the policy remains valid.

Costs and charges

11.4 All costs incurred in perfecting the security shall be charged to the customer.

12 Rights of a legal assignee of a life policy

On default by the borrower

12.1 In these circumstances the bank may:

- *Surrender the policy.* The policy and the assignment/mortgage form are sent to the insurance company, along with a standard surrender request form which is completed by the bank. The insurance company will remit the proceeds to the bank.
- *Sell the policy* to a specialist company who may pay more than the current surrender value.

  Note: the two courses of action above apply in accordance with the usual power of sale clause in the assignment form.
- *Convert the policy to a fully paid-up policy.* In such cases a reduced sum assured and a reduced surrender value will be applied in return for the cessation of the need to pay premiums.

  This course could be adopted if the reduced surrender value was well in excess of the loan, and if the bank anticipated that the customer could service the borrowing at a future date.
- In addition, the insurance company could agree to grant a mortgage of the policy and the proceeds could then pay off the bank borrowing.

  On receipt of the proceeds, the bank would vacate its own mortgage/assignment, and would send these documents and the policy to the insurance company. The policy holder's formal consent to this would be needed.

On the death of life assured

12.2 The bank may collect the proceeds of the policy from the insurance company. The policy, and mortgage/assignment forms are sent to the insurance company, along with the death certificate.

Realising a life policy

12.3 Realisation means either:

- Surrender of the policy;
- Sale to a specialist company;
- Claiming the proceeds from the insurance company on the death of a life assured;
- Claiming the proceeds from the insurance company at maturity.

12.4 Whatever form of realisation applies, the proceeds will be paid directly to the bank.

Direct security

12.5 If the security is direct security, the proceeds will be credited directly to the customer's account. If there is a surplus, i.e. the receipt of the proceeds will take the account into credit, then the customer, or his personal representatives if he is deceased, can withdraw the surplus proceeds. However, if the bank has received notice of a second assignment, then it must pay over the surplus proceeds to the second assignee, rather than allowing the customer to withdraw them.

Third-party security

12.6 The proceeds will be paid into a suspense account, in accordance with the clause in the charge form which was upheld in *Re Sass* (1986).

12.7 In the event of bankruptcy, the bank will thus be able to prove as an unsecured creditor for the full amount of indebtedness on the customer's account and then use the proceeds to meet any shortfall. Any surplus proceeds will be returned to the assignor, unless the bank has notice of a second assignment/mortgage.

12.8 If bankruptcy does not apply, the bank will be able to transfer the proceeds from the suspense account to the customer's account. However, the bank will only do this if it has been unable to obtain repayment from the customer's own resources. Once again, any surplus proceeds will be returned to the assignor, unless notice of a second assignment has been received.

12.9 *Note*: similar principles as regards surplus proceeds and suspense accounts apply when stocks or shares are realised.

Summary

Now that you have studied this unit, you should be able to:

- **understand the advantages and disadvantages of stocks and shares and life policies as security;**
- **understand the advantages and disadvantages of legal and equitable mortgages of stocks and shares and life policies;**
- **explain how stocks and shares and life policies are charged as security;**
- **know the clauses in the appropriate charge forms and appreciate their significance;**
- **know the rights of a legal assignee of a life policy;**
- **appreciate what is meant by realisation of a life policy.**

Self-assessment questions

Note: there may be more than one correct answer.

1 Which of the following is most valuable as security, other things being equal?

(a) Quoted shares.

(b) Unquoted shares.

(c) Shares in private companies.

2 Which of the following is an equitable mortgage of quoted shares?

(a) Bank holds the certificate and a signed undated stock transfer form.

(b) The shares are registered in the name of the bank's nominee company.

(c) The certificate is deposited without any written charge by the registered owner to secure his overdraft of facility of £20,000.

(d) The bank holds a certificate in the name of x and the borrowing is in the name of Y (no written authority is held).

3 A bonus issue of shares adversely affects the bank's security:

(a) When it has an equitable mortgage.

(b) When it has a legal mortgage.

(c) in the case of both (a) and (b).

(d) A bonus issue never effects the value of shares held as security.

4 What are the advantages of quoted shares as security (signed, undated transfer held)?

(a) Easy to value.

(b) Stable in value.

(c) Easy to sell.

(d) Take priority over prior equities.

5 An endowment policy has a capital value of £10,000 without profits. What is the amount paid on death of the life assured?

(a) £500 (the surrender value).

(b) £200 (the amount of premiums paid).

(c) £10,000.

(d) £100 (the amount of premiums, less the insurance company's expenses).

6 A simple deposit of a life policy with the intention to charge it as security will create a valid equitable mortgage:

(a) When the account to be secured and the beneficiary are different.

(b) When the beneficiary and the account holder are the same person and the borrowing limit is £20,000.

(c) As in (b) but for a loan of £14,000.

(d) A simple deposit with the required intention will always create a valid equitable mortgage.

7 You are offered a duplicate life policy as security. What is the bank's position if it subsequently turns out that the original has already been mortgaged elsewhere?

(a) The bank's mortgage will take priority if it has given notice to the insurance company.

(b) The bank's mortgage is invalid.

(c) The bank has a second mortgage and ranks after the mortgagee who holds the original policy.

8 As valuable security, which value concerns a bank when it has a mortgage over an endowment policy?

(a) Nominal value.

(b) Capital value.

(c) Surrender value.

9 The advantages of a life policy as security are that:

(a) It is easy to value.

(b) Its value is stable or increases with payment of premiums.

(c) Surrender is quick and easy with a legal mortgage.

(d) The procedure for taking the security is easy, quick and cheap.

10 Joe Green has given the Traviata Bank a legal assignment of an endowment policy on his own life as security for his overdraft. State what action the bank should take if:

(a) Joe is unable to comply with the bank's formal demand for repayment of his indebtedness.

(b) Joe dies.

Further reading

•	Milnes Holden, J	Chapters 11–15, *The Law and Practice of Banking*, Vol 1, 5th edition 1991, Pitman
•	Laidlaw, A and Roberts, G	Chapters 14 and 15, *Law Relating to Banking* Services, 2nd edition 1992, Bankers Books
•	Raby, P	Chapter 16 and 17, *Law Relating to Banking Services*, 2nd edition 1992, Pitman

Unit 15

Land as Security

Objectives

After studying this unit, you should be able to:

- **appreciate the difference between estates and interests in land;**
- **differentiate between unregistered and registered land;**
- **understand the significance of searches and registration and the implications of minor interests and overriding interests;**
- **appreciate the implications of the Law of Property (Miscellaneous Provisions) Act 1989;**
- **differentiate between the creation of legal and equitable mortgages;**
- **understand the significance of the clauses in a legal mortgage form;**
- **appreciate the implications of case law and statute for the matrimonial home;**
- **differentiate between a joint tenancy and a tenancy in common;**
- **understand the significance of leasehold, as opposed to freehold land;**
- **understand and evaluate the various remedies of a legal mortgagee;**
- **appreciate the legal position of second mortgagees.**

1 Introduction

1.1 In England and Wales, the primary sources of land law are:

- The Law of Property Act 1925 which applies to all property, not just land.
- The Land Charges Act 1972 which applies to unregistered land.
- The Land Registration Act 1925 which applies to registered land.

1.2 You must be able to apply the above statutes, along with relevant cases, to all aspects of land. In addition you must be able to distinguish between estates and interests in land, and must appreciate the significance of these terms to mortgagees of land.

1.3 Whilst the origins of land law date back at least to the Norman Conquest, modern land law stems from the Property Acts of 1925.

1.4 All references are to the Law of Property Act 1925 unless otherwise stated.

2 The nature of land – estates and interests

Estates in land

2.1 At law, title is to land itself, and any permanent structures or crops on the land are part of the land. An estate is commonly thought of as amounting to ownership of land, but this is not strictly true since all land in England and Wales belongs to the Crown.

2.2 Under s.l, only two legal estates in land can be created:

- Freehold;
- Leasehold.

Freehold

2.3 Freehold is formally the *fee simple absolute in possession*, and these words have the following meanings:

- *Fee*: the land can be inherited;
- *Simple*: the land can be inherited by the general heirs, i.e. those nearest in line, of the present owner, as opposed to, say, only male heirs;
- *Absolute*: the estate is owned unconditionally as opposed to being only a life interest, which will cease on death.
- *In possession*: the freeholder is in actual possession, or he has leased the property to a tenant. A freeholder who has leased the property is still said to be 'in possession' because he is entitled to receive rent.

2.4 Freehold in effect, means that the owner has absolute ownership of the land (despite the theoretical ownership by the Crown) and ownership will pass to his heirs unless he sells the land. The owner can do whatever he wishes with his land, subject only to planning legislation, bylaws, various restrictions at common law, e.g. the tort of nuisance, and restrictive covenants in the conveyance (the deed transferring title to the purchaser). The last of these restrictions are usually of a minor nature, for example a restriction on the height of any fence which may be erected. However, a covenant will be binding on any subsequent purchaser or mortgagee. (Restrictive covenants may be recorded at one of the land registers.)

Leasehold

2.5 A freeholder may from his own estate grant a lesser estate to another person. The freeholder is the lessor or landlord, the other person is the lessee. The freeholder holds a reversion, which means that the estate will revert to him at a set future date or on breach of any conditions by the leaseholder.

2.6 A leasehold estate is a *term of years absolute*. This means:

- *Term of years*: the leasehold estate lasts for a set time unless ended by forfeiture or breach;
- *Absolute*: the leasehold estate is owned unconditionally, i.e. it is not a life interest.

2.7 When a leasehold estate is granted, a formal agreement, known as a head lease or lease is created between the freeholder and leaseholder (lessee). The lessee has absolute rights over the property, subject to the same conditions as a freeholder *plus* the conditions of the lease. The lease will provide an expiry date, at which the estate will revert to the freeholder, and it will usually give details of the rental payable by the lessee.

2.8 Under the Leasehold Reform Act of 1967, a leaseholder has the right to compel the freeholder to sell him the freehold, or to extend the lease. However, this Act applies only to certain properties, usually ones of low value and only a very small proportion of leasehold properties come within this Act.

2.9 With freehold land a freeholder can sell his interest to another person and the deed transferring ownership is called a conveyance. A leaseholder can sell his leasehold estate, so long as the head lease does not prevent this. The document transferring the legal estate is an assignment. This transfers the rights of the original lessee to the subsequent purchaser.

Interest in land

2.10 A legal interest is a right over land not amounting to an estate. A common form of legal interest is an easement which can take the form of a right of way, say, to walk across land belonging to another. An interest in land can be thought of as a right against the land which does not amount to ownership, i.e. a right against the land of another rather than a right to the land itself.

2.11 From the perspective of lending bankers, the most important type of interest in land is a mortgage.

3 Unregistered land

Evidence of title

3.1 Evidence of title to unregistered land is a bundle of deeds and documents showing changes in ownership and other matters over the years. With leasehold land, the head lease is required, together with all documents transferring the title to the lessee.

3.2 On sale or mortgage of the property, the purchaser or mortgagee will usually insist that the deeds and documents must be examined by a solicitor to ensure that they are genuine and that a valid root (chain) of title dating back 15 years can be established. Under s.44, a purchaser of land has the right to have deeds produced to him or to his solicitor.

The Land Charges Department

3.3 The Land Charges Department (or Land Charges Register) is a register of the names of the proprietors of unregistered land. Holders of an interest in unregistered land who do not have possession of the deeds can register their interest at the LCD against the name of the proprietor.

3.4 The various classes of registration which may be made are:

- *Class A:* Land improvement or drainage charges.
- *Class B:* Statutory Charges which are imposed automatically.
- *Class C:*

(i) *Puisne mortgage* – a legal mortgage of unregistered land unsupported by a deposit of the deeds.

(ii) *Limited owner's charge* – an equitable charge which a tenant for life may have because he has paid off certain taxes or other liabilities in connection with the land.

(iii) *General equitable charge* – an equitable mortgage of unregistered land unsupported by a deposit of the deeds.

(iv) *Estate contract* – a contract for the sale of land by the present owner may be registered by the other party. Such registration will mean that any subsequent purchaser or mortgagee is subject to this contract.

- *Class D:*

  (i) A *charge in favour of the Inland Revenue* securing inheritance tax.

  (ii) Any *restrictive covenants.*

  (iii) Any *equitable covenants*, e.g. rights of way. (Legal easements which are perpetual and are included in the wording of the deeds are not registrable.)

- *Class E:* Certain annuities, few exist.
- *Class F:* Spouse's right of occupation under the Matrimonial Homes Act 1983.

3.5 Other registers which will be covered by a search at the LCD are:

- *Register of Pending Actions.* This register records actions pending in a court relating to any interest in land, for example a bankruptcy petition against the owner. Failure to register such actions will render them void against subsequent purchasers for value. In *Whittingham v Whittingham – National Westminster Bank Intervening* (1978) a wife sought a court order to transfer the property into her name from that of her husband. The bank took a mortgage from the husband whilst the action was pending. It was held that the bank's mortgage took priority over the wife's action since the action had not been recorded in the register of pending actions.
- *Register of Annuities.* Only annuities created before 1926 can be registered, hence such entries are now rare.
- *Register of Writs and Orders.* This records orders of the court, such as bankruptcy orders against the owner of the land.
- *Register of Deeds of Arrangement.* Such entries are likely to be rare.

Significance of registration

3.6 Under s.97 the general rule is that priority of mortgages over unregistered land is determined by whichever comes first, either possession of the title deeds with no notice of other interest at the time or the date of registration by a mortgagee who does not have the deeds at the Land Charges Department.

3.7 A mortgagee who has possession of the deeds cannot register his mortgage, and if he has a clear search at the LCD dated on or after the date of his mortgage, he will retain priority so long as he retains possession of the deeds.

3.8 As regards subsequent mortgagees, priority is determined by the date of registration. Registration of the mortgage does not amount to notice to an earlier mortgagee, and an earlier mortgagee who has the deeds or one who does not have them but has registered will continue to have priority. The only way in which the subsequent mortgagee can fix the monetary priority of an earlier mortgagee is to give direct notice to the earlier mortgagee. Such direct notice will fix the priority of the earlier mortgagee to monies already lent, unless he is under an obligation to make further advances (known as tacking): s.94.

3.9 An unregistered charge which is registrable is void against purchasers for value, e.g. other mortgagees or a trustee in bankruptcy: Land Charges Act 1972.

Student Activity 1

1 A bank has an equitable mortgage dated 1 October 1995 and holds the deeds. A finance company has a puisne mortgage over the same property dated 15 September 1996 and registered on 20 September 1996. Direct notice to the bank has not been given. Which mortgage has priority?

2 The position is the same as in 1, but the finance company gave notice to the bank which was received by the bank on 20 September 1996. How will the position differ from 1, and what action will the bank take on 20 September 1996?

3 A finance company took a legal mortgage dated 10 January 1996, but did not register, despite not having the deeds. A bank took an equitable mortgage dated 10 October 1996 and took possession of the deeds. Which mortgage takes priority?

4 What constitutes evidence of ownership of unregistered land? *(Paragraph 3.1)*

5 What is the purpose of the Land Charges Department? *(Paragraph 3.2)*

4 Registered land

4.1 Registered land, or more correctly registered title to land, is where proof of title by inspection of deeds has been replaced with a title investigated and guaranteed by the state and registered in one of number of district land registries (DLR). Registered title is governed by the Land Registration Act 1925 and its subsequent amendments.

4.2 All changes of ownership or legal interests, e.g. mortgages, are recorded at the DLR. Evidence of title is a land certificate, proof of title is the register. The details on the land certificate can be brought up to date by sending it to the DLR who will certify that the details on the certificate agree with those on the register. The DLR deals *only with registered land.*

4.3 Eventually all land in the UK will be registered, at present most land is in 'compulsory registration' areas where the title to land must be changed to registered if the property changes hands. The detail of compulsory registration are outside the scope of this syllabus.

Advantages of registered land

4.4 These are that:

- Title is state guaranteed. Anyone who suffers through an incorrect entry made on the register by the DLR will receive government compensation.

- There is no need for a solicitor to investigate the title when a charge is taken as there is with unregistered land. The certificate can be sent to the DLR for writing up to date. The DLR will date stamp the certificate to show the latest date of comparison with their records.
- Legal fees are generally lower on sales of registered land.
- With unregistered land, title is evidenced by a large bundle of deeds. Every time the property is sold, another document is added to the bundle. With registered land, a single land certificate (with a head lease if leasehold land) is all that is required as evidence of title. Changes are simply noted on the land certificate by the DLR.

Details appearing on a land certificate

Property register

4.5 This gives the title number, together with a short description of the land, and states whether it is freehold or leasehold. The appropriate reference number relating to the land registry map is quoted.

Proprietorship register

4.6 This gives the class of title, and the name and address of the owner.

There are four types of title:

- *Absolute:* this is state guaranteed title of ownership and can apply to freehold and leasehold land. With absolute title the only document required is the land certificate.
- *Good Leasehold:* this guarantees the leaseholder's title to leasehold land, but does not guarantee the freeholder's right to create the lease. Nevertheless good leasehold title is perfectly acceptable for leasehold land. The land certificate and head lease are required as evidence of title, and nowadays the head lease is often combined with the land certificate in a single document.
- *Possessory:* this indicates that the DLR is not completely satisfied that the owner's title is valid. Title is guaranteed in respect of dealings after registration of the land, but no guarantee is given concerning title prior to registration. A prospective purchaser or mortgagee would obtain a solicitor's report as if the land were unregistered. Provision is made for the DLR to convert possessory title into absolute title or good leasehold title, after a lapse of 15 years and 10 years respectively, provided the registrar is satisfied that a proprietor is in possession.
- *Qualified:* this is very rare and indicates reservations on the part of the DLR as to the title of the owner. A bank would not normally be prepared to accept a mortgage over land with a qualified title.

Charges register

4.7 A note of all mortgages or other interests in the land appears here.

4.8 *Note:* the land certificate can be sent to the DLR at any time to be written up to date. All charges which appear in the register of the DLR will be inserted on the land certificate (as would any changes of ownership on the proprietorship register).

Searches at the district land registry

4.9 One method of searching is to send the land certificate to the appropriate DLR to be written up to date.

4.10 An alternative method is to request an official search by submitting a Form 94A. If an official search is made by a mortgagee, he has a 30-working-day period of priority in which he can register his mortgage. The 30 days run from the date of the official search.

Minor interests in registered land

4.11 Minor interests over registered land are any interests which are not:

- Registered within two months as legal titles or as legal charges;
- Protected by entry on the register within two months; and which
- Are not overriding interests (see below).

4.12 Minor interests are equitable and a subsequent purchaser (a purchase includes a mortgagee) acquires the land free from any minor interests, unless they are protected by entry on the register: Land Registration Act 1925.

4.13 Examples of minor interests are:

- Inhibitions (court orders forbidding dealings in land);
- Charges originally effected by way of legal mortgage, but not registered within the statutory two months.

Overriding interests

4.14 Under the Land Registration Act 1925 an overriding interest is one which is binding on a subsequent purchaser, even if that interest is not protected by entry on the register.

4.15 The most important overriding interest is found in s.70, Land Registration Act 1925 as:

> The rights of every person in actual occupation of the land or in receipt of rents and profits thereof, save where enquiry is made of such a person and the rights are not disclosed.

4.16 Thus a person in actual occupation of the property is protected, even though that interest is not entered on the register.

4.17 From a bank's perspective, a legal mortgagee:

- Will have priority over minor interests which are not recorded on the register;
- May not have priority over any earlier overriding interest.

5 Law of Property (Miscellaneous Provisions) Act 1989

5.1 Section 2 provides that a contract for the sale or other disposition of an interest in land can only be made in writing and by incorporating all the terms which the parties have agreed in one document or, where contracts are exchanged (as in a sale of land), in each. In addition, the contract must be signed by each party and not just the party charging the property. The consequences are that:

- Equitable mortgages by way of simple deposit of land certificate or of deeds are no longer valid. A signed memorandum of deposit should be taken in all cases, and this memorandum must be signed by both the customer and an official of the bank.
- The bank should sign both copies of facility letters relating to borrowing which is secured on land, and so should the borrower.

5.2 Section 1 provides that an individual may execute a document as a deed without it being under seal, provided that document is described as a deed.

6 Methods of creating a legal mortgage

6.1 Under the Law of Property Act 1925 there are two methods of creating a legal mortgage.

- By a charge expressed to be by way of legal mortgage. This can be used for both freeholds and leaseholds.
- By a lease in favour of the lender for a term of years.

6.2 These methods apply to both registered and unregistered land.

7 Methods of creating an equitable mortgage

Equitable charge by deed

7.1 This will normally contain an irrevocable power of attorney clause agreeing to convey the legal estate if the mortgagor defaults. Its practical effect is similar to that of a legal mortgage. This form of mortgage applies to unregistered land because all mortgages of registered land must be registered at the appropriate DLR.

7.2 Alternatively, there may be a declaration of trust under which the mortgagor declares that he holds the property in trust for the bank and authorises his own removal and the appointment of a new trustee as directed by the bank.

Equitable charge in writing

7.3 This will contain a promise to create a legal mortgage in the case of default, but a court order will be required to enforce this promise.

A memorandum attesting to the mortgagor's intention

7.4 This can be completely informal, providing it attests to the mortgagor's intention that the land is to be considered as security for the advance. As with all contracts relating to land, including the methods noted above, this memorandum must be signed by both the bank and the mortgagor. Again a court order will be required before the mortgagee can enforce his remedies.

Lodging of notice of deposit with registered land

7.5 Before April 1995, it was possible to lodge a notice of deposit, or a notice of intended deposit with the DLR. The effect of this was to retain priority of an equitable mortgage of registered land provided the equitable mortgage was converted into a legal mortgage within 30 days of notice to the mortgagor by the DLR of the creation of any subsequent mortgage. It is no longer possible to lodge such notices with the DLR, although any notices lodged prior to that date will be retained as cautions on the register.

7.6 In practice, even before this rule change, banks would rarely take equitable mortgages of registered land, but insist on a legal mortgage.

8 Procedure for taking a legal mortgage

Table 15.1

Unregistered		*Registered*	
1	Value the land.	1	Value the land.
2	Obtain the deeds.	2	Obtain the land certificate if title is absolute, and land certificate and head lease if good leasehold title. Search at DLR.
3	Have the bank's mortgage form signed by the owner.	3	Have the bank's mortgage form signed by the owner.
4	Obtain solicitor's report on title.	4	Send land certificate to DLR with mortgage form and fees, within 30 days of the date of the official search.
5	Search at the LCD to see if there are any other mortgages.	5	The DLR will retain the original land certificate and send the bank a charge certificate showing the bank as mortgagee.
6	Search at the local land charges register of the local authority to ensure there is no detrimental town planning for the area.	6	As for unregistered land.
7	Ensure the property is insured and retain the insurance policy.	7	As for unregistered land.

*Note: special forma*lities regarding land as security for borrowing within the Consumer Credit Act 1974 are covered in Unit 19 and the special formalities for land owned by limited companies are covered in Unit 17.

9 Clauses in a bank's form of legal mortgage

9.1 The form will contain the standard clauses covering:

- **A** ll monies.

- **C** ontinuing security.
- **R** epayment on demand.
- **A** dditional security.
- **C** onclusive evidence.
- **S** uccession.

9.2 Additional clauses which are specially relevant to land are:

- Power of sale.
- Appointment of a receiver.
- Cesser on redemption.
- Insurance and repair.
- Agreement not to create or surrender leases.
- Consolidation clause.
- Consent to further charges.
- Right to break the account on notice of a second charge.

Power of sale

9.3 The standard power of sale clause excludes s.103. This means that the bank can commence sale proceedings as soon as the time stated in the mortgage form (usually seven days to one month) has elapsed from the making of demand.

9.4 However, if residential property continues to be occupied by the mortgagor, the bank will need to apply to the court for a possession order, and then if the occupants will not peacefully move out, the bank must make a second application for power to evict.

9.5 Under s.103, a receiver can be appointed upon precisely the same events as apply to the power of sale. However, bank mortgages again exclude s.103, and a receiver can be appointed after a specified period.

9.6 A receiver can sell the property, lease it, or collect rents or manage the property in any way he thinks fit.

9.7 The receiver is normally appointed when the property is let and not easily saleable. The receiver will collect the rents from the tenants and after deducting his costs will apply the residue in reduction of bank borrowing.

9.8 The bank's mortgage states that the receiver is an agent of the mortgagor, who in law is thus responsible for the defaults of the receiver. However, if the bank were to appoint someone totally unsuitable as a receiver, or if the bank were to interfere in any way which reduced the sale value or net rental income, then the bank might be held liable for the receiver's actions.

Cesser on redemption

9.9 The bank will undertake to vacate the mortgage on request by the borrower, provided all monies have been repaid. All costs will be borne by the mortgagor.

Insurance and repair

9.10 The mortgagor will undertake to keep the property in good repair and to insure against all normal risks of damage. The clause will give the bank the right to arrange and pay for insurance if the mortgagor does not. All such costs will be at the mortgagor's expense. The 'insurance clause' will usually stipulate that any monies received from claims shall be used to reduce the bank debt.

Agreement not to create or surrender leases

9.11 Under s.99 a mortgagor has the power to grant agricultural or occupational leases or building leases, subject to certain conditions. Such leases, if created after the bank's mortgage, could greatly diminish the value of the property as security. Banks therefore include a clause which states that the mortgagor cannot grant any leases without the bank's written consent.

9.12 Apart from where the land in question is agricultural land, this clause will be valid as regards all leases or tenancies created on or after the date of the bank's mortgage. Under the Agricultural Holdings Act 1948 the statutory power of a mortgagor in possession to grant a lease over agricultural land cannot be excluded by any clause in the mortgage form.

Consolidation clause

9.13 Section 93 allows a mortgagor when redeeming one mortgage to do so without repayment of any sums due under a separate mortgage granted by him.

9.14 This right is removed by an appropriate mortgage clause so the mortgagor must repay all monies before he can redeem any mortgages. (Some would argue that the standard all monies clause in itself would overcome any right of consolidation.)

Consent to further charges

9.15 The bank's consent is required before the mortgagor can create a subsequent mortgage in favour of another lender. This clause may not be enforceable against innocent second mortgagees, since the mortgage is a form of contract between the bank and the mortgagor. However, the clause will encourage the mortgagor, and further mortgagees, if they are aware of it, to keep the bank informed. Under the Land Registration Act 1925, in the case of registered land, if the bank wished it could record a caution at the DLR. The DLR would notify the bank of any attempt to register a subsequent mortgage, and the bank could apply for an injunction.

Right to break the account on notice of a second charge

9.16 When a bank is lending against a mortgage of land, it may receive notice of a second charge. Although the amount advanced by the second mortgagee will rank behind the amount owing to the bank on the date of notice, any money lent by the bank *after* notice of the second mortgage will lose priority to the amount advanced by the second mortgagee, assuming tacking does not apply, and the bank would be adversely affected by the *Rule in Clayton's case* (1816). The bank will therefore break the account.

9.17 To afford further protection, some banks also include a *Westminster Bank v Cond* clause which protects the bank's priority if it fails to break the account.

9.18 *Note: if the* bank is *committed to a further advance* on the date it receives notice, that further advance will retain its priority.

Student Activity 2

Obtain one of your bank's mortgage forms covering land. Highlight the clauses which represent the eight shown above, plus the other ACRACS clauses.

10 The matrimonial home

The Matrimonial Homes Act 1983

10.1 This Act gives a spouse who has been deserted the right of continued occupation for as long as the marriage lasts. This is an equitable interest which must be protected by filing a Class F charge at the Land Charges Department (unregistered land) or by lodging a notice at the District Land Registry (registered land).

10.2 Such an entry gives the spouse the right to occupy the property regardless of the wishes of the other spouse, and it gives an equitable right of occupation against any mortgagee whose mortgage has been created subsequent to the Matrimonial Homes Act entry. New mortgagees will be aware of the entry when they complete their standard searches at the Land Charges Department or at the DLR and they will normally then seek alternative security or insist that the spouse's right is postponed to the mortgage.

10.3 If the deserted spouse gives the bank notice of a matrimonial homes charge, the bank will treat this in the same way as notice of a second mortgage. In other words any existing bank borrowing will take priority, but any subsequent borrowing will rank behind the charge. If the borrowing is on overdraft, the account will be broken to avoid the rule in *Clayton's case*. Failure to break the account may, however, be covered by the *Westminster Bank v Cond* clause.

Williams and Glyn's Bank Ltd v Boland (1980)

10.4 The facts of the *Boland case* were that:

- The land certificate showed one person, the husband, as registered proprietor of a house.
- The bank took a mortgage over the house as security for the liability of the husband, in particular for his liability as guarantor.
- At the date of execution of the mortgage, the wife was living in the house.
- Only the husband signed the mortgage form.
- The wife had not registered a charge under the Matrimonial Homes Act 1983.

10.5 The bank subsequently sought a possession order, but the court refused because the wife had contributed money or money's worth to the original purchase of the house and therefore had an equitable interest in it. It was held that the husband owned the house in trust for himself and his wife and further that the wife's interest was an overriding interest within the terms of the Land Registration Act 1925, because she was in actual occupation at the time the mortgage was taken.

10.6 Since *Boland*, banks have always asked any occupants of property over the age of 18 to sign a consent form to the mortgage if their name did not appear on the deeds or land certificate. An independent solicitor would normally advise the occupants immediately prior to signature to avoid the danger of undue influence.

10.7 Note the following points:

- A mortgagee is only affected if the third party:
  - has contributed money or money's worth to the purchase price (and therefore acquired an equitable interest; *and*
  - was in occupation at the time the mortgage was executed – in other words, third parties who move in after the execution of the mortgage cannot claim priority over the bank.
- *Midland Bank v Dobson* (1985): household or domestic duties do not count as money's worth.
- In *Midland Bank Ltd v Farmpride Hatcheries and Willey* (1980) the managing director negotiated a mortgage over his company's land as direct security for company borrowing. The director occupied a house on the land, but did not advise the bank and the bank was unaware of this. Subsequently the director claimed *Boland-type* rights of occupation, but the court held that he was estopped from such a claim because he failed to disclose his rights to the bank.

  However, if the property had been occupied by another employee who was not involved in the mortgage negotiations, then that employee would have had *Boland-type* rights of occupation.
- *Boland-type* interests are overriding interests because they are equitable interests which can take priority over subsequent legal interests, despite not being registered. An overriding interest can only apply to registered land but, in practice, banks assume that the *Boland principle* applies equally to unregistered land. The court heard comments from the judge such as:

  > If a bank is to do its duty, in the society in which we live, it should recognise the integrity of the matrimonial home. It should not destroy it by disregarding the wife's interest in it.... Monied might must, in this Court, give way to social justice.

  Thus in practice banks obtain consent forms, where applicable, irrespective of whether the land is registered or unregistered.

City of London Building Society v Flegg (1986)

10.8 Where the property vests in joint proprietors, and not in a single proprietor as in *Boland*, and a third person who contributed to the purchase price was in occupation at the time of the mortgage, the mortgagee can exercise his rights even in the absence of a 'consent form'. *Flegg* held that two or more trustees can give a valid discharge over the rights of the beneficiary, whereas a sole trustee cannot. Table 15.2 summarises the position.

Table 15.2

Names in which property is vested	*Name of borrower's account*	*Signatories to mortgage/ consent form*	*Person in occupation when mortgage executed*	*Has the occupier contributed money to purchase price?*	*Mortgagee's position*
A	A	A	A & B	Yes	A holds the property in trust for A & B. Possession order will not be granted. (Boland applies.)
A & B	A & B	A & B	A ,B, C	Yes	A & B are joint trustees and joint trustees can overreach the interests of a beneficiary. Possession order will be granted. (Flegg applies.)
A	A & B	A	A & B	Yes	Possession order will be granted because the bank has lent money to the owner and occupier jointly.

Note: the word 'vests' is simply a legal term meaning that the name appears on the deeds or land certificate as owner.

Lloyds Bank v Rossett (1990)

10.9 The facts were that:

- Mr Rossett borrowed £15,000 on overdraft to meet renovation costs of a house for which he had exchanged contracts to purchase.
- Mr Rossett told the branch manager that the property was to be acquired in his sole name.
- Mr Rossett signed the bank's mortgage on 17 December 1982 and the bank registered the mortgage at the District Land Registry on 7 February 1983.
- Mrs Rossett knew nothing of the mortgage or of the overdraft.
- Mrs Rossett did not make any financial contribution to the purchase price.
- Mrs Rossett was not living in the house at the date of the bank's mortgage, but she was engaged almost daily in decorating work on the property whilst the builders were completing renovations.
- The bank sought a possession order in 1984, but Mrs Rossett claimed an overriding interest which, she said, took priority over the bank's mortgage. Mr and Mrs Rossett had parted by this date.

10.10 The court held that:

- A wife cannot have an overriding interest against the bank, unless she can show that prior to purchase her husband agreed that the property should be jointly owned, or that by her conduct she contributed to its acquisition, indicating a common intention that the husband should hold the property for their joint benefit.

- Decorating work does not class as a monetary contribution to the acquisition of the property. (An initial lump sum towards the purchase price or mortgage instalments would have been sufficient to create a constructive trust in favour of the wife.)
- 'Actual occupation' must exist at the date the bank's mortgage is completed, as opposed to the date of registration at the DLR.

Abbey National Building Society v Cann (1990)

10.11 In this case the main point which was decided was:

- The mere fact that the belongings of the person claiming an overriding interest were on the premises at the time the mortgage was signed does not mean that that person can be classed as being 'in actual occupation'. In this case the belongings were on the premises in preparation for subsequent occupation, and the person claiming overriding interest was abroad at the time the mortgage was completed. Thus, the overriding interest claim failed.

11 Co-ownership of land

Joint tenancy

11.1 Title to land can be held by one person alone, or it can be held jointly. Under the LPA 1925, where there are two or more owners, their legal title will be joint but no more than four persons can be shown as holders of a joint legal estate in land.

11.2 When one of two joint tenants dies, the title will then vest in the survivor alone. If the property is already mortgaged, all that is required is that a copy of the death certificate be held with the title documents. There is no need to recharge the security. Likewise if the survivor subsequently wishes to sell, the only formality required as regards passing on the title of the deceased is the production of a copy death certificate.

11.3 Under the Law of Property (Miscellaneous Provisions) Act 1989, all joint owners (as well as the bank) must sign the mortgage form.

Tenants in common

11.4 Tenants in common have an *equitable interest only* in land. Each tenant owns a share of the land, not the whole of the estate jointly as with joint tenancy. These shares need not be equal.

11.5 There is no right of survivorship for tenants in common. Thus, where one of these tenants dies his share will be dealt with by the executors, if there is a will, or by the administrators if no will exists. Either way, the share of a deceased tenant in common will pass to the heirs of the deceased.

11.6 With a tenancy in common, an individual tenant can mortgage his equitable tenancy in common, and this will result in severance of the joint tenancy.

Any such mortgage would be equitable as the tenant in common has only an equitable title. A court could order the sale of the property if requested to do so by the bank, which would then receive that tenant's share of the sale proceeds.

11.7 However, in the case of registered land, the other tenant in common will have an overriding interest under the *Boland* doctrine if he is in actual occupation. Hence, the court would not order a sale. Thus, with tenants in common, the bank would only wish to proceed if all the tenants were prepared to mortgage the land.

12 Problems for mortgages of leaseholds

12.1 The head lease may prohibit assignments (transfers of lease) or mortgages of the lease. *Solution:* check the head lease; usually the relevant clause simply requires the prior permission of the freeholder or notice of mortgage to the freeholder. If so, the mortgagee can simply comply with the instructions. Under the LPA, the consent of the freeholder to the granting of a mortgage by the leaseholder cannot be unreasonably withheld.

12.2 The head lease may say that the freeholder can forfeit the lease if the ground rents are not paid to date, or if other covenants of the lease are broken by the lessee. *Solution*:

- Diarise to ensure ground rents are paid. If the lessee does not pay, the bank's mortgage will give authority for the bank to pay and debit the lessee's (mortgagor's) account.
- Ask the freeholder to confirm in writing that he will not commence forfeiture proceedings without first notifying the bank.

12.3 If the mortgaged leasehold property is a flat, then there are problems if the bank wishes to exercise its power of sale. *Solution:* check that the lease is drawn in such a way that the bank can enforce its power of sale under the LPA. If the lease is not drawn up in such a way, then the bank would not proceed with the security.

12.4 The lease may call for fire insurance premiums to be paid by the leaseholder, and may specify the insurance company. *Solution:* ensure the terms of the head lease are followed.

12.5 The value of the lease will decline as the expiry date approaches. *Solution:* do not lend more than the likely valuation at the perceived maturity date of the borrowing.

12.6 Short leases, with an original term of under 21 years, usually contain a clause which makes them lapse upon the insolvency of the lessee. There is little that can be done here, and such leases have little monetary value as security. *Note:* the Leasehold Reform Act is an advantage to mortgagees of leasehold property, since it gives leaseholders the right to purchase the freehold. If this right is exercised, the bank's mortgage will continue even after expiry of the original lease. However, the Leasehold Reform Act only applies to a small percentage of domestic leasehold properties.

13 Remedies of a mortgagees

13.1 The remedies available to a mortgagee on default by the mortgagor are contained in the LPA 1925 as amended by the mortgage form.

- *Sell the property*: this will apply if the property is occupied by the mortgagor.
- *Appoint a receiver*: this will normally apply where the property is not occupied by the mortgagor, but is let to tenants. The tenants will then pay the rent to the receiver, rather than to the landlord who is also, of course, the mortgagor.
- *Foreclosure*: the ownership of the property is transferred from the mortgagor to the mortgagee irrespective of the amount owing and the mortgagor loses his equity of redemption. A court order is required before the transfer can be carried out since it would be unfair to allow this if the debt was small in relation to the value of the property. In practice, forfeiture is never sought and would be unlikely to be granted since a sale achieves the same objectives.
- *Enter into possession*: the costs of entering into possession are to be met by the mortgagee. In addition, a court order is required if the mortgagor is in occupation; if he refuses to go an eviction order will be needed. A mortgagee in possession incurs various responsibilities and therefore this is an unlikely course of action.
- *Sue*: the bank has a right to sue on the debt independently of the security if it wishes.

13.2 If the equitable mortgage contains clauses such as the power to appoint a receiver, or power to enter into possession, a court order will be required prior to enforcement unless the mortgage was created by deed (see 7.1).

13.3 If the bank exercises its power of sale over unregistered land, and if there are surplus proceeds, i.e. the net sale proceeds exceed the amount due from the borrower, then the bank must search at the Land Charges Department before placing the surplus proceeds at the disposal of the mortgagor. There may be subsequent mortgages recorded (Class C(i) or Class C(iii)) which have not been notified to the bank. If any such mortgages are shown, the surplus proceeds must be placed at the disposal of such mortgagees.

13.4 Failure to search at the LCD is no excuse, and the bank would be liable to reimburse such mortgagees up to the amount of the surplus proceeds if the money had been paid over to the mortgagor direct by the bank. The fact that the subsequent mortgagee had not informed the bank of the mortgage is irrelevant.

13.5 In the case of registered land, a surplus proceeds search is unnecessary. The bank will have been advised by the District Land Registry of any subsequent entries, so long as the bank's mortgage is expressed to cover 'all monies'. In any case, the solicitor of the purchaser will have had the land certificate written up to date, and will be aware of all mortgages recorded at the DLR.

13.6 In *Swing Castle Ltd v Gibson* (1990) it was held that a surveyor who negligently values a house for mortgage purposes so that its forced sale value is less than the amount lent, is liable in damages for the mortgagee's entire loss, including unpaid interest at the default rate specified in the mortgage agreement.

13.7 In *Banque Bruxelles Lambert SA v Eagle Star Insurance Co et al* (1995), the implications of the general property market slump and negligent valuation were examined. It was agreed from the facts that the valuation figure had been negligently exaggerated, but the question of the amount of compensation to award was complicated by the property market slump. The amount lost by the mortgagee on realisation of the property had been the amount of the negligent over-valuation plus the loss attributable to the general market fall in prices. The court decided that the important factor in deciding the amount of compensation, i.e. should the general fall in market prices be included or not, was whether the 'no transaction' test or the 'successful transaction' test applied.

13.8 For the 'no transaction test' to apply, the lender would not have given any loan at all had he received a proper valuation, whereas for the 'successful transaction' test the transaction, i.e. the loan, would have proceeded, albeit on different terms had a proper valuation been given.

13.9 Where the 'no transaction' test applied, then the lender could claim the full amount of the loss, that is the difference between the negligent valuation and a proper valuation plus the amount lost because of the fall in the market. This can be seen as fair, since any rise in market values would have reduced the claim of the lender in a 'no transaction' situation.

13.10 The court also confirmed that the duty of a valuer was:to take reasonable care to give a reliable and informed opinion on the open market value of the land in question at the date of valuation.

13.11 This is an important decision, but care must be taken as every case will turn on its facts. In subsequent cases, the position when the 'successful completion' test applies will no doubt be considered in regard to the amount of compensation to a lender.

13.12 Notes:

- Remember the word SAFES (sell; appoint a receiver; foreclosure; enter into possession; sue).
- Sale of property is the normal remedy if the property is owner occupied, and appointing a receiver is used if the property is rented to tenants.

  Foreclosure requires a court order and would involve adverse publicity, and entering into possession involves the bank in unnecessary expense and legal responsibilities.
- In *Standard Chartered Bank v Walker & Walker* (1982) it was held that on realisation of security the bank must act reasonably and obtain a fair price. In practice the bank will comply with these conditions if it employs a reputable estate agent and does not interfere with his work.

  Before the bank sells or appoints a receiver, it must make formal demand for repayment from the customer.
- In *China and South Sea Bank v Tan Soon Gin* (1990) it was held that the tim-

ing of any realisation of security was entirely a matter for the bank. The court said that no bank could carry on the business of lending if it could become liable to a mortgagor or surety for a decline in the value of mortgaged property unless the bank was responsible for that decline. This judgement is applicable to a mortgage over any type of asset, and it is not just confined to land.

- In *Palk v Mortgage Services Funding plc* (1992) it was held that a court had the power to order the sale of a mortgagor's property, even though the mortgagee had refused consent because the sale would have realised insufficient funds to pay off the money advanced. The lender had wanted to obtain a possession order and would then have waited in the hope that the property market would improve. The Court insisted on sale because the rented income would have been below the interest on the mortgage.
- In *Target Home Loans Ltd v Clothier* (1992), following the default of the Clothiers in meeting monthly mortgage repayments on a loan for the purchase of a property, Target Home Loans Ltd applied to the court for a possession order over the mortgaged property. The court held that the possession order should be deferred for three months in order to allow the Clothiers the opportunity to try to sell the property. The court's view was that an occupied house is more attractive to a potential buyer than a repossessed property. This postponement of repossession was granted in accordance with s.36, Administration of Justice Act 1970. If at the end of the three-month period no sale had been agreed which would discharge the whole debt then Target could take immediate possession of the house.
- In *Parker-Tweedale v Dunbar Bank plc and Others* (1989) it was held that a bank does not have any duty towards a beneficiary of a trust on realisation of security when the mortgagor is a trustee.

14 Second mortgages of land

14.1 A second (or subsequent) mortgage arises when a mortgagor has mortgaged his property and then wishes to borrow additional money from another lender. The second lender can then take a 'second mortgage' over the property.

14.2 Provided the property is worth enough to cover both mortgages there should be no problems. If the property has to be sold the first mortgagee will have a first claim on the net sale proceeds to cover the amount owed to him as at the date of notice of the second mortgage. The surplus proceeds (equity) will be available to the second mortgagee towards repayment of the borrowing.

Procedure for taking a legal second mortgage

See Table 15.3.

Table 15.3

Unregistered	*Registered*
1 Search at LCD to ensure no mortgage there and obtain owner's authority to first mortgagee, disclose information to the bank.	1 Ask for owner's authority for first mortgagee to disclose.
2 Send the bank's standard questionnaire to the first mortgagee.	2 Send the standard questionnaire to the first mortgagee and search at DLR.
3 The first mortgagee will advise how much he is owed and whether his mortgage compels him to make any further advances to the mortgagor.	3 As for unregistered land.
4 The valuation of the second mortgage for securities purposes is manager's valuation of property less amount owing to first mortgagee.	4 As for unregistered land.
5 Have the bank's charge form signed by the owner and search at LCD. At the same time register at the LCD as a puisne mortgage (Class c(i)).	5 Have the bank's charge form signed by the owner.
6 Give notice to the first mortgagee and ask him to advise the amount owing on receipt of notice. Any money lent by the first mortgagee after receipt of notice will rank after the bank's mortgage, unless the first mortgagee is committed to making further advances.	6 As for unregistered land.
7 Check that the first mortgagee has made sure the property is insured.	7 As for unregistered land.
8 Make local searches with the local authority.	8 As for unregistered land.
9 Search at LCD to ensure bank's puisne mortgage is registered there.	9 The bank will send its charge form with fees and land registry forms to the DLR. The DLR will send a certificate of second charge.

Student Activity 3

What questions would you include in the standard questionnaire to a first mortgagee and why? Do not read further until you have completed this task.

Questionnaire

14.3 The bank's standard questionnaire addressed to the first mortgagee will ask the following questions:

- How much is owing and what are the repayment instalments?
- In whose name is the title vested?
- Is the first mortgagee under an obligation to make further advances (sometimes referred to as 'tacking')? (If so, such advances would take priority over the bank's second mortgage under s.94.)
- Has the power to redeem mortgages separately under s.103 been removed by the terms of the first mortgage?
- Has the first mortgagee any knowledge of any other mortgages over the property'?

Searches

14.4 With *registered land*, a search at the District Land Registry can be made on a standard form. On receipt of a search certificate, the bank has 30 days' protection from the date of the certificate. If there is only the first mortgage shown, nobody will be allowed to register a mortgage during the 30-day period and the bank's mortgage will take priority, if registered in this time, over any mortgage other than the one already registered.

14.5 With *unregistered land*, the bank would expect a clear search at the Land Charges Department if the first mortgagee has the deeds. Thus, if the bank registers a Class C(i) puisne mortgage and holds a clear search it should have priority over all mortgages other than the first mortgage. There is some doubt as to the position if another mortgagee registers in between the date of the bank's search and the date of registration by the bank. Some authorities think that the search at the LCD will give the bank 21 days' priority in which no other mortgage could be registered. Others are not sure of the exact position. Many banks therefore search again once their Class C(i) has been registered. Provided this search shows only the bank's mortgage, the bank will have priority apart from money due to the first mortgagee.

Valuation

14.6 The basic valuation for securities purposes is the value of the property less the amount owing to the first mortgagee. In practice, banks reduce this basic valuation for the purposes of their securities records, but a detailed knowledge of these considerations is outside this syllabus.

14.7 The first mortgagee will advise the bank of how much is owed at the date of receipt of notice. This is the amount, together with interest, for which the first mortgagee will take priority, unless tacking applies.

Summary

Now that you have studied this unit, you should be able to:

- **describe the various estates and interests in land;**
- **describe the difference between unregistered and registered land;**
- **understand the search and registration procedures and appreciate the practical difference between a minor interest and an overriding interest;**
- **understand the effect of the Law of Property (Miscellaneous Provisions) Act 1989;**
- **describe how legal and equitable mortgages are created;**
- **detail the procedure for taking a legal mortgage;**
- **identify and explain the clauses in bank's legal mortgage form and the importance of these clauses;**
- **understand the legal effect and problems of taking a charge over the matrimonial home, co-owned land and leasehold land;**
- **explain the remedies of a legal mortgagee;**
- **describe the process of taking a second mortgage by way of legal charge;**
- **understand the procedures regarding 'surplus proceeds' from the realisation of land.**

Self-assessment questions

1 Your customer's house is valued at £30,000 and there is an outstanding building society mortgage of £10,000. What is the security valuation of your second mortgage? (Assume the above figures are correct and do not adjust them in any way.)

(a) £30,000.

(b) £20,000.

(c) £10,000.

2 The bank has a mortgage over domestic property which is in the name of Mr X. Only Mr X signed the mortgage. Mrs X claims the mortgage is subject to her rights because of her domestic and household work. Which of the following applies?

(a) She is correct.

(b) She is incorrect.

Which case supports your answer?

3 Name the two legal estates which can be created in land.

4 Name the statute which states that a disposition of an interest in land must be made in writing, and must be signed by both parties.

5 What constitutes evidence of ownership of unregistered land?

6 For which type of land (unregistered/registered) is the Land Charges Department used?

7 What is the purpose of the Land Charges Department?

8 What constitutes evidence of ownership of registered land?

9 What document does the bank hold if it has a legal mortgage of registered land?

10 What is the purpose of 'local searches'? Does it matter whether the land is registered or unregistered?

Further reading

- Milnes Holden, J — Chapters 2–5, 10, *The Law and Practice of Banking*, Vol 1, 5th edition 1991, Pitman
- Laidlaw, A and Roberts, G — Chapter 13, *Law Relating to Banking* Services, 2nd edition 1992, Bankers Books
- Raby, P — Chapter 15, *Law Relating to Banking Services*, 2nd edition 1992, Pitman

Unit 16

Guarantees

Objectives

After studying this unit, you should be able to:

- **define a guarantee and explain the difference between a guarantee and an indemnity;**
- **understand the position regarding contractual capacity of guarantors;**
- **understand the purpose of the clauses in bank guarantee forms;**
- **appreciate the effect and implications of undue influence, mistake or misrepresentation;**
- **understand the reasoning behind the way interviews with guarantors are conducted;**
- **appreciate the rights of a guarantor against the creditor, principal debtor, and co-guarantors;**
- **understand the principles which apply to the determination of guarantees;**
- **appreciate the consequences of mental incapacity, death or bankruptcy of guarantors;**
- **understand the consequences on notice of determination by a co-guarantor;**
- **appreciate the dangers in release of guarantees in a preference situation;**
- **understand the nature of various special types of guarantee;**
- **understand the nature of the duty of a bank to the surety.**

Note: before reading this unit reread your workbook on preferences (Unit 6), limited companies and ultra vires (Unit 7), and clauses in direct charge forms (Unit 13).

1 Guarantees: an introduction

Definition

1.1 A guarantee is a promise to answer, 'for the debt, default or miscarriage of another' if that person fails to meet their obligation: s.4, Statute of Frauds 1677.

Guarantees and indemnities

1.2 A guarantee is a contract between a guarantor and a lender (usually a bank) whereby the guarantor undertakes secondary liability for the debts of the principal debtor (usually the bank's customer). 'Secondary' liability means that the guarantor undertakes to pay only *if* the principal debtor defaults.

1.3 Under a pure guarantee, the guarantor is liable only if the principal debtor is liable. Thus, if the bank cannot enforce the debt against the customer, then it cannot claim from the guarantor. A guarantor says in effect, 'I will pay what your customer owes (up to a stated maximum), if the customer does not pay, but only if the customer is liable.?

Indemnities

1.4 An indemnity goes further than a guarantee. The person giving the indemnity promises to pay for the debts of someone else, even if the principal debtor is not liable at law. Thus, the indemnifier undertakes *primary* liability.

1.5 An indemnity need not be evidenced in writing but a guarantee must be: Statute of Frauds Act 1677.

Position of bank guarantees today

1.6 A bank guarantee is a combination of a guarantee and an indemnity. It is worded in the manner of a guarantee, in that the guarantor says he will be responsible (up to a stated maximum) for the debts of the customer, if the customer is liable and if he defaults. However, in addition, the standard bank guarantee contains an indemnity clause, a typical example of which reads:

> Where any monies or liabilities hereby agreed to be paid or discharged may not be recoverable from the guarantor on the footing of the guarantee, whether by reason of any legal limitation, disability or incapacity of the customer ... this guarantee shall nevertheless be valid and binding on the guarantor and such monies and liabilities shall be recoverable from the guarantor as principal debtor ...

1.7 There are various reasons why money owed by a principal debtor could not legally be enforced against him, for example money lent after notice of mental incapacity, but the two main reasons which used to be encountered in practice were where the principal debtor was a:

- Minor; or a
- Limited company and its borrowing was *ultra vires* its memorandum of association.

1.8 Since the Companies Act 1989, the *ultra vires* doctrine has become far less onerous for banks. However, the indemnity clause aims to protect a bank when the principal debtor has borrowed *ultra vires* on a 'just in case' basis.

1.9 As regards borrowing by minors, since 1987 the position has been that the indemnity clause is unnecessary. The Minors Contracts Act 1987 states that a guarantee cannot be avoided solely because the principal debtor is a minor.

Legal capacity of guarantors

1.10 The usual principles regarding contractual capacity apply. Guarantees given by minors are void: Minors Contracts Act 1987; and guarantees given by a guarantor who was mentally incapacitated at the time the guarantee was signed are also void: Mental Health Act 1983.

1.11 When the guarantor is domiciled outside England and Wales, the laws of the guarantor's own country will determine whether he has contractual capacity to act as guarantor. This applies even if the guarantee contains a clause stating that it is to be construed under English law. In such cases, the terms of the guarantee will indeed be governed by English law, but the law of the country of the guarantor will determine whether he has contractual capacity.

2 Clauses in the standard bank form of guarantee

2.1 Common law provides extensive protection of the rights of guarantors, and the aim of the clauses in the standard bank form of guarantee is to restrict that protection.

2.2 Note that the standard bank guarantee form does not apply where the borrowing of the principal debtor comes within the Consumer Credit Act 1974. Note also that the 'conclusive evidence' the 'successor' clauses described in Unit 13 also apply to guarantees.

Student Activity 1

Obtain a copy of your bank's standard guarantee form and compare the clauses in it with those discussed below.

Principal clauses

Consideration clause

2.3 A typical clause would read:

> In consideration of the Bank at the request of (the Guarantor) granting, or continuing time credit and or banking facilities and accommodation to (customer), the guarantor hereby agrees ...

2.4 As a guarantee is a contract between the bank and guarantor, there must be consideration if it is to be binding. Under the Mercantile Law Amendment Act 1856, the consideration need not be stated in the guarantee document, but it must exist, unless the guarantee is by deed, which is very rare.

2.5 Where the customer was not borrowing at the time the guarantee was signed, consideration automatically exists as regards any subsequent borrowing. Where the customer was already overdrawn, the fact that the bank has not called in the borrowing will count as consideration for the guarantee. In *Clegg v Bromley* (1913) the court reasoned that, by implication, the failure of the bank to exercise its right of demand regarding borrowing which existed at the time the security was executed was valid consideration.

Agreement to pay on demand

2.6 The words 'on demand' mean that the guarantor's liability does not commence until demand has been made on him: *Bradford Old Bank v Sutcliffe* (1918). Hence the statutory limitation period of six years for suing the guarantor (Limitation Act 1980) does not start to run against the bank until demand has been made on the guarantor.

All monies clause

2.7 The guarantor's liability is for all monies owing by the customer, sometimes subject to a monetary maximum. Thus, if the customer owed £40,000 to the bank and if the guarantee had stipulated a monetary maximum of £25,000, the position would be that:

- The most the bank could enforce against the guarantor would be £25,000.
- If the guarantor paid the £25,000 to the bank, he still could not claim from the customer, nor could he claim against the trustee in bankruptcy in the event of bankruptcy.

2.8 In addition, 'all monies' would normally include any monies owed by the principal debtor to the bank on any other account. For instance in *Bank of Scotland v Wright* (1991) the position could be summarised as follows:

- Principal debtor holding company X Ltd.
- Guarantor for liabilities of X Ltd: Mr Wright.
- X Ltd and its subsidiary Y Ltd had entered into a cross-guarantee arrangement whereby each company guaranteed the liabilities of the other to the bank.

2.9 It was held that Mr Wright's guarantee covered not only the money owing by X Ltd on its bank accounts, but also the guarantee liability of X Ltd in connection with the guarantee for the borrowing on Y Ltd's account.

2.10 In order to rely on this judgment, the bank must be able to demonstrate that it was the intention of all parties that the personal guarantee should cover all inter-group liabilities to the bank. In the *Bank of Scotland* situation this was clearly the case since Mr Wright was a director who had full knowledge of the group situation with regard to the bank.

Right of bank to use a suspense account for monies from guarantor

2.11 Any money received by the bank from the guarantor can be placed to a suspense account. (This clause was upheld by *Re Sass* (1896).) Hence, if the guarantor had paid £25,000 to the bank, and if the customer had become bankrupt, the bank would have credited the £25,000 to a suspense account and would have then been able to prove for the full £40,000 from the trustee.

2.12 The guarantor, on the other hand, could not claim at all for the £25,000, since this would amount to two proofs, or 'double proof' for the same debt.

Guarantor's right to claim in the bankruptcy or liquidation of the customer

2.13 The only way the guarantor could prove in bankruptcy or liquidation, or sue the customer in the absence of bankruptcy or liquidation, would be for him to pay off the whole debt, including interest and charges. Thus, referring back to the 'All monies' clause (above), if the guarantor paid off the full £40,000, the bank would simply credit the customer's account and close it off. Under the doctrine of subrogation, the guarantor would then, but only then, take over all the bank's rights against the customer, including any securities held.

Indemnity clause

2.14 This clause turns the document into an indemnity should the debt prove to be unenforceable. Bear in mind, for example, that clubs and associations (unless incorporated as companies) are not separate legal entities, and normally the bank would be unable to enforce repayment. Sometimes banks are happy to lend to such unincorporated bodies against a guarantee given by respectable, trustworthy and creditworthy members or officers.

Partnerships and changes in the partners

2.15 Guarantors will continue to be bound when the principal debtor is a partnership and there are changes in the partners. In the absence of such a clause, the change in the composition of the partnership would invalidate the guarantee.

Continuing guarantee

2.16 This is the standard continuing security clause which prevents the rule in *Clayton's case* from operating against the bank. The effect of the clause is that the guarantee will secure whatever is the ultimate debt when the bank enforces it. Sometimes a bank may use a specific guarantee form. This guarantee covers a particular transaction and does not contain a continuing security clause.

Variation of arrangement with principal debtor

2.17 At common law, any change in the conduct of relations with the customer (such as varying the agreed repayments or releasing some securities) would render the guarantee void. The above clause gives the bank discretion to vary its arrangements without invalidating the guarantee.

Termination of the guarantee

2.18 The guarantee will continue to be effective until three months after receipt of written notice of determination by the guarantor or by his personal representatives. Once the period of notice has expired, the guarantee will be valid, at common law, only for such borrowing which existed at the date of expiry of notice.

2.19 If the customer's borrowing was on overdraft, the bank should break the account on expiration of notice to prevent the rule in *Clayton's case* from reducing the amount which could be claimed. However, there is a clause which protects the bank if it fails to break the account. *Westminster v Cond* (1940) upheld the clause's efficacy.

Bank's right of set off

2.20 Some banks word their guarantees so that the guarantor maintains a credit balance at the bank in support of his liability. The guarantor undertakes not to withdraw from such accounts if the effect would be to reduce the balance below the amount agreed. The bank has the right to refuse to sanction any such withdrawals.

Restriction on guarantor as regards taking customer security

2.21 At law, the guarantor is entitled to take security from the principal debtor if the guarantor and debtor agree. However, this clause purports to prevent the guarantor from exercising this right. Usually it is so worded that any security taken in breach of the terms of the guarantee will be held in trust for the bank.

Joint guarantors

2.22 The guarantee form will be worded in such a way that when more than one guarantor has joined in the charge form their liability shall be joint and several. (Some banks have special 'joint and several' guarantee forms for use when two or more guarantors guarantee the same account.)

2.23 *Note:* Joint and several guarantees are not binding against any guarantor until all have signed: *National Provincial Bank of England v Brackenbury* (1906); nor against any guarantor if the signature of one guarantor is forged: *Graham James & Co (Timber) Ltd v Southgate-Sands* (1985).

Student Activity 2

Obtain a copy of the bank's standard guarantee form used in connection with borrowing which comes within the Consumer Credit 1974. Make a note of the major differences between the two forms of guarantee and retain the two documents until you come to study the CCA unit.

Practical application of the clauses

2.24 The following examples illustrate the practical value of one of the clauses in the bank's guarantee.

Guarantees and Clayton's Case

Your customer has a current account with an overdraft limit of £25,000 secured by his friend, G.

Three months ago the guarantor's notice of determination expired. Since that time the customer's account looks as follows:

Date	*Dr*	*Cr*	*Balance*
Three months ago	£	£	£
Balance forward	24,000		24,000 Dr
Notice of determination expired			
One month ago Credit		15,000	9,000 Dr
Two weeks ago Withdrawal	12,000		21,000 Dr

To what extent can the bank rely on the guarantee in the following circumstances?

(a) If the guarantee document had been in simple form without any clauses except for the one covering determination.

(b) If the guarantee had been the bank's standard form.

Answer

(a) Under *Clayton's case* the £21,000 balance consists of £12,000 debited after expiry of notice of determination and £9,000 from the £24,000 opening balance. Hence the guarantee is now valid for only £9,000.

(b) The standard bank guarantee contains a clause which protects the bank if it omits to break the account after expiry of notice of determination. The clause was upheld in *Westminster v Cond.* Hence the bank is protected and can claim the full £21,000 from the guarantor.

3 The effect of undue influence on guarantees

The basis of undue influence

3.1 The modern leading cases are the House of Lords decisions in:

- *National Westminster Bank Plc v Morgan* (1985); and
- *CIBC Mortgages Plc v Pitt* (1993); with
- *Barclays Bank Plc v O'Brien* (1993) giving clear judicial guidance on the procedure which should be adopted by a lender when the relationship between the borrower and the surety who are cohabitees raises the possibility of undue influence (or misrepresentation) being used by the borrower to obtain the surety's agreement to the charge.

3.2 In *National Westminster Bank Plc v Morgan* (1985) Mr and Mrs Morgan were joint owners of their home. They mortgaged it to the bank to secure the refinancing of a previous loan from a building society, on which they had fallen behind with the repayments when Mr Morgan's business got into difficulties. Mrs Morgan did not want the new mortgage to extend to advances for her husband's business activities and she was assured, wrongly but in good faith, by the bank manager that it did not. The lender sought possession of the house when the couple fell into arrears with the repayments. Mr Morgan died soon afterwards without any business debts to the lender and Mrs Morgan appealed against a possession order on the grounds that she had signed the legal charge because of undue influence from the bank manager.

3.3 The appeal was dismissed and the possession order upheld by the House of Lords. The mortgage Mrs Morgan had signed was not to her disadvantage because it had enabled her to remain in her home. Nor, indeed, had the bank exploited its position, on the facts no special relationship had arisen.

3.4 The legal principle of the case is that a contract will only be set aside for undue influence where:

- The weaker party was subject to the dominance of the stronger party; and
- They suffered a real and obvious disadvantage as a result.

3.5 In *CIBC Mortgages Plc v Pitt* (1993) Mrs Pitt was induced by the undue influence of her husband to agree to charge the matrimonial home as security for a loan made to the Pitts jointly. The loan was stated to be for the purchase of a holiday home but was actually used to buy shares. Mrs Pitt did not read any of the documents she signed and the CIBC's solicitor acted for all parties to the transaction. CIBC sought possession of the property when the Pitts could no longer make repayments.

3.6 Concerning the basis of undue influence, the House of Lords stated that:

- Where *actual* undue influence is proved (as in *Pitt* as opposed to *presumed* undue influence as in *Morgan*) there is no need to also establish that the transaction resulted in a real and obvious disadvantage to the weaker party.

3.7 Thus, where undue influence is *proved* to have been exercised, that is sufficient grounds for a court to set aside a contract, but where it is *presumed* to have been exercised, by virtue of the relationship between the parties, that alone is insufficient – the weaker party must *also* suffer a real and obvious disadvantage. (It is not clear, however, exactly what relationships will give rise to a presumption of undue influence.)

3.8 Note that in *Barclays Bank Plc v O'Brien* (1993) the House of Lords held that there was no need to introduce a 'special equity' to protect wives in relation to surety transactions (a wife 'guaranteeing' her husband's borrowing – as had been implied in the Court of Appeal), i.e. wives do not require special protection as wives provided the doctrine of notice is properly applied).

Third party involvement

Agency

3.9 In a rare case the dominance will be exercised by the lender directly (see *Bundy*) but more likely it is exercised by someone who is considered to be acting as agent for the lender, e.g. a debtor who persuades, say, a relative to stand surety for their proposed borrowing from the lender, or one joint owner of a house who persuades the other joint owner – typically a husband persuading his wife – to execute a mortgage deed over it.

3.10 In *Avon Finance Co Ltd v Bridger* (1985) Mr and Mrs B bought a retirement home partly with a mortgage and partly with money from their son. What they did not know was that their son had raised a loan from AV to help him provide his contribution. This loan was secured by a second charge on the property and the son persuaded his parents to execute the charge at the office of AV's solicitor by misleading his parents as to its nature and by exerting influence over them. The son later defaulted on the loan and AV sought possession of the house.

3.11 A possession order was refused because, on the facts, AV had used the son as its agent to obtain the Bs' signatures on the charge. Clearly, the Bs had also suffered a real disadvantage as a result of the transaction.

3.12 In contrast, in *Coldunell Ltd v Gallon* (1986) C advanced short-term business finance to the son of the Gs on security of a charge over their home executed by Mr G, the registered proprietor, and consented to by Mrs G. C's solicitor prepared the necessary documents and intended to post them to the Gs together with a letter advising them that they should obtain independent legal advice before signing. However, the son intercepted the letters at some stage, withheld the solicitor's advice from his parents and persuaded them to sign the charge and the consent respectively. The son defaulted on repayments and C sought a possession order against the Gs.

3.13 Although the Gs had clearly signed the documents under the influence of their son and had suffered a real disadvantage as a result, their son was equally clearly not acting as C's agent. The solicitor had not handed the letters to him and even if they had this in itself would not necessarily have constituted his appointment as their agent. The possession order was therefore granted.

3.14 In both Avon and Coldunell the parents had suffered a manifest disadvantage which, although relevant at the time, would not now, since *Pitt*, be of the essence.

Doctrine of notice

3.15 In *Barclays Bank Plc v O'Brien* (1993) the House of Lords held that if a wife is induced by the undue influence, misrepresentation or other legal wrong of her husband to stand surety for her husband's debt, the creditor would, in circumstances which should have put the creditor on enquiry, be fixed with constructive notice of the wife's right to set aside the transaction unless the creditor had warned the wife, at a meeting not attended by the husband, of the risks involved and had advised the wife to take independent legal advice.

3.16 The same principles apply to any situation where there is an *emotional relationship* between cohabitants.

3.17 In *O'Brien* the O'Briens executed a legal charge over their jointly owned matrimonial home as security for overdraft facilities extended by the bank to a company in which the husband, but not the wife, had an interest. The Bank prepared the security documents and sent them to a branch for execution with instructions to make sure that both husband and wife were fully aware of their nature and to advise them that, if in doubt, they should take independent legal advice before signing. The instructions were not carried out and Mrs O'Brien signed the legal charge without reading it, relying on her husband's false misrepresentation that it was limited to £60,000, it was in fact for £130,000, and would last only three weeks. The bank sought to enforce the charge after the company's overdraft exceeded £150,000 and Mrs O'Brien's defence was that she had been induced to execute the charge by the undue influence and misrepresentation of her husband.

3.18 On the facts, undue influence was not proved but because the bank should have had constructive notice of the risk of undue influence or misrepresentation in the situation, her husband had misrepresented the facts, and the bank had not given her proper advice, Mrs O'Brien was entitled to set aside the legal charge.

3.19 The House of Lords stated that a lender would be *put on enquiry* where a wife is offering to stand surety for her husband's debts if:

- The transaction is on its face not to the financial advantage of the wife; and

- There is a substantial risk that when the husband procured the wife to act as surety he may have committed a legal or equitable wrong (misrepresentation or undue influence) that would entitle the wife to set aside the transaction.

3.20 A lender who ignores the risk, and does not take steps to ensure that the wife is acting with full informed agreement and consent, will be deemed to have constructive notice of the wife's rights, as against her husband, to set aside the transaction on the basis of undue influence or misrepresentation. A lender must take *reasonable steps* to satisfy itself that the surety entered into the obligation freely and in the knowledge of the true facts.

3.21 In *O'Brien* the lender had been put on enquiry by the facts but in *Pitt* it had not. As far as the lender was concerned *Pitt* was a straightforward joint mortgage application and the lender had no idea that Mr Pitt intended to use the loan for anything other than the stated purpose. As such it could be distinguished from a surety situation which was not to the wife's benefit. Hence, in *Pitt* the charge was not set aside.

3.22 In *TSB Bank Plc v Camfield* (1994) the Court of Appeal held that a legal charge entered into as the result of a third party's innocent misrepresentation of which the chargee had constructive notice, was *wholly unenforceable* by the chargee. In the case Mr C had persuaded his wife to jointly charge their home to secure an advance to repay his business debts. In doing so, he innocently misrepresented to her that her maximum liability was limited to £15,000 when in fact it was unlimited. The Bank unsuccessfully argued that the charge was valid security for £15,000.

3.23 Note that it is clear that the existence of *actual or constructive notice* by the lender of undue influence or misrepresentation being used to obtain a surety's agreement to a charge is the crucial factor when determining whether the surety's charge is to be set aside. As such, it to some extent subsumes the agency situations discussed above and certainly dismisses any suggestion that third party security given by a wife will be set aside simply on the ground that the wife did not fully understand the transaction.

Independent legal advice

3.23 For many years it has been common banking practice to insist that a person providing security, particularly a third-party surety such as a relative of the borrower, obtains independent legal advice on the nature of and the obligations incurred under the charge before executing it and further that it is executed in the presence of the adviser. Since *O'Brien* this practice *must* be followed to prevent a surety who is a cohabitee of the borrower, and with whom an emotional relationship exists, setting aside a charge if the surety can establish that the borrower had used undue influence or had misrepresented the facts in obtaining the surety's agreement to the charge.

3.24 It would seem that lender's and their legal advisers should adopt the following procedure before accepting a charge:

- Where a surety is involved, full details of the proposed surety should be taken and of the surety's relationship with the borrower;

- The circumstances of the transaction should then be investigated, in particular:
  - does the transaction appear to be in the surety's financial interest; and
  - given the relationship between surety and borrower, is there a substantial risk that the borrower might have exercised undue influence or have misrepresented the facts in order to get the surety to stand;
- A private meeting between the surety and a trained representative of the lender should be arranged in the absence of the borrower at which the representative explains the nature of the transaction, the risks involved and advises the surety to take independent legal advice – the advice being confirmed in writing.

3.25 It is perhaps worth concluding by noting that in *National Westminster Bank plc v Morgan* (1985) Lord Scarman stated that '... there is no precisely defined law setting limits to the equitable jurisdiction of a court to relieve against undue influence'.

Lloyds v Bundy (1975)

3.26 Mr Bundy was an elderly man with little financial acumen. He had given the bank a guarantee for £1,500 to secure his son's business and had also completed a mortgage over his house as supporting security. The business fared badly and at a meeting between the bank, Mr Bundy senior and Mr Bundy junior, the bank representative suggested that Mr Bundy may wish to give a further guarantee and a further charge over the property for £6,000. Mr Bundy's own solicitor recommended that the maximum Mr Bundy should guarantee should be £5,000. Despite this advice, Mr Bundy senior signed a new guarantee and further charge, and thus his total contingent liability was £7,500.

3.27 Matters continued to deteriorate and a new bank representative went to see Mr Bundy senior in the presence of the son. It was explained to Mr Bundy that the son could continue to operate his business overdraft up to a limit of £10,000, provided Mr Bundy senior executed a new guarantee for £11,000 coupled with a further charge on the house. Mr Bundy joined in these charges and the forms were witnessed by the bank official. No legal advice was given.

3.28 Later the son was made bankrupt and the business became insolvent. The court held that the guarantee for £11,000 from Mr Bundy was voidable at Mr Bundy's option, and hence the mortgages, which were in support of Mr Bundy's guarantee, were also voidable.

The court's reasons for invalidating the guarantee were that there was:

- Inequality of bargaining power between Mr Bundy and the bank. This was defined as 'where one party is grievously impaired by his needs, or desires, or ignorance, or infirmity, coupled with influences or pressure brought to bear on him for the benefit of another'.
- A relationship of trust between the guarantor and his bank manager. This relationship cannot be automatically presumed when the guarantor is a customer of the same bank as the principal debtor, but the bank must always be wary in these circumstances, especially when the bank has

previously acted as a financial advisor to the guarantor.

4 Avoidance of a guarantee for mistake or misrepresentation

Saunders v Anglia Building Society (1970)

4.1 A guarantor may wish to avoid liability by claiming that he did not realise that he was signing a guarantee but thought that it was some other form of legal document. Alternatively a guarantor may have believed that he was simply signing as witness whereas he had actually signed as guarantor.

4.2 In *Saunders* it was held that this defence (known as *non est factum*) is only available if the guarantor has not been negligent. Thus, provided a guarantor can read and is of full mental capacity, he will not avoid liability on a guarantee under the *non est factum* doctrine. 'The burden of proving *non est factum* is on the party disowning his signature. This includes proof that he or she took care.' *per* Lord Hodson.

Lloyds Bank plc v Waterhouse (1989)

4.3 A father was asked to sign a guarantee for his son's liabilities to the bank. The father did not read the guarantee because he was illiterate, but he was too shy to tell the bank that he could not read. He asked the bank's representatives about the terms of the guarantee, and the explanation he received gave him the impression that the guarantee simply covered the son's loan account. In fact, the guarantee contained the standard 'all monies' clause and covered the son's other debts to the bank.

4.4 The court ruled that the guarantee was voidable on the grounds of misrepresentation. The court believed that the father would not have signed the guarantee if he had known the true extent of the liability thereunder.

4.5 *Note:* the principles regarding undue influence, *non est factum,* and misrepresentation occur most often in practice in connection with guarantees or third-party security. However, these principles also apply to direct security.

Student Activity 3

Study your bank's guarantee form again. You are going to attend an interview with a prospective guarantor who does not need to have independent legal advice. Assume that your bank's internal rules do not prevent you from conducting such an interview. Which clauses would consider ought to be explained, and what other considerations might apply. Now read on.

5 Conduct of interview when a guarantor calls to sign a guarantee at the bank

5.1 The following assumes that independent legal advice is unnecessary, and the bank's internal rules permit bank officials to witness the signing of guarantees.

Disclosure of information

5.2 The bank cannot disclose information before the guarantee is signed unless the customer authorises disclosure. It may be helpful to arrange a tripartite meeting so the customer can authorise disclosure if the guarantor asks about the account.

5.3 A guarantee is not a contract *uberrimae fidei*, so that the bank has no duty to inform the guarantor of facts which may discourage him from signing. In *Cooper v National Provincial* (1945), for example, it was held that the bank had no obligation to inform a prospective guarantor that an undischarged bankrupt had authority to sign *per pro* on the customer's account, and that the account was already overdrawn.

Silence may amount to misrepresentation

5.4 When a prospective guarantor is obviously under an erroneous impression, the banker cannot remain silent. If the guarantor does sign when the banker remains silent, the guarantee will be voidable at the guarantor's discretion.

5.5 Thus, when a guarantor is obviously under the wrong impression concerning the affairs of a customer, the bank must postpone signing the guarantee and arrange for the customer's authority to disclose the true facts.

6 Rights of the guarantor against the creditor

6.1 The rights of the guarantor against the creditor (bank) are:

- To be told by the creditor the amount of his liability under the guarantee. The guarantor is not entitled to any other information such as copy statements.

  For example, if a guarantor has guaranteed a customer who is borrowing on overdraft, and if the guarantee contains a clause which imposes a monetary maximum of, say £20,000, the bank would advise the guarantor as follows:

  - Balance £40,000 Dr: 'Guarantee fully relied upon.'
  - Balance £10,000 Dr: 'Your monetary maximum is at present limited to £10,000, plus accrued interest and charges, but the position can change from day to day.'
  - Balance £5,000 Cr: 'At present there is no monetary liability, but the position can change from day to day.'

  Note: where the borrowing comes within the terms of the Consumer Credit Act 1974, there are special rules governing the information to which guarantors are entitled: see Unit 19.

- If the guarantor pays off the whole debt he may sue the principal debtor in the bank's place. This is an example of the doctrine of subrogation where the guarantor 'steps into the bank's shoes' if he pays off the whole debt. Likewise the doctrine of subrogation extends to any securities which the bank may hold: s.5, Mercantile Law Amendment Act 1856.

7 Guarantor's rights against the principal debtor

7.1 The guarantor has the following rights:

- If the bank claims from the guarantor, the guarantor has the right to petition the court for an order that the principal debtor repays the bank.
- If the guarantor pays the bank, he can claim the money back from the principal debtor, but only if the bank has been paid off in full. This stipulation that the bank must be paid off in full before the principal debtor can be sued by the guarantor is contained in the 'all monies' clause, (sometimes known as the 'whole debt' clause).
- If the guarantor pays off the whole debt, he can take over any rights of set off or any counterclaims which the customer may have had against the bank under the doctrine of subrogation.

8 Rights of co-guarantors inter se

8.1 A paying guarantor is entitled to reimbursement on a *pro rata* basis from his co-guarantors. This applies whether there is a single joint and several guarantee, or whether the guarantors have entered into separate guarantee forms. If the principal debtor is solvent, he must be joined in any action against the guarantors: *Hay v Carter* (1935).

8.2 Similar considerations as apply for a paying guarantor also apply if someone else has deposited third party security as opposed to giving a guarantee. The following question illustrates the point.

8.3 A customer had an overdraft which was secured by:

- A guarantee limited to £10,000; and
- Shares valued at £10,000 deposited by a third party. The customer was bankrupt at a time when he owed the bank £10,000. The guarantor paid off the whole of this debt to the bank. He asks the bank to assign the shares to him.

Is he entitled to these shares, and for what purpose?

Answer
The guarantor is entitled under the doctrine of subrogation to take over any securities held by the bank if he pays off the whole debt: s.5, Mercantile Law Amendment Act 1856.

As the guarantee was for £10,000 and the shares were worth £10,000, the guarantor and third party were, between themselves, equally liable for the borrowing.

If the guarantor pays off the full £10,000 he could sell the shares, use £5,000 to recoup his payment under the guarantee, and pay the balance of £5,000 to the third party.

The guarantor and third party would then each claim £5,000 as unsecured creditors in the bankruptcy of the customer, because the bank has been fully repaid.

9 Determination of a guarantee

Determination by the guarantor

Where the debit balance exceeds the amount of the guarantee

9.1 The bank will advise the guarantor of the amount required. The guarantor should pay this sum at the expiration of the period of notice. The customer's account would normally be broken and a new account opened for future transactions. However, the bank guarantee is so worded as to make this unnecessary: *Westminster Bank v Cond* (1940).

9.2 If the bank believed that insolvency proceedings were likely, then it could make demand on the customer and place any proceeds from the guarantor into a suspense account.

Where the debit balance is below the amount of the guarantee

9.3 If the customer has been behaving in an unsatisfactory manner, the bank could call for repayment on demand, unless the borrowing was on a separate loan on which instalments were up to date. If the bank did make demand, it would advise the guarantor of the amount due, and would ensure no further withdrawals were allowed from the account.

9.4 If the customer has been behaving in a satisfactory manner, and if the guarantor is good for the full amount, there is no reason why the bank cannot make further advances during the period of notice. The bank would arrange a meeting between bank officials, customer and guarantor, to decide which of the customer's future commitments should come within the guaranteed borrowing. Once notice has expired, the bank will break the account to prevent the rule in *Clayton's case* from operating against it. However, failure to break the account will not invalidate the guarantee because of the standard clause which was upheld in *Cond.*

Notice of death or mental incapacity of the guarantor

9.5 Most bank guarantees contain a clause which states that in the event of death of a guarantor, three month's notice of determination is required by the personal representatives. However, in the absence of such a clause the guarantee would be determined not by the date of death but by the date of notice to the bank: *Bradbury v Morgan* (1862).

9.6 Similar considerations apply in the case of mental incapacity of the guarantor. In the absence of any special clause, the liability will be determined by notice of mental incapacity. Some banks have a clause which requires three months' notice of determination by the Court of Protection or other representative.

9.7 In any event, once the guarantee has been determined, whether by notice of death or mental incapacity, or whether by completion of any notice period after written notification from the appropriate representatives of the guarantor, then the customer's account will be broken to prevent the rule in *Clayton's case* operating against the bank. (In practice the *Westminster v Cond* clause will protect the bank anyway if it fails to break the account.)

9.8 *Note*: in practice the bank may be willing to release the guarantor's estate if the customer can provide alternative security.

Bankruptcy of guarantor

9.9 The guarantee is determined by notice of a bankruptcy petition against the guarantor. The bank may prove as an unsecured creditor against the bankrupt guarantor's estate. The amount for which a claim is made will be the amount due from the customer on the date of notice of the bankruptcy petition. The bank will obtain a dividend in the pound for the amount due. The bank would normally make demand on the principal debtor to clarify the amount due.

9.10 *Note:* in practice the bank may be prepared to release the guarantor's estate if the principal debtor can provide alternative security.

Notice of determination by one joint and several guarantor

9.11 Most bank guarantee forms contain a clause which allows one guarantor to give notice of determination without determining the liabilities of the co-guarantors. On expiry of the notice by one guarantor, his liability is determined.

9.12 If the bank wishes to retain the liability of that guarantor, it will break the account to prevent the rule in *Clayton's case* operating to the bank's detriment. (Once again the *Cond* clause will protect the bank if it fails to break the account.) Normal procedure would then be to ask the remaining guarantors to sign a new guarantee to clarify the position. However, the remaining guarantors will continue to be liable for all debts of the customer which were covered by the terms of the original guarantee. The usual clauses allowing banks to vary the arrangements with the principal debtor or co-sureties will remain in force on the original guarantee. Unless these remaining guarantors themselves give notice, they will continue to be jointly and severally liable.

10 Danger of preferences on release of guarantee or third-party security

10.1 You should be very familiar with the concept of preferences as set out in s.340, Insolvency Act 1986. If you need to recap, refer to Unit 6.

Student Activity 4

Simon, who runs a small garage, has an overdraft facility of £20,000 at the South Bank, fully covered by stocks and shares lodged as third party security by his brother, Peter. In the past four weeks few cheques on the account have been drawn by Simon and sufficient credits have been paid in to place the account in credit for the first time for years. Today, with the account still in credit, Simon and Peter call at the bank, and Simon asks for the stocks and shares to be released to Peter, who will shortly be emigrating to Australia. What action should the bank take and why?

Write some notes to answer this question.

11 Special types of guarantee

Supported guarantees

11.1 Where the guarantee is supported by security from the guarantor the bank can take one of the following:

- A third party charge covering the security being offered. This charge form is signed by the guarantor, and it states that the security is lodged to cover the liabilities of the principal debtor.

  The guarantor signs the guarantee form in addition to the third party charge form.

- A direct charge over the asset lodged as security signed by the surety, i.e. guarantor, as well as the guarantee. The direct charge form will cover all the liabilities of the guarantor including his liability to the bank in connection with the guarantee.

  Where the guarantor is also a customer, it is preferable to use this method, since the security offered will cover the guarantor's own borrowing as well as the liability under the guarantee.

Joint and several guarantees

11.2 Each guarantor is jointly and severally liable. If a joint and several guarantee with a monetary maximum of £20,000 were signed by two guarantors, G1 and G2, the guarantors as between themselves would be liable to pay £10,000 each.

11.3 However, the bank would be at liberty to sue G1 and/or G2 for £20,000 each if it wished, and then leave it to the court/them to sort out how much they should each pay. The maximum the bank could retain would be £20,000.

11.4 The clauses in the joint and several guarantee are similar to those already covered. However, there is a clause which specifically allows the bank to release one of the co-guarantors whilst retaining the liability of the others. At common law the release of one co-surety would releases the other(s); the bank guarantee clause overcomes this problem.

Partnership as guarantor

11.5 Whether a partnership is a trading or a non-trading partnership, an individual partner does not have implied power to give a guarantee on behalf of his partnership unless the firm's business is that of giving guarantees: s.5, Partnership Act 1890. Therefore all partners should sign a guarantee given by the partnership. This provides actual, express authority for the partnership to give the guarantee.

Partner offers to guarantee the partnership account

11.6 Guarantees must not be taken from partners to secure the borrowing of the partnership. The partner will already be jointly and severally liable for the whole of the partnership borrowing because of the clause in the standard bank mandate, and any guarantee from the partner could imply a limitation on his personal monetary liability for partnership borrowing.

12 Duty of a bank to protect a surety

China and South Sea Bank v Tan Soon Gin (1990)

12.1 In *China and South Sea Bunk v Tan Soon Gin* (1990), the bank made an advance against shares and a guarantee from a third party. When the debtor defaulted the bank did not enforce its mortgage over the shares, although when default first occurred the shares' value appeared to cover the borrowing. The shares subsequently became worthless and the bank claimed from the guarantor. The guarantor claimed that his liability was extinguished or greatly reduced by the bank's breach of duty of care to him.

12.2 The court ruled that:

- The bank owed no duty to the guarantor in deciding when to exercise its power of sale, and could decide in its own interest when to do so.
- The only exceptions to this would be if the bank was responsible for the decline in the value of the security, or if the bank did any act injurious to the surety, or if the bank omitted any duty it was obliged to do and the omission caused injury to the surety.

Standard Chartered Bank v Walker and Walker (1982)

12.3 When a bank holds a guarantee and has other direct security deposited by the customer, the bank has a duty to exercise reasonable care if it realises the security. This duty to exercise reasonable care extends to both the mortgagor and to the guarantor. If the asset charged consists of land, the bank must appoint a reputable estate agent to sell and the bank must not interfere.

12.4 The Unfair Contract Terms Act 1977 will render void any clause in the guarantee which seeks to restrict the bank's responsibility to a guarantor as regards acting with reasonable care.

Summary

Having studied this unit, you should be able to:

- **define a guarantee and distinguish it from an indemnity;**
- **describe the contractual capacity of guarantors;**
- **list and understand the clauses in a standard bank guarantee form;**
- **understand the meaning and effect of undue influence and what steps should be taken to avoid it;**
- **understand the effects of mistake and misrepresentation on a contract of guarantee;**
- **describe how an interview with a prospective guarantor is carried out;**
- **describe the rights of a guarantor;**
- **explain how a guarantee is determined;**
- **appreciate the effect of death, mental disorder or bankruptcy of a guarantor on a guarantee;**
- **understand the possibilities of preferences in relation to guarantees;**
- **describe the special types of guarantee;**
- **outline the duty of a bank to a surety.**

Self-assessment questions

1 Which Act states that a guarantee cannot be avoided solely because the principal debtor is a minor?

2 If a guarantee is to be given by James, John and Philip is it valid when James and Philip have signed it, and John is unavoidably called abroad before he can sign?

3 If Keith, David and Paul signed a guarantee, and the bank later discovers that David's signature has been forged, is the guarantee valid?

4 In your opinion, what are the most important clauses in a guarantee?

5 In the course of the interview for a prospective guarantor to sign a guarantee, the prospective guarantor says 'I am pleased that James is starting up his own business after he was made redundant, and I was only too pleased to guarantee his account to help him set up in business.'

You (the bank) know that the money is being lent to pay for a world cruise, not to set up a business. What action, if any, would you take?

6 In which of the following situations is there no presumption of undue influence ?

(a) Parent and child.

(b) Guardian and ward.

(c) Doctor and patient.

(d) Husband and wife.

7 Under a guarantee, the guarantor is entitled to:

(a) Inspect the debtor's bank statement.

(b) Be informed of the balance of the debtor's account.

(c) Be able to see any cheques issued by the debtor.

(d) Make repayment at any time.

8 Which of the following can give a valid guarantee?

(a) A son, aged 25, for his father's borrowing.

(b) A daughter, aged 17, for her father's borrowing.

(c) A mentally incapable person so deemed under the Mental Health Act 1983.

Further reading

- Milnes Holden, J — Chapters 18–21, *The Law and Practice of Banking*, Vol 1, 5th edition 1991, Pitman
- Laidlaw, A and Roberts, G — Chapters 11–12, *Law Relating to Banking* Services, 2nd edition 1992, Bankers Books
- Raby, P — Chapter 14, *Law Relating to Banking Services*, 2nd edition 1992, Pitman

Unit 17

Security Given for Company Borrowing

Objectives

On studying this unit you, should be able to:

- **appreciate the characteristics of the various types of security to cover the liabilities of limited companies;**
- **understand the procedures for registration of charges given by companies;**
- **appreciate the consequences for banks for failure to follow correct registration procedure;**
- **differentiate between the relative merits of fixed and floating charges;**
- **understand the legal problems connected with floating charges and *Romalpa* clauses;**
- **appreciate the significance of intercompany guarantees;**
- **understand the potential difficulties caused by release of third party security.**

1 Introduction

1.1 When a company needs to borrow money, the lender will often require some form of security. This enables the lender to realise the security to repay the borrowing if the company defaults.

1.2 The company can give a charge over any of its assets, and that charge can be either fixed or floating. Briefly, a fixed charge gives the lender a charge over specific assets, e.g. the land and buildings, whereas a floating charge gives the lender a charge over all assets that are not charged elsewhere.

1.3 In addition a third party can also guarantee the borrowing of the company. The guarantee may be given by a director or if the company is one of a group of companies, by the other companies in the group (intercompany guarantees).

1.4 Note that under s.130, Companies Act 1989, a company need no longer have a company seal, but may use one if it so wishes. Any document signed by two directors, or by one director and a secretary, has the same effect as if it had the company's seal on it.

1.5 *Note*: all references are to the Companies Act 1985 unless otherwise stated.

2 Registration of securities given by companies

2.1 In the Companies Act 1989, various changes were proposed to the registration of securities given by companies. However, the new procedures have not been implemented and, currently (1996) the position is governed by the companies Act 1985, unamended by any of the 1989 Act's provisions. Hence, the position under the 1985 Act is set out in this unit.

2.2 Similar agreements can be made between a lender and a third party that an asset belonging to the third party shall be security for the borrower's borrowing (collateral security).

2.3 Charges given by a company over certain types of asset need to be registered at Companies House within 21 days of creation, in accordance with ss.395 and 396. The terms 'charge' and 'property' are defined as:

> ... 'charge' means any form of security interest (fixed or floating) over property, other than an interest arising by operation of law; and 'property', in the context of what is the subject of a charge, includes future property.

2.4 An example of an interest arising by operation of law is shown in *London and Cheshire Insurance Co Ltd v Laplagrene Property Co Ltd* (1971), where the unpaid seller of the property had a lien over the price of the land sold.

2.5 The definition of 'property' including future property is of particular relevance if the security held is by way of floating charge. Property does not simply mean, 'bricks and mortar', but any assets of the company.

2.6 Registration consists of supplying the charge form (if any) and the prescribed particulars of the charge on the prescribed form 395 to Companies House where the Registrar of Companies maintains a charges register for each company. This information on the register is available to anyone for inspection, and the Registrar will provide a certificate stating the date on which any form 395 and a charge were delivered to him.

2.7 Registration at Companies House is required in addition to any other formalities which are required for security deposited by individuals. The purpose of registration is to enable interested parties, such as potential lenders or suppliers of goods on credit terms, to be able to ascertain whether there are any charges in existence over a company's assets.

Charges requiring registration

2.8 Section 396 requires the following charges to be registered:

- A charge for the purpose of securing any issue of debentures;
- A charge on uncalled share capital of the company;
- A charge on land (wherever situated) or any interest in it, but not including a charge for rent or other periodical sum issuing out of land;
- A charge on book debts of the company;
- A floating charge on the company's undertaking or property;
- A charge on calls made but not paid;

- A charge on a ship or an aircraft or any share in a ship (note shares only apply to ships);
- A charge on goodwill, on a patent or a licence under a patent, or a trademark or on a copyright or licence under a copyright.

Charges not requiring registration

2.9 It is important to know what charges must be registered under s.396, and for clarity for examination purposes, this unit lays out clearly what charges do *not* require registration. Remember, registration of charges only applies when it is the company creating the charge. It does not apply to charges given by third parties, e.g. a director, to secure company borrowing.

2.10 The charges that do not need registering are over:

- Stocks and shares;
- Goods (pledges);
- Insurance policies;
- Negotiable instruments; and
- Guarantees; and
- Letters of set off.

The mnemonic SPINGS will help you remember the above list.

Stocks and shares

2.11 Stocks and shares are those which are held by the company as assets in its balance sheet: this does not refer to the company's own stocks and shares which form part of the capital of the company. The only time those stocks and shares would need registering is if they formed part of the security caught under a floating charge.

Pledges

2.12 Pledges over goods applies particularly to banks when they lend under a facility called a 'produce loan'. The bank holds the documents of title to the goods as security and only releases the goods against either the money or a trust receipt from its customer. A trust receipt is issued when the customer holds the goods and their proceeds in trust for the bank as the bank's agent.

Insurance policies

2.13 Insurance policies may be held by a company over the life of a keyman (one whose illness or death would have severe consequences on the likelihood of the survival of the company), thus, there is insurable interest. Such life policies can be charged to the bank as security for lending, without requiring registration.

Negotiable instruments

2.14 Negotiable instruments include cheques and bills of exchange which are deposited as security against book debts.

Guarantees

2.15 Guarantees are a contractual liability on the part of the company. The company will be guaranteeing the borrowing of (usually) another company, and will only be liable if that other company fails to repay the borrowing. A guarantee is a contingent liability which is shown as a note to the company's accounts.

Letters of set off

2.16 Letters of set off are authorities whereby the company agrees formally that the bank can set off two or more of the company's accounts to arrive at a net position of debit or credit.

Why banks should comply with registration formalities

2.17 Failure to comply with the registration formalities as laid down by the Act will mean that the charge is void against a liquidator or creditor. Charges must be registered within 21 days of their creation.

2.18 In *Esberger & Son Ltd v Capital & Counties Bank* (1913) a company lodged the deeds of its property as security and executed a formal legal mortgage. However, the form was held undated for several months until the company actually required the borrowing facility. Then and only then the current date (the date when the borrowing was required) was inserted on the charge form and the charge was registered in the normal way. Later the company went into liquidation and the liquidator claimed that the charge was void, not having been registered within 21 days of its creation. The court agreed that the charge was void as creation occurred at the actual date of execution when the form had originally been signed and sealed.

2.19 The practical consequences of this decision are that if a bank has retained an executed but undated charge for more than 21 days without registering it, then it should start afresh and take a new charge form which would be registered within the requisite time. There is a procedure for late registration (see below) but this is cumbersome and starting afresh is much simpler.

Late Registration

2.20 Under s.404(2) late registration may be possible. This section states that:

> The court may, on application of the company or a person interested, and on such terms and conditions as seem to the court just and expedient, order that the time for registration shall be extended, or as the case may be the omission or misstatement shall be rectified.

If late registration would detrimentally affect any creditor then the court would refuse such registration.

2.21 An illustration of the court's decision can be found in *Re Telomatic Ltd* (1993), where Barclays Bank sought to register a mortgage out of time at the Companies Registry. The sequence of events was as follows:

- 4 January 1989 Legal charge created over Telomatic's property in favour of Barclays Bank.
- 19 July 1989 Charge registered at HM Land Registry, but not at the Companies Registry.
- July–December 1989 Barclays unsuccessfully attempted to obtain a new charge which it could have then registered properly at Companies House.
- October 1989 Cyprus Bank took a second charge over the same property.

2.22 After the above events Barclays attempted to register its original charge out of time. However, the court refused to exercise its discretion to allow late registration because:

- Omission to register might have prejudiced other creditors and no case was made on the evidence to contradict this possibility;
- Barclays had only applied to the court when it had become obvious that it would not be possible to obtain another charge from Telomatic Ltd;
- In any event, the second charge in favour of Cyprus Bank would have retained priority, even if the circumstances had been such that the court had exercised its discretion in favour of Barclays.

Note: the fact that Barclays had registered its charge at the District Land Registry was irrelevant.

Certificate of Registration as conclusive evidence

2.23 Under s.401(2) the certificate of registration is taken as conclusive evidence that the requirements of the Act as to registration have been complied with. In *R v Registrar of Companies ex parte Esal (Commodities) Ltd* (1985) the solicitors had failed to complete the form of registration correctly and had overlooked the need to send the original form of charge (as opposed to a copy). The Registrar returned the copy and the form without registering the charge, but later issued a certificate of registration dated 29 February 1984 of the charge dated 9 February 1984. The court held that the certificate was conclusive evidence that the registration formalities had been complied with and allowed the charge to stand.

2.24 Presumably *Telomatic* can be distinguished from *Esberger* under the inadvertence provisions of s.404(1) which provides that:

> The following applies if the court is satisfied that the omission to register a charge within the time required by this chapter or that the omission or misstatement with respect to any such charge ... was accidental or due to inadvertence or to some such sufficient cause, or is not of a nature to prejudice the position of creditors ... or that on other grounds it is just and equitable to grant relief.

Position when the details on the register do not contain all the details of the charge form

2.25 In *Re Mechanisations (Eaglescliff) Ltd* (1964) it was held that the whole terms of a charge granted by a company are binding on the world, provided registration has been effected, even though all the terms of the charge are not recorded on the register.

Summary of bank procedures for registration at Companies House

2.26 In summary:

1 Search the register at Companies House to ensure that there are no prior charges registered.

2 Execute the security.

3 If the security is such that registration is required, register by sending form 395 and the form of charge to Companies House. Registration is required within 21 days of the creation of the charge.

4 Ensure that the Registrar returns a certificate of registration and that the charge form is returned bearing the Registrar's stamp which duly notes the date of registration.

5 Registration at Companies House is in addition to all other formalities required to perfect the security.

3 Fixed and floating charges

Fixed charges

3.1 A fixed charge covers a specific asset of the company such as land, buildings, plant and machinery and book debts.

3.2 A fixed charge relates to assets that are valuable, easily identifiable and not subject to regular change or turnover. However, book debts (both present and future), current asset, can be secured by means of a fixed charge: *Siebe Gorman and Co Ltd v Barclays Bank Ltd* (1979).

3.3 A book debt is defined as a debt owing to the company which arises out of the normal carrying on of its business, so that they would appear in the books of the company, if well kept: *Shipley v Marshall* (1863). However, a credit balance in a bank account is not classed as a book debt, thus is not caught under a *Siebe Gorman* clause in a debenture: *Re Brightlife Ltd* (1986).

3.4 Fixed charges do not cover future property, except in the case of a fixed charge over book debts. Book debts change on a daily basis, and the company has a free rein in dealing with the debts. However, if book debts are taken as security under a fixed charge, the company agrees to pay all monies received in respect of such debts into the bank account. They also agree not to charge or assign these book debts to any other person or body unless the bank gives its written consent. The court held, in *Siebe Gorman and Co Ltd v Barclays Bank Ltd* (1979), that this restriction on the company freely dealing with the asset (book debts) created a fixed charge, even though the charge related to future book debts.

3.5 Further light was cast on the position of a credit bank balance in the case of *Northern Bank v Ross* (1990) when the implications of *Siebe Gorman* and *Re Brightlife* were analysed. A borrowing company which had granted a fixed charge with a *Siebe Gorman* type clause subsequently held a closing-down sale. The proceeds of the closing-down sale were paid into an account at another bank.

3.6 It was held that the lending bank's fixed charge did not cover the entire bank balance at the other bank as this could not be construed as a book debt. Nevertheless, the moneys in that account which represented the proceeds of cheques and credit card payments were subject to the fixed charge, since such payments represented 'book debts and other debts' owing to the company.

Floating charges

3.7 A floating charge covers all assets not otherwise charged, by way of a fixed charge, including future assets. A floating charge enables the company to deal with these assets in whatever way they wish, without requiring them to obtain the bank's permission in advance.

3.8 A floating charge has certain characteristics as described in *Re Yorkshire Woolcombers Association* (1903):

- It is a charge on a class of assets of a company, both present and future.
- If that class of assets is one which in the ordinary course of the business of the company would be changing from time to time.
- If it is found that by the charge it is contemplated that, until some future step is taken by or on behalf of those interested in the charge (e.g. the bank), the company may carry on its business in the ordinary way so far as concerns the particular class of assets charged.

3.9 Thus, the main characteristic is the fact that the company is free to deal with the assets caught under a floating charge until the holder of the charge takes action to enforce the security to repay the borrowing. This action results in crystallisation, a process whereby a floating charge fixes on the assets covered and the company is no longer free to deal with them

3.10 Only when a floating charge has crystallised does the company's right to deal with those assets cease, and there cannot be any disposals without the bank's or administrative receiver's authority.

3.11 A floating charge will pick up any asset not already charged. It picks up both assets at the time the charge was created, and future assets. One of the main items caught under a floating charge is stock.

Student Activity 1

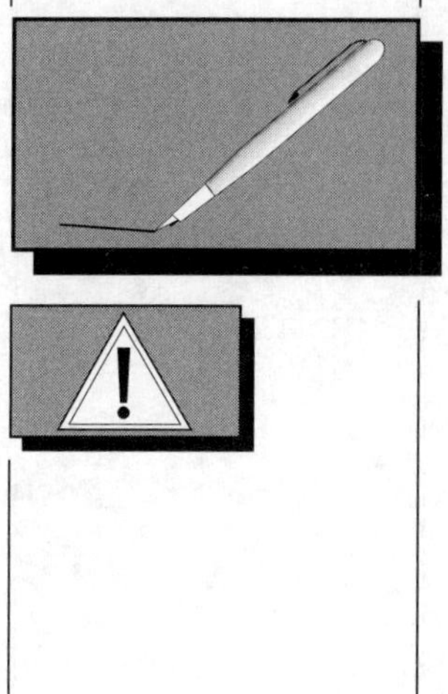

Now that you have read about fixed and floating charges, think about the potential benefits and drawbacks of a floating charge to both the bank and the company and then read on.

Advantages of a floating charge to the company

3.12 The company is free to deal with the assets caught under a floating charge without having to obtain the prior permission of the bank. The advantage can be clearly seen if you consider the problems that would arise for both the company and the bank if every time an item was sold out of stock the company had to obtain the permission of the bank to sell that specific item!

Advantages of a floating charge to the bank

3.13 Because a floating charge also covers future property, it means that any future property is caught under the floating charge as soon as the company acquires it. This is the case even if the bank is unaware that the asset has been purchased.

3.14 Another major advantage of a floating charge is that under the Insolvency Act 1986, it enables a bank to appoint an administrative receiver. The appointment of an administrative receiver can prevent other parties from appointing an administrator.

Disadvantages of a floating charge to the bank

3.15 One of the main problems a bank faces when it has taken a floating charge as security is 'that it is worth least when it is wanted most'. When a company is insolvent, it will usually have run down all its liquid assets prior to winding up, in order to pay off its creditors. Thus, items such as stock and book debts (if not caught under a fixed charge), will have virtually vanished because they have been turned into cash, and that cash has been paid out by the company to its creditors.

3.16 Another problem is that another creditor may have obtained a court judgment in respect of unpaid debts. If those debts are not paid, the court may order its officials to seize certain assets to repay the debt. If the bank does not become aware of this unsatisfied judgment debt soon enough, the assets will have been sold, and thus the value of the bank's security will have fallen. If the bank is aware of an unsatisfied judgment debt, it should crystallise the floating charge prior to the sale of the assets or before the proceeds of the sale are handed over to the judgment creditor.

3.17 A third problem faced by the bank is that the floating charge will rank behind a fixed charge created after the floating charge. This problem can be easily overcome by including a 'negative pledge' clause in the floating charge. A 'negative pledge' is a promise by the company not to charge its assets elsewhere without the prior agreement of the bank. This negative pledge (although not a charge in itself) will form part of the floating charge form and will usually be registered at Companies House as part of the floating charge. This registration is taken as being notice to the whole world of the bank's charge and thus any subsequent charge cannot rank before a floating charge if the registration procedure has been carried out correctly.

Validity of a floating charge – the 12-month rule

3.18 Under s.245, Insolvency Act 1986 a floating charge is valid if any one (or more than one) of the following applies:

- The company was able to pay its debts at the time and immediately after the floating charge was created, in which case the charge is fully valid.
- New money was lent in consideration of the floating charge. The floating charge would be valid to the extent of such 'new money'.

  When the company has a current account, 'new money' is the debit turnover on or after the date of the charge.

  Example: X Ltd

Date	Details	Dr	Cr	Balance
30 Nov 96	Balance			20,000 Dr
1 Dec 96	Floating charge created			
1 May 97		17,000	13,000	24,000 Dr
10 May 97	Company goes into liquidation			

Student Activity 2

Consider the situation above. Bearing in mind *Clayton's case*, what would you consider to be the amount of 'new money' advanced since the creation of the floating charge. Now read on.

In this case, under *Clayton's case*, the £24,000 balance consists of £17,000 lent since the floating charge was created and £7,000 lent before it. (The £13,000 of credits have repaid £13,000 of the original £20,000 debit balance.)

Thus, the floating charge will be valid for at least £17,000 and of course would cover the full £24,000 if the company could be proved capable of paying its debts on 1 December, 1990.

The floating charge would also cover interest on the £17,000, or interest on the full £24,000 if the company had been proved solvent on 1 December, 1990.

- There was no liquidation or administration order made within one year of the creation of the floating charge. Hence, in the example above, the floating charge would automatically have been fully valid if liquidation had not commenced until 2 December 1996. (*Note*: if company was solvent at date of creation of floating charge, then the floating charge is fully valid even if an administration order is made within one year of creation of the floating charge.)

3.19 The 12-month period applies as follows:

- In the case of a compulsory liquidation, the date of the presentation of the petition (date of the resolution in a voluntary liquidation);
- In the case of an administration order, the date of the presentation of a petition.

Note: if the floating charge is created in favour of a 'connected person', e.g. a director, the relevant period is two years, not one. However, the bank is unlikely to be a 'connected person': *Re M C Bacon Ltd* (1989).

3.20 If the company became insolvent because of the creation of the floating charge, then this charge will be invalid, save for 'new monies' advanced.

3.21 The 'new monies' advanced will be looked at carefully by the liquidator to ensure that they are genuine advances and not just paper transactions. If a creditor enters into a transaction purporting to be an advance of new monies secured by a floating charge on the understanding that the money was used to repay the old debt of the same amount, this would be classed as a 'paper transaction'. This would be invalid because there is no new consideration for the giving of the security: *Re G T Whyte and Co Ltd* (1982).

3.22 However, if the transaction was in any sense genuine, it would not affect the validity of the floating charge, for example if a creditor were owed £5,000 and he was the sole supplier of the goods on credit terms. The company may wish to buy more goods, but the creditor will only sell more goods if it has security. If the creditor lends the company £7,000, £5,000 of which is repaid to the creditor to discharge the old debt, and £2,000 retained in cash by the company, the charge could be valid. The court would take the view that the transaction was undertaken as a real attempt to keep the company in business: *Re Matthews Ellis Ltd* (1933).

3.23 When a bank lends new monies on a separate loan account it should ensure that the advances are not made until the charge has been executed. This will establish beyond all doubt that the advances are new monies. In *Re Shoe Lace Ltd* (1992) the court held that literal meaning should be given to the words 'at the same time as, or after, the creation of the charge'.

Crystallisation of a floating charge

3.24 A floating charge crystallises, i.e. fixes on the assets covered, and the company ceases to be able to deal with its assets as it wishes under the following circumstances, if:

- Winding up commences, whether compulsory: *Re Colonial Trusts Corporation ex parte Bradshaw* (1879), or voluntary: *Re Roundwood Colliery Co* (1897);
- An administrative receiver is appointed;
- The company ceases to carry on business: *Re Woodroffes (Musical Instruments) Ltd* (1986), or disposes of all of its assets and business with a view to ceasing trading: *Hubbock v Helms* (1887).

In all the above situations, the floating charge crystallises due to the operation of law. A floating charge can also crystallise if:

- One of the contractual provisions in the charge form is breached, e.g. charging an asset caught under the floating charge elsewhere, without obtaining the prior permission of the bank: *Re Brightlife Ltd* (1986).

Romalpa clauses

3.25 Sellers of goods on credit try to protect themselves as much as possible against nonpayment. One method of doing so is to insert a *'Romalpa'* clause into the sales contract. A typical example of such a clause in a sales contract could be:

> All goods will remain the property of the vendor until the price has been paid in full and the purchaser will remain the bailee only until payment is made.

3.26 Under the Sale of Goods Act 1979 and in accordance with *Aluminium Industrie Vaasen v Romalpa* (Date) (known as the *Romalpa* case) such clauses can be inserted in sales contracts, and will be effective provided the wording is properly drawn up.

3.27 However, various other cases have subsequently extended the original decision so that the position is now as follows.

Validity of a Romalpa clause

3.28 Where a *Romalpa* clause applies, the clause will have to be worded in such a way that it does not constitute a registrable charge on the goods, otherwise when the purchaser is a limited company the Romalpa clause will be void for lack of registration.

3.29 The test set out in *Armour v Thyssen Edelstahlwerke AG* (1990) is as follows:

Table 17.1 Summary of differences between fixed and floating charges

Fixed	*Floating*
1 Covers a specific asset, e.g. land.	1 Covers all assets of the company except those which are covered by a fixed charge.
2 The company cannot deal with the asset concerned in any way at all unless the lender consents.	2 The company has a free hand to deal with the assets in any way it wishes so long as it remains a going concern.
3 A fixed charge normally takes priority over a floating charge, even if the fixed charge is created after the floating one. (But see opposite.)	3 To prevent the company giving a subsequent fixed charge over an asset, the bank has a clause (called a 'negative pledge') in the floating charge agreement prohibiting the creation of a fixed charge in favour of another lender without the bank's consent. This clause will normally be recorded at Companies House and so any subsequent mortgage in favour of another lender will lose priority to the bank's floating charge. Even if the clause is not recorded on the register, any other potential lender will be deemed to have notice of it: *Re Mechanisations Ltd* (1964).
4 The charge will only cover a particular asset or assets.	4 The floating charge covers all assets both present and future.
5 Fixed charges can be given by either individuals, partnerships, or by companies,	5 Only limited companies can give floating charges. (Although a farmer can give a special form of agricultural floating charge.)

- In the event of liquidation of the purchaser, where the value of the goods exceeds the amount owing, e.g. because part payment has been made already, to whom would surplus proceeds belong?
- If the 'surplus proceeds' belong to the seller, then the *Romalpa* clause will be valid, since the clause is not a charge over the goods and it would not require registration at Companies House
- If the 'surplus proceeds' would belong to the liquidator of the purchaser then the *Romalpa* clause would be void, being a charge over goods which had not been registered
- The specimen clause shown above is valid, because it says that *ownership* remains with the seller until payment.

3.30 The following assumes that the clause is drawn up in such a way as to be valid.

Position where the goods have been mixed with other goods

3.31 The position is that:

- Where the purchased goods are attached to other goods but can be detached without causing damage, a *Romalpa* clause will be effective: *Hendy Lennox v Grahame Puttick Ltd* (1984).
- Where the goods are mixed with other goods and have lost their separate identity, the *Romalpa clause* will be void, e.g. iron ore smelted into steel: *Borden UK v Scottish Timber Products* (1979).
- Where the goods are attached to other goods and cannot be detached without causing damage, the *Romalpa* clause will be void.

Position of sale proceeds if the goods have been sold by the original purchaser to a third party

3.32 In *Compaq Computers v Abercorn Ltd* (1991) it was held that any clause would be void for lack of registration which purported to retain title to the sale proceeds or to the debtors when the goods had been sold by the original purchaser.

Significance of Romalpa clause for banks with floating charges over the assets of the purchaser

3.33 One of the main assets of a limited company caught by a floating charge is its stock. However, where the bank holds a floating charge and the bank's customer has purchased goods under valid *Romalpa* terms, then the bank's rights to that stock will be totally lost if the bank's customer has not paid for that stock in full.

Conclusion

3.34 Where the main asset of a limited company borrower is stock, and where the bank holds a floating charge as security, that bank must bear in mind that its security may not be 'watertight'. The stock in the customer's warehouse may, effectively, not belong to the customer if it has not been paid for and if it has been bought on *Romalpa* terms.

3.35 Similar considerations apply when a bank examines the borrower's balance sheet. The stock shown in that balance sheet may not belong to the customer if it has been purchased on *Romalpa* terms and has not been paid for. Lending banks often make enquiries of the customer when examining the balance sheet to try to ascertain whether the stock is subject to *Romalpa* terms.

4 Debentures

4.1 A debenture is a written acknowledgement of debt by a company: *Levy v Abercorris Slate and Slab Co* (1887). In the context of this unit we do not consider a debenture which raises capital for the company, but at a debenture which a bank takes to secure borrowing. This form of debenture means that a bank has a fixed and floating charge over assets of the company.

4.2 A bank debenture is in a standard form. It will contain certain standard clauses if it is used as an 'all monies debenture'. 'All monies' means that the debenture secures the borrowing of the company in all forms and on any type of account or other facility, e.g. where money is advanced against a bill of exchange due at some future date.

Standard clauses

Repayment on demand

4.3 The company agrees to repay on demand existing or future debts or liabilities, on any account, whether it is solely or jointly liable, whether as principal or guarantor, and including charges, interest and any costs to the bank.

4.4 The clause agreeing to repay on demand relates not just to overdrafts but to any form of loan except that which has a specific time when it is granted. Such a loan would only become repayable on demand if it were in arrears of the stated terms or if the terms of the loan specified that it was repayable on demand.

4.5 When a company is required to repay on demand, it is quite easy for the bank to engineer a default by making a demand for repayment and only allowing the company a very short time to obtain the money. In *R A Cripps and Son Ltd v Wickenden* (1973), it was held that the debtor need only be given time to get the money from a nearby place, supposing of course that he actually had any money in such a place. If the debtor is obviously without resources, a very short time is reasonable: *Bank of Baroda v Panessar* (1987).

Charges clause

4.6 The company charges specific property (the fixed charge) which is specified in the debenture. A floating charge is taken over all other assets, both present and future, that are not already charged.

4.7 The taking of a floating charge is important, even if the majority of the company's assets are covered by a fixed charge, because a floating charge enables the bank to appoint an administrative receiver under a floating charge.

4.8 The clause agreeing to create a fixed charge over specific property and a floating charge over all other assets, both present and future, gives the bank a very comprehensive form of security over all the company's assets that are not charged elsewhere.

4.9 The fixed charge covers or can cover:

- Freehold and leasehold property;
- Fixed plant and machinery;
- Uncalled or unpaid capital;
- Shares in and securities of subsidiaries;
- Book debts;
- Goodwill and patents.

4.10 All the above can be taken as a fixed *legal* charge. In addition, a fixed *equitable* charge can be taken over any of the above assets, and a charge covering future assets must be taken by way of a fixed equitable charge.

Negative pledge

4.11 This prohibits the company from charging an asset elsewhere or creating a lien over an asset, without the prior permission of the bank.

Documents of title

4.12 In relation to land, the bank must hold all documents of title. If the charge is an equitable charge, the company must execute a fixed legal charge if called upon to do so by the bank.

Disposal of the business

4.13 The company agrees not to dispose of any part of the business without the prior permission of the bank.

Book debts

4.14 With a fixed charge over book debts, the company must pay any money received into the bank account.

Crystallisation

4.15 This specifies the events on which the bank debt becomes repayable on demand and the security enforceable. This can be:

- When a demand is made by the bank for repayment; or
- When the company breaches one of the prohibitive clauses; or
- If the company fails to repay interest on capital as agreed; or
- On presentation of a winding up petition; or
- Appointment of a receiver or administrative receiver by another creditor; or
- If the company ceases to carry on its business either completely or in the major part.

Irrevocable power of attorney

4.16 This appoints the bank as agent to do what is necessary to enforce the debenture, and to appoint others as substitute agents for the bank.

Repair, maintenance and insurance

4.17 In relation to land there are covenants to repair, maintain and insure (both land and buildings), and on default the bank is authorised to take action to remedy the deficiencies and recover the costs incurred from the company.

Administration

4.18 The company must pay all debts as they fall due and inform the bank of any proceedings against the company. It must keep its records in good order and supply copies of accounts and notices of meetings to the bank.

Continuing security

4.19 The security is a continuing security for all debts, liabilities and obligations from time to time owed by the company to the bank. It is unaffected by any payment of monies into the account. Thus, the Ru*le in Clayton's case* (1816) does not operate against the bank by creating new borrowing that is not secured simply because of the paying in of credit items which, under *Clayton's case*, would extinguish the original debt.

Accounts

4.20 The bank has the power to break the account and open a new account if it learns of charges made to others. The bank also has the right to combine accounts if there is a credit balance elsewhere.

Memorandum and articles

4.21 It is certified that the charges do not contravene the memorandum or articles of association, although this has less import with the abolition of the *ultra vires* rule in relation to the memorandum of association.

Student Activity 3

Look at your bank's standard debenture form and see how the clauses differ from the above list, if at all.

Remedies of a debenture holder

4.22 A secured debenture holder has five remedies available if a formal demand for repayment has been made but not satisfied:

- To sue for the debt.
- To apply to the court for a foreclosure notice. This vests the title of the company's assets in the debenture holder's name. (In practice, this remedy is rarely pursued.)
- To exercise the power of sale. As a secured creditor the debenture holder has the right to sell the asset so secured to gain repayment. The maximum sum the debenture holder can take from the sale proceeds is the amount of the debt, including interest and charges. Any surplus proceeds must be handed over to:
  - the company (if liquidation has not commenced);
  - the liquidator if liquidation has commenced; or
  - a second mortgagee, if a second mortgage has been created.
- To petition for the winding up of the company.
- To appoint an administrative receiver under the floating charge.

The effect of liquidation on fixed and floating charges

4.23 To recap, the order of repayment of company creditors in liquidation is:

- Secured creditors;
- Liquidator's expenses;
- Preferential creditors;
- Floating charges;
- Unsecured creditors;
- Interest on debts due since the date of liquidation;
- Members of the company.

4.24 Thus, a bank that has a debenture as security will rank first in relation to its fixed charge, and fourth (after liquidator's expenses and preferential creditors) in relation to its floating charge. The bank will only receive money under its floating charge if the three prior claims are satisfied in full. Likewise, creditors ranking after the floating charge will only receive payment if the floating charge has been paid in full.

5 Administrative receiver, administrator, and receiver

Administrative receiver

5.1 An administrative receiver is appointed under a floating charge: s.29(2), Insolvency Act 1986.

5.2 The administrative receiver must be appointed in writing by the debenture holder. He must accept the appointment by the end of the business day following receipt of the letter appointing him. The confirmation of acceptance must be given within seven days, in writing.

5.3 In practice, when a bank has become concerned about a company account, it may suggest that the directors invite the bank to appoint an administrative receiver. If the directors have asked the bank to appoint the administrative receiver, then there will be no danger of the administrative receiver being classed as a trespasser on the company's property, even if it subsequently turns out that the appointment was invalid. If the directors decline to request the appointment, the bank can put the appointment in place anyway.

5.4 The administrative receiver must:

- Advertise his appointment in the *London Gazette* and in a local newspaper;
- Give specific notice of his appointment to creditors within 28 days of appointment;
- Ensure that the company stationery, e.g. letterheads or invoices, contains the notice of his appointment.

5.5 The powers of an administrative receiver are laid down in Schedule 1, Insolvency Act 1986. (They are also usually reiterated and extended in the debenture.) The main powers are to:

- Take possession and get in the charged property;
- With the permission of the court, sell charged property where the charge ranks ahead of that under which the administrative receiver is appointed, and distribute proceeds in accordance with creditors' priorities;
- Carry on the business and borrow money;
- Present or defend a petition for the winding up of the company;
- Do all things (including the carrying out of works) as may be necessary for the realisation of the property of the company.

5.6 There are in total 23 powers detailed in Schedule 1, Insolvency Act 1986, but any of these powers can be overridden by the terms of the debenture under which the administrative receiver was appointed. However any person dealing with the administrative receiver in good faith and for value does not need to enquire as to whether the administrative receiver is acting within his powers: s.42(3) Insolvency Act 1986.

5.7 It is not uncommon for an administrative receiver to carry on the business of the company with a view to selling it as a going concern (which should mean that more money is raised for creditors than would be raised if the company ceased trading). It is, legally, coincidental that liquidation usually follows the appointment of an administrative receiver.

5.8 Although it is the bank that appoints the administrative receiver, albeit sometimes at the invitation of the directors, the administrative receiver is deemed to be the agent of the company until the company goes into liquidation. This means that he has the power to bind the company contractually in any transaction he initiates. However, he will deal with the security held at the bank's instruction. More importantly, the company, as opposed to the bank, is liable for the actions of the administrative receiver, unless the bank interferes in any way.

5.9 The administrative receiver is personally liable on all contracts, unless he specifically contracts out of liability. This is one of the few situations where an agent becomes personally liable for his deeds. This liability is the standard agency provision found in most commercial debentures.

Administrator

5.10 An administrator is appointed under a court order which is applied for by the company, its directors or a creditor. Under s.8, Insolvency Act 1986, an administration order may be made where, in the opinion of the court, the:

- Company is or is likely to become unable to pay its debts; and the
- Making of the order is preferable to a liquidation in terms of the realisation of assets or the survival of part of the business.

5.11 Under rr.2.6 and 2.7, Insolvency Rules 1986, at least five days notice of a hearing for an administration order must be given to a creditor entitled to appoint an administrative receiver. If the bank appoints an administrative receiver before the hearing, the court will not appoint an administrator.

5.12 Under ss.14–16, Insolvency Act 1986, the administrator's powers are wide and include the right to:

- Carry on the business;
- Deal with and dispose of assets;
- Borrow money and grant security;
- Bring and defend proceedings on the company's behalf;
- Establish subsidiaries and transfer them to the whole or part of the company's business;
- Employ and dismiss employees;
- Appoint and remove directors;
- Call meetings of members and creditors;
- Deal with property.

5.13 Where a bank holds a fixed charge without any floating charge (which would be unusual), it cannot block the appointment of an administrator. During the administration, the fixed chargeholder cannot exercise his power of sale unless the administrator agrees. However, if the administrator does realise assets over which the bank has a fixed charge, he must account to the bank for the proceeds.

5.14 A further problem can arise if the administrator sells assets caught under a fixed charge at below market price to effect a quick sale. In such a case, the administrator must have applied to the court. The authority for sale may only be made if the fixed chargeholder is protected by an order to make sums available to make up the deficiency. The only source of such funds are assets caught by a floating charge or assets available to unsecured creditors.

5.15 The administrator must, within three months, produce proposals for creditors: s.23, Insolvency Act 1986; and a meeting of creditors is then summoned to approve the proposals: s.24, Insolvency Act 1986. If the creditors do not approve, the administration order may be discharged. To approve the proposals a simple majority of unsecured creditors voting in person or by proxy is required. Secured creditors can only vote if part of their debt is not covered by security, and thus is unsecured.

Receiver

5.16 A receiver is appointed under the Law of Property Act 1925 by a fixed charge holder. He is appointed to sell the assets caught under the fixed charge and uses the proceeds to repay the fixed charge holder. Any surplus proceeds are returned to the company, which may then be put into liquidation by some other creditor.

5.17 The problem with the appointment of a receiver, is that if an administrator is subsequently appointed, he can force the receiver to vacate his office: s.11(2), Insolvency Act 1986.

Practical points for the bank

5.18 Banks include a floating charge clause in all forms of charge covering limited company assets so as to overcome the problems of relying on a fixed charge only. This will give the bank the flexibility to prevent the appointment of an administrator if it wishes. In *Re Croftbell Ltd* (1990) it was held that even if all of the borrower's assets were covered by the fixed charge, a clause in the debenture which incorporated a floating charge could enable the debenture holder to block the appointment of an administrator.

5.19 In *Shamji and Others v Johnson Matthey Bankers Ltd* (1986) it was held that the bank can appoint an administrative receiver under the terms of its floating charge without the need to concern itself with any other aspects e.g. whether or not the action taken by the bank is in the general interests of the borrower.

5.20 All bank floating charge forms incorporate a clause entitling the bank to appoint an administrative receiver on notice of a petition for an administration order.

5.21 Legal opinion is that any bank floating charge dated before 29 December 1986 will also entitle the bank to appoint an administrative receiver on notice of an administration order petition.

Action on notice of a petition for an administration order

5.22 On notice of a petition for an administration order, telephone head office at once if the bank holds a floating charge. This will enable guidance to be given regarding the appointment of an administrative receiver within five days.

5.23 The procedure for appointing an administrative receiver is:

- Ensure the conditions in the debenture (floating charge) have been fulfilled to give the bank the right to appoint an administrative receiver;
- The appointment must be in writing and must be formally accepted by the administrative receiver before the end of the next business day after receipt;
- Register at Registrar of Companies within seven days;
- The administrative receiver must be a licensed insolvency practitioner;
- In practice, the bank will ask the directors to appoint the AR. This avoids the risk of being classed as a shadow director and avoids liability for trespass. If the directors refuse, the bank will arrange the appointment itself.

Action when the bank receives notice of a petition to appoint an administrator when the account is in credit

5.24 When the account is in credit and the bank receives notice of a petition to appoint an administrator, the bank should stop the account, and ask the directors to obtain an interim order from the court to cover the operation of the bank account pending the hearing.

5.25 Once an administration order has been made, the powers of the directors cease. The bank will require sight of the administration order, and will note details in its records. Thereafter the bank must accept the instructions of the administrator, although it is not obliged to allow the bank account to go overdrawn.

Fixed and floating charges and preferences and transactions at an undervalue

5.26 Under ss.238–240, Insolvency Act 1986, a fixed or floating charge may be invalid because it amounts to a preference or a transaction at an undervalue.

5.27 If the court felt that the bank was being preferred by the giving of such security, then it would set aside the security as a preference. The bank is protected against the claim that such security is a preference if the only reason for the advance of further money or for the decision not to call in the debt was that security was given by the company. Likewise a debenture in favour of a director will not be classed as a preference if the director has taken the debenture as security for new money advanced to keep the company in business: *Re Fairways Magazines Ltd* (1992).

5.28 A transaction at undervalue could affect a company if another company in the group gave a guarantee to secure the borrowing. However, if the transaction was entered into in good faith, for the reason of carrying on its business, and if at the time the transaction was entered into there were grounds for believing that the transaction would benefit the company, then it is not a transaction at an undervalue: s.128(5), Insolvency Act 1986.

6 Intercompany (group) guarantees

Student Activity 4

Your bank holds the accounts of three companies, A plc which is the parent company of B plc and C plc. The three companies form the ABC group of companies and your bank has been asked to lend against the strength of the consolidated group balance sheet and profit and loss account. The request is for a net limit to cover the net borrowing position of the three companies. Do you think such an arrangement could be justified in the absence of special arrangements? If not why not? Now read on.

6.1 In the case of a group of companies, each one must be treated as a separate legal entity in the absence of special arrangements. Thus, if one company in the group is overdrawn at the bank and becomes insolvent, that bank will have rights only against that company and will not be able to look to the assets and cash flow of the group as a whole.

6.2 The most common way for the bank to be legally a creditor of the group as a whole is for the bank to arrange intercompany guarantees. If the guarantees are not supported by way of any fixed or floating charges, then the bank will effectively rank as an unsecured creditor against the group as a whole in the event of liquidation of one of the companies which is borrowing from the bank. If, however, the bank also holds fixed and floating charges from all members of the group in support of the guarantees, then the bank is a secured creditor with rights against the assets of the group as a whole.

6.3 Within a group of companies each one will have some effect on the profitability and, possibly, even on the survival of the others. Thus, there is consideration available for guarantees across the group. Intercompany guarantees mean that each member of the group is guaranteeing the borrowing of every other member of the group. Provided no new companies are brought into the group there will be no problems with the guarantees if they have been taken in accordance with the articles of association of the group of companies and providing the bank has a certified copy of the resolution authorising the guarantees.

6.4 If another company joins the group then great care needs to be taken in adding it to the guarantees, as incorrect procedure will invalidate the guarantee: *Ford and Carter Ltd v Midland Bank Ltd* (1979). If a new member is to be added to the guarantee, consideration must be given to the following:

- Whether the original agreement contemplates and allows for the addition of new guarantors, or whether all the original members must agree to the addition of the new member, or the new member must sign a separate guarantee;
- There must be consideration for the new member, or the guarantee must be executed by deed;
- The new member must follow the procedures which are correct for it, i.e. it must comply with its own articles of association.

7 Company security for directors' liabilities

Student Activity 5

Recap Unit 7, section 11.

7.1 Under s.303, 'financial assistance to directors is prohibited ... by way of guarantee or other security'. For such security to be valid under ss.332–338, the security or guarantee must come under the exceptions listed.

7.2 If a guarantee was given by the company to secure directors' liabilities, and these liabilities did not fall under ss.332–338, then the guarantee would be unenforceable against the company. Thus, the bank needs to take great care when such security is offered against directors' liabilities.

8 Discharge of security deposited for company borrowing

Security deposited by the company

8.1 Once the lending has been repaid, the bank will release the security back to the company. The bank will send a 'memorandum of charge ceasing to affect company's property', signed by both the chargee (bank) and the company, to the Registrar of Companies. The Registrar will file the correctly completed memorandum in the company charges register relating to that specific company, and note in such form as he thinks fit the date on which it was delivered to him: s.403(1)–(3). The Registrar must send a copy of the memorandum filed by him and of the note made by him as to the date on which it was delivered to the company and to the bank (if the bank was the chargee).

Collateral security

8.2 If a third party has deposited security to secure the company borrowing, this (of course) will not have been registered at Companies House. However, care must be taken that such security is not released in a preference situation. Such collateral (or third-party) security is usually deposited by a director who is a person connected with the company. Thus, the period for a preference is two years, against six months for security deposited by someone who is not connected with the company. If the borrowing has been paid in accordance with normal arrangements, all is well. The Insolvency Act 1986 protects innocent third parties who have no reason to suspect preferences. Likewise, the bank is safe if it has exerted pressure on the customer to repay: *Re M C Bacon Ltd* (1989).

8.3 If funds have come from the guarantor, all is well, since it is not the customer's money which has been diverted.

Request to release third-party security when an account goes into credit

8.4 If the reason for the improvement in the bank's position is that money has been diverted from other creditors, and if a winding up order is made within six months (non-connected person) or two years (connected person), the court could rule that a preference has arisen. The customer will have preferred the bank to ensure that his guarantor would not be called upon to pay.

8.5 If a preference is suspected, the bank must refuse to release the third-party security, relying on the period of notice set out in the charge form. If the company is in financial difficulty the winding up will probably occur very soon. If the liquidator claims a refund from the bank, the bank can use its third-party security to meet such a claim.

8.6 The bank should be able to rebut any claim for preference if the reason for the reduction in the bank overdraft came as a result of pressure from the bank: *Re M C Bacon Ltd* (1989).

Summary

Now that you have studied this unit, you should be able to:

- **understand the types of security given to secure company borrowing;**
- **list and describe the types of charges that need registration;**
- **differentiate between fixed and floating charges, and the effects of insolvency procedures on these charges;**
- **understand the effect of guarantees given by directors to secure company borrowing;**
- **describe the procedures for taking intercompany guarantees;**
- **understand the effect of a company giving security for directors' liabilities;**
- **describe how security deposited to secure a company's borrowing is discharged.**

Self-assessment questions

1 Which of the following mortgages requires registration at Companies House?

(a) An equitable mortgage over the company's factory.

(b) A legal mortgage over the director's house which secures the borrowing of the company.

(c) A mortgage over the factory of AB & Co (Partners A and B).

(d) A mortgage over a life policy taken out by a company on the life of a director.

2 You have a floating charge over the assets of Y Ltd, dated March 1995. You now learn that a legal mortgage over their factory was created in November 1996 in favour of a finance company. What is the position?

(a) The finance company mortgage takes priority as it is a legal one.

(b) The bank's floating charge takes priority because it was created first.

(c) The bank's floating charge takes priority because of the 'prohibition' clause registered at Companies House.

3 Which of the following are preferential creditors under Schedule 6, Insolvency Act 1986?

(a) VAT (six months).

(b) Uniform Business Rates unpaid for the past 12 months.

(c) Loans from directors for general purposes.

(d) Loans from directors to pay wages (maximum £800 per employee).

4 In a liquidation, where does a floating charge rank amongst the following: trade creditors; shareholders; rates; liquidation costs?

(a) First.

(b) Second.

(c) Third.

(d) Fourth.

(e) Fifth.

5 Sections 395–396, Companies Act 1985 state that all mortgages (with the certain exception) must be registered at Companies House within ... days of their creation. Within how many days must mortgages be registered?

(a) 30.

(b) 21.

(e) 14.

(d) 12.

6 The director and secretary of a limited company signed a bank mortgage form granting a floating charge over the company's property. Liquidation followed. The liquidator claims the floating charge is void because the company's seal was not used. Is the liquidator correct?

(a) Yes.

(b) No.

7 What is the name of the official whom a bank can appoint under a floating charge?

(a) Receiver.

(b) Liquidator.

(c) Administrative receiver.

(d) Administrator.

8 A bank holds a fixed charge. What is the name of the person whom it can appoint?

(a) Receiver.

(b) Liquidator.

(c) Administrative receiver.

(d) Administrator.

9 There are the following creditors in a company liquidation:

(i) Unpaid wages (maximum £800 per employee, money due within four months of liquidation).

(ii) A bank with a fixed charge.

(iii) A bank with a floating charge.

(iv) Rates.

(v) Nine months' VAT.

(vi) Trade creditors.

Set out the order of priority:

(a) Wages. Fixed charge. Floating charge. Rates. VAT. Trade creditors.

(b) Wages/six months' VAT. Fixed charge. Floating charge. Trade creditors/rates/three months' VAT.

(c) Fixed charge. Wages/six months' VAT. Floating charge. Trade creditors/rates/three months' VAT.

(d) Fixed charge. Wages/nine months' VAT. Floating charge. Trade creditors/rates.

10 A bank holds a valid third party security with a guaranteed value of £5,000 and a winding up order is made against its customer. The balance is £7,000 debit. How does the bank prove in the liquidation?

(a) Unsecured for £7,000.

(b) Unsecured for £2,000.

(c) As for (b), but only if the security has been realised.

(d) No proof submitted as the bank is fully secured.

11 The bank holds a fixed charge over the factory of a limited company. It has received notice of a petition for an administration order. What action can it take to overcome the administration order?

(a) Appoint a receiver within five days.

(b) Appoint an administrative receiver within five days.

(b) Appoint an administrative receiver within 10 days.

(d) The bank cannot do anything.

12 What can the bank do in 11 above, if the bank's fixed charge had been part of a debenture which also gave a floating charge as well?

(a) Appoint a receiver within five days.

(b) Appoint an administrative receiver within five days.

(b) Appoint an administrative receiver within 10 days.

(d) The bank cannot do anything.

13 Three years ago the North Sea Bubble Co Ltd gave to its bank as security a debenture in the usual bank form, including a fixed charge on all fixed assets and goodwill and a floating charge on all other property and assets. Last week the bank was surprised to see in a commercial gazette that amongst charges registered with the Registrar of Companies was a legal mortgage on land given by the company to a building society. On enquiry, the bank finds that the mortgage was on a house recently purchased by the company for occupation by a new executive.

Briefly discuss the legal position of the bank in relation to the house.

14 List the securities given by a company that do not require registration.

15 One of your bank's customers is a holding company, X Ltd, with a subsidiary, Y Ltd which is also a customer of yours. There is a combined limit of £1,000,000 to cover the net position.

You hold as security group guarantees supported by debentures with fixed charges over all property. The directors advise you that X Ltd wish to transfer ownership of their factory to Y Ltd for a consideration of £50,000. The market value is £500,000, but the transfer is at a lower price for tax reasons. Once the transfer is complete, Y Ltd will execute a mortgage over the factory.

What specific legal problems could arise as a result of the transfer?

Further reading

- Milnes Holden, J — Chapter 32, *The Law and Practice of Banking*, Vol 1, 5th edition 1991, Pitman
- Laidlaw, A and Roberts, G — Chapter 16, *Law Relating to Banking* Services, 2nd edition 1992, Bankers Books
- Raby, P — Chapter 18, *Law Relating to Banking Services*, 2nd edition 1992, Pitman

Unit 18

Regulation of Investment Business

Objectives

On studying this unit, you should be able to:

- **appreciate the background to the introduction of the Financial Service Act 1986;**
- **understand the main principles of that Act in relation to investment business;**
- **appreciate what is meant by the phrase 'people carrying out investment business';**
- **understand the significance of authorised or exempt;**
- **appreciate the impact of the main rules governing the conduct of investment business;**
- **understand the need to know your customer;**
- **appreciate the position regarding unsolicited calls.**

1 Background to the Financial Services Act 1986

1,1 The Financial Services Act 1986 (FSA) was passed in order to provide the investor with a higher and more up-to-date level of protection. With the growth in the financial services industry, new financial products have been created, and new ways of marketing financial service products have been developed. Under previous legislation, many of these products and marketing techniques were inadequately covered.

1.2 The Act has radically changed the way that the financial service industry operates, in particular, it:

- Established a new regulatory framework which is operated via industry based self-regulatory organisations (SROs), and which is overseen by the Securities and Investments Board (SIB).
- Requires all persons carrying on 'investment business' as defined by the Act to be authorised or exempted.
- Regulates the conduct of investment business and restricts the marketing of investments in accordance with, amongst other things the regulatory regime and regulatory framework.

2 Position prior to the FSA

2.1 Much of the old legislation covered specific areas of financial services, but there was no overall cover to provide for investor protection. The old legislation included, amongst others, the Companies Acts 1948–85, Banking Act 1979, Insurance Companies Act 1982, and the Prevention of Fraud (Investments) Act 1958.

2.2 Self-regulation was not mandatory throughout the financial services industry. The Council of the Stock Exchange, National Association of Securities Dealers and Investment Managers (NASDIM), and the various accountancy and legal bodies all regulated their own members. However, banking is not, and never was, regulated by its own professional body, The Chartered Institute of Bankers.

2.3 The need for change, and the run up to the FSA, came from the Gower Report – chaired by Professor Gower – which looked at three areas, the:

- Statutory protection required by both private and business investors in securities and other property, both directly and indirectly in regard to investment companies operating within the UK.
- Need for statutory controls of dealers in securities, investment consultants and investment managers.
- Need for new legislation.

2.4 This report, along with other changes taking place in the City, resulted in the Financial Services Act 1986.

2.5 The FSA established the framework for investor protection, including wide-ranging statutory powers and new criminal offences. Most of the powers have been delegated to the Securities and Investments Board (SIB). The main provisions of the Act came into force on 29 April 1988.

2.6 Within the FSA there are specific self-regulatory organisations (SROs), recognised professional bodies (RPBs) and recognised investment exchanges (RIEs) which regulate their own members. The SROs, RPBs and RIEs are recognised by the Securities and Investments Board (SIB), and are answerable to it.

3 Main purpose and effect of the FSA in connection with investment business

3.1 This can be summarised as follows.

1. People carrying out investment business must be authorised or exempt.
2. The FSA established a structure of industry based self-regulatory organisations (SROs) and recognised professional bodies (RPBs) overseen by the Securities and Investments Board.
3. The FSA regulates the carrying on of investment business through conduct of business, finance and other rules.
4. The FSA imposes restrictions on the marketing of investments and regulates the marketing of unit trusts and other collective investments.

3.2 The overall aim of the regulatory framework is to ensure healthy, internationally competitive markets in which users and practitioners can have confidence. As with all forms of regulation, there is a need to keep a balance between two conflicting objectives. On the one hand, too light a regulation will mean that malpractice can easily arise and this will damage the reputation of the market. On the other hand, if the regulation is too complex and costly to administer, then this could stifle initiative and raise costs to such an extent that business will move to a less stringently regulated market of a competitor.

What is meant by people carrying out investment business?

3.3 This is very broadly defined in the Act, and covers everything from one-man operations to the major clearing banks. It includes dealers in securities, advisors and arrangers of investment transactions. The range of financial service providers set out in paragraphs 1–11 of Schedule 1 of the FSA is extremely wide and covers:

- Banks – investment, merchant and commercial;
- Market makers;
- Stockbrokers;
- Unit trust managers;
- Investment trust managers;
- Portfolio managers;
- Commodity dealers;
- Solicitors;
- Accountants;
- Estate agents;
- Corporate treasurers;
- Building societies;
- Insurance brokers;
- Financial advisors.

3.4 Part II of Schedule 1 lists the activities constituting investment business, i.e. 'those activities which would require authorisation if carried on as a business and the Act contained no exemptions', as:

- *Dealing*: buying or selling a regulated investment as principal or agent.
- *Arranging*: arranging for a third party to deal.
- *Managing*: managing the regulated investments of another.
- *Advising*: giving specific advice on the merits of dealing.
- *Establishing, operating* or *winding up* collective investment schemes, e.g. unit trusts.

What is meant by investments?

3.5 The full list of regulated investments is found in Part I, Schedule 1. The investments to which the Act applies are, in general terms:

- Shares in companies or other bodies corporate, or in overseas unincorporated bodies (but not shares in open-ended investment companies or in building societies): paragraph 1.

- Eurobonds, gilts, loan stock, certificates of deposit, commercial paper and other debentures, or debt securities (but not bills of exchange, letters of credit, mortgages or trade finance instruments): paragraphs 2 and 3.
- Warrants and other rights to subscribe for shares or debentures: paragraph 4.
- Depository receipts or other certificates representing securities: paragraph 5.
- Shares in or securities of offshore funds, units in unit trusts and participation in other 'collective investment schemes' (including schemes for common management of physical investments) whether or not these schemes invest in regulated investments: paragraph 6.
- Traded options or other put or call options over securities (but not subscription rights, which fall under paragraph 4), currency options, gold or silver options, futures options and options over such options: paragraph 7.
- Financial and commodity futures, if the futures contract is for investment rather than commercial purposes, with regard to which the Act contains certain presumptions or indications: paragraph 8.
- Interest rate or currency swaps, stock market 'bets' and other contracts for differences, including perhaps interest rate futures: paragraph 9.
- Life assurance contracts with an investment element and personal pension policies, but not pure protection policies falling within very restricted criteria: paragraph 10.
- Rights to and interests in the above 'investments', but not interests under the trusts of an occupational pension scheme (or subscription rights, which fall in paragraph 4): paragraph 11.

Note: as a generalisation, tangible investments such as stamps, antiques and coins, are now classed as 'investments' for the purposes of the FSA.

4 The regulatory regime and main principles of the FSA

4.1 Investment business can be carried out only by those who are either authorised or exempt under the Financial Services Act 1986. The relevant SRO must be satisfied as to the integrity, competence and solvency of the business before it will grant authorisation. Authorisation can be given by the SIB of one of the SROs. Figure 18.1 illustrates the position.

4.2 The SIB has also granted authorisation to certain professional bodies (RPBs) and certain recognised clearing houses. Each RPB imposes a limit on the quantity of investment business which a member may carry out. This is intended to ensure that the member's main business is the practice of the profession and not that of investment business. The Chartered Institute of Bankers is *not* an RPB. The RPBs issue investment business certificates to those members whom they are prepared to authorise.

Which bodies do not require authorisation because they are exempt ?

4.3 The following bodies are wholly or partly exempt for the purposes of the FSA; the reasoning being that the investor is felt to be at no risk, or is felt to be otherwise adequately protected.

Figure 18.1 The regulatory framework for investment protection

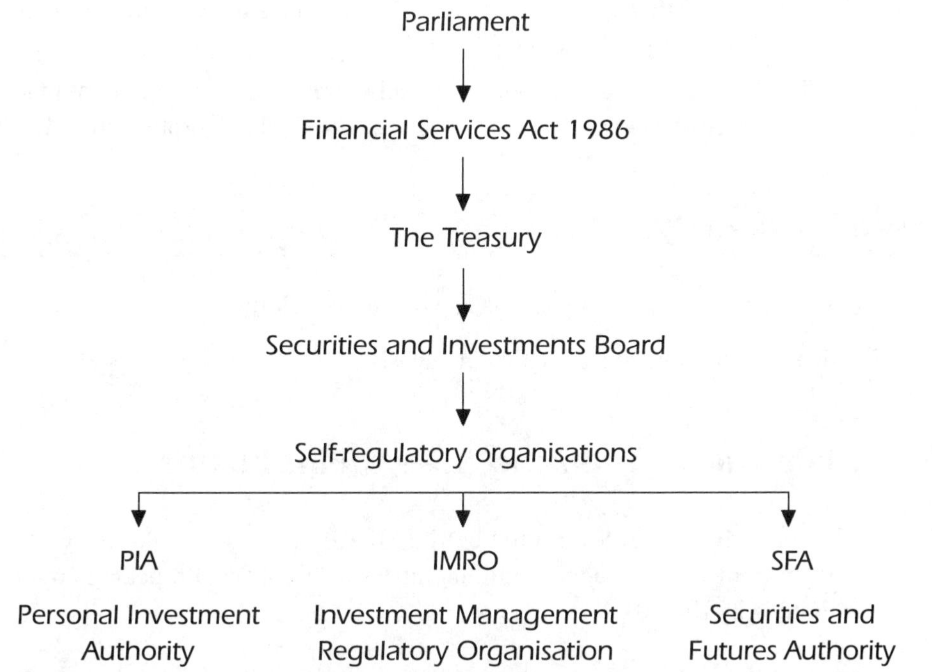

Notes

1 PIA covers organisations part of whose business is concerned with advising on or selling unit trusts, life assurance, or the provision of general financial advice and financial management. Some unit trust managers come under this category.

2 IMRO covers businesses whose activities include among others pension fund management, arranging deals and advising on investments in general.

3 SFA covers organisations which, among other things, give advice on transactions in futures and options.

- The Bank of England: s.35;
- Recognised investment exchanges and clearing houses (RIEs): ss.36–41.

  Individual exchanges may apply to the SIB to be classed as RIEs and hence become exempted persons for the purpose of the FSA. The SIB must be satisfied that the rules of the applicant exchange conform to the requirements of s.37 and Schedule 4 of the FSA. An example of an RIE is The London Stock Exchange.
- *Lloyds.* The Society of Lloyds and Lloyds underwriting agents are exempted persons in relation to investment business which they carry on for the purpose of insurance business at Lloyds: s.42.
- *Listed money market institutions.* Transactions between certain parties in the wholesale money, bullion and foreign exchange markets because they are supervised by the Bank of England: s.43.
- *Appointed representatives (tied agents).* This is the largest category of exempt person and consists of representatives who are exclusively or semi-exclusively sales agents of an authorised person. The exemption applies to investment business carried on in connection with the products of the organisation to which the authorised representative is tied: s.44.

An appointed representative must disclose his tied status and the company to which he is tied is bound by all his representations, acts and omissions. The appointed representative can be either an employee of the organisation or an agent.

- There are also miscellaneous exemptions consisting of a number of judicial and other officers such as the Master of the Court of Protection: s.45.

Student Activity 1

1 To which of the SROs listed above does your bank belong?

2 Why does it belong to those particular SROs?

5 Main rules governing investment business

5.1 There are 40 core rules drafted by the SIB and approved in January 1991. They are intended to apply to all members of all SROs and persons directly regulated by the SIB.

Financial rules

5.2 To qualify for and to retain the authorisation of an SRO, the firm must satisfy the SRO that it has available the amount and type of financial resources required by its regulator. The specific requirements are set out in the rule books of the various SROs.

5.3 A firm must maintain adequate financial records to accurately disclose its financial position and these records will normally include records of assets and liabilities, receipts and expenses, bank reconciliation statements, reconciliation statements in connection with any brokers or clearing houses used, and details of transactions made on behalf of clients. A firm must have adequate internal financial controls so as to be able to ensure that all transactions and commitments are properly reported and that customer assets are protected.

5.4 A firm must notify its regulator immediately if it becomes aware of any breach of the financial rules relating to solvency, records and internal controls.

5.5 The SIB Financial Services (Clients Money) Regulations 1991 lay down detailed rules regarding the keeping of clients money. These rules provide that firms must:

- Keep clients money separate from their own money and promptly pay it into a designated clients' account at an approved bank.
- Pay interest on the money as set out in the rules, unless otherwise agreed.
- Account for the money to the client.
- Follow prescribed rules for record keeping and auditing requirements.

5.6 These rules do not apply to an approved bank which is an authorised person and which holds money with itself. Nor do they apply to friendly societies which are governed by the arrangements of the PIA or of the Friendly Societies Commission.

Independence

5.7 A firm must not give or take any inducement which is likely to significantly conflict with its duty to its clients. When a firm has a material interest in a transaction or a conflict of interest, it must take reasonable steps to ensure fair treatment for its customer.

5.8 The term *polarisation* applies to a firm which advises a private customer on a packaged product, e.g. a unit trust/life policy. Such a firm must advise the client whether it is doing so in the capacity of product company/tied agent (advising only on its own products) or as an independent intermediary.

5.9 Most financial services organisations are tied agents, but many also have subsidiaries which are designated independent intermediaries. A client who wants independent advice may request advice from the subsidiary, and in such cases the representative of the organisation who is a tied agent cannot comment on the advice from the subsidiary. This would be known as conduit advice.

The regulation of employees

5.10 The SIB principle is that firms who employ staff must ensure that they are suitable, adequately trained and properly supervised. This obligation extends to the firm's appointed representatives. A firm is obliged to ensure that its personnel act in such a way that the firm will itself comply with the provisions of the FSA and of the relevant SRO. The following are examples of rules from SRO rule books:

- Staff must be registered with the SRO: which means that they must have passed a prescribed examination or be exempt from it because they hold an equivalent qualification or because of prior experience.
- A firm must take reasonable steps to ensure its staff and directors observe restrictions on insider dealings – dealing for personal gain having acted upon confidential information acquired during the course of employment. The firm must give every registered employee a personal notice which regulates the way in which the employee deals in securities, including any dealing for their own personal account.

Student Activity 2

If you have already passed an examination which allows you to be registered, consider how that examination would help you as an employee involved in investment business. If you have not already passed such an examination, then discuss this point with a colleague who has.

Complaints procedure

5.11 Every authorised firm must have a formal written complaints procedure and all complaints must be recorded and monitored. The detailed procedures vary from SRO to SRO, but in general:

- Complaints must be handled by a responsible officer not directly concerned with the matter.
- A response must be given promptly with a clear statement as to whether the complaint is accepted (and if so what remedy is proposed) or rejected.

- The customer must be told of his right to complain to the relevant ombudsman.
- The ombudsman will attempt to conciliate and achieve a mutually acceptable agreement. If unsuccessful, he can adjudicate the complaint and if he finds in the customer's favour he can require the firm to pay compensation or make other amends. There are various restrictions and other differences depending on which Ombudsman is involved. For example, the Banking, Building Society and Insurance Ombudsmen generally only deal with private customers.

5.12 Clients are free to pursue other legal remedies if they are dissatisfied with the award of the Ombudsman.

Advertising

5.13 When a firm issues or approves an advert, it must take such steps to apply expertise to ensure that the advert is fair and not misleading. Indeed a firm may only make any promotional communication about investment business provided it reasonably believes that the advert is fair and not misleading. A key SIB principle is that a firm must:

- Understand the subject matter of an advert.
- Appraise the advert critically.
- Be able to show that it has reasonable grounds to believe that the advert is fair, factually accurate and that any opinions expressed are reasonably held.
- Include risk warnings, for example, where the:
  - value of the investment might fluctuate
  - investment is not readily realisable
  - income yield is variable, or where the
  - investment may involve the client in a contingent liability, such as could arise from becoming a counter-party to a derivative.

5.14 There are other codes which govern the use of adverts in general. Under The Control of Misleading Advertisements Regulations 1988, the Director General of Fair Trading can take action against misleading adverts if he considers that it is in the public interest to do so. He may apply for an injunction requiring the advertiser to substantiate any factual claims.

5.15 The British Code of Advertising Practice requires that members of the public must be able from the advert to fully grasp the nature of any commitment they might enter into as a result of the advert.

Compensation scheme

5.16 Every SRO member must pay a levy to support the SIB compensation scheme, which can make awards of up to £48,000 to investors in appropriate circumstances.

Student Activity 3

Obtain a copy of any article in an appropriate publication (*Financial Times, Investors Chronicle*) on any 'scandal' where investors have been defrauded. Try to find out what the victims thought of the speed with which their compensation claims were settled.

Best advice

5.17 A firm is obliged to give the 'best advice' to its customers at all times. In the case of a company representative, this means providing advice on the most suitable investments available from the range of its company products. For the independent intermediary, this means the best advice from the whole range of investment products available. In both cases, the advice must be adequate and suitable. A firm is obliged to keep records to back the basis for its recommendations. These rules are laid down in the SIB rule book.

Best execution

5.18 The 'best execution' rule requires a firm to take all reasonable steps to ensure that its customers' orders are executed on the best available terms. Normally, the main consideration is price, but other factors, such as whether additional advantages apply, may also be taken into account.

5.19 This SIB rule does not apply to all investors. It does not apply to the professional, business or experienced investor who agrees that the firm does not owe him any fiduciary duties other than giving advice. This is clearly stated in the customer agreement letter.

5.20 When a firm acts as a broker/dealer, it can only make a deal with its market-making arm if that arm can offer the client a better price than that available elsewhere.

5.21 A broker/dealer is a firm which has two sections, a broking arm and a dealing arm. The broker acts as the agent of the investor, taking his instructions to buy or sell stocks and shares. The dealer is a principal who actually owns the stocks and shares and makes the market in them (market-making). The conflict that could arise is when the dealing arm would prefer to buy or sell stocks and shares to the investor via its broking arm. In such a case the investor may not get the best price. To prevent this, the 'best execution' rule states that the two arms can only deal together if the dealing arm can provide a better price than that available elsewhere. To ensure this rule is complied with, the deals can be randomly checked because all the information about prices ruling throughout the day is stored on computers.

Fair allocation

5.22 When a firm has aggregated orders for customer transactions in stocks and shares, it must not giver any unfair preference to itself or to any customer.

Safe custody of investments

5.23 A firm which has safe custody of client investments must keep the title documents safe and ensure that any registrable investments are properly registered.

Chinese walls

5.24 Sometimes a financial services company may have a conflict of interest or duty between two of its clients. Suppose, for example, that a clearing bank has a corporate finance section which provides advice and finance to major quoted companies. In addition, assume that the same bank has a market-making division and a broker/advisory function for its private clients. In these circumstances, it is quite possible that the bank could have a major quoted company as a client of its corporate finance division, whilst the broker/dealer arm of the bank could be concerned with advice and transactions in the shares of that same company for its personal clients.

5.25 The potential conflict of interest could arise if the corporate finance division of the bank became aware of confidential financial data about the company and then passed on that data to the broker/dealer arm of the bank. If such information were to be passed on between the two departments of the bank, then this could amount to 'insider dealing', a criminal offence under the Company Securities (Insider Dealing) Act 1985.

5.26 To prevent insider dealing occurring, financial services companies who may have a conflict of interest as described above are obliged to follow the concept of 'Chinese Walls'. This means that there must be no flow of confidential information between different divisions of a financial services company when such data could cause a conflict of interest or result in insider dealing. This barrier to the passing of information is known as a 'Chinese Wall'.

6 Know your customer

6.1 A firm cannot do anything for a customer, with the exception of 'execution only' customers, unless it knows what sort of customer an individual would be. An 'execution only' customer is one who simply gives a firm an instruction and the firm carries out the instruction exactly as given, without providing any advice or explanation. This is covered in the SIB rules.

6.2 A firm must take reasonable care to determine whether a customer is a professional investor, business investor, experienced investor or ordinary investor.

6.3 A *professional investor* is one who is authorised or exempted to carry out investment business.

6.4 A *business investor* is one who in the course of a business which is not an authorisable business customarily buys or sells investments. A business investor is only a business investor with respect to the type of investment he normally deals in, or advises on, in the course of his main business. For example, a company which uses currency futures as part of its treasury management function would be classed as a business investor for that investment. However, if a business had no foreign business or foreign currency, it would not be regarded as a business investor in currency futures.

6.5 An *experienced investor* is one who has gained experience of particular types of investment by actively managing his own investments over a period of a year or more on such a scale that he has exposed himself to significant risks.

By such action he can be expected to understand the nature of the risks involved. An investor must agree to be treated as an experienced investor, it is his decision, not that of the firm with which he is dealing.

6.6 An *ordinary investor* is one who does not fall into any of the above three categories. It is to the ordinary investor that the highest level of protection is given, as he is taken as having little or no knowledge of any investments.

Student Activity 4

Obtain a copy of your bank's 'know your customer' form and study the questions on it. How do these questions meet the legal requirements laid down in the FSA?

Suitability rule

6.7 This complements the 'know your customer' rule (covered in the SIB rule book). The rule requires that a firm which recommends to a customer the purchase, sale or exchange of any investment must have:

> ... reasonable grounds for believing that the transaction is suitable for the customer, having regard to the facts known, or which ought reasonably to be known, to the firm, from such answers as the customer has given to the firm's enquiries, as to the customer's other investments and his personal and financial situation.

6.8 This rule means that a firm should find out as much information as possible from the client before making any recommendations. The information gained will be recorded, but the firm does not have to check the accuracy of such information given. If the customer refuses to give full information, the firm can still make recommendations.

6.9 An example of unsuitable information would be where a customer who has recently retired with a lump sum of money plus a pension requires growth of income and capital from his lump sum. You would not suggest that he put his money into investments such as warrants, options and futures because these are very high risk, no income, investments. Any investor who is adversely affected by unsuitable advice may sue the firm for damages under s.62, FSA 1986.

Customer agreements

6.10 A firm must only provide services to a customer *after* they have obtained a signed customer (or client) agreement letter, which lays down the nature of the services provided. There are three types of customer agreement:

- Full customer agreements, essential for ordinary investors;
- Occasional customer agreements;
- Terms of business letter for business, professional or experienced investors.

All three types of agreement must disclose the nature of services provided, and the basis, method and frequency of payment by the customer to the firm.

7 Unsolicited calls (cold calling)

7.1 Section 56(8) defines an unsolicited call as 'a personal visit or oral communication made without express invitation'.

7.2 'Oral communication' covers unsolicited telephone calls. 'Personal visit' does not apply when a prospective investor comes to a financial advisor's office to discuss one matter and the financial advisor then talks about another matter without invitation.

7.3 The main areas that are banned under s.56 are door-to-door selling and selling under the guise of market research, i.e. a person is stopped in the street and given the impression that the interviewer is carrying out market research, but the interviewer then launches into an investment sales pitch.

7.4 *Note*: s.56(1) and (7), FSA 1986 allow the SI, an SRO or RPB to exclude or modify the prohibition on cold calling.

7.5 Unsolicited calls, more commonly known as cold calls, are effectively banned for all persons, even though they are authorised or exempted persons. Anyone who contravenes the prohibition on cold calling is not guilty of a criminal offence but will be subject to certain civil sanctions.

Civil sanctions for cold calling

7.6 The sanctions are that:

- Any resulting investment contract will be unenforceable against the person called: s.56(2).
- The person called will be able to recover any money or other property transferred, as well as interest or other compensation: s.56(2).
- In the case of life assurance and unit trusts, there is a 14-day 'cooling-off' period, during which time the person called can cancel the contract and recover any money or property paid over (SIB rules). Cooling off in relation to unit trust bargains and single premium life assurance contracts will not be allowed on execution-only cases, i.e. when the order is simply given by the customer and carried out without any advice of any nature being given. It also does not apply to bargains entered into on the basis of money-off-the-page advertisements or following a written customer agreement.

7.7 These are civil sanctions, and even where there has been a contravention of the prohibition on cold calling, a court may allow the investment contract to be enforced, or money or property retained in certain circumstances. These situations are covered in s.56(4) and are if the:

- Person on whom the call was made was not materially influenced by anything done in the course of, or in consequence of, the call;
- Agreement was entered into after discussions other than those made during the 'unsolicited call', provided the investor was aware of the nature of and risks involved in the agreement.

Summary

Now that you have studied this unit, you should be able to:

- **understand the rationale of the Financial Services Act 1986;**
- **appreciate the main principles and terminology of the FSA;**
- **understand the implications of the FSA as regards customer agreements;**
- **appreciate the rules and sanctions imposed by the FSA on unsolicited calls ('cold calling').**

Self-assessment questions

1 What is the term used to describe the duty of a financial services organisation to choose between being a tied agent and being an independent intermediary?

2 Does 'best advice' mean that the advisor must always give advice on the most suitable investment for the client from all investment available? If not, why not?

3 What does 'best execution' mean?

4 Where there is a possible conflict of interest between two arms of a bank regarding information about a business customer that could, if known, influence an investment decision by another client of the bank, what would this information be classed as if it were passed on to the investor? What has been 'erected' to stop this flow of information?

5 If information is passed on to an investor as described in question 4, what is the possible legal offence and under what Act?

6 Under the 'know your customer' rule, there are four categories of investor. What are they?

7 Define 'unsolicited calls'.

8 A court may allow an investment contract to be enforced even if it was cold called. What gives the court this power?

Further reading

- Laidlaw, A and Roberts, G — Chapter 4, *Law Relating to Banking* Services, 2nd edition 1992, Bankers Books
- Morris, S — Chapters 1–10, 13, *Financial Services Regulating Investment Business*, 1995, Sweet & Maxwell
- Raby, P — Chapter 4, *Law Relating to Banking Services*, 2nd edition 1992, Pitman

Unit 19

Regulated Lending: Consumer Credit Act 1974

Objectives

After studying this unit, you should be able to:

- **appreciate the rationale behind the Consumer Credit Act 1974 (CCA);**
- **understand the meaning of the terms credit, regulated agreement, consumer credit agreement, debtor and creditor in the CCA;**
- **appreciate the consequences of failure to comply with the documentary requirements of the CCA;**
- **differentiate between different types of regulateed agreement;**
- **identify the exempt credit agreements;**
- **understand what is meant by security in connection with regulated lending;**
- **appreciate the special formalities which apply to regulated agreements secured on land;**
- **understand what is meant by a credit token and why it is important to be able to decide whether a particular plastic card is a credit token;**
- **appreciate the significance of connected lender liability;**
- **understand how the CCA rules are applied to overdrafts;**
- **understand the debtor's rights if he wishes to make early repayment;**
- **understand the legal position when a bank wishes to terminate a regulated agreement;**
- **understand what is meant by canvassing and how this is regulated by the CCA;**
- **understand what is meant by credit brokerage and how this is regulated by the CCA;**
- **appreciate the implications of the CCA in connection with advertising.**

1 Introduction to the Act

1.1 The Consumer Credit Act 1974 (CCA) was enacted following the Crowther Report (Report of the Committee on Consumer Credit 1971). The key paragraph in the report summing up the rationale behind the Act states:

> Many consumers have no understanding, or no adequate understanding, of the nature of the commitment into which they are entering or of the cost and other terms, or of alternatives that are available to them. They are also ignorant of their legal rights. This lack of knowledge may be due to want of intelligence or education on the part of the consumer concerned, or it may result from the fact that information which he is conscious of needing in order to make an intelligent choice is not made available to him, or alternatively is not presented to him in an intelligible form.

1.2 The CCA seeks to protect non-corporate borrowers over a whole range of areas covering consumer credit up to £15,000. It protects individuals in a private capacity, as sole or joint traders, as trustees or executors, or when acting in any capacity for an unincorporated body, or as partners in a partnership.

1.3 Many parts of the Act were brought into force over a period of time by statutory instrument. In particular, for banks, the implementation of the Act has meant that special forms must be used for all borrowing which is regulated by the Act. These forms must draw the debtor's attention to his rights, and copies of the forms, including copies of any security forms, must be supplied to the borrower and to any surety. In particular, guarantees and third-party charge forms for borrowing which comes within the Act must be in a form prescribed by the Act.

1.4 All references in this unit are to the 1974 Act unless stated otherwise.

Terms defined

Credit

1.5 Section 9(1) defines credit as a 'cash loan and any other form of financial accommodation'. If the credit is provided in the form of foreign currency, it is still within the Act: s.9(2).

Regulated agreement

1.6 A regulated agreement is defined by s.189(1) as any consumer credit agreement or consumer hire arrangement which is not an exempt agreement.

Consumer credit agreement

1.7 A consumer credit agreement is an agreement under which an individual is provided with credit not exceeding £15,000, so long as the agreement is not an exempt agreement: s.8.

Debtor and creditor

1.8 A debtor is an individual receiving, and a creditor is the person providing, credit under a consumer credit agreement: s.189(1).

1.9 For the purpose of the Act any loan with a qualifying credit limit (basically £15,000 or less) which is not exempt under s.16, covered below, will be a consumer credit agreement if the debtor is:

- An individual;
- A partnership; or

- Consists of two or more individuals borrowing on a joint account; or
- Is an unincorporated body of individuals such as a club or society.

Consequences of any breach of CCA documentary regulations

1.10 Under s.170 any breach of the terms of the documentary requirements of the Act shall incur no criminal or civil sanction as being such a breach, except to the extent, if any, as provided by the Act. However, under s.170(2) the Director General of Fair Trading may take account of any such breach in exercising his functions under the Act and under s.170(3) the courts have the power to grant injunctions to enforce compliance with the Act.

1.11 However, whilst there may be no civil or criminal sanctions except as provided above, failure to fulfil the documentary requirements of the CCA will mean that a resulting regulated agreement will be 'improperly executed' and, under s.65, this means that the agreement is enforceable against the debtor only if a court so orders. Under s.127, the general guidelines stipulate that the court should *not* make an enforcement order unless it considers it just having regard to:

- Whether anybody has suffered as a result of the contravention of the Act;
- Who is at fault;
- Whether the amount should be reduced or discharged to compensate the debtor for what he has suffered as a result of the breach;
- Whether any security agreement should be modified or rendered void.

2 Loan agreements

2.1 Section 60(1) states that:

> ... the content of documents embodying regulated agreements shall contain such provisions as ... to ensure that the debtor is made aware of:
>
> (a) the rights and duties conferred or imposed on him by the agreement;
>
> (b) the amount and rate of the total charge for credit;
>
> (c) the protection and remedies available to him under this Act; and
>
> (d) any other matters which, in the opinion of the Secretary of State, it is desirable for him to know about in connection with the agreement.

2.2 'Regulated agreements' apply only to personal credit agreements not exceeding £15,000 which come under the Act and which are not exempted by the Act, or which are an overdraft. The document produced under a regulated agreement must be in writing, s.61(1) requires that the document be signed, thus there cannot be a binding oral CCA agreement.

2.3 To recap, if the agreement is not executed in the manner specified in the Act and subsequent Consumer Credit (Agreement) Regulations 1983, then it will only be enforceable on an order of the court: s.65(1).

The Consumer Credit (Agreement) Regulations 1983

2.4 These came into force on the 19 May 1985, some 11 years after the Act was passed and have had a far-reaching effect on lenders' documentation.

2.5 They specify the information which must be disclosed in particular circumstances. The basic information that must be included in all regulated agreements is:

- Creditor's (i.e. lender's) name and address;
- Amount of credit or credit limit;
- Classification of the agreement, e.g. if it is cancellable, that the debtor has the right to cancel within a certain number of days of signing it.

Depending on the type of lending, other information must also be included.

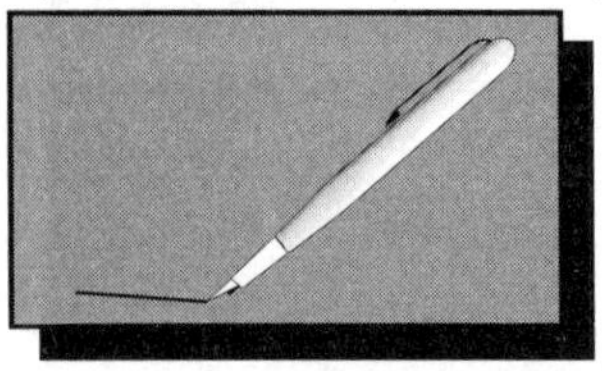

Student Activity 1

Obtain a copy of your bank's agreement form for regulated lending. Compare the information given in that form with the information in the following text.

Types of consumer credit agreement

2.6 The agreement can be between two parties – the debtor (the borrower) and the creditor (the lender) – or between three parties – the debtor, the creditor and the supplier (the person who supplies goods or services under a pre-*existing agreement bet*ween himself and the creditor).

- Section 13 covers debtor-creditor agreements, e.g. a bank overdraft.
- Section 12 covers debtor-creditor-supplier agreements, e.g. a credit card agreement.

2.7 There are two ways in which money can be lent: as a fixed sum, e.g. a personal loan, or as a running account, e.g. overdraft. The lender can either specify the usage of the money, i.e. a restricted use such as purchase of a specific asset, or can allow the debtor to use the money for any purpose, i.e. unrestricted use.

2.8 This results in eight basic combinations of agreement:

- Debtor-creditor/restricted use/fixed sum;
- Debtor-creditor/unrestricted use/fixed sum;
- Debtor-creditor/restricted use/running account;
- Debtor-creditor/unrestricted use/running account;
- Debtor-creditor-supplier/restricted use/fixed sum;
- Debtor-creditor-supplier/unrestricted use/fixed sum;
- Debtor-creditor-supplier/restricted use/running account;
- Debtor-creditor-supplier/unrestricted use/running account.

In addition, the agreements may be cancellable, non-cancellable, modifying, multiple or credit token.

Cancellable agreements

2.9 These are regulated agreements that can be cancelled by the debtor within five days of the signing of the agreement by the debtor. The unexecuted agreement must be signed by the customer *off trade premises.*

2.10 If the agreement is concluded on the spot, i.e. right away, then a copy of it must be sent to the debtor by post within seven days together with details of his right of cancellation: s.64.

2.11 The cancellation period is five days: s.68(a). The period runs from the *signing* of the agreement by the debtor. Finance is not available to the borrower(s) until the cancellation period has expired. Thus, the effective time period is seven plus five days (12 days). This is called the 'cooling-off' period.

2.12 In a banking context, cancellable agreements usually arise where there have been face-to-face negotiations between the bank and borrower(s), and where the agreement form has not been signed on bank or trade premises, or has not been signed by all borrowers on bank or trade premises.

2.13 The potential borrower is not required to give a reason for cancelling. He is merely required to give written notice to the creditor during the five-day period after receipt of the cancellation notice.

Non-cancellable agreements

2.14 Under s.67, an agreement is non-cancellable if it was:

- Signed on trade premises; or
- Secured on land.

Modifying agreements

2.15 These are agreements which vary or supplement an earlier agreement. They revoke the earlier agreement and contain provisions reproducing the combined effects of the old and new agreements: s.82. Notice of modification must be served on the debtor not less than seven days before the variation takes effect.

2.16 In the case of bank overdrafts, where the interest is in line with bank base rate, this would be a cumbersome process. The Act therefore allows banks to notify the change by means of an advertisement placed in three national papers, or if this is not practicable, in the London Gazette. The notice will also be displayed on bank premises. This saves the bank from having to contact every overdraft customer individually.

Multiple agreements

2.17 These are hybrid agreements under the Act, or an agreement that is partly regulated and partly unregulated: s.18. A hybrid agreement is one which falls under two or more sections of the Act.

Credit-token agreements

2.18 These are agreements for the provision of credit in connection with the use of a credit token, e.g. a credit card: s.14(1).

Statutory forms

2.19 The different types of agreement require different forms. To be valid under the Act the wording must be reproduced 'without alteration or addition': Regulation 5(1), Consumer Credit (Agreement) Regulations 1983. However, the words 'the creditor' can be replaced by the creditor's name. The word 'debtor' can be replaced by 'borrower' or 'customer'.

2.20 The agreement must be signed by the debtor or his agent, in the space provided for the purpose (usually a box), and it must also be dated in the same place. The creditor or his agent must sign the agreement outside the space or box provided, and date the signature.

2.21 If the agreement is cancellable a statement to that effect, giving the number of days allowed for cancellation, must be included in the agreement. If the agreement is not cancellable, the date on which the unexecuted (unsigned) agreement becomes an executed agreement may be inserted.

The general information required in regulated agreements

2.22 The following information is required in regulated consumer credit agreements:

- A heading, e.g. 'Credit Agreement regulated by the Consumer Credit Act 1974';
- The name and address of the debtor and creditor;
- The amount of credit (fixed sum) or credit limit (running account);
- The timing of repayments;
- The amount of each repayment;
- The APR (annual percentage rate of charge for credit).

Other information required will depend upon the type of agreement entered into by the debtor.

Exempt credit agreements

2.23 Some credit agreements, even though they are made with individuals, are exempt from the provisions of the Act. They are:

- Mortgage lending by building societies, banks, including foreign banks, wholly- owned subsidiaries of banks, local authorities, insurance companies, friendly societies and church charities: s.16(1), and redefined by the Consumer Credit (Exempt Agreements) Order 1989.

  The exemptions under s.16(1) only apply where the agreement is:

  - a debtor-creditor-supplier agreement for the purchase of land, or the provision of dwellings on any land, and is secured by a land mortgage on that land, or
  - a debtor-creditor agreement secured by a land mortgage. *Note*: second mortgage type lending is not exempt.
- Debtor-creditor-supplier fixed sum agreements, where the number of repayments does not exceed four.
- Debtor-creditor-supplier running account agreements under which credit provided in a given period must be repaid in not more than one instalment.
- A foreign trade agreement.

- Low-cost credit under debtor-creditor agreements. Low cost is taken as the higher of base rate plus 1% or 13%: s.16.

Definition of security

2.24 Section 189(1), defines security as:

> ... a mortgage, charge, pledge, bond, debenture, indemnity, guarantee, bill, note or other right provided by the debtor, or at his request (express or implied), to secure the carrying out of the obligation of the debtor under the agreement.

2.25 If security is provided by the debtor, i.e. the borrower, it is direct security. If security is provided 'at his request' (express or implied), someone other than the debtor depositing the security, thus it is third-party (or collateral) security.

2.26 Care must be taken with 'bond' and 'bill', this does not apply to bearer bonds or bills of exchange (including cheques), as they are negotiable instruments. Under s.123 negotiable instruments cannot be taken as security for a regulated agreement.

Student Activity 2

Obtain a copy of your bank's land secured agreements which come under the Consumer Credit Act. Also obtain a copy of your bank's timetable and compare this with the one given in this unit.

Where the provision of credit for any purpose is to be secured wholly or partly by a charge over land, the agreement is always non-cancellable.

Land secured agreements

Timetable

2.27 An advance copy of the agreement is despatched to the prospective borrower. This copy is marked 'Copy of proposed credit agreement containing notice of your rights to withdraw. Do not sign or return this copy.' The lender must not contact the borrower during the consideration period of seven days, which commences when the advance copy is sent to the prospective borrower. The prospective borrower is free to contact the lender during the consideration period.

2.28 Next, and not earlier than seven days later, the regulated agreement form is sent by post, together with the borrower's copy of the agreement and completed copies of the security documents mentioned in it. Again there must be no contact during the consideration period of eight days, except at the request of the prospective borrower. The time runs from posting of these documents.

2.29 If the borrower returns the documents, duly signed before the end of this eight-day period, the consideration period ends. The documents can be signed either on or off the bank's premises.

2.30 As with all agreements, the lender must also sign the agreement forms, and if there is more than one borrower, each party must receive his own copy of the agreement form and a copy of any other security form mentioned in the agreement.

2.31 In total, for land secured agreements, the consideration period extends to a maximum of 15 days. Once the process has been completed, the loan can be drawn down.

Student Activity 3

Obtain blank copies of your bank's regulated agreement forms covering borrowing secured on land, other forms of security and guarantees. Compare the details in your bank form with the details in this unit. Are there any differences?

Security agreements other than land

2.32 Security can take two forms, direct and third party (collateral). For both, if the lending falls within the CCA, the regulations apply. Note that the requirements regarding the provision of independent legal advice, as set out in the Code of Banking Practice, must also be followed.

2.33 If it is direct security, i.e. deposited by the borrower, the security must be scheduled in the regulated agreement and a copy of the agreement and charge form must be given to the borrower.

CCA: guarantees and other third party security

2.34 The Consumer Credit (Guarantees and Indemnities) Regulations 1983 require the inclusion of a:

- Description of the regulated agreement secured;
- Statement of the third party's rights;
- Note of the names and addresses of all parties to the security;
- Box (as prescribed) for the signature of the guarantor/third party.

2.35 If a guarantee is to be supported by any other security, e.g. shares, the supporting security must be included in the guarantee form.

2.36 All third-party security forms in relation to regulated agreements must carry prominent warnings, such as 'sign only if you want to be legally bound', and 'Important you should read this carefully'.

2.37 All third parties pledging their security for the liabilities of the customer must receive a copy of the agreement form and copy of the security form.

Information to which guarantors are entitled under the CCA

2.38 Under the Act, provided the guarantor requests the information in writing and pays the 15p fee, a bank must provide a guarantor of a fixed-sum credit agreement with a:

- Copy of the agreement form;
- Signed statement showing the total sum which:

- has become payable by the debtor under the agreement but remains unpaid
- is to become payable under the agreement by the debtor, and the various amounts comprised in that total sum, with the date when each becomes due.

2.39 Under s.108, which covers overdrafts or 'running credit agreements', the guarantor who has paid the fee and made a written request is entitled to a:

- Copy of the executed agreement, if any;
- Signed statement showing the:
  - state of the debtor's account
  - amount, if any, currently due from the principal debtor to the bank
  - amounts and due dates of any payments which if the debtor does not draw further on the account will later become payable under the agreement by the debtor to the creditor.

2.40 If the bank fails to provide this information, it will be unable to enforce the security whilst the default continues. The bank commits an offence if the default lasts for one month.

Negotiable instruments

2.41 Under s.123, negotiable instruments cannot be taken as security for a regulated agreement. Negotiable instruments include cheques, bills of exchange and bearer shares (bonds).

3 Credit tokens

3.1 Section 14(1) of the Act defines a credit token as:

> a card check, voucher, coupon, stamp, form, booklet or other document or thing given to an individual by a person carrying on a consumer credit business who undertakes:
>
> (a) that on the production of it, he will supply cash, goods and services on credit; or
>
> (b) that where, on production of it to a third party, the third party supplies cash goods and services, he will pay the third party for them, in return for payment to him by the individual.

3.2 You should be able to decide which of the five main types of plastic card below are credit tokens.

Cheque guarantee cards

3.3 These are *not* credit tokens. The cheque itself is the means of payment for the goods and services. The card simply guarantees payment, provided the conditions have been fulfilled.

Cash cards

3.4 These may or may not be credit tokens, but all are *exempt* from CCA regulation.

3.5 When the card is used to obtain cash from an ATM of the issuing bank it is not a credit token as there is no question of credit being granted, even if the effect of the withdrawal is to create or increase an overdraft as this would be under a totally separate agreement.

3.6 If the card is used at another bank's ATM it is not a credit token if the other bank is an agent of the card issuer. If the other bank is not an agent, then the cash card will be a credit token, but it will be exempt from CCA regulations in accordance with s.89, Banking Act 1987.

Debit cards

3.7 Debit cards such as SWITCH or Connect are credit tokens, but they are exempt from CCA regulations in accordance with s.89, Banking ACt 1987.

Charge cards

3.8 A charge card such as American Express is a credit token. Clearly, a period of credit is involved, although payment is made in full to the card issuer, it is only due on receipt of statements which are usually sent at monthly intervals. However, the Consumer Credit (Exempt Agreements) Order 1989 exempts such cards from regulation, primarily because 'the number of payments to be made by the debtor in repayment of the whole amount of credit provided in each period shall not exceed one'.

Credit cards

3.9 Credit cards such as Visa or Mastercard differ from charge cards in that the cardholder normally need pay off only a specified minimum percentage of the debit balance as shown on the periodic statements. Thus, such cards are credit tokens and they do not fall within the exemptions set out for charge cards because the credit provided in each period can be paid off in more than one instalment.

3.10 *Note* 1 Connected lender liability can apply only to credit cards, since the other cards are either not credit tokens, or are exempt from CCA regulations.

2 Banks can insert 'reasonable' exclusion clauses in customer agreements concerning cards which are not credit tokens. Such exclusions must pass the test of reasonableness as set out in the Unfair Contract Terms Act 1977 and must not conflict with the Code of Banking Practice.

Student Activity 4

Draw up a chart summarising the status of the five types of plastic cards discussed above under the CCA.

4 Connected lender liability

4.1 When a person wishes to buy goods from a certain supplier, and requires credit, and the supplier introduces the customer to the provider of the loan, then the provider of the loan can become jointly and severally liable with the supplier on the contract: s.75. Thus, if the goods are the subject of misrepresentation or breach of contract, the customer (borrower) can take action against both the supplier of the goods and the lender. If the lender has to recompense the borrower, then the lender can take action against the supplier to recoup the loss.

4.2 The two main types of agreement carrying connected lender liability are credit cards and personal loans obtained via the retailer of the goods from a finance house.

4.3 Note that these provisions do not apply to items costing £100 or less, or more than £30,000. Also, that cheque cards, cash cards, charge cards and debit cards are outside the scope of the provisions of connected lender liability,, either because they are not credit tokens or because they are not regulated under the CCA.

5 Overdrafts on current accounts

5.1 Section 74(1) applies to overdrafts on current accounts. It specifically identifies this type of lending as 'a debtor-creditor agreement, enabling the debtor to overdraw on a current account. There is no definition of a current account in the Act, but the test of a current account is likely to be:

- Can the debtor get at his money, or pay it to another, by cheque or other written order from this account?
- If so, can he overdraw?

If the answer to both questions is 'Yes', the conditions for s.74(1) are met.

5.2 Under s.74, regulated agreements relating to overdrafts do not have to comply with the agreements regulations; the Director General of Fair Trading has exempted banks from the documentation relating to the provision of the finance via overdraft, but not from documentation relating to any security deposited against such borrowing.

5.3 The bank must inform the customer in writing, at or before the time the overdraft is granted, of the:

- Credit limit;
- Annual interest rate and charges, and the conditions under which they may be amended;
- Procedure to terminate the overdraft, i.e. the fact that it is repayable on demand.

5.4 In the case of agreed overdrafts the above details must be provided to the customer before or at the time an overdraft is granted.

Unagreed overdrafts

5.5 In addition to agreed overdrafts, *unagreed* overdrafts can arise by tacit agreement of the bank when, without contacting the customer, it pays a cheque which creates an overdraft. For the purposes of the CCA an unagreed overdraft is one which was not agreed in advance, but which has continued for three months without the bank taking positive efforts to have it reduced or repaid. For such unagreed overdrafts the above details must be given before, or within seven days after the end of the three-month period: s.74(1).

Preventing avoidance

5.6 The CCA rules prevent banks from avoiding its regulations by granting overdrafts with an artificially high credit limit in excess of £15,000. Overdrafts are subject to regulation if the:

- Credit limit is £15,000 or below; or
- Credit limit exceeds £15,000 but no more than £15,000 can be withdrawn on any one occasion; or
- Debit balance is unlikely to exceed £15,000 at any one time.

Student Activity 5

Your regional office has instigated an inspection of your branch and the inspectors have misgivings about the following account.

- John Smith (wealthy customer).
- Overdraft £4,500.
- No formal arrangements, but the branch manager paid a cheque for £4,800 four months ago which created the initial overdraft. Since that date the account has fluctuated between £4,700 debit and £4,400 debit.
- Dividends of £10,000 are expected in the next months which will clear the overdraft.

Why do you think the inspectors may be concerned?

6 Early repayment

6.1 Under s.94 the debtor has the right to repay the full amount owing before the agreed expiry date if he wishes.

6.2 If the debtor so requests in writing, he is entitled to:

- Be informed of the amount required to pay off the borrowing in full at the present time;
- Full details of the method of calculation;
- Details of the rebate of interest on a structured loan, i.e. the difference between the total charge for credit which would have applied had the loan run its full course, and the actual amount charged.

7 Termination of agreement by the bank

7.1 If a bankruptcy order is made against a customer who owes money under a regulated agreement, then the whole amount due under the agreement automatically becomes due at once.

7.2 However, in the absence of bankruptcy, the bank will be able to terminate such borrowing only if the borrower has failed to meet one or more terms of the agreement. In practice, the most likely breach will be failure of the borrower to meet an agreed instalment on a loan account.

7.3 Before the bank can call in the borrowing, it must:

- Issue a warning notice which must:
  - set out the consequences of the customer's default
  - state that if the default is not rectified within a certain period (minimum seven days) the whole of the borrowing will be called up
  - show the amount for which demand will be made and the date on which it will happen
  - state that the warning notice has been issued under the terms of s.87;
- Issue a call-up notice if the default has not been rectified before the stated expiry date.

7.4 Note that the position regarding the right of a bank to call for repayment on demand of overdrafts which come within the terms of the Act, depends upon whether or not the overdraft was granted for a specified term. If, as usual, the overdraft has no specified term, then it is repayable on demand. If it is for a fixed term, then the above procedure must be followed.

8 Position if the borrower does not comply with a call-up notice

8.1 The bank may serve a default notice on the customer and on all guarantors or depositors of third-party security if the call-up notice has not been satisfied.

8.2 Default notices must be served simultaneously on all borrowers and sureties or guarantors. The aim of the Act is to ensure that all borrowers/guarantors/sureties are fully aware of the situation.

8.3 Once this procedure has been completed, the bank can apply for a court order for recovery of monies due or for the realisation of security.

9 Advertising

9.1 A fundamental principle of the CCA is that an advertiser, i.e. a potential creditor, commits an offence if an advertisement governed by the regulations conveys information which is false or misleading or which does not convey the information required by the Act: s.46. In addition the publisher or producer of such an advertisement will commit an offence: s.47. This could result in a fine or imprisonment.

9.2 Advertising is covered by the CCA provisions. This includes radio, television, displays, notices, circulars, leaflets and all similar forms of advertising. However, the CCA will not apply, if it is made clear that the lending:

- Can only be unsecured and has a minimum amount in excess of £15,000; or
- Is restricted to companies;
- Is exclusively for business purposes.

9.3 There are three categories of advert: *simple, intermediate* and *full.*

Simple advertisement

9.4 The only information which can be shown in a simple advert is the advertiser's name, logo, address, telephone number, and occupation. The simple advert must not indicate that the advertiser is willing to extend credit, so there must be no reference to interest rates, repayment periods or security.

Intermediate advertisement

9.5 This is the most frequently seen advert. It must contain:

- The name, address and telephone number of the advertiser.
- A statement that security or insurance is required if that is the case.
- If applicable, a statement that a sum of money must be deposited into an account.
- Any credit broker's fees which may be payable.
- The APR.
- A statement that written quotations are available.
- Any restriction if the offer is limited to particular class or group of the public.
- Where a mortgage over the borrower's house may be required a 'warning' that the home is at risk if payments fall in arrears or that the sterling equivalent of the repayments may vary if the loan is in foreign currency.

Full advertisements

9.6 For full adverts, where the advertiser wishes to include more information than is allowed in intermediate adverts, the advertiser will usually wish to show some illustrative details of loans, credit limits, or repayment tables. The regulations aim to ensure that such examples are typical in practice. The usual details required for an intermediate advert (such as the warnings shown above) must be included.

Annual Percentage Rate (APR)

9.7 The APR is meant to be a reflection of the true rate of interest and thus to be a valid figure of comparison between one institution and another. The calculation of the APR must include any fees incurred in arranging the facility or in perfecting the security.

9.8 APR calculates an annualised interest rate taking account of compounding and repayments and the other fees shown above. The full details are set out in the Consumer Credit (Total Charge for Credit) Regulations 1986.

10 Canvassing

10.1 Canvassing is an oral attempt by a lender (the canvasser) to persuade a potential borrower to enter into an agreement to borrow money from the lender. Under s.49(1), it is an offence to canvass debtor-creditor agreements off trade premises without prior written invitation.

10.2 Trade premises are the bank's normal premises, or any temporary premises such as a stand in a show ground, or the business premises of the customer.

10.3 A private individual does not have business premises, thus a bank cannot canvass in his home unless it has a prior written invitation. However, a general discussion of financial matters can take place off trade premises provided the discussion is initiated by the third party and not by the bank, and provided the bank has not gone along to the meeting with the intention of canvassing.

10.4 Section 49(3) allows canvassing of overdrafts for existing customers who already have any type of account (not just a loan account) with the bank. In this type of lending the canvassing does not have to be on trade premises, provided it falls within the limits of s.49(3)(a).

10.5 Any credit agreements which have been arranged via unauthorised canvassing are valid, but the bank and the officials responsible are guilty of a criminal offence and could face a fine.

11 Credit brokerage

11.1 Credit brokerage is defined in s.145 as business of introducing individuals seeking credit, or goods on rental, to businesses involved in:

- Consumer credit;
- Housing finance;
- Consumer hire (not in the syllabus);

or to other credit brokers.

1.2 Credit broking is not necessarily the sole business carried on, indeed in many cases it forms a small part of other business, e.g. the sale of new or used cars.

11.3 A bank which arranges for a third party to market or sell its personal loan facilities must ensure that the third party holds a credit brokerage licence. Any regulated agreement entered into following an introduction made by an unlicensed credit broker will be enforceable only if the Director General of Fair Trading so directs. In making his decision, the Director General will consider the:

- Extent of the third party's influence on the debtor; and
- Degree of blame on the part of the bank.

11.4 *Note*: a retailer who accepts credit cards and who advertises this fact is not a credit broker. Such retailers do not introduce prospective card-holders to the card issuers.

Summary

Now that you have studied this unit, you should be able:

- **appreciate the rationale behind the CCA 1974;**
- **describe the wording which must apply to regulated loan agreements;**
- **define what is meant by an exempt credit agreement;**
- **describe agreements relating to land and guarantees;**
- **define a credit token and explain which plastic cards are credit tokens;**
- **know the CCA regulations relating to overdrafts;**
- **understand the process of early repayment;**
- **describe the procedure and effects of a bank terminating regulated borrowing;**
- **know the rules on canvassing;**
- **understand the meaning of credit brokerage.**

Self-assessment questions

1 Under s.49(1) what would be defined as trade premises?

2 Under what circumstances is a loan agreement non-cancellable?

3 On payment of £5, Eagle Co issues to Thomas Smith a trading check under which he can spend up to £60 at any shop which has agreed, or in future agrees to accept Eagle Co's, trading checks. Analyse the implications of this statement for the purposes of the CCA.

4 Which types of agreement are classed as exempt credit?

5 Which of the following is not eligible as security for a regulated agreement under the Consumer Credit Act:

(a) ICI ordinary shares.

(b) Midland Bank subordinated unsecured loan stock.

(c) Rio Tinto Zinc bearer shares.

(d) A bill of exchange.

6 If a Mrs Johnson purchases a washing machine costing £800 using her credit card and the washing machine is faulty when it is installed, whom can she sue for recompense?

7 The manager of Midshires Bank agrees orally with Dennis Jones to open a current account in Jones's name. Nothing is said about overdraft facilities. After maintaining the account in credit for some months, Jones draws a cheque in favour of Smith for £500. His credit balance upon presentation of the cheque was £450. The bank pays the cheque upon presentation. Analyse these facts in accordance with the Consumer Credit Act 1974.

8 Define credit brokerage.

Further reading

- Laidlaw, A and Roberts, G — Chapter 3, *Law Relating to Banking* Services, 2nd edition 1992, Bankers Books
- Raby, P — Chapter 3, *Law Relating to Banking Services*, 2nd edition 1992, Pitman

Unit 20

External Regulation of Building Societies and Banks, and Customer Protection

Objectives

After studying this unit, you should be able to:

- **explain the statutory basis of the Building Societies Commission;**
- **list and describe the functions and powers of the Building Societies Commission;**
- **understand the purpose of capital and the broad framework of the capital adequacy requirements of building societies;**
- **list and summarise the criteria for prudent management;**
- **differentiate between the relative merits of the Building Societies Investor Protection Scheme and the Deposit Protection scheme covering authorised banks;**
- **understand the role of the Building Societies Ombudsman Scheme and how complaints are dealt with under the Scheme;**
- **understand the rationale behind the supervision of banks under the Banking Act 1987;**
- **appreciate the importance of the Board of Banking Supervision;**
- **understand the impact of EU Directives on banking supervision.**

1 The Building Societies Commission

1.1 The Building Societies Commission was established under s.1, Building Societies Act 1986. It replaced the Chief Registrar of Friendly Societies as regulator of the building society industry.

1.2 The Commission is made up of between four and 10 members, with the Chairman called the First Commissioner. Schedule 1 of the Act lays down matters such as the tenure of Commissioners, their payment and the appointment of staff. Section 2 Act specifies how the operations of the Commission are funded. This is achieved by a charge on societies and by the payment of fees by societies when the Commission exercises in powers relating to them.

1.3 The Commission is responsible to the Treasury. It also advises other government departments on building society matters.

Functions

1.4 The Commission has five functions, it:

- Promotes the protection of investments held on behalf of shareholders and depositors;
- Promotes the financial stability of building societies;
- Ensure that societies retain their principal purpose of raising mainly retail funds and making advances secured on residential land;
- Administers the system of regulation under the 1986 Act;
- Advises and make recommendations to the Treasury and other government departments on building society matters.

Protection of investments

1.5 As building society liabilities are mainly short-term investments and their liabilities are long-term mortgages, there can be occasions when the industry is vulnerable to the effects of rumour and outside events. One such occasion occurred shortly after the BCCI collapse when it was rumoured that the Southdown Building Society had investments in the failed bank. Although the rumour was unfounded, the Society suffered a run on its funds. The Commission monitored this situation closely until the short-term crisis passed. (Eventually, the Society sought a merger partner in the Leeds Permanent.)

1.6 Such crises are rare, but the Commission knows they will arise occasionally. An earlier scare involved the Derbyshire Building Society which was rumoured to have investments in the collapsed Rolls-Royce Aero Engine company in 1971. On that occasion the Society was empowered by the Registrar (then the regulator) to borrow from other societies to maintain the confidence of investors.

Financial stability of building societies

1.7 The role here is to ensure that societies do not endanger the interests of customers in any way by inappropriate policies. The Commission was involved in monitoring the situation which arose in the Town and Country Building Society, which was bearing its own risk on high percentage mortgages rather than using indemnity guarantees to insure against losses, which is the usual practice. The society was persuaded to seek a merger partner (the Woolwich) when it was revealed that there would be a trading loss.

Retention of the principal purpose

1.8 There have been no modern day problems here, but the lessons of the New Cross Building Society in the early 1980s serve as a warning of what can occur. That society was a growth-oriented organisation, paying premium rates for investments and charging more for mortgages. When the mortgage market tightened, the society was unable to achieve the lending volumes necessary, and at the time of the takeover by the Woolwich, the society had over 60% liquidity – hardly fulfilment of the principal purpose.

Regulation under the 1986 Act

1.9 The Commission ensures that societies comply fully with the law by scrutinising their annual accounts and requiring regular financial reports during each trading year. Representatives of the Commission visit every society each year to assess the quality of performance and efficiency of management.

Advising the government

1.10 The Commission makes an annual report to the Treasury and is involved in discussions regarding new developments and potential expansion or changes in powers which can be altered by statutory instrument.

Powers

1.11 The Commission has numerous powers which can be used to discharge its functions.

Breach of statutory limits

1.12 If a society breaches any statutory limits, s.36 empowers the Commission to:

- Direct the society to submit a restructuring plan within a specified period and demonstrate that it can regularise the position within 12 months;
- Direct the society to call a general meeting within six months to consider a transfer to plc status;
- Carry out either of the above actions directly.

1.13 The limits concerned are the:

- Non-retail funds limit of 50% maximum;
- Loan capital limit, 50% maximum;
- Lending nature limits (classes 1, 2 and 3);
- Maximum liquidity figure, currently 33.3%.

Enforcement of principal purpose

1.14 If the society is apparently not complying with its principal purpose, s.37 empowers the Commission to:

- Petition the High Court for a winding up order;
- Apply to the High Court to enforce a restructuring plan or otherwise require the society to modify its business.

Determination of vires

1.15 Section 38 empowers the Commission to determine whether an activity is *intra vires* (within the powers of) a society. The Commission will make an investigation here if the:

- Directors are unsure of whether that activity is allowed;
- Central Office has requested guidance on an activity prior to registering a power;
- Commission finds that a society is already carrying out an activity and wishes to require the society to apply for a determination;
- Society does not make an application when directed as above; here the Commission can make its own determination.

1.16 If the Commission makes a prohibition order regarding activities which are *ultra vires* the society and assets are then disposed of by the society, s.40 does not prejudice the claims of any person who has an interest in those assets.

Authorisation

1.17 The Commission has the power to authorise societies conditionally and unconditionally, and to revoke authorisation if appropriate: ss.41 and 42. Section 41 empowers the Commission to require a society to apply for a renewal of authorisation.

Appointment of inspectors

1.18 Sections 55 and 56 enable the Commission to appoint inspectors to investigate a society's affairs or the businesses of subsidiary and associated bodies. Such inspectors have wide powers to gather information, and the society and its past and present officers must cooperate fully with their requirements.

Advertising

1.19 A society can be required to cease advertising in a particular way, and can be prevented from advertising at all if the Commission deems it appropriate: s.50. In addition, there are the general controls on advertising enforced by the Advertising Standards Authority (ASA), which require all advertisements to be 'honest, decent and legal'.

Student Activity 1

Summarise the statutory basis of authority and the functions of the Building Societies Commission, and the powers of the Commission if one of the statutory limits is breached.

2 Prudent management

2.1 Section 45 of the 1986 Act sets down seven criteria for prudent management, relating to:

- Reserves and capital resources;
- Structure of commercial assets;
- Liquidity;
- Security for advances;
- Books of account, control and inspection;
- 'Fit and proper' persons;
- Professional skills.

Reserves and capital resources

2.2 A society must maintain adequate reserves and other designated capital resources. This criterion refers to 'capital adequacy', see below.

Structure of commercial assets

2.3 A society must maintain a structure of commercial assets which satisfies the requirements of Part III of the Act. This requirement relates to the nature limits on commercial assets, described in the Unit 2, section 4.

Liquidity

2.4 There must be adequate liquidity within the society's asset structure. The Commission only lays down a maximum level of liquidity, but all societies are expected to maintain sufficient liquidity to manage cash flow comfortably.

Security for advances

2.5 There must be arrangements in place to ensure that property considered as security for advances is adequate for the loan sought. Section 13 requires societies to have each and every security offered valued by a competent person who is not disqualified under the Act.

Books of account, control and inspection

2.6 Societies must keep proper books of account and maintain proper systems of control and inspection: s.71. This is arguably the most important aspect of the legislation.

'Fit and proper' persons

2.7 The society must be managed and directed by a sufficient number of persons who are 'fit and proper' and who must discharge their responsibilities with prudence and integrity. This criterion reiterates the more important aspects of the First Banking Coordination Directive of the EU.

Professional skills

2.8 The business must be conducted with adequate professional skills. This relates to executive expertise as well as functional competencies, such as accountancy, surveying and IT.

Guidance

2.9 The criteria for prudent management form the basis of continued authorisation. If the Commission felt that a society was failing in its obligations under s.45, it could effectively be closed down.

2.10 To guide societies further on prudent management and best practice, the Commission issues Prudential Notes. These are guidelines on specific business areas, such as lending and capital. Prudential Notes are not legally binding, though failure to observe their recommendations could be interpreted as a failure to comply with s.45 of the Act. In effect, a society would ignore a prudential note at its peril.

2.11 The Commission also issues what are known as 'Dear Chief Executive (DCE)' letters which advise on certain courses of action to be followed, or matters to be considered, by building societies. Addressed to the chief executive of each society, their contents tends to be more general in nature than that of prudential notes. However, like prudential notes, whilst not legally binding, failure to observe their contents could be interpreted as a failure to comply with s.45.

3 Capital adequacy requirements

Purpose

3.1 All financial institutions are required to maintain reserves, or capital, in order to:

- Provide a buffer against unforeseen losses;
- Ensure continued viability;
- Maintain the confidence of investors.

3.2 The Commission requires building societies to maintain adequate capital, with regulations laid down by Prudential Note.

3.3 Capital represents the difference between income-earning assets (such as mortgages) and liabilities on which expenditure is paid (such as savings accounts). It therefore serves as a cushion to absorb any squeeze on margins.

Measures

3.4 The Commission lays down two measures, the:

- Minimum acceptable level of capital relating to the current business of the society, any level below this puts the society and its customers at risk;
- Desirable level of capital which should be the basis for planning, budgeting and decisions on the extent to which activities will be broadened.

Framework

3.5 The framework takes into consideration the following factors:

- Character of the lending book;
- Maturity structure of investments as part of liquidity;
- Mix of business activities;
- Extent to which the society has or plans to diversify into new activities;
- Structure of fixed assets, notably premises and IT;
- Concentration of business by market segment and geographical area;
- Levels of staffing and expertise, especially in smaller societies.

3.6 The framework laid down is summarised below:

Activity	*Capital required %*
Core business mortgages	1–2% of mortgage balances
High percentage mortgages and loans to housing associations	4%
Other loans	6%
Liquid assets	1–2% depending on maturity and risk
Fixed assets	50%
Loans other than mortgages	10–20% depending on type
Development property	10–50% depending on type

Student Activity 2

Explain the criteria for prudent management and consider what factors would influence the level of capital held by a building society.

4 Investor Protection Scheme

4.1 In common with other groups of financial institutions, building societies have a scheme which provides a minimum level of protection for savers and investors.

4.2 The building society scheme was set up originally on a voluntary basis following the crash of the Grays Building Society in 1979. This resulted in losses of over £6 million, caused mainly by the criminal activity of its former chief executive. The Society was taken over by the Woolwich, but the industry shared the losses to prevent the Woolwich having to bear the loss itself. The societies then created a voluntary scheme under the auspices of the Building Societies Association.

4.3 The voluntary scheme was short lived. Section 24 of the 1986 Act created the Building Societies Investor Protection Board as a body which would administer a statutory scheme called the Building Societies Investor Protection Scheme. Societies must belong to this, although they may join additional schemes if they wish: s.31.

4.4 The First Commissioner, as Chairman of the Building Societies Commission, is Chairman of the Protection Board. Two further members are appointed by the Commission and four others by the Treasury in consultation with the Commission.

Statutory functions

4.5 The statutory functions of the Board are to:

- Hold, manage and apply the Building Societies Protection Fund;
- Levy contributions to the Fund from building societies in the event of insolvency of a society.

Protection available

4.6 The Fund provides protection for private investors who are either shareholders or depositors. The only shareholders not covered are those who hold Permanent Interest Bearing Shares (PIBS), a type of capital raised by issuing paper which can be traded on the London Stock Exchange.

4.7 The Scheme provides protection of 90% of an investor's balance, up to a maximum balance of £20,000. The maximum cover is therefore £18,000 per individual.

Funding

4.8 The Scheme is funded only when required. Unlike the banks' scheme, in which member banks contribute to a fund in advance, the building society scheme calls for the levy only if required to make payments to investors of an insolvent society.

4.9 Each society can be asked to contribute up to 0.3% of its share and deposit base to the fund.

4.10 The Board can also raise funds by additional levies and by borrowing.

Payments

4.11 Payments made to investors in the insolvent society are called 'insolvency payments'. The Board then has a claim upon the assets of the insolvent society against payments made in this respect.

4.12 The building society scheme has much in common with the parallel bank scheme, including the same maximum payment and percentage cover.

Student Activity 3

1 Explain the structure and statutory basis of the Building Society Investor Protection Scheme. *(Paragraph 4.1–4)*

2 How much would be paid in insolvency payments to

(a) an investor with £26,000

(b) an investor with £10,000? *(Paragraph 4.7).*

5 Complaints

5.1 The 1986 Act established the Building Societies Ombudsman Scheme. Under the Act, each society must belong to one or more ombudsman schemes.

5.2 The purpose of an ombudsman is to give an independent judgement on complaints between an institution and its customer. It is usual for an ombudsman to have a legal background. All ombudsman schemes operate on the principle that before a case is considered the customer and institution must first exhaust all avenues open to them to resolve the issue.

Investigatory powers

5.3 The ombudsman investigates any complaint from an individual, provided that:

- The incident took place in the UK;
- Related to a building society or one of its subsidiary or associated bodies;
- Related to one of the activities specified in the Act.

5.4 The complainant must have been subjected to an action that caused 'pecuniary loss, expense or inconvenience'. Complaints which the ombudsman considers to be frivolous or vexatious are set aside, as too will actions that are subject to court proceedings or those which occurred more than six months previously. The ombudsman does not consider matters of commercial judgement, such as the refusal of lending facilities due to inadequate income or security offered.

5.5 The ombudsman has discretion in respect of methods of investigation but has an obligation to act impartially and fairly. He can request any information and documentation necessary to investigate the complaint.

5.6 In forming a judgment, the ombudsman must consider the rules, the deed or contract, any applicable code of conduct, advertisements where relevant, and all communications between the society and the complainant.

Decision

5.7 The ombudsman must give one months' notice of his intention to make a decision and indicate the general nature it is likely to take. He can direct a society to take an action or desist from taking an action. He can also award up to £100,000 by way of compensation for loss or expense to the complainant.

5.8 The determination of the ombudsman must be in writing. The complainant has 28 days to accept this, after which it becomes binding. If it is not accepted, the complainant has recourse to the courts.

5.9 If the society does not accept the judgment, it must inform the ombudsman of this within 28 days and give notice in the next directors' report of the reasons for noncompliance. It must also give notice of its reasons to the public in a manner prescribed by the ombudsman. There are obvious public relations implications here but, in a small minority of cases, some societies have taken this course of action.

Matters of complaint

5.10 Matters of complaint are laid down by Schedule 12. They include the operation or termination of an account and the grant or refusal to grant a member facilities normally available in respect of:

- Share accounts;
- Deposit accounts;
- Class 1 and 2 advances, including further advances;
- Loans on mobile homes;
- Other s.16 (class 3) loans;
- Initial or further advances from an appropriate mortgage company (subsidiary lender);
- Banking, trusteeship and executorship services.

Grounds of complaint

5.11 The ground of complaint must relate to:

- Breach of statutory obligations, the rules or a contract;
- Breach of a subsidiary company's obligations under the contract or rules;
- Unfair treatment;
- Maladministration.

5.12 Typical matters of complaint include:

- Withdrawals from ATMs (incorrect dispensing or withdrawals purported not to have been made);
- Fees and other conditions of fixed rate mortgages;
- Interest entitlement on investment accounts;
- Mortgage redemption and part redemption fees.

6 Fair trading and restrictive practices

Office of Fair Trading

6.1 The Office of Fair Trading (OFT) was established by the Fair Trading Act 1973 to protect consumers and those in business against unfair trading practices. The head of the OFT is the Director General of Fair Trading.

6.2 The OFT has several duties which impact on financial institutions. These include:

- Regulator under the Consumer Credit Act 1974:
    - regulation and supervision of lenders who provide loans which fall within the definition of regulated loans;
    - regulation of advertising and quotations, including interest rates and use of annual percentage rate (APR).
- Monitoring of the provision of insurance services: the OFT requires lenders to offer a choice of at least three property insurers.
- Making recommendations on trading practices: the OFT is especially concerned with matters such as codes and statements of practice. (It was critical of the Code of Banking Practice when this was introduced and similarly criticised the proposed Code of Mortgage Lending Practice developed by the Council of Mortgage Lenders in 1996.)

Monopolies and Mergers Commission

6.3 The Monopolies and Mergers Commission (MMC) is concerned with ensuring that monopolies and firms which propose to merge will continue to serve the public interest. The MMC can prevent a monopoly from taking place and can intervene if it discovers price or output fixing through a cartel.

6.4 The MMC would consider a proposed merger of two very large banks or building societies extremely carefully before allowing it to go ahead. The key determinants of decisions are whether such an action will result in less competition and create a poorer deal for the customer.

6.5 The MMC considers recommendations made by the OFT and instigates investigations where appropriate.

6.6 Survey and valuation services provided in connection with properties to be mortgaged was the subject of MMC recommendations in a 1994 report. Most home buyers are content to rely on a basic valuation, which only confirms the suitability or otherwise of the property for mortgage purposes. Some borrowers, however, commission a full structural survey at the same time. The MMC found that savings could be made here by getting the person carrying out the valuation to undertake the survey also. The problem arises when the borrower commissions the survey only to find that the surveyor is not recognised by the lender. It was therefore suggested that potential borrowers be made aware of this potential problem as early in the application process as possible. The MMC also recommended that survey and valuation fees be made more transparent, so that the borrower would know what element would be paid over for the professional service and what element constituted administration fees or other income for the lender. This recommendation has been implemented by members of the Council of Mortgage Lenders in a statement of practice.

7 The Bank of England's supervisory role

Banking Act 1987

7.1 Under s.1(1), the Bank of England:

> ... shall have the powers conferred upon it by this Act and the duty generally to supervise the institutions authorised by it in the exercise of those powers.

7.2 Under s.1(2) the Bank has a duty to:

> keep under review the operations of this Act and to monitor developments in the field of banking which appear to it to be relevant to the exercise of its powers and the discharge of its duties.

7.3 Section 1(4) states that:

> neither the Bank nor any person who is a member of its court of directors or who is, or is acting as, an officer or servant of the Bank shall be liable in damages for anything done or omitted, in the discharge or the purported discharge of the functions of the Bank under this Act unless it is shown the act or omission was in bad faith.

7.4 The Act introduced a unified system of regulation for banks. There is now just a single category of authorised banking institutions, every member of which must operate within the same statutory supervisory framework.

7.5 Schedule 3 of the Act sets out the minimum criteria which a banking institution must satisfy in order to obtain authorisation as a bank. These are that:

- An institution's directors, controllers and managers must be *fit and proper persons* to hold their positions.
- The business must be *effectively directed* by at lease two individuals.
- In the case of UK incorporated institutions, there must be as many *non-executive directors* as are considered appropriate by the Bank of England.
- The business must be *conducted prudently* in respect of:
  - capital adequacy
  - liquidity
  - foreign currency exposure
  - provisions for bad and doubtful debts
  - accounting and other records
  - internal management controls.
- The institution must have *net assets* of not less than ECU5m when authorisation is granted.

7.6 Also, under the Act:

- The Bank of England retains the discretion to set *prudential standards on a case-by-case basis* (see later sections on liquidity and capital adequacy);
- The Bank of England has the power to *object to proposed takeovers and mergers* involving UK banking institutions;
- It is a criminal offence to provide *false or misleading information* to the Bank of England;

- Banks' *auditors* must co-operate with the supervisory requirements;
- Banks must give notice to the Bank when their *exposure to individual borrowers* is expected to exceed 25% of their capital, and exposures of between 10% and 25% must be reported to the Bank.

Board of Banking Supervision

7.7 The Banking Act also established a Board of Banking Supervision, full details of which are set out in Schedule 1 of the Act. Two-thirds of the members of this Board are independent of the Bank of England (although they are selected by the Chancellor of the Exchequer in consultation with the Governor of the Bank), and are chosen on the basis of their legal, accounting or banking backgrounds.

7.8 The independent members of the Board have a duty to advise the Governor on the operation and administration of supervision and the formulation of policy: s.2(3). The Governor may ignore the advice, but must justify doing so to the Chancellor. Hence, ultimate responsibility for supervision remains firmly with the Bank and the Treasury and this has led to the criticism that banking regulation is too closely aligned to City interests and that there is little independent scrutiny of supervisory practices.

7.9 Section 2(7) refers to s.1(4) and states that this section will apply to any act or omission by any member of the board in the discharge or purported discharge of his functions. In other words, the position regarding immunity is the same for both the Bank's officers and the members of the Board of Banking Supervision.

Deposit protection scheme

7.10 The Banking Act 1979 provided for the establishment of a deposit protection scheme, aimed at offering a degree of insurance for ordinary depositors against the failure of authorised banking institutions. The scheme was extended by the 1987 Act and by the EU Directive on Deposit Guarantee Schemes. Since 1 July 1995 the Scheme has provided cover for the first 90% of protected deposits up to a maximum of £20,000 for each depositor (unless the sterling equivalent of ECU22,222 is greater).

7.11 The UK scheme covers branches of UK-incorporated institutions throughout the EEA (European Economic Area, which consists of the EU plus Iceland, Liechtenstein and Norway), and includes deposits denominated in any EEA currency and in ECU. Qualifying deposits placed with a UK branch of a credit institution incorporated in another EEA country are covered by that country's deposit protection arrangement.

7.12 The UK scheme is paid for by a levy on all authorised institutions, set according to the size of their deposit balances. This approach has been criticised in that it fails to reflect the inherent risk of different institutions' activities, although the need to maintain confidence in the banking system as a whole is seen as being critical.

Banking regulation within EU

7.13 Prior to the late 1980s, EU (at the time EC) legislation had little impact on banking activities in the UK. Requirements were fairly general, and were broadly in line with the Bank of England's own position on the issues covered. However, the *Single European Market (1992) initiative* gave a major boost to the relevance of EU legislation.

Second Banking Co-ordination Directive

7.14 The single most important piece of legislation is the Second Banking Coordination Directive, which was adopted in January 1988. This Directive introduced the concept of a *single European banking licence*, whereby a bank authorised in one EU state is now able to operate freely in any other state without further authorisation. This mutual recognition of authorisation gives the home country supervisors the responsibility for the overall supervision of the EU-wide operations of banks based within their respective countries.

7.15 The provisions of the Directive came into force on 1 January 1993, by means of secondary legislation within the framework of the Banking Act 1987. At this time a new definition of bank controllers was introduced and the minimum capital required for new authorisations was raised to ECU5m.

Harmonisation of supervisory standards

7.16 In order for mutual recognition of authorisation to be acceptable to EU member states, it is necessary for there to be also the harmonisation of certain key supervisory standards. The Second Banking Directive includes requirements in respect of capital bases, major shareholders in banks, banks' participation in the non-banking sector, and accounting and internal control mechanisms. Other Directives and Recommendations deal with such matters as the definition of capital and the risk weighting of assets, reporting requirements for branches, capital movements, investment services, and stock exchange listing procedures.

Other Directives

7.17 In December 1990, the Bank of England implemented the *Solvency Ratio Directive* (relating to credit risk and capital ratios) and the *Own Funds Directive* (defining capital for supervisory purposes). On 1 January 1996 the *Capital Adequacy Directive* became effective. This sets minimum capital requirements for market risks in the trading books of banks and investment firms and is expected to precede by about two years a BIS requirement relating to market risks. An interesting aspect of this development is that the authorities have agreed, subject to certain conditions, to allow banks to use their own inhouse 'value-at-risk' models to calculate the relevant capital charges.

7.18 The impact of the changing regulatory framework is likely to be substantial. Certainly, banking markets in Europe are likely to become more competitive, with many opportunities for expansion. Nevertheless, in the shorter-term the cost of adjustment and preparation for new activities may be high, and UK banks cannot ignore the possible competitive threats to domestic market from other EU states' banks.

Student Activity 4

1 Consider the role of the Building Society ombudsman. Write a couple of paragraphs about whether or not you think the Scheme provides a fair method of resolving disputes ?

2 What role does the Office of Fair Trading have in relation to building society trading practices? Do you consider that the impact of the OFT on building society practice to be significant?

Summary

Now that you have studied this unit, you should be able to:

- **describe the role and functions of the Building Societies Commission;**
- **explain the powers of the Commission;**
- **understand the concepts relating to prudent management and be able to list and explain the criteria for prudent management;**
- **understand the principles behind the capital adequacy requirements;**
- **understand how the Building Societies Investor Protection Scheme operates;**
- **describe the role of the Ombudsman, the method by which complaints are investigated and give examples of complaints that the Ombudsman might consider;**
- **understand the roles of the Office of Fair Trading and the Monopolies and Mergers Commission in relation to financial institutions.**

Self-assessment questions

1 Which of the following are statutory limits on a building society's financial structure?

(a) Minimum liquidity ratio;

(b) Maximum liquidity ratio;

(c) Maximum class 1 assets as a percentage of commercial assets;

(d) Minimum class 2 assets as a percentage of commercial assets.

2 The body responsible for registration of changes in memorandum, rules and other matters relating to building societies is the:

(a) Building Societies Commission;

(b) Central Office;

(c) Bank of England;

(d) Office of Fair Trading.

3 An investor has £31,000 in a building society retail account and a further £20,000 in permanent interest bearing shares. The society becomes insolvent. The cover provided by the Building Societies Investor Protection Scheme is:

(a) £31,000;

(b) £20,000;

(c) £18,000;

(d) £45,900.

4 Which of the following would be considered as a complaint by the Ombudsman? A customer:

(a) Who is aggrieved that his application for a loan has been turned down on status grounds;

(b) Whose account has been debited with an ATM withdrawal that he alleges he did not make;

(c) Who complains about charges made to his account 12 months ago;

(d) Who feels that he was overcharged in respect of redemption fees when his mortgage was redeemed three months ago.

5 If a building society wishes to make a combined charge for administration and valuation, it:

(a) Is not permitted to do so;

(b) Can do so but is legally required to separate out the two elements;

(c) Can do so but should separate out the elements under the CML statement of practice;

(d) Can do so and needs to take no further action.

6 List and describe briefly the functions of the Building Societies Commission, commenting in each case on the possible consequences of noncompliance with each.

7 What are the relationships between the Building Societies Commission, the Central Office, the Building Societies Investor Protection Scheme and the Treasury?

8 What are the similarities and differences between the respective bank and building society investor/depositor protection schemes?

9 What is the purpose of capital and what would be the possible consequences of a building society having inadequate capital?

10 What factors would be important when considering the capital requirements of a local building society of £50 million total assets, employing 40 staff and working in a tightly defined catchment area within a radius of 50 miles of its head office?

11 What are the major considerations of the Office of Fair Trading when it sets out to investigate trading practices?

12 (a) Explain what is meant by the statutory requirement in connection with building societies for prudent management.

(b) Explain the consequences of failure to comply with the criteria for prudent management.

Further reading

- Boleat, M, Armstrong, R French, C and Coogan, M — Chapters 10–14, *Building Societies, the Regulatory Framework*, The Building Societies Association

Unit 21

Examination Questions

1 North Bank received a court order under the Police and Criminal Evidence Act 1984 which stated that the bank had to advise the police of any credits in excess of £1 million on customer Y's account. North Bank complied with the court order, and did not advise Y regarding its actions. Subsequently Y discovered what had happened when he was prosecuted by the police for serious fraud.

Y's solicitor now claims compensation from the bank on the basis that the bank:

(a) Should not have divulged the information.

(b) Should have opposed the court order.

(c) Should have advised its customer of receipt of the order.

Advise the bank. [Total 20 marks]

2 Alice Street, a widow aged 75, has maintained a current account and a deposit account at your branch for 40 years. In recent times her health has deteriorated, and in May 1984 she entered an old people's home. At that time, whilst of sound mind but physically frail, she executed a power of attorney under the Powers of Attorney Act 1971 in favour of her son, Alan Street, and this was shown to you, as manager of the branch. Since then Alan has operated both of his mother's bank accounts.

Today Alan Street has called to see you and says that his mother has now been transferred to a hospital as she is mentally very confused and there is no hope for her recovery. He says that he will continue to operate the accounts, and requests your confirmation that this is acceptable in the circumstances.

(a) Explain what a Power of Attorney is, and how it is executed under the Powers of Attorney Act 1971. [6]

(b) State how you would have handled matters in May 1984. [3]

(c) State how you would deal with Mr Street's request today, indicating any advice you might give him. [5]

(d) State how the situation would differ if the power of attorney had been drawn up under the Enduring Powers of Attorney Act 1985. [6]

[Total 20 marks]

3 A bank has, as a customer, a certain partnership. Fully explaining the legal principles, discuss the main problems (and their solutions) that may arise for the bank when one partner dies. In your discussion include

reference to as many of the following points as you can (it is not essential to include them all):

(a) Should the bank pay on a cheque signed by the deceased?

(b) Is the deceased's estate liable for past partnership debts?

(c) Is the deceased's estate liable for new partnership debts?

(d) Can personal securities previously given by the deceased be relied upon for new partnership debts?

(e) What residual powers (if any) have the partners on dissolution?

(f) Do the surviving partners have power to charge partnership property for new debts for which the deceased's estate is not liable?

(g) Can the deceased's representatives complain if the bank pays the surviving partners from the account (which the representatives think should have been paid to them)?

(h) If the surviving partners continue in business, is a new bank mandate needed?

(i) If the surviving partners continue in business, should the bank take new securities from them in replacement of old securities?

(j) Must the assets of the partnership be distributed amongst the deceased's estate? [20 marks]

4 A professional partnership has three members: Alan, Betty and Charles. Alan is quite wealthy, but Betty and Charles are not. The following matters occur in relation to the partnership and its members:

(a) A bank, Blackbank, is a personal creditor of Charles and it makes him bankrupt. Assuming the partnership is not wound up, what rights, if any, would Blackbank have over the partnership assets or any part of them? [5]

(b) Another bank, Whitebank, is a creditor of the partnership, and is owed a large sum of money which significantly exceeds the value of the partnership's assets. Assuming the partnership is not wound up, what rights, if any, would Whitebank have in relation to the personal assets, and partnership assets, of the partners, and how could it enforce its rights? [5]

(c) In the circumstances of (a) and (b) above, can either Whitebank or Blackbank wind up the partnership or take any other action? What course of action should the banks, in your opinion, follow here? [10]

[Total 20 marks]

5 (a) Maggie, Nigel and Alan are partners in a firm of economic consultants. What powers does Maggie have to bind the partnership? [12]

(b) Nigel wishes to cease to be a partner in the firm, which has a large bank overdraft. What steps should he take to avoid legal liability for the overdraft after his retirement? [8]

[Total 20 marks]

6 (a) Lock, Stock and Barrel are partners in a firm. During the past year Barrel has become aggressive and bad tempered. Recently Barrel was convicted of drunken driving and Lock got married. Lock and Stock would like to take the opportunity of Barrel's conviction to get rid of

him from the firm and Lock would like to introduce his wife into the firm as a new partner. Advise them. [9]

(b) How would the legal position differ if (instead of being partners) Lock, Stock and Barrel were directors of Gun Ltd, in which each owned a third of the issued share capital, so that Lock and Stock wished to remove Barrel as a director, and Lock sought to have his wife appointed as a director? [6]

(c) Lock's wife is appointed a director of Gun Ltd. She is required to have a qualification holding of shares, but cannot purchase these from her own resources. Can Gun Ltd offer any financial assistance, and what procedure would they need to go through to give this assistance? [5]

[Total 20 marks]

7 Arthur Fagge runs a tobacconist's shop, Arthur Fagge Ltd, and employs an assistant at a wage of £200 a week, which the company pays by cheque. The company has an overdraft on its current account at its bank. The tobacconist's business runs into financial difficulties and the bank decides to open a separate wages account, to which the bank debits the shop assistant's weekly wages cheques.

Discovering that the company's unsecured trade creditors are owed £75,000, the bank makes formal demand on Arthur Fagge Ltd for £4,600 on overdraft and £1,000 on the wages account. The company also has a deposit account with a credit balance of £700.

(a) How should the bank combine the balances on the three bank accounts? [9]

(b) How would your answer to (a) differ if, before the bank made formal demand, a winding up order had been made against Arthur Fagge Ltd on a trade creditor's petition? [6]

(c) How would your answers to (a) and (b) differ if, instead of Arthur Fagge Limited, Phil Turr, an individual, owned and ran the tobacconist's shop and employed the assistant, and if (for the purposes of reconsidering (b) above) a bankruptcy order had been made against Phil Turr? [5]

[Total 20 marks]

Note: for the purposes of this question you are not required to consider the implications, if any, of the Consumer Credit Act 1974.

8 (a) Discuss the doctrine of estoppel in relation to the forgery of the drawer's signature on a cheque. [10]

(b) Two months ago X paid into his account with the North Bank a cheque in his favour for £1,000 (apparently drawn by Y on a branch of the South Bank) and asked for it to be specially presented. This was done, and once the cheque had been paid by the South Bank, X withdrew nearly all the balance on his account. The South Bank now finds that Y's signature on the cheque had been skilfully forged, and seeks repayment of the £1,000 from the North Bank. Consider the legal position. [10]

[Total 20 marks]

9 Advise the Omega Bank whether it may safely pay the following cheques presented to it (each drawer having a sufficient credit balance).

(a) A cheque drawn by customer X in favour of Mr Y and crossed 'A/c payee only'. The cheque appears to have been negotiated to a well known department store. [5]

(b) Cheque number 117285 drawn by customer Z in favour of the same payee and for the same amount as cheque number 117283, payment of which the customer stopped by letter a few days ago. The bank is unable to contact Z, as he has just gone away on holiday. [5]

(c) A cheque drawn by Zed Ltd in payment of the electricity bill for its factory. Last week the bank learned that a petition for the winding up of the company had been presented, and the petition will be heard by the High Court at the beginning of next month. [5]

(d) An open cheque in favour of 'A Jones' which is presented for encashment at your counter by a stranger. The cheque is endorsed 'A Jones'. [5]

[Total 20 marks]

10 (a) 'A bill, of itself, does not operate as an assignment of funds in the hands of the drawee available for payment thereof, and the drawee of a bill who does not accept as required by this Act is not liable on the instrument. This subsection shall not extend to Scotland.' (Section 53(1), Bills of Exchange Act 1882.)

Explain the significance of this provision as regards the paying by a bank of its customers' cheques. [10]

(b) Owing to lack of funds on its customer's account, the Downtown Bank is unable to pay on the due date a standing order for the customer's subscription to a London club, in consequence of which he has now been expelled from membership. The customer claims that the bank should have kept an eye on the situation and made the standing order payment as soon as there were sufficient funds. Advise the bank. [4]

(c) Jason, a wealthy stamp collector, bought a valuable stamp from Golden Fleece Stamps Ltd and paid for it by a cheque drawn on his account at the Argonaut Bank. On a closer examination of the stamp later that day, he thought there was a flaw in it and stopped payment of the cheque before it had been presented. However, because of an oversight the bank paid the cheque and Jason now requests a refund of the amount. Consider the legal position of the bank. [6]

[Total 20 marks]

11 It was said in a leading case on conversion that 'Persons deal with the property in chattels or exercise acts of ownership over them at their peril'.

Consider this statement in relation to the tort of conversion in general and to its application to collecting bankers in particular. How far does the law mitigate this 'peril' as regards collecting bankers?

12 Adrian is a customer of Aggrobank. He draws a cheque on his account for £1,000 made out to 'B Brown or order'. The cheque has two parallel transverse lines on its face, and the words 'not negotiable'. Brown, the

payee, has been pressed for payment by a creditor, C Chalmers, and, as a sort of security until he can pay the money, he hands the cheque without alteration to C Chalmers to hold in the meantime. Chalmers, however, presents the cheque to his bank, Whitebank, which asks that he endorse it, which he does. Whitebank collects the cheque, which is paid by Aggrobank.

Answer the following, giving a full explanation of the legal principles:

(a) Adrian tells Aggrobank that the cheque should not have been paid, and demands reimbursement. Aggrobank says it will do so only if Chalmers repays the bank. Can Aggrobank insist on this, or must it repay Adrian immediately? [10]

(b) Brown demands that Whitebank compensate him for the £1,000. Must it do so? [10]

[Total 20 marks]

13 (a) The directors of DIY Works Ltd resolved to seek an overdraft facility of £10,000 from the company's bank. The bank agreed with Mr Fixit, the company's managing director, to grant the facility provided its three directors guaranteed the company's account.

Mr Fixit signed the bank's standard guarantee form and took it to Mr Glue, one of his co-directors. After explaining the bank's requirements, Mr Fixit asked Mr Glue to sign the guarantee, which Mr Glue did. Mr Fixit could not find Mr Bodger, the third director, so Mr Fixit forged Mr Bodger's signature on the guarantee and sent it back to the bank. DIY Works Ltd commenced winding up and the bank made demand on the company and on all three guarantors. Mr Fixit has absconded and cannot be found.

Are Mr Glue and Mr Bodger liable on the guarantee? [5]

(b) Gordon, Percy and Thomas have given a guarantee to Controller Bank for all the indebtedness and liabilities at any time owing to the bank by Sodor Railway Ltd, but subject to their liability under the guarantee being limited to a maximum amount of £50,000.

The guarantee provides that the guarantors and their successors and assignees shall be jointly and severally liable and that the rights of one guarantor, who has paid monies under the guarantee, to sue any other guarantor or the principal debtor shall not be exercisable until the guarantee has been fully discharged.

The guarantee also provides that the bank can keep any payment by the guarantors on a suspense account until it has recovered the full guarantee liability.

Sodor Railway Ltd is in liquidation, owing Controller Bank £80,000. Under the guarantee, Gordon has paid the bank £30,000, which Controller Bank has placed on a suspense account. Percy died and Thomas has become bankrupt; both of these events occurred after Controller Bank had made demand on the company and all three guarantors.

Discuss the respective rights of Controller Bank and Gordon. (It is not necessary to specify the amounts of claims.) [15]

[Total 20 marks]

14 A bank gives a mortgage of land to a customer and, as additional security, takes from him an assignment of a life policy over the customer's life (the policy monies being payable to the customer's wife, on his death). The policy is a 30-year term policy (a non-endowment one). Discuss the following:

(a) How is a legal assignment of the policy taken? Supposing that someone else, at a later date, also takes an assignment of the policy, which of the two assignments has priority? [10]

(b) What would happen to the bank's security if the customer stopped paying the premiums? [5]

(c) Would the policy monies be payable if the customer committed suicide? [5]

[Total 20 marks]

15 A bank's customer is freehold owner of registered land. On the security of this he wishes to borrow money from the bank, with a 25-year repayment term.

Answer the following, assuming in each case that the bank has a registered legal mortgage:

(a) The mortgage form contains a prohibition on the creation of subsequent mortgages (to other creditors). To what extent is this effective to prevent such subsequent mortgages? [6]

(b) If a subsequent mortgage is made and registered, and the bank has notice of it, what procedures should be followed, and why? [11]

(c) Assuming that a standard bank mortgage form has been completed, if the customer makes no default, can the bank call for repayment after, say, three years? [3]

[Total 20 marks]

16 (a) James is seeking substantial overdraft facilities from his bank, but the only security he can offer is his shareholding in John Ltd, a small and prosperous private company of which he is a director. In what ways might the bank obtain a charge on his shares, and would there be any particular defects in them as security? [12]

(b) Advise Whizzo Limited, a small but growing pharmaceutical company, whether it can insure the life of its chief chemist, on whom its prosperity largely depends. If so, could the policy be subsequently charged to the company's bankers as security, and would it make any alteration to the legal position if during the currency of the policy the chief chemist left the company's employment? [8]

[Total 20 marks]

17 Rags Limited, clothing manufacturers, maintains an overdrawn current account and a loan account at your branch against the security of an unlimited joint and several *guarantee by the two directors.* Control of the borrowing has proved difficult.

Last March the directors called with their audited accounts as at 31 October 1995 which showed a loss of £15,000 for the previous year's trading on turnover of £150,000. However, they assured you that this was because of one particular line of stock which had been difficult to sell, and they believed that they were again trading on a profitable basis. You therefore agreed to continue the overdraft facilities of £10,000 fluctuating on current account and £13,000 on loan account reducing at £1,000 per month, subject to further security in the form of a *debenture incorporating a legal mortgage over the company's freehold factory and a floating charge over all other assets. This security was received on 8 March 1996.*

The account continued to give trouble and on *15 September 1996*, with the balance at *debit £21,000* on current account and debit *£ 7,000 on loan account*, the company went into *creditors' voluntary winding up.* Today you have received a letter from the liquidator claiming that:

(a) The floating charge is invalid, as it was taken within the last year. [10]

(b) The giving of the fixed charge was a preference, and is void on those grounds. [5]

(c) As the directors were personally interested in the giving of the debenture, it is also void on those grounds. [5]

What has the liquidator in mind in respect of each of his claims, and what matters will the bank need to investigate to determine whether or not he is correct?

[Total 20 marks]

18 You are the manager of Happy Bank and your securities clerk asks you the following questions:

(a) We submitted an application to advances department showing the following details:

Account: X Ltd

Proposed limit. £1,000,000

Proposed Security: Fixed charge over factory, minimum forced sale value £3,000,000 on a professional valuation.

Advances department have agreed to lend, but they are not happy with the security. They require us to take a debenture which will give a floating charge over the company's assets, as well as the fixed charge over the factory.

Explain to the clerk why advances department require this extra security when the bank appears to be fully secured already.

(b) I have read some correspondence about the appointment of an administrative receiver for Z Ltd. Can you explain what this means, what the administrative receiver does and how he is appointed? [10]

[Total 20 marks]

19 Tom Putter has a small deposit account at Readibank's City Branch. He has never met or corresponded with Mr Green, the branch manager. One day he met Mr Green at the local golf course. On learning that Mr Putter was a customer of his, Mr Green asked if Readibank could offer an overdraft or a personal loan or, perhaps, some life assurance.

(a) What is the legal position governing Mr Green's offer of financial facilities to Tom Putter? [15]

(b) Would it make any difference if the conversation had taken place in Readibank's hospitality tent at the British Open Golf Championship? [5]

[Total 20 marks]

20 Mr and Mrs Archer want to buy Target Company Limited, a profitable trading company which is wholly owned by Arrow Limited. A bank agrees to lend Mr and Mrs Archer £100,000 for the purchase of all Target Company's shares from Arrow Limited, provided that Mr and Mrs Archer submit satisfactory repayment and security proposals to the bank.

Mr and Mrs Archer propose to the bank that on their acquisition of the shares they will get Target Company to give the bank a floating charge over all Target Company's assets and to declare a dividend, within three months of acquisition, sufficient to reduce the loan substantially.

(a) What problems should the bank consider and how could they be solved? [17]

(b) What would be the position if Mr and Mrs Archer were already directors of Target Company Limited? [3]

[Total 20 marks]

21 When taking a guarantee as security for its customer's indebtedness, a bank faces the hazard of the guarantor eventually attempting to avoid liability on the grounds of undue influence, either on the part of the principal debtor or on the part of the bank. Discuss the meaning and effect of undue influence, and explain the steps a bank can take to deny this loophole to a guarantor.

22 Whit Drawl inserted his cash card in Techni Bank's cash dispensing machine (ATM), entered his personal number (PIN) and pressed the keys to request £50. Whit made no mistakes but, due to an internal mechanical error, the ATM dispensed only £40. The ATM's internal tally roll recorded £50 as having been dispensed to Whit, and his account with Techni Bank was debited with £50.

(a) What are Techni Bank's legal obligations to Whit Drawl in respect of its ATMs? [13]

(b) To what extent can Techni Bank limit, by express agreement, its liability to Whit Drawl for breach of those obligations (for instance, by a clause, in its cardholder terms and conditions, relating to use of its cash cards)? [7]

[Total 20 marks]

23 *January 1996*

(1) Lendalot Bank gave Downslide Limited a £30,000 overdraft facility;

(2) The bank took a fixed legal mortgage over the company's factory.

January 1996

(3) Downslide Limited's overdraft facility was increased to £100,000;

(4) The bank took a £70,000 guarantee from Mr Sharp, director and majority shareholder of Downslide Limited.

March 1996

(5) Downslide Limited was told by Lendalot Bank it must keep within the

£100,000 limit, despite recent excesses;

(6) The bank took a floating charge over all the company's assets.

May 1996

(7) Downslide Limited sold its factory for full market value (and moved to a rented site);

(8) £40,000 net proceeds of sale were paid into current account at Lendalot Bank;

(9) the overdraft limit was reduced to £60,000.

December 1996

A winding up order was made against Downslide Limited, on an unsecured creditor's petition, and a liquidator was appointed.

The liquidator has told Lendalot Bank that he thinks one or more of the nine numbered events described above constituted a preference and was therefore invalid under s.239 of the Insolvency Act 1986.

In the case of each of the following four events state whether or not a preference was constituted: (2), (4), (6), (8). Give reasons for your answer.

[Total 20 marks]

24 Joe Soap is Finance Director of Snow White Ltd, a detergent manufacturer. Mr Soap was authorised, by board resolution, to negotiate bank borrowing for his company's purchase of a new factory. Joe Soap made an appointment with Melanie Yellow, the branch manager of Metro Bank plc's City branch. Joe Soap showed Melanie Yellow a copy of the board resolution and she agreed that Metro Bank would advance £300,000 for the purchase. Joe Soap accepted the terms required by Melanie Yellow and they signed Metro Bank's standard facility letter. Unknown to Joe Soap, Melanie Yellow only had authority within Metro Bank to agree loans up to £50,000.

At Joe Soap's request, Melanie Yellow also obtained life assurance cover on Joe Soap, his wife being named as the beneficiary. The policy showed Snow White Ltd as the owner, and Joe Soap signed a direct debit mandate to enable the premiums to be deducted from Snow White's bank account. The policy was issued by Metro Life Ltd, a subsidiary of Metro Bank. All Metro Bank's managers were authorised 'tied agents' of Metro Life Ltd, for the purposes of the Financial Services Act 1986.

(a) In relation to (i) the loan agreement, and (ii) the life policy, are Snow White Ltd and Metro Bank plc bound by the acts of their respective agents, Joe Soap and Melanie Yellow? [12]

(b) On the assumption that (i) Metro Bank is not bound by the loan agreement, and (ii) Snow White Ltd is not bound by the life policy, would ratification of either be possible? [8]

[Total 20 marks]

25 Brian Kule was the accountant at Freshair Limited, a company which manufactures fans. This is known to Grass Bank, where Mr Kule maintains his personal current account. Freshair Limited maintains its current account at a branch of the Flower Bank, and Mr Kule was authorised to sign alone on the company's account.

Mr Kule paid in to Grass Bank a £3,000 cheque for the credit of his personal current account. The cheque had been drawn in favour of 'Freshair Limited or order' by a customer of the company and crossed 'account payee'. The cheque had been endorsed in blank, the endorsement being signed 'pp Freshair Limited, B Kule'.

When paying in the cheque to his account, Mr Kule asked if he could draw against it. On enquiry by Grass Bank, Mr Kule said his managing director had authorised him to keep the cheque in lieu of expenses. Grass Bank credited the £3,000 to Mr Kule's account and allowed him to draw against it. The bank was later challenged by the managing director of Freshair Limited, who said that Mr Kule's story was untrue. The managing director required payment of £3,000 from Grass Bank. Mr Kule has disappeared without trace.

Explain whether Grass Bank can refuse to pay Freshair Limited £3,000. Give the legal reasons for your answer. [20 marks]

26 (a) A bank takes a memorandum of deposit over shares in a private limited company, together with a deposit of the share certificates. What risks will the bank have which would not apply to a legal charge on the same shares? [11]

(b) Joe mortgaged his freehold unregistered house to a bank. Later, he granted a lease of the house to Fred. What are the bank's rights against Fred if he is still in occupation of the house when the bank makes formal demand on Joe under the mortgage? [9]

[Total 20 marks]

Appendix 1

Clayton's Case

When Clayton's Case helps a bank

1 With a floating charge when a company goes into liquidation within 12 months. The charge is automatically valid if the debit balance consists of 'new' borrowing.

2 With a potential preference situation, but here the period is six months, unless the preference was to a 'connected' person, when the period is two years.

3 When a minor borrows on current account. Once he becomes 18, under Clayton's case the borrowing will eventually consist of 'new' borrowings.

When Clayton's Case works against a bank

1 When the bank fails to open a separate wages account, its preferential claim can be reduced, as some of the borrowing on current account will have been 'repaid'.

2 When the bank fails to break a current account on notice of a second mortgage. Eventually the borrowing becomes 'new' and the bank loses priority of mortgage. The bank may be protected if the charge form contains a *Westminster Bank Ltd v Cond* type clause.

3 Death of partner or joint account holder and the bank fails to break the overdrawn account.

4 Failure to break the account when the notice of determination of a guarantee expires – but the bank is protected by *Westminster Bank Ltd v Cond* type clause.

Note
In *Barlow Clowes International v Vaughan* (1992), it was held that the rule in Clayton's case should not be applied by a court where the result would be manifestly unjust to creditors of an insolvent debtor. In this particular case it was held that investors in the failed Barlow Clowes company should share any available funds *pari passu*, as the rigid application of Clayton's case would have been impractical and unjust.

Appendix 2

Code of Banking Practice

1.0 Introduction

1.1 This second edition of the Code has been prepared by the British Bankers' Association (BBA), The Building Societies Association (BSA), and the Association for Payment Clearing Services (APACS) in the light of a review carried out by an independent committee following the receipt of submissions from Government Departments, consumer and other organisations, the Banking and Building Societies Ombudsmen and members of the public.

1.2 The Code has been written to promote good banking practice. Specific services may have their own terms and conditions which will comply with the principles contained in the Code.

1.3 The Code is in three parts:

Part A – Governing Principles.

Part B – Customers, their Banks and Building Societies – is addressed to banks and building societies who adopt the Code and offer personal customers ('customers' for short throughout the Code) banking services such as current accounts, deposit and other savings accounts, overdrafts and loans, and various services delivered by the use of plastic cards.

Part C – Customers and their Cards – is addressed to banks, building societies and others who adopt the Code and provide financial services by means of plastic cards. All such providers are called card issuers in the Code.

Part A – Governing Principles

2.0 Governing principles

2.1 The governing principles of the Code are:

(a) to set out the standards of good banking practice which banks, building societies and card issuers will follow in their dealings with their customers;

(b) that banks, building societies and card issuers will act fairly and reasonably in all their dealings with their customers;

(c) that banks, building societies and card issuers will help customers to understand how their accounts operate and will seek to give them a good understanding of banking services;

(d) to maintain confidence in the security and integrity of banking and card payment systems. Banks, building societies and card issuers must recognise that their systems and technology need to be reliable to protect their customers and themselves.

2.2 Banks, building societies and card issuers will comply with all relevant legislation, judicial decisions and codes of conduct or similar documents which are observed by members of the BBA, BSA and APACS.

2.3 The Code requires banks, building societies and card issuers to provide certain information to customers. This will usually be at the time when an account is opened. Information will also be available to customers from branches, if any, of the bank, building society or card issuer. Banks, building societies and card issuers will provide additional information and guidance about specific services at any time on request.

Part B – Customers, their Banks and Building Societies

3.0 Opening an account

3.1 Banks and building societies are required by law to satisfy themselves about the identity of a person seeking to open an account to assist in protecting their customers, members of the public and themselves against fraud and other misuse of the banking system.

3.2 Banks and building societies will provide to prospective customers details of the identification needed.

4.0 Terms and Conditions

4.1 Written terms and conditions of a banking service will be expressed in plain language and will provide a fair and balanced description of the relationship between the customer and bank or building society.

4.2 Banks and building societies will tell customers how any variation of the terms and conditions will be notified. Banks and building societies will give customers reasonable notice before any variation takes effect.

4.3 Banks and building societies should issue to their customers, if there are sufficient changes in a 12 month period to warrant it, a single document to provide a consolidation of the variations made to their terms and conditions over that period.

4.4 Banks and building societies will provide new customers with a written summary or explanation of the key features of the more common services that they provide. This will include an explanation, when accounts are held in the names of more than one customer, of the rights and responsibilities of each customer.

4.5 Banks and building societies will not close customers' accounts without first giving reasonable notice.

4.6 To help customers manage their accounts and check entries, banks and building societies will provide them with regular statements of account. Except where this would be inappropriate to the nature of the account (e.g. where passbooks are issued) this should be at no less than 12 monthly intervals but customers will be encouraged to request statements at shorter intervals.

5.0 Charges and debit interest (payable by customers)

5.1 Banks and building societies will provide customers with details of the basis of charges, if any, payable in connection with the operation of their accounts. These will be in the form of published tariffs covering basic account services which will

- be given or sent to customers: (a) when accounts are opened; (b) at any time on request;
- and be available in branches.

Details of any changes will also be given or sent to customers and be available in branches before the changes are implemented.

5.2 Charges for services outside the tariff will be advised on request or at the time the service is offered.

5.3 Banks and building societies will introduce systems to come into effect by 31 December 1996 to ensure that they will give no less than 14 days' notice of the amount to be deducted from their customers' current and savings accounts in respect of interest and charges for account activity that have accumulated during the charging period.

Banks and building societies which have not introduced such systems will disregard the charges to be applied to customers' accounts for any charging period if those were incurred solely as a result of the application of charges for the previous charging period.

5.4 Banks and building societies will tell customers the interest rates applicable to their accounts, the basis on which interest is calculated and when it will be charged to their accounts. These will include the rates applicable when accounts are overdrawn without prior agreement or exceed the agreed borrowing limit. Banks and building societies will explain also the basis on which they may vary interest rates.

5.5 When banks and building societies change interest rates with immediate effect they will effectively publicise those changes, for example by notices in their branches, if any, or in the press, or on statements.

6.0 Credit interest (payable to customers)

6.1 Banks and building societies will make information about the rates on interest bearing accounts which they offer (whether or not these are open to new customers) freely available and accessible to customers by one or more effective means, for example:

(a) notices and/or leaflets in branches;

(b) press advertisements;

(c) personal notice;

(d) a branch/central telephone service.

6.2 Banks and building societies will tell customers the interest rates applicable to their accounts, the basis on which interest is calculated and when it will be paid to their accounts. Banks and building societies will explain also the basis on which they may vary interest rates.

6.3 When banks and building societies change interest rates with immediate effect they will effectively publicise those changes, for example by notices in their branches, if any, or in the press, or on statements.

7.0 Handling customers' complaints

7.1 Each bank and building society will have its own internal procedures for handling customers' complaints fairly and expeditiously.

7.2 Banks and building societies will inform their customers that they have a complaints procedure. Customers who wish to make a complaint will be told how to do so and what further steps are available if they believe that the complaint has not been dealt with satisfactorily either at branch or more senior level within the bank or building society.

7.3 Banks and building societies will ensure that all their staff who deal directly with customers are made aware of their institution's internal complaints procedure and are able to help customers by giving correct information about it.

7.4 Banks subscribing to the Code will be expected to belong to one or other of the following:

The Banking Ombudsman Scheme;

The Finance and Leasing Association Conciliation and Arbitration Schemes; or

The Consumer Credit Trade Association Arbitration Scheme.

Building societies have to belong to the Building Societies Ombudsman Scheme or another authorised scheme.

Banks and building societies will provide details of the applicable scheme to customers using such methods as leaflets, notices in branches or in appropriate literature, showing their current addresses and telephone numbers.

8.0 Confidentiality of customer information

8.1 Banks and building societies will observe a strict duty of confidentiality about their customers' (and former customers') affairs and will not disclose details of customers' accounts or their names and addresses to any third party, including other companies in the same group, other than in the four exceptional cases permitted by the law, namely:

(i) where a bank or building society is legally compelled to do so;

(ii) where there is a duty to the public to disclose;

(iii) where the interests of a bank or building society require disclosure;

(iv) where disclosure is made at the request, or with the consent, of the customer.

8.2 Banks and building societies will not use exception (iii) above to justify the disclosure for marketing purposes of details of customers' accounts or their names and addresses to any third party, including other companies within the same group.

8.3 Banks and building societies will give customers at least 28 days' notice if they intend to disclose to Credit Reference Agencies information on undisputed personal debts which are in default and where no satisfactory proposals for repayment have been received following formal demand.

Banks and building societies will inform customers that, where they have acquired the legal right to sell mortgaged or charged property, this information may be disclosed to Credit Reference Agencies.

Any other disclosure to Credit Reference Agencies shall be with the customer's consent.

8.4 Banks and building societies will at all times comply with the Data Protection Act when obtaining and processing customers' data.

Banks and building societies will explain to their customers that customers have the right of access, under the Data Protection Act 1984, to their personal records held on computer files.

9.0 Status enquiries (bankers' references)

9.1 Banks and building societies will on request:

(a) advise customers whether they provide bankers' references or bankers' opinions in reply to status enquiries made about their customers;

(b) explain how the system of Status Enquiries (Bankers' References) works.

10.0 Marketing of services

10.1 Except in response to a customer's specific request, banks and building societies will not pass customers' names and addresses to other companies in the same group for marketing purposes, in the absence of express written consent. Banks and building societies will not make the provision of basic banking services conditional on customers giving such written consent. For this purpose 'basic banking services' include the opening and the maintenance of accounts for money transmission by means of cheques and other debit instruments.

10.2 Banks and building societies will give new customers at the time they open their accounts the opportunity to give instructions that they do not wish to receive marketing material.

10.3 Banks and building societies will remind customers from time to time, and at least once every three years, of their right to give instructions at any time that they do not wish to receive marketing material.

10.4 Banks and building societies will not use direct mail indiscriminately and in particular will exercise restraint and be selective:

(a) where customers are minors; and

(b) when marketing loans and overdrafts.

11.0 Marketing and provision of credit

11.1 Banks and building societies in their advertising and promotional material will tell customers and potential customers that all lending will be subject to appraisal of their financial standing by the banks and building societies concerned.

11.2 Banks and building societies will act responsibly and prudently in marketing. All advertising will comply with the British Code of Advertising Practice, The British Code of Sales Promotion Practice, and other relevant Codes of Practice of similar standing.

In particular banks and building societies will ensure that all advertising and promotional literature is fair and reasonable, does not contain misleading information and complies with all relevant legislation.

11.3 In considering whether or not to lend, banks and building societies will take account of information which may include:

- prior knowledge of their customers' financial affairs gained from past dealings;
- information obtained from credit reference agencies;
- information supplied by applicant;
- credit scoring;
- age of applicants; and
- applicants' ability to repay, with the aim of avoiding overcommitment by an applicant.

11.4 Banks and building societies will give due consideration to cases of hardship. They will encourage customers who are in financial difficulty to let them know as soon as possible and will use their best endeavours to give practical information and, subject to normal commercial judgment, will try to help.

12.0 Availability of funds

12.1 Banks and building societies will provide customers with details of how their accounts operate, including information about:

- how and when they may stop a cheque or countermand other types of payments;
- when funds can be withdrawn after a cheque or other payment has been credited to the account;
- out of date cheques.

13.0 Foreign exchange services and cross-border payments

13.1 Banks and building societies will provide customers with details of the exchange rate and the charges which will apply to foreign exchange transactions or, when this is not possible, the basis on which they will be calculated.

13.2 Banks and building societies will provide customers wishing to effect cross-border payments with details of the services they offer. In doing so, they will provide, as a minimum:

(a) a basic description of the appropriate services available and the manner in which they can be used;

(b) information as to when money sent abroad on customers' instructions will usually reach its destination or, when an exact date cannot be given, the latest date by which the money might be expected to arrive;

(c) the details of any commission or charges payable by customers to their bank or building society including a warning where agents' charges may also be incurred.

14.0 Guarantees and other types of third party security

14.1 Banks and building societies will advise private individuals proposing to give them a guarantee or other security for another person's liabilities:

i) that by giving the guarantee or third party security he or she might become liable instead of or as well as that other person;

ii) whether the guarantee or third party security will be unlimited as to amount or, if this is not the case, what the limit of the liability will be;

iii) that he or she should seek independent legal advice before entering into the guarantee or third party security.

14.2 Guarantees and other third party security documentation will contain clear and prominent notice to the above effect.

Part C – Customers and their Cards

15.0 Opening an account

15.1 Card issuers are required by law to satisfy themselves about the identity of a person seeking to open an account or to obtain a card to assist in protecting their customers, members of the public and themselves against fraud and other misuse of the banking and card processing systems.

15.2 Card issuers will provide to prospective customers details of the identification needed.

16.0 Terms and conditions

16.1 The written terms and conditions of a card service will be expressed in plain language and will provide a fair and balanced description of the relationship between the customer and the card issuer.

16.2 Card issuers will tell customers how any variation of the terms and conditions will be notified. Card issuers will give customers reasonable notice before any variation takes effect.

16.3 Card issuers should issue to their customers, if there are sufficient changes in a 12 month period to warrant it, a single document providing a consolidation of the variations made to their terms and conditions over that period.

16.4 Card issuers will publish changes to their credit card interest rates in their branches or in the press or in the statement of account sent to credit card holders, or by all those methods when such changes are made with immediate effect.

16.5 Card issuers will tell credit card holders how frequently they will receive a demand for payment and the period within which payment should be made.

17.0 Issue of cards

17.1 Card issuers will issue cards to customers only when they have been requested in writing or to replace or renew cards that have already been issued.

17.2 Card issuers will tell customers if a card issued by them has more than one function. Card issuers will comply with requests from customers not to issue Personal Identification Numbers (PINs) where customers do not wish to use the functions operated by a PIN.

18.0 Security of cards

18.1 Card issuers will issue PINs separately from cards and will advise the PIN only to the customer.

18.2 Card issuers will tell customers of their responsibility to take care of their cards and PINs in order to prevent fraud. Card issuers will emphasise to customers that:

(a) they should not allow anyone else to use their card and PIN;

(b) they should take reasonable steps to keep the card safe and the PIN secret at all times;

(c) they should never write the PIN on the card or on anything usually kept with it;

(d) they should never write the PIN down without making a reasonable attempt to disguise it;

(e) they should destroy any PIN advice promptly on receipt.

18.3 When customers are provided with an opportunity to select their own PIN, card issuers should encourage them to do so to help them remember the PIN.

19.0 Lost cards

19.1 Card issuers will inform customers that they must tell their card issuers as soon as reasonably practicable after they find that:

(a) their card has been lost or stolen;

(b) someone else knows their PIN.

19.2 Card issuers will tell customers, and will remind them at regular intervals on their statement or by other means, of the place and the telephone number where they can give the details of a lost or stolen card at any time of the day or night. Card issuers will arrange for that telephone number to be included in British Telecom Phone Books.

19.3 Card issuers will act on telephone notification but may ask customers also to confirm in writing any details given by telephone.

19.4 Card issuers, on request, will inform customers whether they accept notification of loss or theft of a card from card notification organisations.

19.5 Card issuers on being advised of a loss, theft or possible misuse of a card or that the PIN has become known to someone else will take action to prevent further use of the card.

20.0 Liability for loss

20.1 Card issuers will bear the full losses incurred:

(a) in the event of misuse when the card has not been received by the customer;

(b) for all transactions not authorised by the customer after the card issuer has been told that the card has been lost or stolen or that someone else knows or may know the PIN (subject to 20.4 below);

(c) if faults have occurred in the machines, or other systems used, which cause customers to suffer direct loss unless the fault was obvious or advised by a message or notice on display.

20.2 Card issuers' liability will be limited to those amounts wrongly charged to customers' accounts and any interest on those amounts.

20.3 Customers' liability for transactions not authorised by them will be limited to a maximum of £50 in the event of misuse before the card issuer has been notified that a card has been lost or stolen or that someone else knows the PIN (subject to 20.4 below).

20.4 Customers will be held liable for all losses if they have acted fraudulently. They may be held liable for all losses if they have acted with gross negligence. Gross negligence may be construed as including failures to comply with any of the requirements of paragraph 18.2 if such failures have caused those losses.

20.5 In cases of disputed transactions the burden of proving fraud or gross negligence or that a card has been received by a customer will lie with the card issuer. In such cases card issuers will expect customers to co-operate with them in their investigations.

21.0 Records

21. 1 To help customers manage their accounts and check entries, card issuers will provide customers with a written record on their statement of account of all payments and withdrawals made.

21.2 Card issuers will inform customers that they should tell them as soon as reasonably practicable if they receive a statement of account that includes an item which seems to be wrong.

22.0 Handling customers' complaints

22.1 Each card issuer will have its own internal procedures for handling customers' complaints fairly and expeditiously.

22.2 Card issuers will inform their customers that they have a complaints procedure. Customers who wish to make a complaint will be told how to do so and what further steps are available to them if they believe that the complaint has not been dealt with satisfactorily by the card issuer.

22.3 Card issuers will ensure that all their staff who deal directly with customers are made aware of their internal complaints procedures and are able to help customers by giving correct information about them.

22.4 Card issuers subscribing to the Code will be expected to belong to one or other of the following:

The Banking Ombudsman Scheme;

The Building Societies Ombudsman Scheme or another authorised scheme;

The Finance and Leasing Association Conciliation and Arbitration Schemes;

The Consumer Credit Trade Association Arbitration Scheme; or

The Retail Credit Group Mediation and Arbitration Schemes.

Card issuers will provide details of the applicable scheme to customers using such methods as leaflets, notices or in appropriate literature, showing their current addresses and telephone numbers.

Appendix 3

Answers to Student Activities and Self-Assessment Questions

Unit 1

1 (b) The cheque must be dishonoured.

2 (a) The bank must give reasonable notice.

3 (i) (e) *Prosperity v Lloyds.*
(ii) Code of Banking Practice.

4 (i) (e) All of the above.
(ii) Code of Banking Practice.

5 (a) *Joachimson v Swiss Bank Corporation.*

6 (i) (c) *Tai Hing Cotton Mill.*
(ii) (a) The bank must refund.

7 (i) (b) *Greenwood v Martins Bank*
(ii) (b) The customer must stand the loss because estoppel applies.

8 (a)

9 (a) and (c).

10 (b) *Hedley Byrne.*

11 (i) (b) *Tournier* (but the BBA say this is now outmoded).
(ii) Code of Banking Practice.

12 *Commercial Banking Co of Sydney* case.

13 Section 6, Statute of Frauds Amendment Act 1828.

14 *Banbury v Bank of Montreal* (1918).

15 Data Protection Act 1984.

16 The Unfair Contract Terms Act 1977.

17 £100,000.

18 This question refers to the bank's liability when it gives status replies. If the bank could prove the reply to have been reasonable all is well, but here the bank has acted negligently but honestly. Therefore the bank will rely on the disclaimer clause which will have been incorporated on its reply form.

Hedley Byrne states that the disclaimer will be valid provided the bank has acted honestly. However the Unfair Contract Terms Act of 1977 may invalidate the disclaimer if the bank has been particularly lax and has not followed normal procedures. Therefore, the bank would advise the HP company that its disclaimer would free it of all liabilities. The HP company could consider suing relying on the Unfair Contract Terms Act 1977, but probably would not as the amount is insufficient to justify the legal costs.

Unit 2

Student activities

1 You should have considered in particular:

- Larger amounts of funds available for mortgages because building societies could raise additional deposits by deposits by offering higher interest rates;
- Borrowers had to pay higher interest rates if demand for mortgages outstripped supply.

3 (2) You should have considered the

- Greater scope for profit making for societies;
- Potential conflict of interest between sales targets and customer needs.

Self-assessment questions

1 c

2 b and d

3 b

4 All are true.

5 a

6 b

7 When the Building Societies Act 1986 came into effect, societies had little and sometimes no experience of the powers that became available to them. The nature limits ensured that societies retained their principal purpose as defined by section 5(1) of the Act and 'eased' themselves into new operational areas which carried greater potential risk (hence the sliding scale relating to the classification of assets).

8 Deregulation has meant that the government has become progressively less concerned with direct controls over the balance sheets of financial institutions. Minimum liquidity ratios can constrain positive business activity. Also, as a tool of monetary policy they are both ineffectual and inconsistent with the government's economic philosophy. The maximum liquidity ratio ensures that building societies cannot become too over-reliant on profits from investments or be tempted to 'play' the gilt market. A major reason for the introduction of the maximum liquidity ratio was the New Cross Building Society situation in the early 1980s. The society had over 60% liquidity at the time it was forced to be taken over by the Woolwich.

9 (a) *Banking.* Societies have moved quickly into mainstream banking services for personal customers but not corporates. This may change with the relaxation of constraints under the Treasury Review, as societies can now provide corporate banking services. Particular successes have been enjoyed in providing interest-bearing current accounts (for example, Halifax 'Maxim' account and Nationwide 'Flexaccount') and other money transmission services. The larger societies have also diversified into new lending services.

(b) *Land.* Societies have increased their activity in survey and valuation services. They have had mixed success in estate agency, possibly due to their market entry coinciding with the property slump. Some societies have retained their estate agency chains while others have divested them.

(c) *Investment.* The larger societies provide investment services such as unit trusts and corporate bonds. Many societies have both tied arrangements and IFA subsidiary companies to provide services regulated by the Financial Services Act 1986. Some societies offer stockbroking through subsidiaries, e.g. Norwich and Peterborough, whilst others provide 'execution only' services, e.g. Skipton and Yorkshire.

(d) *Insurance.* Most societies provide an array of insurance services either organically or through arrangements with insurance companies. Many large organisations have embraced the b*ancassurance* concept, setting up their own life assurance companies or buying existing ones, e.g. Woolwich Life, Britannia Life. Schedule 8 restricted the holding in a general insurer to 15% of the equity, but this has been removed (1996) in respect of 'personal lines' insurances, so societies are expected to move into this area quickly. Some societies have formed captive MIG companies.

(e) *Executorship and trusteeship.* Societies have made few inroads into these areas.

10 The 1986 Act is seen by most societies as too restrictive, despite it being hailed as revolutionary when it was first introduced. In the absence of proposals for new legislation, the government has adopted a flexible approach to easing the restrictions on societies, but change has come only gradually. The inequality in the respective legislative frameworks of banks and building societies have undoubtedly hastened the desire of several societies to convert.

Mutuality will certainly survive, at least in the medium term. Despite conversions and proposed conversion announcements, large players such as Bradford and Bingley, Britannia and Nationwide have all confirmed no intention to convert in the foreseeable future. In addition, most of the smaller societies will certainly remain mutual, if only because many could not meet the requirements necessary for a Stock Exchange quotation.

11 To convert to plc, a society must:

- Agree a framework and strategy;
- Communicate this to the members (shareholders and borrowers);
- Obtain a resolution of the shareholders and the borrowing members;
- Hold the meeting necessary to ratify the conversion;

- Communicate the outcome to the Building Societies Commission;
- Obtain sanction from the Commission for the proposal;
- Register the necessary documents with the Central Office.

12 (a) *Building society membership and mutuality*

Membership is a key concept within the statutory framework of building societies. Section 5(1) of the 1986 Act refers to raising a fund primarily from members and making advances to members secured mainly on land for residential use.

It follows that there are two types of members:

- Shareholders, or investing members; and
- Borrowing members.

Shareholders are the owners of the society. They have rights laid down by the Act, including to receive statutory statements and notices and to attend, vote and speak at general meetings.

Borrowing members enjoy few rights other than relating to mergers and proposed conversion (see below).

Membership of a building society operates on the basis of 'one member, one vote'. No building society can therefore be controlled by an individual or small group of individuals.

Mutuality means 'interdependence'. The original purpose of societies was to intermediate between those with funds to invest and those seeking to facilitate home ownership. Although the 'club' ethos has largely disappeared, the basic purpose of serving mutual interests remains.

(b) *Rights and liabilities*

Investing members, to:

- Receive a summary financial statement;
- Receive a copy of the rules;
- Inspect the register of members;
- Receive notice of the AGM;
- Attend, speak and vote at general meetings;
- Demand a poll;
- Appoint a proxy;
- Move a special resolution;
- Receive interest;
- Make withdrawals subject to the conditions of investment;
- Receive the annual accounts.

Borrowing members:

- Rights laid down in the legal charge;
- To vote on resolutions relating to amalgamations, transfers of engagements and transfers to plc.

(c) *Shareholders and depositors*

Shareholders	*Depositors*
Owners' of the society	Creditors of the society
Right to receive various notices	No rights to receive notices
Right to vote	No right to vote
Right to attend meetings	No right to attend meetings
Repaid after depositors in event of winding up	First call on society in event of winding up

Both shareholders and depositors have recourse to the ombudsman in the event of complaints and are protected by the Building Societies Investor Protection Scheme (except holders of PIBS).

Unit 3

Student activities

6 Only if the damage arose as a result of the bank's negligence, e.g. failure to secure vents or make arrangements for proper drainage inspection, would the bank be liable. However, if the vault has previously been flooded and no action was taken, the bank would almost certainly be liable.

In *Port Swettenham Authority v T W Wu and Co* (1978), it was held that the onus is on the bank to prove it had acted properly. Most banks do not ask for details of items in a deed box but issue a receipt 'contents unknown to bank' and advise the customer to insure. Any attempt to deny liability because of the 'disclaimer' on the safe-custody receipt would probably fail: Unfair Contract Terms Act 1977. In practice, it is unlikely that the customer would have advised the bank that a stamp collection had been deposited; if he had done so the position could be altered.

The practical steps to take would be to ascertain whether or not the collection was insured and, if so, advise the customer to claim under their insurance. If the collection was not insured the bank could probably resist any claim, but might make an *ex gratia* payment.

Note. if the insurance company paid out on a claim for damage to the stamp collection, it could claim compensation, from the bank, under the doctrine of subrogation if the bank's negligence caused the damage.

Self-assessment questions

1 (b)

2 (b)

3 (d)

4 (b)

5 (a), (b), (d), (e) and (f), i.e. not (c).

6 (b)

7 (i) (b)
(ii) (d)

8 (d)

9 (a) and (b)

10 (d)

11 (b)

12 (c)

13 (d)

14 The question asks about the doctrine of undisclosed principal, where the agent has not disclosed but has acted within his authority. Once the facts are discovered, the bank can sue either the agent or the principal. Thus, bank can sue either Arthur or Percy, but not both, and therefore must make a choice.

15 This question asks about the doctrine of undisclosed principal when the agent has not disclosed, but has acted outside his authority. In this case, the agent is liable. An undischarged principal is not liable on contracts made on his behalf without authority. Hence the bank can sue only Arthur.

16 This question refers to the position when a principal gives the impression that an agent is authorised to act on his behalf, when that is not the case. Agency or estoppel applies here and the bank can sue Peter only. The bank cannot sue Albert, but Albert is liable to Peter for breach of duty.

17 A wife's right to act as an agent for her husband is covered under 'agency from cohabitation'. Under this doctrine a wife has implied authority to pledge her husband's credit for necessaries which (traditionally) fall within her domestic responsibilities in the relationship, e.g. food and clothing. If a wife habitually contracts on behalf of her husband in other matters, the husband will also be bound, and is estopped (prevented) from denying her agency. If the husband wishes not to be bound by his wife he must give specific notice to every third party, otherwise he will be bound as regards necessaries which fall within the wife's domestic responsibilities.

18 (a) Because the wife has habitually collected the statement, Mr Jones is estopped from denying his wife's agency. Now that he has complained, his authority will be needed in future.

(b) Bankruptcy of an agent does not terminate his agency. Signing on behalf of his wife is a form of agency on the part of Mr Roger. In practice the bank may prefer the mandate to be cancelled to prevent possible misuse by the husband, but it has no legal duty to have the mandate cancelled.

Unit 4

Student activities

5 Under *Garnett v McKewan*, set off can apply provided the accounts are:

- For certain sums;
- In the same right;
- Between the same parties.

The problem arises as regards the last of these requirements. In *Uttamchandi* it was held that the bank must bring clear and indisputable evidence to the court to prove that one party is a mere nominee of the other.

Thus, the bank cannot combine the accounts. If it did so, Y could claim wrongful dishonour of any unpaid cheques subsequently presented.

Self-assessment questions

1 It runs the risk of being liable for conversion, i.e. collecting cheques for someone who is not entitled to them.

2 *Marfani and Co Ltd v Midland Bank Ltd* (1968).

3 Under s.3, Minors Contracts Act 1987, a minor can ratify the debt on attaining his majority. The debt must be ratified in full and within a reasonable time of attaining majority.

4 The bank takes over the rights of another person in relation to a third party. If the third party would have been able to enforce a debt against the bank's customer, and the bank lent the customer the money to pay the debt, the bank takes over the other party's rights: *Orakpo v Manson Investments Ltd* (1978).

5 No; a sole trader and his business are one and the same as far as their assets and liabilities are concerned.

6 All parties to a joint account are fully liable, both on their own (i.e. severally) and jointly for any debt incurred on the account.

7 This would amount to notice of dispute, which cancels a mandate. You would, tactfully, explain to Mary Brown that in future all withdrawals from the account must be made by both parties signing the withdrawal authority. No withdrawals can be allowed pending instructions completed by both parties, and this includes the withdrawal she wishes to make now.

8 Either party to a joint account can stop a cheque. The bank would return the cheque 'Payment stopped by order of drawer'.

9 The bank must stop the account on notice of death, and return any cheques not drawn in conjunction with a cheque card, marked 'Drawer deceased'. The bank will then wait for receipt of letters of administration or probate before paying the balance over to the estate. If any credit items are received, they will be placed either to the account or to a suspense account, and the executors or administrators of the estate will be notified.

10 With a joint account the balance of the account vests in the survivor under the doctrine of survivorship. Any credits in connection with pensions or annuities must be returned to the remitter. Whilst cheques drawn by the deceased could be returned marked 'Drawer Deceased', the surviving party may countersign them, or give authority for any such cheques to be paid.

11 *Prosperity Ltd v Lloyds Bank Ltd* (1923), and Code of Banking Practice in the case of personal customers.

12 (a) No
(b) Yes
(c) Yes
(d) No
(e) No
(f) No
(g) Yes
(h) Yes: *Re K* (1990).

Unit 5

Self-assessment questions

1 (c)

2 (d)

3 (a)

4 (c)

5 (d)

6 (b)

7 (a)

8 This question refers to the liability of a partner for partnership debts incurred after he has retired.

(a) (i) A is not liable for any overdraft incurred after he has given the bank notice of retirement. The debit balance as at 8 January is comprised of the item of £100 debited on 7 January. The credits paid in have extinguished the debts prior to 7 January (*Clayton's case*). Therefore A is no longer liable for any partnership overdraft, since the debit balance as at 2 January has been repaid.

(ii) The bank should have broken the account, and opened a new account for future transactions after 2 January, to be kept in credit in the absence of agreement to the contrary. A meeting should have been arranged with A, B and C to discuss how the £300 could be repaid or secured.

(b) This question refers to the liability of the deceased partner's estate in connection with partnership debts.

(i) In the absence of a mandate the liability is joint and death would free B's estate. However, the standard bank mandate would impose joint and several liability which would ensure B's estate is liable for the debt as at date of notice. However, the debit balance consists of an item charged after notice, therefore B's estate is no longer liable for the same reasoning as in (a)(i).

(ii) On notice of death the account should have been broken, see (a)(ii) above.

9 This question asks about the significance of various events as regards relations between the partners. Unless there is any agreement to the contrary, the Partnership Act of 1890 will apply.

(a) In a non-trading partnership, a partner has implied authority to bind the other partners by signing a cheque on behalf of the firm, but does not have implied authority to bind the firm by accepting a bill of exchange.

However, in a trading partnership, a partner has implied power to accept bills of exchange on behalf of his firm. In every case, however, the partnership's bank will follow its mandate, since express authority overrules implied authority.

(b) The other partners are not bound or liable for the overdraft. It is not in the normal course of business to open an account for a partnership in the name of one of the partners: *Alliance Bank Ltd v Kearsley* (1871).

(c) The introduction of a new partner requires the consent of all existing partners.

(d) A conviction for dishonesty could be grounds for dismissal of D, because this may affect the firm's reputation *Carmichael v Evans.*

Note: the above is the legal position as set out in the Partnership Act of 1890. The position can be varied if the partners have any specific agreement to do so.

10 The question concerns the position on retirement of a partner and on admission of a new partner.

In all matters between the partners themselves the Partnership Act of 1890 applies, unless there are articles of partnership which cover the position. As regards the partners and creditors, the Partnership Act also applies, unless the creditors agree to the contrary. The answer assumes no special articles or creditor agreements.

New partner
The introduction of a new partner requires the unanimous consent of all the existing partners. The new partner, if he is admitted, is not liable for partnership debts incurred before his admission.

Retirement
The retiring partner will continue to be liable for partnership debts incurred before his retirement. As regards new partnership debts, he can avoid liability by:

(a) Giving notice in the *London Gazette.* This avoids any personal liability to creditors who had never dealt with the firm prior to the retirement.

(b) Giving actual notice of retirement to existing creditors will free him from any personal liability for new partnership debts. Notice in the *London Gazette is* insufficient as regards pre-retirement creditors.

Novation as a possible compromise solution
It may be possible to obtain a tripartite agreement on the date of retirement between creditors, retiring partner and new partnership, whereby all parties agree that the new partnership and partners will take over the liabilities of the old partnership and partners.

11 The question refers to the liability of a partner for debts of the partnership after he has retired. All aspects are governed by the Partnership Act 1890.

(a) If a partner 'holds out' he is still liable (quasi partner).

(b) Otherwise to avoid liability for new partnership debts the partner must:

- Give notice to all creditors who had previously dealt with the firm.
- Give notice in the *Gazette* which binds any new creditors who had not previously dealt with the firm.

(c) If the firm uses old note paper without the retiring partner's knowledge, he is not 'holding out' (*Tower Cabinet* case).

Therefore:

- Tom is liable to Dick if Dick was not aware of the retirement.

Therefore:

- Tom is not liable to Harry as notice in the *London Gazette is* enough.

12 The question asks about the effect of insanity of a partner on a firm. Under the Partnership Act of 1890, insanity of a partner does not automatically dissolve the firm, unless there is a specific agreement to that effect. However, the other partners may petition the court for dissolution if they wish.

Once the bank receives notice of the insanity it will:

- Obtain a new mandate from the other partners.
- Ask for their confirmation regarding any cheques signed by the insane partner which are subsequently presented.
- Break the account only if it is overdrawn, if the bank wishes to rely on the estate of the incapacitated partner. This prevents the *Rule in Clayton's case* from operating against the bank.

Unit 6

Student activities

4 Under the Insolvency Act 1986, there is a hierarchy of classes of creditors, in which the bank ranks fifth. The order of priority is:

- Those with direct security;
- Pre-preferential creditors;
- Costs of bankruptcy;
- Preferential creditors;
- Unsecured creditors.

Each class of creditor, according to their position in the hierarchy of creditors, must be paid off in full before the next category of creditor can receive any proceeds.

Whilst we have no information on the composition of the first three categories above, we know that there is a preferential creditor for any unpaid VAT for up to six months prior to the bankruptcy order.

The bank, being unsecured, will rank behind the VAT and unless there are sufficient funds to cover all five categories, there is a possibility that the bank will receive only a dividend in the pound, whilst the VAT could be paid off in full if the available funds cover the first four categories.

5 *Method of distribution*

Name of Bankrupt	*Assets available* £	*Liabilities to be met* £	*Surplus or deficit* £	*How surplus or deficit is dealt with*
Tom	20,000	15,000	+5,000	To partnership
Dick	14,000	14,000	NIL	—
Harry	18,000	24,000	−6,000	Harry's creditors receive 75p in £ $\left(\frac{18.000}{24,000} \times 100\right)$
Part'ship	25,000 + 5,000 from Tom = £30,000	50,000	−20,000	If all creditors are unsecured they receive 60p in £ $\left(\frac{18.000}{24,000} \times 100\right)$

Tom's creditors are repaid in full, and the surplus of £5,000 is added to the partnership assets of £25,000 making a total of £30,000 available to partnership creditors.

Dick has only sufficient assets to repay his creditors in full, there is no surplus for the partnership creditors.

Harry has a deficit of £6,000 for his personal creditors, thus they will only receive a dividend of 75p in the pound.

The partnership creditors also only receive a dividend, in this case 60p in the pound.

(A dividend in the case of insolvency is the percentage in the pound that a creditor receives when there are insufficient funds available to meet the liabilities in full. The maximum amount any creditor can receive is 100% of everything he is owed.)

Exam Note
Calculators are not allowed in the law exam, so you will not be asked to calculate dividends. The answer above is given to clarify the position in numerical terms.

6 (1) After the petition is brought against Horace, any payment or disposition of his property is void, unless validated by the court: s.284.

The precise criteria which would influence the court's decision as to whether to validate transactions are unclear: *Re Gray's Inn Construction* (1980) and *Re Barncrown* (1994).

If the bank has received the money in good faith and before commencement of bankruptcy proceedings, i.e. before the bankruptcy order and without notice of the petition, the trustee cannot reclaim the money: s.284(4).

If the petition had not been *gazetted*, and the bank had no other notice, it could retain the £3,000. However, the petition was advertised in the *London Gazette* on 3 May and the fact that the bank did not check this publication is unfortunate for the bank, as the advertisement in the *Gazette* is deemed to be notice. Thus the £3,000 may be reclaimed by the trustee in bankruptcy.

(2) The payment out of £2,000 could also be void against the bank. However, the payment out was made prior to the granting of the bankruptcy order (when bankruptcy actually commences), also the bank can prove for this amount (along with the rest of the overdrawn balance) in the bankruptcy. Because the bank can claim in the bankruptcy in relation to the £2,000, it can debit it to the account.

Self-assessment questions

1 (a) (i)

(b) (ii)

2 (d)

3 (c)

4 (b)

5 (a)

6 (d)

7 (b)

8 (c)

9 (c) and (d)

10 (b), (c), (d) and (f)

11 (c)

12 (b)

13 (c)

14 (a) (*Note.* it is non-compliance with the statutory demand that will mean a petition is presented.)

15 (a)

16 (a)

17 (c)

18 (c)

19 (a) Criminal bankruptcy waiting period five years, and discharge is obtained by application to the court.

(b) Person who has already been an undischarged bankrupt during the last 15 years has to wait for five years and apply to the court for discharge.

(c) Small bankruptcies under a court sponsored voluntary arrangement gain an automatic discharge after two years.

20 (a) The question asks what a bank can do when it suspects a customer is an undischarged bankrupt and what it should do if the information is confirmed.

The legal position is covered by section 307 of the Insolvency Act 1986.

- Phone Head Office, London and ask them to make an immediate search in the Bankruptcy Register at London.
- If the search reveals that he is an undischarged bankrupt:
  - Write to the official receiver at the Department of Trade, London by registered post and act on his instructions.
  - If no reply is received within 42 days allow the account to operate normally.
  - Meanwhile, permit no withdrawals, stop the account and advise the customer.

(b) An undischarged bankrupt cannot act as a company director:

- New mandate required.
- All cheques presented which are signed by Smith must be confirmed by the other directors.

Under the Insolvency Act 1986, Smith will be automatically discharged after three years unless he is a criminal bankrupt, or a second bankrupt.

Unit 7

Self-assessment questions

1 (c) debenture holders and

(d) unsecured loan stock holders

2 (a)

3 (b)

4 (c)

5 (b)

6 (c)

7 (a)

8 (b)

9 (b)

10 (a)

11 (d)

12 (b)

13 (a)

14 (a) *Name of the company*

The name may be changed by a special resolution (requiring a 75% majority of those voting). The Department of Trade can insist on any undesirable or misleading name being changed.

(b) *Domicile*
The domicile cannot be changed.

(c) *Objects clause*
The objects clause can be changed by a special resolution. However, if at least 15% of the shareholders formally object, the consent of the court will be needed.

(d) *Liability of members*
This cannot be changed, except in the case of a private company where all shareholders may vote for a change from limited to unlimited liability.

(e) *Share capital*
Any increase in capital can be authorised by an ordinary resolution. Any reduction must be sanctioned by the court, except for redeemable shares which can be redeemed from profits or from a fresh issue of shares.

(f) *Association clause*
This is historical and cannot be changed.

15 A director is appointed by means of an ordinary resolution passed at a general meeting. An ordinary resolution requires a simple majority of votes passed.

A company may specify that a director has a 'qualification holding' of shares, i.e. a specified minimum number of shares which are required to be held by a director.

16 The question asks whether an account can be opened for a private limited company, prior to completion of registration formalities. A company has no legal existence prior to incorporation.

It is not normal practice to open an account in these circumstances; the bank would not have a valid discharge for sums debited prior to formal incorporation. Any unpaid creditor of John Brown Limited would be able to claim the payments from Brown as he is personally liable to pre-incorporation contracts: s.36(4), Companies Act 1985. He could only avoid personal liability if he had disclaimed any personal liability at the time of signing the contract.

If the bank had debited sums to the account it may be liable to refund these to any unpaid creditors of Brown or John Brown Limited because the bank knew the company did not legally exist. Thus, it could be held that the bank was a constructive trustee of the money in the 'company's' account: *Selangor United Rubber Estates Ltd v Craddock* (1968).

Thus the bank would decline to open an account in the company name prior to incorporation. It could open a new account styled 'J Brown re John Brown Ltd', which would protect the bank from any claims.

Unit 8

Student activities

2 (a) Under schedule 6, Insolvency Act 1986, the order of priority is:

(i) *Liquidator's costs*: £300. (Unless the court specifies differently this will rank first in this liquidation.)

(ii) *Preferential creditors*

- *Wages*: money lent by the director to pay qualifying wages up to a maximum of £800 per employee and four months prior to liquidation. Hence £4,000 (four months) is preferential.
- Income tax deducted but not paid over – £2,000.

(iii) *The bank's floating charge.* Because liquidation has occurred within 12 months of the creation of the charge, the position is:

- Valid for the full £7,000 if the bank can prove the company to have been solvent on the date of the creation of the floating charge; or
- Valid for any money lent on or after the date of creation of the floating charge (under *Clayton's* case) if the bank cannot prove solvency: s.245, Insolvency Act 1986.

(iv) *Unsecured creditors*

- The director for £1,000 (remaining from wages).
- Any bank borrowing not covered by the floating charge.
- Trade creditors: £14,000.

The above classes of creditors rank equally amongst themselves, and will receive the same dividend in the pound if there is insufficient cash to pay them off in full. Subsequent classes of creditors will not receive any money.

(b) If the bank held a legal charge on the property it would be a secured creditor. Thus the order of repayment would be:

(i) *Bank's Legal charge* £7,000.

(ii) *Liquidator's costs*: £300.

(iii) *Preferential creditors.*

- Wages as before: £4,000.
- Income tax as before: £2,000.

(iv) Unsecured Creditors:

- The director for £1,000.
- Trade creditors: £14,000.

Note: this assumes that the fixed charge cannot be classed as a preference, which is unlikely following *Re MC Bacon* (1989).

5 The bank would wish to set off the credit balance on the No 1 account against the loan account, and prove as a preferential creditor for wages.

The bank's proof would be:

Preferential	£5,000
Unsecured (10,000 – 4,000)	£6,000
Total preferential and unsecured	£11,000

In accordance with *Re Unit 2 Windows Ltd* (1985) the liquidator would amend the proof to read:

Preferential (5,000 – 1,333)	£3,667
Unsecured (10,000 – 2,667)	£7,333
Total preferential and unsecured	£11,000

The credit balance of £4,000 has been set off pro rata. The calculation is

$$4{,}000 \times \frac{5{,}000}{15{,}000} = £1{,}333$$

and $$4{,}000 \times \frac{10{,}000}{15{,}000} = £2{,}667$$

(The figure £15,000 being total of debit loan account and wages account.)

Taking into account *Re Unit Two Windows*, whilst the total proof is the same, the bank's preferential claim is reduced and the unsecured claim is increased. This change will detrimentally affect the bank, since there is a strong possibility that the preferential claim will be met in full, whilst the unsecured claim will only receive a dividend.

Self-assessment questions

1 (c)

2 (b)

3 (b) (only six months' VAT is preferential)

4 (b)

5 (d)

6 (a), (b) and (c)

7 The question asks about the bank's rights to set off in liquidation. The Insolvency Act 1986 and *National Westminster v Halesowen* give the bank an automatic right of set off in liquidation, except where a trust is involved.

The bank can set off the tax account, since this is not a trust account. The account is styled 'tax account' for the company's internal purposes, and thus could be set off in exactly the same way as if it had been called a 'Number 2 account'.

The dividend account cannot be set off. In *EVTR Ltd, Gilbert and Another v Barker* (1987), it was held that when money has been paid to a company for a specific purpose, and where the money is kept in a separate account, then if liquidation intervenes that money is held in trust if the purpose has not been fulfilled. Hence the merchant bank is entitled to have the £100,000 returned in full. The liquidator has no right to that money, nor does our bank. This dividend account is a 'Quistclose Trust' (*Barclays Bank v Quistclose Investments Ltd* (1970).

The bank can claim £912,000 as an unsecured creditor, although there may be a part of that sum which could be preferential in respect of wages.

8 (a) The question asks why it is necessary to stop a limited company's account on notice of winding up petition. If the court subsequently grants a winding up order, the liquidation will be deemed to have commenced from the date of presentation of the petition (Insolvency Act 1986.)

In *Re Grays Inn Construction*, it was held that withdrawals from the bank account in the period between the presentation of the petition and the winding up order were void. Consequently, the bank would have to refund these payments to the liquidator.

(b) If the directors wish the bank to continue the company's account, they must obtain a court order under s.127, Insolvency Act 1986. The bank can then safely operate the account in accordance with this order.

9 Under s.123, Insolvency Act 1986 a company is deemed to be unable to pay its debts if a petition is presented based on one of the following:

- A creditor, to whom the company owes more than £750 left at the company's registered office a written demand for payment, and payment or security for the debt is not forthcoming within three weeks. The debt must be an undisputed one.
- A judgment debt against the company is unpaid.
- The court is satisfied that the company cannot meet its debts as they fall due.
- The court is satisfied that the value of the company's assets is less than the amount of its liabilities. Prospective and contingent liabilities are included in the liabilities total. A company whose assets considerably exceed its liabilities could be put into liquidation if the assets are very illiquid. However if the assets are easily saleable a petition for winding up the company will fail.

10 The priority of the claims is determined by the Insolvency Act 1986. Preferential creditors are set out in Schedule 6 to the Act.

- The bank because it is a secured creditor. Any surplus from the sale of the premises will be paid over to the liquidator.
- Preferential creditors who rank *pari passu* are:
  - six months' VAT;
  - wages, provided they are within £800 per employee and within four months of the insolvency.
- Unsecured creditors who rank *pari passu* are:
  - rates;
  - trade creditors;
  - directors' loan.

Preferential creditors must be paid in full before the unsecured creditors receive anything.

Position if the bank had been unsecured and half the overdraft had been incurred because of wages payments

Under Schedule 6, a person who lends money to enable 'qualifying' wages to be paid ranks as a preferential creditor, irrespective of whether the borrower is a limited company, partnership or sole trader. This presumes that *Clayton's case* has not cleared the wages. Thus, half the bank debt would be preferential and would rank *pari passu* with the six months' VAT, whilst the other half would be unsecured and would rank equally with other unsecured creditors.

11 Under s.214, Insolvency Act 1986, directors must not allow a company to continue to trade when there is no reasonable prospect of paying the debts. If the directors do not stop trading, they will be liable for wrongful trading and will incur personal liability for future debts of the company. Once a director knows, or ought to have known, that continued trading will result in insolvent liquidation, he must take every step to minimise losses to creditors.

12 The question asks whether a person who has lent money for a specific purpose can reclaim that money if the purpose fails. In *Re EVTR Ltd, Gilbert and Another v Barker* (1987) it was held that such money is held in trust and can be recovered by the lender. The money does not form part of the general assets of the borrower. The bank must return the £60,000 to the finance company. It will prove for £20,000 as an unsecured creditor, but part of the £20,000 may be preferential being qualifying wages. The covering letter amounts to notice of the trust.

Unit 9

Self-assessment questions

1 (b)

2 (b)

3 (a)

4 (b)

5 (b)

6 (a)

7 (d)

Unit 10

Self-assessment questions

1 (i) Drawer
(ii) Paying Bank

2 (i) (c)
(ii) (c)
(iii) (d)
(iv) (d)

3 (b) and (c)

4 (b)

5 (c)

6 (c)

7 (a)

Unit 11

Self-assessment questions

1 (c)

2 (d) *Note*: the bank is liable for conversion, and having acted negligently, it is deprived of the protection of s.4.

3 (b)

4 (a) 'Not negotiable' means that the transferee does not obtain any better title than his transferor. The transferor can still transfer whatever title he has.

5 (e)

6 (b) *Note*: 'contributory negligence' does not apply to paying banks which pay cheques on forged drawer's signatures.

7 (a), (c), (d), (e). *Note*: these are all analogous instruments. Postal orders are covered by s.21, Post Office Act 1953.

Unit 12

Self-assessment questions

1 (c) Nothing – see *Whitehead v National Westminster Bank.*

2 The normal duty of secrecy applies and disclosure could not come under any of the four exceptions set out in the *Tournier*. The bank would ask the beneficiary to refer to the customer.

3 The bank should return the direct debit and advise the originator that the mandate is cancelled. It would also request written confirmation of the 'stop'.

4 The payer's bank must reimburse the payer for the difference as the excess was paid without authority. The bank can then claim reimbursement from the originator under the terms of the general indemnity.

5 In each situation, the bank will have to refund to its customer. However, under the direct debit, the bank can claim reimbursement under the terms of the general indemnity.

With standing orders, the payer's bank could claim from the beneficiary's bank for reimbursement, but this claim can only succeed as regards monies not withdrawn on the beneficiary's instructions: *National Westminster Bank Ltd v Barclays International Ltd.*

The above assumes that the beneficiary's bank acted in good faith, and without negligence, so that it can claim the protection of ss.4(1) and 4(2), Cheques Act 1957. *(Note:* this assumes that credit transfers can be likened to cheques for this particular instance.)

6 (a) £50.
(b) Customer liable for all losses.

7 Following *Momm v Barclays*, the transfer could not be reversed. Whether the beneficiary has been advised or not is immaterial.

8 The bank's standard agreement form would contain an 'exclusion clause'. In these circumstances, the bank would not be liable, provided it had completed all normal precautions, e.g. ensuring the dispenser was filled with cash in accordance with normal procedures.

The clause would be seen to be reasonable in these circumstances, since it would seem to be in conformity with the Unfair Contract Terms Act 1977 and the Code of Banking Practice.

9
- Failure to destroy the PIN advice promptly on receipt;
- Allowing someone else to use the card and PIN;
- Failure to take reasonable steps to keep the PIN secret and the card safe;
- Writing the PIN on the card or writing down the PIN without trying to disguise it.

Unit 13

Self-assessment questions

1 Mrs Jones will sign a third-party security charge form.

2 Mrs Smith could sign a first-party charge form which would cover her liability on the joint account and on her personal account. Alternatively a third-party form could be used.

3 (a) A court order is normally required before the bank can exercise its power of sale.

(b) Equitable mortgages are subject to prior equities, whereas legal mortgages are not, provided the legal mortgagee was unaware of the prior equity when his mortgage was created.

4 The bank will have a valid equitable mortgage. Simple deposit with the intention to charge as security is sufficient: *Harrold v Plenty* (1901).

5 Remember the mnemonic ACRACS:

- All monies.
- Continuing security.
- Repayment on demand.
- Additional security.
- Conclusive evidence.
- Successor.

Unit 14

Self-assessment questions

1 (a)

2 (a) and (c)

3 (a)

4 (a) and (c)

5 (c)

6 (b) (Take care! (c) is within the terms of the Consumer Credit Act 1974)

7 (c)

8 (c)

9 (b)

10 (a) (b) (c) (d)

Unit 15

Student activities

1 (1) The bank's mortgage will take priority for all monies advanced, whatever the date of such advance because it has possession of the deeds.

(2) In this case the bank will have priority for all monies advanced to 20 September 1996, but any advances after that date will rank behind the finance company, unless tacking applies. If the bank is lending on current account, it will break the account on 20 September 1996 to prevent the rule in *Clayton's case* from affecting its priority.

(3) In this case the finance company's mortgage will be void against the bank or against any subsequent purchaser for value as it has not registered its interest.

Self-assessment questions

1 (b)

2 (b) *Midland v Dobson.*

3 Leasehold and freehold.

4 The Law of Property (Miscellaneous Provisions) Act 1989.

5 Deeds. (Remember DUN = Deeds Unregistered Land.)

6 Unregistered.

7 The Land Charges Department exists to record the interests in unregistered land of people who do not have possession of the deeds.

8 Land certificate (or land certificate and head lease if title is good leasehold).

9 A charge certificate.

10 Local searches are made at the local authority to see if there are any developments which could affect the value of land. The local authority registers are not concerned with title to land and thus it is immaterial whether the land is registered or unregistered.

Unit 16

Student activity

4 The question asks about the risk that the bank will run if it releases third party security when the customer's account goes into credit.

The danger is that the situation could amount to a preference under the Insolvency Act 1986. When there is a sudden, dramatic change in the borrower's account, the borrower may have diverted money into the bank account at the expense of his other creditors so that the bank account is now in credit. If Simon were to be made bankrupt on a petition presented within two years, the trustee in bankruptcy could claim that the bank had been preferred (although, of course, it was the brother who was intended to be the one to benefit from the repayment), and could insist that the bank repaid all the diverted funds. The two-year period applies because the guarantor is classed as an 'associate' of the customer under the Insolvency Act 1986.

Section 342(2), Insolvency Act 1986 would protect the bank in the event of Simon's bankruptcy within two years, provided payment had been received:

(a) in good faith;

(b) for value;

(c) without notice of bankruptcy proceedings or that the transaction was a preference.

However, the circumstances here are such that the bank knows, or should know, of the possibility of a preference. (If the borrowing had been paid off in the normal course of business and the bank had had no reason to suspect a preference then all would be well.)

Under *MC Bacon*, it would appear that the bank would be protected if repayment had come because of the bank's pressure on the customer. However in this question as the repayment was voluntary this defence cannot apply.

If the bank had released the shares to Peter, the practical position would be that the bank would be an unsecured creditor for the monies which it had to refund to the trustee in bankruptcy, should bankruptcy occur within the two-year period. The court could order the restitution of the security, but this would be of little practical benefit if Peter had sold the shares and gone to Australia. The bank should, therefore, tell Peter that it insisted on retaining the shares in accordance with the clause which would be incorporated into the charge form.

If Simon goes bankrupt in this two-year period, and if the trustee claims the diverted monies as a preference, the bank can ultimately use the shares to recoup any payments.

If Simon is not made bankrupt at the end of the two years, release the shares to Peter.

Self-assessment questions

1 Minors Contracts Act 1987.

2 No: *National Provincial Bank of England v Brackenbury* (1906)

3 No: *Graham (James) and Co (Timber) Ltd v Southgate-Sands* (1985)

4 All money (up to a maximum in some cases), continuing security, retention of security, agreement to pay, consideration, set off, determination.

5 You must postpone the signing of the guarantee and suggest that the customer (James) must be contacted in order that the true reason for the borrowing is disclosed. 'Silence may amount to misrepresentation', and if you allow the guarantee to be signed, knowing that there is a misunderstanding relating to the purpose of the loan, then the guarantee may not be enforceable.

6 (d) Husband and wife (although the risk is greater than in ordinary cases where no sexual or emotional ties affect the exercise of free will).

7 (d)

8 (a)

Unit 17

Self-assessment questions

1 (a)

2 (c)

3 (a) and (d)

4 (b)

5 (b)

6 (b)

7 (c)

8 (a)

9 (c)

10 (a)

11 (c)

12 (d)

13 The question asks whether a fixed charge, created by a borrower over property already the subject of a floating charge in favour of the bank, will take priority over the bank's floating charge.

The normal legal position is that the fixed charge will take priority over a floating charge, even if the floating charge has been created first. However, the standard bank floating charge will contain a clause prohibiting the creation of any other mortgages or charges without the bank's consent. This will have been registered at Companies House within 21 days of creation of the charge, in accordance with ss.395–396, Companies Act 1985.

If the normal procedure has been followed, the bank's floating charge will take priority. Registration of the prohibition is constructive notice to all secured charges, who will be deemed to be aware of the existence of the charge, and of any other matters which are required to be included in the registered particulars.

14
- Stocks and shares.
- Pledges over goods.
- Insurance policies.
- Negotiable instruments.
- Guarantees.
- Set off letters.

15 The transfer could be a *transaction at an undervalue*. If so, s.238, Insolvency Act 1986 applies.

If X Ltd went into liquidation within two years (group companies are connected persons), the transfer of the factory would be voidable. Thus, the bank's mortgage from Y Ltd would be voidable, since the bank is aware of the undervalue.

The bank will not have the benefit of the fixed charge, since it will have released the mortgage for which X Ltd was the mortgagor. In addition, even if X Ltd stays solvent for over two years, the charge from Y Ltd could be void as a preference if Y goes into liquidation within two years.

Follow normal precautions:

- *Transactions at undervalue*

  There is no problem if the transferor can be proved to be solvent immediately after the transfer of assets. See if the auditors of X Ltd will provide a certificate to this effect.

- *Preference*

  See if Y's auditors will provide a certificate of solvency. Alternatively, if the lending to Y Ltd is on overdraft, *Clayton's case* will help the bank. All 'new monies' are covered by security even if the company goes into liquidation within two years.

  In addition, if the bank could prove that it had only agreed to allow the borrowing to continue on condition that Y granted the mortgage, then the fixed charge would not be classed as a preference: *Re M C Bacon Ltd* (1989).

Unit 18

Self-assessment questions

1 Polarisation.

2 No; best advice for a tied agent means that he must give advice on the most suitable investment from those available from the range of company products. An independent intermediary must look at all products available.

3 The best execution rule requires a firm to take all reasonable steps to ensure that its customers' orders are executed on the best available terms.

4 Insider information. Chinese Walls.

5 Insider dealing is a criminal offence under the Company Securities (Insider Dealing) Act 1985.

6 Professional, business, experienced and ordinary.

7 An unsolicited call is a personal visit or oral communication made without express invitation: s.56(8), FSA 1986.

8 Section 56(4), Financial Services Act 1986.

Unit 19

Student activities

5 Refer back to the reference in the text to s.74(1)(b). Presumably the branch manager has failed to provide written details of the annual rate of interest and of the charges.

Self-assessment questions

1 The bank's normal premises or any temporary premises, e.g. a stand at an exhibition, or the business premises of the customer.

2 When it is signed on bank premises and the loan is unsecured lending or secured lending – except that on land.

3 (a) The trading check is a credit token under s.14(1).
(b) The credit-token agreement is a debtor creditor-supplier restricted use, fixed-sum agreement.
(c) Thomas Smith is the debtor.
(d) Eagle Co is the creditor.
(e) The shops that have agreed, or agree to accept the trading checks in the future, are the suppliers.

4 (a) Mortgage lending by banks, building societies, local authorities, insurance companies, friendly societies and charities.
(b) Debtor creditor-supplier credit fixed sum agreements where the maximum number of repayments does not exceed four.
(c) Debtor creditor-supplier running account agreements where credit given must be repaid in one instalment.
(d) Foreign trade agreements.
(e) Low cost credit under debtor creditor agreements.

5 Under s.123, the Rio Tinto Zinc bearer shares and the bill of exchange are negotiable instruments, thus cannot be taken as security.

6 She can sue the supplier and the credit card company under s.75, Consumer Credit Act 1974. This section covers connected lender liability and states that the supplier of the goods and the provider of the loan are jointly and severally liable for any defect in the goods. The credit card is a credit token.

7 In drawing the cheque, Jones, by implication, requests the bank to grant him an overdraft on its usual terms and conditions. In deciding to honour the cheque, the bank by implication agrees to grant the overdraft. This constitutes a regulated agreement for a debtor creditor fixed sum, unrestricted use agreement.

As it is an overdraft, under s.38, Banking Act 1979, the bank does not have to provide any documentation. However, the bank must, within three months and seven days from the granting of the unagreed overdraft, advise Jones of the:

- Credit limit;
- Annual interest rate and charges and the conditions under which they can be amended;
- Procedure to terminate the overdraft, i.e. that it is repayable on demand.

8 Under s.145, Consumer Credit Act 1974, credit brokerage is the business of introducing individuals seeking credit, or goods on rental, to businesses involved in consumer credit, housing finance, consumer hire or to other credit brokers.

Unit 20

1 b

2 b

3 c

4 b and d

5 c

6 c

7 *Functions of the Commission*:

- To protect investors;
- To promote stability in the building society industry;
- To ensure that societies comply with their principal purpose;
- To regulate and supervise;
- To make recommendations to government and other government departments.

You could expand one each of these as described in the text.

Regulatory bodies:

- The Treasury is the body to which the Building Societies Commission is accountable.

- The Chairman (First Commissioner) is appointed by the Treasury.
- The Commission's Chairman can be the Chief Registrar of Friendly Societies, who is the Chief Executive of the Central Office.
- Whilst the Commission is the regulatory and supervisory body, the Central Office is mainly an administrative one, responsible for registration of particular of societies.
- The Investor Protection Scheme is administered by a Board, the Chairman of which is the First Commissioner.

8 Both schemes provide 90% protection, up to a maximum balance of £20,000 per customer. They have different statutory bases. The bank scheme requires banks to pay a levy, whilst the building society scheme requires contributions only if a society becomes insolvent.

9 The purposes of capital are to:

- Provide a buffer against unforeseen losses;
- Maintain the confidence of customers.

The consequences of inadequate capital are:

- Losses;
- Potential insolvency;
- Pressure by the regulator to modify the structure of the business, and possibly direct action against the society.

10 The factors which would influence the level of capital held by the society include the:

- Minimum acceptable level laid down by the Commission;
- Minimum desirable level suggested by the Commission;
- Risk profile of commercial assets;
- Risk profile of activities other than lending;
- Spread of managerial expertise and specialisms in the society;
- Concentration of business risk relative to the geographical area in which the society operates.

11 The OFT's primary consideration is the 'public interest'. It needs to be assured that unfair trading practices, such as price agreements and unreasonable business practices cannot take place. In many instances, the OFT accepts that it is reasonable to make charges for commercial reasons, but these should be transparent and known to the customer before contractual obligations arise. The OFT also regards freedom of choice of services to be important, so that customers cannot be 'locked in' to institutions when open competition would provide a better service.

12 (a) The *criteria for prudent management*

Adequate reserves
All societies must maintain adequate reserves to protect against losses and maintain the confidence of investors. Reserves provide a solvency margin – the difference between assets and liabilities. For this reason, minimum capital adequacy requirements are laid down.

Structure of commercial assets

The nature limits are in place to ensure that a society retains its principal purpose as laid down by statute. A society which lends over-zealously on high risk propositions can endanger the investors' funds.

Liquidity

Liquidity has to be adequate. The Commission would probably regard any level less than 10% as inadequate. At the same time, the liquidity level cannot exceed a statutory maximum laid down by statutory instrument, currently 33%.

Adequacy of security

It is the responsibility of the directors to ensure that securities considered for advances on land are valued by a suitably competent person not disqualified under the Act.

Accounting records/control and inspection

This criterion relates to s.71 of the Act. Each society must keep comprehensive records and have in place systems of control and inspection.

Direction

The society must be managed by a sufficient number of persons and the business must be conducted with prudence and integrity.

Adequate professional skills

This criterion relates to the range and scale of business activities. It concerns both technical and professional skills.

(b) *Failure to comply*

Failure to comply with any of the criteria for prudent management may result in the Commission assuming that the interests of the society's investors is compromised. Conditions may be imposed on authorisation under s.42 or authorisation may be revoked altogether under s.43. In addition to these powerful sanctions, breach of some of the criteria, e.g. adequacy of security, constitutes a criminal offence under the respective sections of the Act.

Appendix 4

Answers to Examination Questions

Question 1

The question involved here is the bank's duty of secrecy, and in particular whether a bank has a duty to oppose court orders to divulge information and whether it should advise the customer of receipt of such orders.

The general case governing secrecy is *Tournier*. The case said the duty of secrecy applied apart from the four exceptions, i.e:

- Compulsion of law;
- Public interest;
- Bank's interest;
- Customer's authority.

The above points are also set out in the Code of Banking Practice, which applies to personal customers.

Compulsion of law obviously applies here, and in view of the amounts involved, public interest may well be relevant. If the fraud was being committed against North Bank, then it could be argued that bank's interest could apply. There is insufficient detail in the question to cover this point. Obviously there is no question of the customer having given express or implied authority.

Another relevant case is *Barclays v Taylor* which held that the bank had no duty to oppose a court order unless it knew relevant information not available to the court. In addition, the case expressly stated that banks should not advise customers of the receipt of such court orders.

To conclude, the bank is not liable in any way to its customer, Y, because it is definitely acting under compulsion of law.

Question 2

(a) A power of attorney creates an agency. Alan Street is the agent of his mother under this power of attorney. The deed is signed by the donor (Alice Street) and witnessed by at least one person.

Under s.1, Powers of Attorney Act 1971, the deed can be signed by another person if the donor is present and instructs this to be done, e.g. the donor cannot read or write. In such a case there must be two witnesses to the deed.

(b) The bank would have checked the power of attorney to see if it was a special power of attorney which limits the agent (Alan) to certain acts, or if it was a general power of attorney which gives the agent the right to bind the principal (Alice) in all matters.

Once the bank had ascertained the type of power of attorney, it will have run the bank account in accordance with its instructions.

(c) A power of attorney drawn under the Powers of Attorney Act 1971 is revoked on the mental incapacity of the donor. Thus Alan can no longer operate the account under this power of attorney and the bank must stop the account.

Mental incapacity is governed by the Mental Health Act 1983, and admission to a hospital or recognised nursing home on a certificate signed by two doctors in evidence of mental incapacity. Alan will need to apply to the Court of Protection to have a receiver appointed to look after his mother's affairs. He can request that he be appointed receiver.

Whilst the receivership is being created, the bank can only allow withdrawals on the account for necessaries, such as medical care. Provided all withdrawals necessary are for Alice's care, the bank is protected under *B Liggett v Barclays Bank Ltd* (1928) under the doctrine of subrogation.

Any cheques presented after notice of mental incapacity must be returned marked 'insufficient mandate', except in the case of cheques drawn for necessaries. *B Liggett v Barclays Bank Ltd* (1928) protects the bank if cheques are drawn for necessaries, e.g. medical bills.

Once the receiver has been appointed, the bank will open a new account in the receiver's name and act in accordance with the instruction given by the court.

(d) If the power of attorney had been drawn up under the Enduring Powers of Attorney Act 1985 the procedure would have been:

- On notice of mental incapacity the agent (Alan) must apply to the Court of Protection for registration of the deed, giving notice to the donor (Alice) and any other specified relatives.
- As soon as Alan has made the application, he has limited powers to act. These powers allow him to maintain Alice, paying such items as medical bills. He can also act to prevent any loss to Alice's estate. Under s.3(4) he is also allowed to maintain himself if the donor might have previously done so.
- When the Court of Protection registers the power of attorney, the agent's (Alan's) powers are restored in full, in accordance with the original deed. The bank would need to ensure that the power of attorney had been registered with the Court of Protection, and check the powers granted to Alan (which would be the same as previously granted).

Question 3

(a) A partner is a general agent of a partnership. The death of an agent does not prevent the paying bank from honouring cheques signed on the principal's behalf. However, it would usually obtain the confirmation of the remaining partners. It could return the cheque marked 'Drawer deceased', but is unlikely to do so.

(b) The deceased partner's estate is liable for past partnership debts, i.e. debts incurred up to the date of death: Partnership Act 1890.

If the partnership account is overdrawn, the bank will break the account to prevent the *Rule in Clayton's case* from operating.

(c) Under the Partnership Act of 1890, a deceased partner's estate is not liable for future partnership debts. This applies irrespective of whether creditors are notified of the death.

(d) Any personal security of a deceased partner is only available to cover partnership debts existing at date of death. If the bank account is overdrawn, break it to prevent the *Rule in Clayton's case* from applying.

(e) Under the Partnership Act of 1890:

- The partnership is dissolved, unless the articles of partnership expressly state this is not the case.
- If the partnership is dissolved, the surviving partners may carry on the business with a view to winding up the estate, and paying the deceased partner's share to his estate.

(f) Any lender/mortgagee who acts in good faith may assume that the surviving partners have authority to mortgage partnership assets after the death of one partner.

(g) The bank may pay any credit balance on a partnership account to the surviving partners, under the law of survivorship. The bank is not a constructive trustee and it is not required to make detailed enquiries to see if the surviving partners intend to pass over the deceased's share to his estate. *(Lipkin Gorman,* a bank is *not* a private detective agency.)

(h) Banks will follow normal practice, which is to obtain a new mandate.

(i) Legally, partnership assets continue to be security for the surviving partners if they continue the partnership. There will be a clause in the mortgage form to this effect. However, if there is no special clause in the articles of partnership, then the partnership will be automatically dissolved. In such cases the surviving partners cannot continue the partnership.

(j) If the partnership is dissolved, then the partnership assets, after meeting all outside liabilities, must be distributed amongst the individual partners and the estate of the deceased.

Question 4

(a) The question asks about the rights of a creditor against partnership assets when that creditor is owed money by a bankrupt partner. Under the Insolvent Partnerships Order 1994, the bankruptcy of an individual partner does not involve the bankruptcy of the partnership. Unless there is a clause to the contrary in any articles of partnership, bankruptcy of a partner dissolves the partnership. If the partnership agreement, i.e. articles, say that the partnership is not to be dissolved in these circumstances then it is not dissolved.

The partnership may continue. The trustee in bankruptcy of the bankrupt partner cannot claim against the assets. However, the trustee of Charles could claim Charles's share of profits of the partnership as long as Charles remained an undischarged bankrupt.

(b) The question asks about the rights of a bank to recover money owing by a partnership. Bankruptcy of the partnership has not yet arisen.

The bank may sue the partnership, and it may sue the individual partners because its mandate gives joint and several liability. The bank could sue any or all of the above, but in practice it would be most cost effective to sue the wealthy partner under joint and several liability.

Any failure to meet a court order for payment would enable the bank to make a statutory demand. Failure to comply with the statutory demand within three weeks would mean the bank would present a bankruptcy petition to the court, thus commencing winding up proceedings against the partnership, or bankruptcy proceedings against each partner.

(c) Blackbank cannot wind up the partnership, because the partnership has no liability to Blackbank. Only Charles has any liability to Blackbank. Blackbank could, however, take a charging order over Charles's share of the partnership assets.

As regards Whitebank, the question asks about the action a bank should take when a partnership account is overdrawn, and repayment, having been demanded, is not forthcoming. Whitebank has three options, to:

- Wind up the partnership alone, if it is owed more than £750 and the partnership is unable to pay its debts; or
- Petition for the personal bankruptcy of the individual partners who have unlimited liabilities for the firm's debts; or
- Wind up the partnership and also to bankrupt all the partners.

Since the assets of the partnership are significantly less than its liabilities, option (i), the winding up of the partnership alone, will not see the bank fully repaid. Options (ii) and (iii) are both possible, though if Alan is able to meet his debts, including all the partnership debts, he could not be made bankrupt. The bank would therefore sue Alan personally for the whole of the partnership debt because:

- Winding up the partnership alone is not worthwhile when there are insufficient assets to cover partnership liabilities.
- Winding up the partnership and bankrupting all the partners will incur unnecessary legal costs. It will be cheaper to proceed against Alan alone. It would then be up to Alan to proceed against his fellow partners for reimbursement.

Question 5

(a) The question asks about the powers of a partner to bind the partnership. Under the Partnership Act 1890 a partner is a general agent who has implied authority to bind the firm in normal partnership business. Third parties are not affected by an internal limitation on the authority of the partners unless that third party is aware of the limitation.

The implied powers of a partner under implied authority are to:

- Buy and sell goods, employ staff, give receipts for money;
- Draw cheques on the firm's account.

The partnership is not a trading partnership because its main business is not buying or selling goods *(Beecham case).*

In order to bind the partnership, the partner must expressly contract as an agent of the partnership and must be acting on what appears to be normal partnership business. The third party must also be unaware of any limitation on the implied authority of the partner.

(b) The question refers to the personal liability of a partner for partnership debts after he has retired. Under the Partnership Act of 1890, a partner will be jointly liable with the other partners for all partnership debts which existed at his retirement. The only way to avoid such liability is by novation, when all remaining partners *and* the creditors agree that the new firm can take over liability for the debts which existed at retirement.

As regards partnership debts incurred after retirement, the partner will avoid any personal liability provided he:

- Gives direct notice to all creditors who had dealt with the firm prior to his retirement;
- Inserts a notice in the *Gazette* which will protect him against any new creditors who commence dealings with the firm after retirement;
- Does not knowingly allow his name to remain on the firm's note paper: *Tower Cabinets* case.

Nigel must therefore notify the bank and all existing creditors of his retirement and he should ask Maggie and Alan to delete his name from the firm's note paper. He could ask the bank, Maggie and Alan to agree to novation.

Tutorial Note
On receipt of notice of retirement the bank would break the partnership account to avoid the rule in *Clayton's case.* Failure to break the account would eventually mean that the debit balance on the account would consist of 'new money' debited after receipt of notice. In this situation Nigel would cease to be liable. If the bank agreed to novation, Maggie and Alan would complete a new mandate and authorise a transfer of the overdraft to the new account.

However, this information is not required. The question asks what steps should *Nigel* take!

Question 6

(a) *Barrel's conduct*
This question asks:

- Whether the incompatibility of Barrel is grounds for dissolution of a partnership.
- Whether a conviction for dangerous driving is grounds for expulsion of a partner.

In both cases, if a partnership agreement (articles of partnership) exists, then its terms will apply if these matters are covered. Otherwise the Partnership Act 1890 will cover all matters between the partners. The Act applies as follows:

- Incompatibility does not give automatic grounds for dissolution. The other partners must obtain a court order under s.35. The court is unlikely to grant an order just because of incompatibility. The court must consider dissolution to be 'just and equitable'.
- Again, a court order will be required and an order will be granted if it can be shown that the conviction was 'prejudicial to the firm's business' under s.35. If the firm's business were in transport, then the order would probably be granted: *Carmichael v Evans* (1904). If the firm is in the transport business then a drink-driving conviction could be deemed 'conduct prejudicial to the firm's business'. Otherwise it is unlikely that the court would agree. (This can be compared with a conviction for dishonesty, for which a court order to dissolve will almost always be granted.)

In the circumstances described, it would appear that there is 'managerial deadlock', and if this could be proved to the satisfaction of the court, the partnership may be dissolved under s.35.

Admission of a new partner
In the absence of specific partnership articles on this matter, the Partnership Act 1890 requires the consent of all existing partners before a new partner can be admitted.

If the old partnership has been dissolved as described above, then Lock, Stock and Lock's wife will form a new partnership. If the old partnership has not been dissolved, and Barrel has been expelled from the partnership, then Lock and Stock will have to both agree to the admission of Lock's wife as a partner.

(b) This question asks how a director can be removed. Under the Companies Act 1985 the position is as follows:

- An ordinary resolution requiring a simple majority of votes cast is all that is required to remove a director. This can be passed at a general meeting.
- The passing of an ordinary resolution assumes that there is nothing to the contrary in the articles of association.

Thus, Lock and Stock can convene a general meeting and pass an ordinary resolution to remove Barrel as a director. However, as a director Barrel has the right to participate in the management of the company, and he may claim that he is being denied this right by Lock and Stock – that they are 'freezing him out'. Thus, Barrel could petition the court to have the company wound up under s.122, Insolvency Act 1986. This would only be granted if the court felt it was 'fair and equitable' to do so: *Re Lundie Bros Ltd* (1965)

Appointment of new director
Lock's wife can be appointed, subject to the terms of the articles of association. A director is appointed by an ordinary resolution passed at a general meeting.

(c) Under ss.151–158, Companies Act 1985, giving of financial assistance to enable a person to purchase the company's shares is invalid unless it is 'incidental to some larger purpose of the company': s.153(1), Companies Act 1985.

As Gun Ltd is a private company, provided they can certify that its net assets will not be reduced by such financial assistance or that the assistance is given from its distributable profits, then they can give such assistance by way of either money or guarantee by following this procedure:

- The directors must make a statutory declaration of solvency;
- The auditors' must report on the accuracy of the declaration;
- The shareholders must pass a special resolution;
- The above details must be filed with the registrar of companies within 15 days.

If a guarantee is given by the company to secure bank borrowing this must be given within eight weeks of the above procedure being completed.

Question 7

(a) On making formal demand, and before commencement of winding up, the bank can combine the accounts and appropriate the credit balance to whichever account it wishes: *Garnett v McKewan* (1872).

The deposit account can be set off against the current account overdraft of £4,600. This is advisable, for when Arthur Fagge goes into liquidation, some or all of the wages account would rank above the unsecured creditor (overdraft) as a preferential creditor.

The assistant earns £200 per week. The maximum claim as a preferential creditor is £800 per employee over a period of four months (whichever comes first). Thus, of the balance on the wages account of £1,000, only £800 is preferential: Schedule 6, Insolvency Act 1986.

Any lender can rank as a preferential creditor for wages: s.386, Insolvency Act 1986. Thus the bank should set off the £700 on the deposit account, leaving £3,900 as an unsecured creditor on that account, and £200 as an unsecured creditor on the wages account. The bank could, if it wishes, transfer £200 from the overdraft to the wages account to leave a purely preferential debt on that account.

(b) At the commencement of winding up the bank must set off credit and debit balances: *National Westminster Bank Ltd v Halesowen Presswork and Assemblies Ltd* (1970).

In liquidation where there are three accounts (or more), one of which is credit, the credit balance must be appropriated *pro rata* to the preferential and non-preferential debts: *Re Unit 2 Windows Ltd* (1985).

The £700 will be appropriated:

Total debit £5,600

		£
Wages account (preferential) (800–100)	=	700
Unsecured (4,800–600)	=	4,200
		4,900

Workings

$$700 \times \frac{800}{5600} = £100 \text{ (only £800 of wages account is preferential)}$$

$$700 \times \frac{4800}{5600} = £600$$

(c) Wages are preferential creditors whether the insolvency involves a sole trader, a partnership or a limited company.

Set off applies equally to individuals, sole traders, partnerships and limited companies. Thus the answer to parts (a) and (b) remains unchanged.

Question 8

(a) A bank cannot normally obtain a valid discharge if it pays a cheque in which the drawer's signature has been forged, under s.24, Bills of Exchange Act 1882 a forged or unauthorised signature is wholly inoperative. Whether or not the forgery is a good likeness, is irrelevant. Whether or not the drawer has been careless is irrelevant. The doctrine of contributory negligence does not protect a bank which pays against a forged drawer's signature.

The relevant case here is *Tai Hing Cotton Mill.* The only time a customer can be validly debited when his signature has been forged is when he is estopped (prevented) from denying the validity of the signature. Examples of estoppel are where the customer knows of the forgery and does not advise the bank within reasonable time.

Cases are: *Greenwood v Martins Bank* where the husband did not at first advise the bank when he knew his signature was being forged on cheques by his wife; and *Brown v Westminster Bank* where the customer in reply to enquiries from the bank insisted that her signature was genuine, when she knew it was being forged.

Generally speaking, when the person who benefited from the forgery is closely related to the customer, the bank will wish to see if the customer could have advised the bank sooner and thereby prevented payment against forged signatures. If so, the doctrine of estoppel will apply.

(b) The question asks about the position of a drawee bank which has paid a cheque against a forged drawer's signature.

Provided the doctrine of estoppel does not apply, South Bank must refund the money to Y, since the signature was a forgery: *Tai Hing Cotton Mill.*

In *National Westminster Bank v Barclays Bank International* (1975) it was held that the collecting bank need not refund the money if the payee had withdrawn the funds, provided the collection bank was unaware of the forgery. Thus South Bank must stand the loss.

South Bank may have a claim against the payee for deceit or breach of warranty of authority, but it would appear that the payee does not have any funds.

Question 9

Omega Bank
Omega Bank is the paying bank in all cases.

(a) The words 'account payee' on a cheque render it non-transferable: Cheques Act 1992. Thus, whilst the collecting bank is put on enquiry, there will be no legal problems if the person whose account was credited is entitled to the cheque: s.3, Cheques Act 1992. If conversion did apply, the responsibility would be the collecting bank's.

Thus, Omega Bank can safely pay the cheque, and will be protected by ss.60 and 80, Bills of Exchange Act (if the cheques crossed) and by s.1, Cheques Act 1957, provided payment is in good faith and in the ordinary course of business. Section 2, Cheques Act 1992 extends the protection of s.80 of the Bills of Exchange Act to non-transferable cheques.

(b) The vital information which identifies a 'stopped cheque' is the cheque number: *Westminster v Hilton.* It is quite common for duplicate cheques to be issued if the original has gone astray. The bank can therefore safely pay the cheque. Any loss will be the drawer's.

(c) The bank should return the cheque 'winding up petition presented'. If the petition is upheld, winding up will be backdated to the presentation of the petition, and the bank will have to refund the amount of the cheque to the liquidator: *Re Grays Inn Construction.*

Only pay the cheque if the court agrees under s.127, Insolvency Act 1986 to issue an order to allow the bank to continue the account.

(d) This question asks whether a bank can cash an open cheque for a stranger which purports to be endorsed by the payee.

Under s.60, Bills of Exchange Act 1882, the bank is protected if the endorsement is forged or unauthorised. To be protected the bank must simply pay the cheque in the ordinary course of business and in good faith, there is no requirement to pay without negligence. In addition, under the recommendation of the Committee of London Clearing Banks, the cheque must purport to be endorsed by the payee.

Question 10

(a) (i) *A cheque is not an assignment of funds in the hands of the drawee*
The customer is the drawer and his bank is the drawee bank of the cheque. If a cheque for £50 is presented and there is only £20 in the account the drawee bank can return the cheque. However, this does not 'freeze' the £20 in the account, so that if subsequently a cheque for, say, £15 is presented, that cheque can be paid.

(ii) *Only those who sign negotiable instruments are liable on them*
A cheque is a bill of exchange, drawn on a banker, payable on demand. The drawee only becomes liable on a bill when he accepts it. As banks do not accept cheques, a drawee bank is *never* liable to the holder of a cheque if it refuses to pay it.

(b) The question asks whether a bank has a duty to check an account for funds after it has withheld payment of a banker's order.

In *Whitehead v National Westminster* it was held that there is no duty for the bank to check subsequent to the due date to see if there are funds available to meet the standing order. Hence there is no liability whatsoever on the bank.

(c) The question asks about the position of a bank which has paid a stopped cheque in error.

The bank must refund as it has debited its customer without authority. In addition there could be a liability for wrongful dishonour of other cheques because Jason's balance had been depleted by the unauthorised payment. Any charges or interest incurred must be refunded.

The bank can obtain reimbursement by one of two means:

(i) claim the stamp from Jason under the doctrine of subrogation and sell it to recoup the loss, or

(ii) claim from the payee under *Barclays v Simms.* The bank will succeed provided Golden Fleece has not altered its financial position *vis-a-vis* Jason because it believed the cheque to have been paid.

Question 11

Conversion is defined as 'an unauthorised act which deprives another person of his property'. Thus, if the person whose account has been credited is not entitled to the proceeds of the cheque, then the true owner of the cheque can sue for conversion. The true owner will sue the collecting bank as agent of the wrongdoer.

Section 4, Cheques Act 1957 protects a collecting bank from liability to the true owner for conversion, providing that a collecting bank is not liable for conversion if it collects a cheque:

- In good faith;
- For a customer;
- Without negligence.

Under the Bills of Exchange Act 1882, good faith is defined as 'something which is done honestly, whether it is done negligently or not'. No bank worthy of its name would knowingly become associated with its customer's fraud, and the bank is invariably assumed to have met the requirements of good faith.

Whether the wrongdoer is a customer depends on whether he had some sort of bank account with the collecting bank. The length of time the account had been opened is immaterial provided there are no suspicious circumstances.

The difficult problem is to decide whether the collecting bank has acted without negligence.

Position with cheques made payable to payee or order
In the *Commissioners of Taxation case* it was stated that:

... the test of negligence is whether the transaction of paying in any given cheque, coupled with the antecedent and present circumstances, was so out of the ordinary course of business that it ought to have aroused doubts in the banker's mind and to have caused him to make enquiry.

When the circumstances are such that enquiries should be made, the answers received must appear satisfactory in the light of the circumstances surrounding the transaction and the customer.

Collecting banks fail the negligence test in three broad areas:

(a) failure to complete account opening formalities properly;

(b) failure to enquire when there is a fiduciary relationship between customer and drawer or customer and payee;

(c) failure to enquire and to receive satisfactory answers when there are suspicious or unusual circumstances.

Position with cheques crossed 'account payee'
There is no legal bar to collecting such cheques for third parties, but the collecting bank would almost certainly fail the 'without negligence' test if conversion did apply.

If s.4, Cheques Act cannot be relied upon, then the doctrine of contributory negligence may apply. This states that when the true owner has contributed to the fraud by his own actions, the damages payable by the collecting bank will be reduced to the extent of such contribution.

Where the true owner has a claim which indirectly arises from a criminal act, the doctrine of *ex turpi causa non oritur actio* will protect the bank: *Thackwell v Barclays* (1986).

Finally, the collecting bank may be able to rely on s.29, Bills of Exchange Act 1882 ,(holder in due course) but this could not apply in the case of non-transferable cheques under the Cheques Act 1992 because it is impossible for a transferee to become a holder.

Note: you should briefly cover the main considerations relating to contributory negligence and holder in due course.

There is no single 'correct' answer to this question. Any reasonably argued answer, with cases and the statutes shown here, would obtain good marks.

Question 12

(a) The question asks whether the paying bank is liable to refund to the drawer if it has paid a cheque which has been credited to the account of someone other than the payee. The cheque had not been endorsed by the payee.

A paying bank is protected by s.1, Cheques Act 1957, provided it pays a cheque in good faith and in the ordinary course of business. Thus, if the bank is protected by s.1, it can then say that the cheque has been discharged under s.59, Bills of Exchange Act 1882, having been paid in due course.

The words 'not negotiable' simply mean that the transferee of the cheque obtains no better title than his transferor. Thus, the paying bank has paid the cheque in the ordinary course of business and is protected.

The bank should advise its customer that he is free of liability to Brown, and should suggest that Adrian tells Brown to claim from Chambers. In conclusion the paying bank is not liable. It is not obliged either to refund to Adrian or to sue Chambers on Adrian's behalf.

(b) This question asks about the position of a collecting bank when sued for conversion by the true owner of the cheque.

The collecting bank is protected by s.4, Cheques Act provided it collects the cheque:

- For a customer;
- In good faith;
- Without negligence.

In this case the collecting bank has failed to make enquiries when collecting a third party cheque, and it has collected that cheque without the payee's endorsement. Thus, the collecting bank has acted negligently and cannot claim the protection of s.4. It will be liable for conversion and must refund to Brown. The collecting bank has a right to recover from Chambers but in practice he will have disappeared and drawn out the money.

As the cheque was crossed 'not negotiable', the collecting bank cannot be a holder in due course. It obtains no better title than its transferor. In any case there is no evidence that the collecting bank allowed its customer to draw against uncleared effects, and therefore has not provided consideration..

Finally, there is no evidence of any criminal action on the part of Brown, hence the collecting bank cannot claim the defence of *ex turpi causa non oritur actio.*

Question 13

(a) The question asks about the liability of joint and several guarantors on a guarantee when the signature of one of the guarantors has been forged.

Mr Bodger's signature has been forged, so he cannot be liable. A joint and several guarantee is totally invalid unless all the named guarantors have signed: *National Provincial v Brackenbury*, and it is also invalid if any guarantor's signature has been forged: *James Graham (Timber) Ltd v Southgate-Sands* (1985).

In addition, because Mr Glue only signed in the expectation that the others would do so, Mr Glue cannot be liable because the guarantee was not the contract he had intended to enter into: *Evans v Brembridge* (1855). Hence neither Glue nor Bodger is liable on the guarantee.

(b) *Rights of the bank*
The question asks about the rights of a bank against joint and several guarantors, when one has died and the other has become bankrupt, whilst a third has made part-payment of the monetary maximum.

With joint and several liability the bank can sue each guarantor for the full £50,000, subject to not being able to recover more than £50,000 in total. Thus the bank may:

- Claim as an unsecured creditor in the bankrupt estate of Thomas;
- Claim from the personal representatives of Percy for £50,000;
- Claim £20,000 from Gordon.

In addition the bank will prove as an unsecured creditor for the full £80,000 in the liquidation of Sodor Ltd (assuming it does not have any security other than the guarantee).

Controller Bank's guarantee has a clause which enables Gordon's £30,000 to be placed upon a suspense account. This clause was upheld by *Re Sass.*

Gordon cannot prove in the winding up unless he pays off the whole of the borrowing. Clauses to this effect were upheld by *Goodwin v Gray* (1874) and *Re Houlder* (1929).

Finally, the bank may release the co-guarantors if it wishes without reducing Gordon's personal liability under the guarantee.

Rights of Gordon
If Gordon pays off the whole £80,000, he can claim as an unsecured creditor in the liquidation. If the bank holds any security, Gordon can take over that security if he pays off the whole debt, under the doctrine of subrogation: s.5, Mercantile Law Amendment Act 1856. Likewise Gordon could claim from the respective estates of Percy and Thomas if he paid off the whole debt.

If the bank is successful in suing the estates of Percy and Thomas (assuming Gordon does not pay any more money to the bank), and if the total from the three guarantors exceeds £50,000, then the surplus will be returned to Gordon. He can then sue his co-guarantors for any deficit in their share of the contribution. Each guarantor is liable for £16,667, as regards claims between themselves.

If Controller Bank receives a dividend in excess of £50,000 from the liquidator, and if no other money is received from the guarantors, then the surplus can be paid back to Gordon. This will reduce Gordon's claim against his co-guarantors.

Question 14

(a) Legal assignments are taken in accordance with the Policies of Assurance Act 1867. The assignment must be in writing and signed by the beneficiary of the policy. The insurance company must be notified in writing of the date and effect of the assignment. Some insurance companies charge a small fee for acknowledgement of notice. The assignment, which must be a legal assignment, can be by deed, but need not be so. Alternatively the assignment can be effected on the policy itself.

Priority dates from receipt of notice by the insurance company. If a legal assignment is held, then notice must have been given because in the absence of such notice only an equitable assignment is held. Thus the normal rule would be that the earlier legal assignment must take priority. However, where the policy is not produced, or where a 'duplicate policy' is offered, then even a legal assignee has constructive notice of a prior equitable interest in the policy. In these circumstances an earlier equitable assignment, which was not notified to the insurance company, would gain priority: *Spencer v Clarke.*

(b) It is necessary to examine the policy itself to see what will happen if premiums are in arrears. Normally the insurance company can either lapse the policy after a period of grace, or deduct the overdue premiums from the surrender value.

The bank could call in the borrowing because of breach of covenant to pay premiums. In this case the bank may pay the premiums to date, and surrender the policy. Alternatively, if the policy was near maturity and if its value was well in excess of the borrowing, the bank could pay the premiums in accordance with the terms of the charge form. A further course of action if the value of the policy is well in excess of the debt is to convert the policy to a fully paid up policy, if the insurance company will agree.

(c) The policy may well state the position, but otherwise the insurance company need not pay out if the life assured, whilst sane, has committed suicide: *Beresford v Royal Insurance.* In practice the insurance company may well honour its obligations to a *bona fide* assignee for value, but will probably not pay out to the beneficiary unless the terms of the policy compel such payment.

Suicide is not a criminal offence under the Suicide Act.

Question 15

(a) The clause in the mortgage form is not, on its own, effective against third parties, and it cannot prevent subsequent mortgages from being created and registered at the District Land Registry: Land Registration Act 1925, s.25.

However, the first mortgagee can record a caution at the DLR, so that the DLR will notify him of any attempt to register a second mortgage. The mortgagee could then apply to the court for an injunction.

(b) If the bank's mortgage is in connection with a loan account, there is no need to take any action other than to make a note in the securities records. The bank's mortgage will take priority as regards money lent at the time of receipt of notice of the second mortgage. It does not matter if the loan account debit balance reduces.

If the account is a current account, the bank should break the account to prevent the *Rule in Clayton's case* from operating against it. Earlier debits could be discharged by new credits, and new debits would be classed as fresh borrowing after notice. If the bank breaks the old account, it will open a new account which will be kept in credit unless some suitable agreement can be made.

However, failure to break the account may not matter if the bank has a *Westminster Bank v Cond* type clause in the mortgages.

Finally, if the bank was committed to making a further advance at the time it received notice, such an advance would retain priority under the 'tacking' provisions of s.94, Law of Property Act 1925

(c) The standard bank mortgage contains a clause which states that the borrowing is repayable on demand. There is no need for any default in such situations.

Mortgages for personal loans or house purchase loans may not be a repayable on demand, and there may be a facility letter which will usually say that repayment is only due if repayments are in arrears.

Question 16

(a) The question asks about the different methods of charging shares in a private company.

Legal mortgage
The shares will be registered in the bank's name. The disadvantage is that it

may deprive James of his 'qualification holding'. Check the articles of association in John Ltd to see if this applies. If it does apply James cannot continue as a director.

Do not take a legal mortgage if the shares are partly paid, because the bank will be liable for any unpaid amounts on these shares in liquidation. Even if the bank sells the partly-paid shares up to 12 months prior to liquidation, the bank could be liable to pay any amount unpaid by a subsequent owner of the shares.

Finally, it may not even be possible to take a legal mortgage, since a private company may adopt articles which forbid the shares from being transferred into the name of a mortgagee.

Equitable mortgage
Shares remain in James's name. The bank may take a memorandum of deposit and signed, undated transfer. The disadvantages are that:

- It is subject to prior equities.
- A court order is needed (but not if signed transfer held) to sell them.
- As the company is a private company, its articles of association may give it a first and paramount lien over its shares. If this applies, and if James owes money to John Ltd, the shares could be forfeited to meet this indebtedness. In order to mitigate the effects of the lien, the bank should send notice of lien. Such notice will mean that John Ltd retains priority for monies lent up to receipt of notice, whilst the bank will keep priority as regards money lent by John Ltd after notice.
- Whether the mortgage is legal or equitable, the disadvantage of private company shares is that they are difficult to value and usually difficult to sell.

(b) The question asks if a life policy taken out by a company on the life of a key employee can be charged to the bank.

The company is the beneficiary, and therefore the company can charge the policy to the bank without requiring the consent of the life assured. As regards insurable interest, the policy is valid because the employee is vital to the company's prosperity: *Hebdon v West* (1863).

Both the policy and the bank's charge will remain valid even if the employee leaves, since insurable interest need only apply at the time the policy was originally taken out: *Dalby v India & London Life Assurance Co* (1854).

Note: registration of the charge at Companies House is unnecessary.

Question 17

Summary of events

- Joint and several guarantee already held;
- 8 March – fixed and floating charge created;
- 15 September – creditors' voluntary winding up.

(a) The liquidator is thinking of s.245, Insolvency Act 1986, which says that a floating charge *could* be void if the company goes into liquidation within 12 months of its creation.

If the bank can prove 'solvency' on the date of creation of the floating charge (8 March 1996), the charge is fully valid. If not, the charge is valid for any 'new money' lent when the charge was created or subsequently and in consideration for it. An existing loan account would not count as 'new' borrowing, but the amount owing on the overdraft could well be classed as such. Thus, the *Rule in Clayton's case* (1816) *helps* the bank as the new money starts from the debit turnover through the account since date of creation of floating charge (to a maximum of the debit balance at winding up).

Since the fixed charge is not affected by the '12-month rule', the bank will appropriate the floating charge to cover the current account and the fixed charge to cover the loan.

(b) The granting of the fixed charge *could* be classed as a preference (to the bank) since it would serve to reduce the director's personal liability: ss.238–240, Insolvency Act 1986, i.e. although it is the director who stands to benefit, it is the bank that is, at law, preferred. The period is two years, and here liquidation commenced less than two years after the date of the fixed charge.

As far as the security is concerned, it is valid because the bank only continued the overdraft and loan facilities subject to further security being given. Thus, under the decision in *Re MC Bacon Ltd* (1989), the fixed charge does not amount to a preference.

(c) Whenever a fixed or floating charge is taken after the date of any director's guarantee, there is a danger that the direct security could be void. The giving of direct security by the company could reduce the liability of the directors if the company were to be wound up. This is because collateral security is only called upon if there is a shortfall from the realisation of any direct security held.

The directors could be classed as interested directors as in *Victors Ltd v Lingard* (1927) and s.317, Companies Act 1985. There is no time limit for *Victors case*, as there is for preferences. *Victors Ltd v Lingard* states that interested directors must declare their interest, and should not vote. However s.35, Companies Act 1985 would appear to protect the bank in this situation.

Conclusion
Advise the liquidator that the bank's charges are all valid.

Question 18

(a) This question refers to the Insolvency Act 1986, and asks about the position of a fixed charge and that of a floating charge if a petition is made to appoint an administrator under s.9, Insolvency Act 1986.

An administration order can be made on a petition presented by various parties (shareholders, directors or creditors), but it will usually be the shareholders or directors who present the petition.

If the administration order is granted, the administrator takes over all the assets of the company, including any assets which are charged to lenders as security. The administrator can try to continue the business: ss.14–16, Insolvency Act 1986. If this occurs, the fixed charge holder will receive at least the market price which could be obtained in an *unforced* sale: s.11(5) and (6),

Insolvency Act 1986. (If this value exceeds the amount of indebtedness, the bank would only receive what it was owed by the customer.)

Even if the bank has appointed its own receiver under a fixed charge, the making of an administration order can end the appointment of that receiver: s.11(1)–(2), Insolvency Act 1986. Thus, on the appointment of an administrator, control of the security passes out of the bank's hands.

However, if the bank holds a floating charge, it has the following rights:

- The bank must be given a minimum of five days' notice – Insolvency Rules 2.6 and 2.7, 1986 – of the presentation of a petition for an administration order, i.e. the court cannot hear the petition until five days after the bank has been notified.
- If the bank appoints its own administrative receiver before the court hears the petition, the petition will be refused.

(b) (i) *What is meant by the appointment of an administrative receiver?*
A floating charge gives the company (i.e. directors) a free hand to deal with the company's assets in the ordinary course of business. However, if a floating charge crystallises, the directors' powers cease. Crystallisation will occur in accordance with the terms of the debenture. The usual criteria are:

- Commencement of winding up compulsory, *Re Colonial Trusts Corporation, ex parte Bradshaw* (1879) or voluntary, *Re Roundwood Colliery Co* (1897);
- If a receiver is appointed out of court: *Evans v Rival Granite Quarries* (1910);
- When a creditor (e.g. a bank) takes possession of assets that are caught under a floating charge: *Re Hamilton's Windsor Ironworks, ex parte Pitman and Edwards* (1879);
- If the terms of the debenture have been breached: *Shamji and Others v Johnson Matthey Bankers Ltd* (1986);
- If a company ceases to carry on trading: *Hubbock v Helms* (1887).

On crystallisation, the administrative receiver takes over the powers of the directors. He is appointed by the debenture holder, but is an agent of the company under the terms of the debenture.

(ii) *What an administrative receiver does*
The purpose of the administrative receiver is to manage the company's affairs with a view to obtaining repayment for the debenture holder. He is appointed under s.29(2), Insolvency Act 1986 and must be a licensed insolvency practitioner: s.230(2), Insolvency Act 1986.

He can continue the business if he wishes, but more often he will realise sufficient of the assets to repay the debenture holder.

Any money so raised must first be applied in discharge of creditors secured by a fixed charge, then preferential creditors, then creditors secured by a floating charge.

(iii) *How an Administrative Receiver is Appointed*
The following procedure must be followed:

- The appointment must be in writing;

- He must formally accept the appointment before the end of the next business day after receipt (the confirmation in writing must be given within seven days).
- He must be a licensed insolvency practitioner: s.230(2), Insolvency Act 1986;
- He must advertise his appointment in the *London Gazette* and in a local newspaper, give specific notice to creditors within 28 days of appointment, and ensure that all the company stationery shows the fact of his appointment;
- The bank must register the appointment at Companies House within seven days of the appointment.

Question 19

(a) The principle involved is the approach by the bank manager to his customer offering him the provision of loan facilities and financial services, i.e. life assurance, and whether the facilities can be offered to a customer off bank premises.

The personal loan and overdraft are covered by the Consumer Credit Act 1974. The life assurance is covered by the Financial Services Act 1986. The meeting was by chance, not at bank premises, so the provisions of the CCA 1974 regarding canvassing, and the FSA regarding unsolicited calls, must be considered.

(i) *Overdraft*
Section 74(1), Consumer Credit Act 1974 applies to overdrafts, and identifies them as a debtor-creditor agreement, enabling the debtor to overdraw on a current account.

Canvassing is the oral attempt by a lender to persuade a potential borrower to enter into an agreement to borrow money. Canvassing of overdrafts is covered in s.49(3), which allows the canvassing of overdrafts for existing customers who already have an account with the bank.

The question states that Tom Putter has a small deposit account with the bank, so he is a customer of Readibank. Provided the overdraft is part of a current account that falls within s.49(3)(a), canvassing can take place off trade premises.

Under s.38 of the Banking Act 1979, the Director General has exempted overdrafts from the need for documentation.

(ii) *Personal loan*
Under s.49(1), it is an offence to canvass debtor-creditor agreements off trade premises. The only exception applies to overdrafts. A personal loan cannot, thus, be canvassed on a golf course.

Because the bank manager, Mr Green, initiated the discussion, he has again breached the Consumer Credit Act 1974 regulations, which only allow the third party (Mr Putter) to initiate discussions regarding financial matters. Even if the third party had initiated the discussions, Mr Green could only involve himself in a general discussion off trade premises, provided he had not gone to the golf course with the specific intention to canvass.

(iii) *Life assurance*
This falls under the Financial Services Act 1986, and the rules governing unsolicited calls (cold calling). Section 56(8) defines an unsolicited call as 'a personal visit or oral communication made without express invitation'.

Unsolicited calls, which would cover the meeting on the golf course, are allowed for the purposes of selling life assurance and unit trusts only. However, the customer does have the right to cancel any contract within 14 days – SIB rules. The customer can recover any money or property paid over during this 14 day cooling-off period – SIB rules.

In conclusion, the discussion regarding the overdraft and life assurance are within the relevant Acts, but discussion regarding the personal loan are in breach of the Consumer Credit Act 1974. The agreements are *all* valid and enforceable, but where canvassing has taken place, both the branch manager and the bank are guilty of a criminal offence and could face a fine.

(b) The principle here is whether the bank's hospitality tent at the British Open Golf Championship constitutes trade premises under the Consumer Credit Act (as only the personal loan in part (a) is in breach of the Act).

Trade premises are the bank's normal premises, or any temporary premises such as a hospitality tent. If the conversation about a personal loan had taken place inside this tent, then there would have been no breach of the Consumer Credit Act. If Mr Putter had signed a loan agreement form in the tent then it would be classed as a non-cancellable agreement because it would have been signed on bank premises. This would apply if the personal loan was unsecured or secured – except in the case of the security being land – which is extremely rare for this type of lending.

Question 20

(a) (i) *Giving of financial assistance*
A company cannot give financial assistance for the purchase of its own shares when such assistance is given before or at the time of acquisition, s.151(1), Companies Act 1985.

Financial assistance covers the company giving the purchaser money or a loan to buy the shares, or giving some form of security, e.g. a guarantee or a floating charge, to secure the borrowing of the purchaser: s.152, Companies Act 1985. Thus, the floating charge offered would also be subject to this prohibition.

Financial assistance can be given to secure the borrowing of Mr and Mrs Archer provided it is within s.153(1), Companies Act 1985, which states that the assistance is valid if:

... the company's purpose in giving the assistance is not solely to assist share purchase, or where assistance is part of some larger purpose of the company.

The assistance must also be given 'in good faith and in the best interests of the company'.

The dividend offered may contravene s.151(3)(a), Companies Act 1985. A lawful dividend depends mainly upon the distributable profits available and, for example, the normal interim and final dividends would be lawful if based upon distributable profits. Thus, this offer of a dividend would not be acceptable as Mr and Mrs Archer cannot commit themselves to paying a dividend before they become directors of the company. The only way it could be acceptable would be if the dividend were decided upon by the existing directors and it was also a lawful dividend.

As Target Co Ltd is a private limited company (if it were a public limited company the title would be Target plc) it can give financial assistance for the right to purchase its shares provided that such assistance does not reduce the net assets of the company, and that it comes from distributable profits, and that it follows the following procedure:

- The directors make a statutory declaration of solvency;
- The auditor's report verifies the statutory declaration;
- A special resolution is passed at a general meeting;
- Copies of the above are filed with the registrar of companies within 15 days.

This procedure would ensure that the assistance was valid under ss.151–158, Companies Act 1985.

(ii) *The floating charge*
Assuming that the assistance given is valid, the bank needs to look at the validity of the floating charge as security. A floating charge is only valid for monies lent on or after its creation: s.245, Insolvency Act 1986.

If the company is wound up within 12 months of creation of the floating charge and is unable to pay its debts, the floating charge will only be valid to the extent of any debit turnover through the account from the date of creation of the charge: s.245.

If the floating charge was created in order to prefer the bank, i.e. to put the bank in a better position than it would otherwise have been in, then it may be set aside as a preference. As Mr and Mrs Archer are 'connected persons' to the company, then the time period runs for 24 months from date of creation of the floating charge. However, if the bank will only lend the money against this security it is not a preference and thus cannot be set aside as valid security in the liquidation: *Re M C Bacon Ltd* (1989).

Assuming that the floating charge is valid, it still suffers from three major defects as security:

- It will rank behind subsequently created fixed charges unless the bank has a prohibition clause in the charge, and that clause is registered at Companies House within 21 days of creation on Form 395 in accordance with s.396(1)(e), Companies Act 1985. Sections 415 and 416 state that 'prohibitions' can be registered and that such registration amounts to notice to the whole world.
- It ranks after all preferential creditors.
- It may not cover any stock brought on *Romalpa* terms and not yet paid for.

(b) If Mr and Mrs Archer were already directors of Target Co Ltd they would not be able to offer this security. In this situation, the security cannot be given by the company because under s.330(2)(b), Companies Act 1985 'a company shall not provide any security in connection with a loan made by any person to a director of the company'. Thus, the floating charge cannot be valid under s.330(2)(b), even though the procedures laid down in ss.151–158, Companies Act 1985 had been followed.

Note: Mr and Mrs Archer would be interested directors in this situation, however they can vote to give security from the company for their own borrowing (as laid out above). The question of interested directors applies when the directors have previously given a guarantee or other security for the company's borrowing, and now wish the company to give security.

Question 21

The meaning of undue influence and its effect
Undue influence arises when one party to a contract is unable to exercise free and independent judgment at the time he joins in the contract. Undue influence is defined as arising when one party to a contract takes advantage of the other: *Allcard v Skinner* (1897).

Undue influence applies when one party to a contract has behaved 'unconscionably' and has obtained benefit by applying unfair pressure to another, weaker, party. In certain cases where a special relationship exists undue influence is presumed, unless the contrary can be proved. Examples are: parent and child, doctor and patient, guardian and ward, trustee and beneficiary. There is no presumption of undue influence between husband and wife, although the risk is 'greater than in ordinary cases where no sexual or emotional ties affect the exercise of free will' *(Barclays v O'Brien)*.

Where undue influence applies the 'junior party' may set aside the contract, but where undue influence is presumed to exist rather than actually proved as fact, the junior party must show that the agreement was 'manifestly disadvantageous' to them.

As regards guarantees, undue influence could apply:

- Where the guarantor had a special relationship with the borrower and where the guarantor was the junior party, unless it is clear beyond all doubt that the guarantor has sufficient business acumen to provide a full understanding of the liability.
- Where the bank had acted as financial adviser to the guarantor, it would be presumed that the guarantor trusted the bank.

If a court accepts the plea of 'undue influence' the guarantee is voidable at the instance of the junior party. In *National Westminster v Morgan* it was said that 'there is no precisely defined law setting limits to the equitable jurisdiction of a court to relieve against undue influence'.

How the bank can protect itself
(a) The potential guarantor must receive independent legal advice. If the prospective guarantor is asked to take such advice and refuses, the bank will be protected: *Bahbra v United Bank*. In *Barclays v O'Brien* it was held that if a potential guarantor has been warned by the bank of the dangers of a guarantee and has been advised to take independent legal advice, but refuses to do so, then the bank will be protected.

Under the Code of Banking Practice banks should now seek a private meeting with any guarantor who is, or could be, a 'junior party' and must warn of the dangers and recommend independent legal advice. If such procedures are followed all will be well. If the guarantor who is a customer does not take independent legal advice, then a declaration must be signed by the guarantor saying that they accept that the bank has recommended independent legal advice.

(b) *Lloyds v Egremont* – Although the bank cannot know what was said by the guarantor's solicitor, it is still entitled to assume that the solicitor has given an adequate explanation of the guarantee to the guarantor.

(c) The independent advice must be given before the guarantee has been signed: *Mackenzie v Royal Bank of Canada.*

(d) The bank will be protected where the guarantor obviously knows the nature of the liability and is not offered independent legal advice: *Midland v Chetwynd Talbot.*

Protection where undue influence could apply from debtor

(a) The bank should be protected if there is no indication of undue influence, even where this has in fact applied: *Coldunnel v Gallon.*

(b) The guarantee must be signed on the bank's premises if independent legal advice is not given, otherwise if the bank uses the principal debtor to obtain the guarantor's signature then that customer is deemed to be the bank's agent and the guarantee would be void if undue influence applied: *Avon Finance v Bridger.*

Note: this is a grey area and new cases come to light at frequent intervals. There is no single correct answer here.

Question 22

(a) The question asked about the legal obligations of a bank to its customer as regards ATMs.

Under the terms of *Joachimson v Swiss Bank*, a bank has a duty to honour all requests for withdrawals, provided these requests are in proper form, there are funds available and there are no stop authorities. These principles were formulated in regard to cheques, but it is reasonable to assume that these principles would also apply to ATMs.

The bank must therefore ensure that:

- As far as is reasonable the ATMs are in working order;
- The ATM payments mechanism must be secure;
- The customer's account must be debited with the right amount on the due date.

Therefore, the customer is entitled to be refunded £50, together with any interest or charges incurred due to the incorrect debit. This is the maximum liability of the card issuer as set out in the Code of Banking Practice.

ATMs are not a 'guaranteed' service and if the ATM had displayed an 'out of order' notice, the bank would have simply had to refund the £50 without refunding charges.

(b) This cash card is not a credit token within the terms of the Consumer Credit Act 1974, as it has been used to obtain cash from the ATM of the issuing bank. Hence, a bank may insert exclusion clauses in the cash card agreement, provided such clauses pass the test of 'reasonableness' under the Unfair Contract Terms Act 1977.

A clause limiting the bank's liability for failure of the ATM to operate would be 'reasonable', so long as the reason for non-operation was beyond the bank's control, e.g. a power cut.

Obviously the bank cannot limit its liability to refund when an underpayment has been made.

In addition, any exclusion clause must not contradict the Code of Banking Practice. The bank will exclude none of its obligations under that Code. In particular the customer agreement will conform to the £50 maximum liability for customers in respect of unauthorised transactions which took place prior to notification to the card issuer that there were problems. However, the customer will stand the whole loss in the event of fraud or gross negligence.

Question 23

A preference occurs when a debtor enters into a transaction which places one creditor in a better position than he would otherwise have been in when the company subsequently goes into liquidation within the relevant period. If the person preferred is an associate, then a preference is always presumed unless the contrary is proved.

When the person preferred is not a connected person, then the relevant period is six months, when the person preferred is an associate then the relevant period is two years.

A bank is not an associate. Prior to the *MC Bacon*, it was thought that a bank could easily be a shadow director. However, this case held that professional advisors were not shadow directors. It is still not fully clear whether a branch manager could be classed as a shadow director, but it is likely that the bank will be safe provided that its manager does not become too involved in the day-to-day running of the company.

On the evidence given here, the bank would not be an associate of the company, and hence the relevant period is six months.

As regards the points in the question:

- *Event No 2: Creation of a fixed charge* The question of preference cannot arise. The time period is in excess of two years (connected person) or six months (unconnected person).
- *Event No 4: Taking a guarantee* A preference constitutes an act by the debtor to prefer a creditor. Mr Sharpe is not the debtor and hence there is no question of a preference arising.
- *Event No 6: Floating charges* This could be a preference because the relevant period is two years for a connected person. The director is a connected person and, as such, a preference is always presumed unless the contrary is proved: s.239(b), Insolvency Act 1986. However if the bank put pressure

on the company to give this security, it would not be a preference: *Re MC Bacon Ltd* (1989).

The bank is protected from the fact that Mr Sharpe is an interested director from the decision in *Victors Ltd v Lingard* (1927) if the company has adopted Table A, Article 84, Companies Act 1948, or Article 94, Companies Act 1985. This article protects the bank even if an interested director has not declared his interest and/or has voted. Thus the security is valid.

The bank would also appear to be protected by s.35, Companies Act 1989.

- *Event No 8: Payment of £40,000 from sale of bank's security* Because of its valid fixed charge, the bank had complete control over the sale proceeds of the factory, and the company had no choice but to allow the money to be paid to the bank. In *Re MC Bacon* (1989), it was held that pressure by the bank on the company was sufficient to prevent the creation of security from being classed as a preference. Presumably the same reasoning applies to receipt of sale proceeds of such security.

Question 24

(a) (i) The question relates to the ostensible authority of an agent. If a third party is influenced by the behaviour of a principal and acts on that presumption, then the principal is estopped from denying the agency.

By appointing Melanie Yellow as branch manager, the bank gave her ostensible authority. In *Box v Midland* it was held that a bank was bound by its branch manager's action in such circumstances, and that failure to honour this obligation would result in the bank being liable to the customer in tort for damages.

(ii) A company director has implied authority to bind his company in normal business transactions because he is a general agent. Any third party is not affected by any limitation unless he knew or ought to have known of it: *Watteau v Fenwick.*

There is nothing unusual about a company taking out a life policy on the life of a key employee, and an insurable interest exists if the company is the beneficiary. However, it was Joe Soap's wife and not the company which was the beneficiary of the policy.

In the circumstances of this question, Joe Soap is acting outside his implied authority. He is a special agent and the third party has a duty to verify the authority of the agent if the principal is to be bound. Hence, Snow White Ltd could cancel the policy and claim a refund of any premiums paid from the insurers.

(b) The question concerns agency by ratification. Ratification occurs when a principal adopts a contract made on his behalf by someone who had no authority to bind the principal, or by someone who was exceeding his authority at the time the contract was made.

For ratification to apply:

- The principal must ratify the whole of the contract unless both principal and third party agree to the contrary, and ratification must take place within reasonable time: *Metropolitan Asylums Board Managers v Kingdom & Sons* (1890).

- The principal must be aware of all the details of the contract unless he deliberately chooses to ratify regardless of details. If the principal deliberately chooses to ratify in total ignorance, the ratification will be binding: *March v Joseph* (1987).
- The third party must have been aware of the agency. An undisclosed principal cannot ratify.
- The purpose of the contact must be legal.
- The principal must exist and have had contractual capacity both at the time of the original contract and at the time of ratification.

Applying the above principles we see that:

- Metro Bank could ratify. An authorised official could examine the terms of the facility letter and would then know the full details of the agreement.
- If the policy had been arranged illegally by Joe Soap, i.e. without proper authority for his wife to be the beneficiary, then Snow White Ltd could not ratify. A principal cannot ratify an illegal contract.

Question 25

The question concerns the collecting bank and conversion. Conversion is defined as 'an unauthorised act which deprives another person of his property'. In such cases the true owner of the cheque will normally sue the collecting bank who has acted as agent of the wrongdoer.

The first defence of a collecting bank is s.4, Cheques Act 1957, which protects it provided the cheque was collected:

- In good faith;
- For a customer;
- Without negligence.

Good faith is defined in the Bills of Exchange Act 1882 as 'something which is done honestly, whether it is done negligently or not'. From the facts given, good faith would seem to apply, as is invariably the case as regards banks. Brian Kule was a *customer*, so there is no problem. The problem for the bank is that it will have failed the 'without negligence test'.

In *Underwood A V v Bank of Liverpool and Martins Ltd* (1924) it was held that collecting cheques payable to a limited company for the private account of an official of that company amounted to negligence for the purposes of s.4, Cheques Act 1957. The fact that Kule purported to endorse the cheque on behalf of Freshair Ltd is irrelevant. Banks who collect 'account payee' cheques for third parties will almost certainly fail without the negligence test.

If the bank cannot rely on s.4, it has three other possible defences:

- Contributory negligence;
- Bank as holder in due course;
- The *ex turpi* defence.

Contributory negligence cannot apply here since there is no evidence to show that the true owner contributed to the fraud by his actions.

If the collecting bank can prove itself a *holder in due course*, it can keep the proceeds of the cheque, because a holder in due course is entitled to the proceeds without being subject to any prior equities, counterclaims or defects in title of the transfer. Under s.29, Bills of Exchange Act 1882 a holder in due course is defined as someone who has taken a cheque:

- In good faith;
- For value;
- Complete and regular on the face of it and without notice of prior dishonour.

Hence, as the bank specifically agreed to allow Kule to draw against the cheque prior to clearance the bank may wish to claim as a holder in due course. Note that under the Cheques Act 1992, the cheque would be valid only between drawer and payee. The bank, as a third party, could have no rights to a cheque crossed 'account payee'. Hence the bank cannot be a holder in due course.

The bank cannot rely on the *ex turpi* defence as there is no evidence that the true owner came by the cheque from any criminal act.

Thus, the bank is liable for conversion and must refund £3,000 to Freshair Ltd.

Question 26

(a) The question asks about the risks which apply to an equitable mortgage of shares, as opposed to a legal one.

(i) An equitable mortgage is *subject to prior equities.* A legal mortgagee takes priority over earlier equitable interests, provided he was unaware of such prior equities at the time the legal mortgage was created. It is too late for an equitable mortgagee to convert his mortgage to a legal mortgage once he has notice of prior equities: *Coleman v London County and Westminster Bank* (1916).

(ii) A private or unquoted company's articles may state that it has a first and paramount lien over its shares. This means that the shares could be forfeited if the shareholder is indebted to the company on some other account. An equitable mortgagee can protect his position to some extent by giving notice of lien to the company. Such notice will not protect the bank as regards any indebtedness of the mortgagor to the company prior to notice, but the bank should be protected as regards any future indebtedness of the shareholder to the company.

With legal mortgages there is no question of lien, since the shares are transferred into the bank's name.

(iii) A share certificate is only *prima facie* evidence of ownership of shares. If the bank has an equitable mortgage, the mortgagor could obtain a duplicate certificate and could sell the shares. This would leave the bank's shares valueless.

With a legal mortgage, the mortgagor cannot obtain a duplicate certificate as the shares are registered in the bank's name.

(iv) If a company makes a bonus issue, there will be a free issue of new shares to existing shareholders on a *pro rata* basis. Other things being equal, the price per share will fall in the same proportion as the issue of shares, but shareholders will hold a greater number of shares in compensation. For example, in a one-for-one bonus issue, the price per share should be halved, but each shareholder would end up owning twice as many shares, and the value would be unchanged.

When a bank has a legal mortgage, the new bonus certificates will be sent to the bank and the value of the bank's security will be unaffected. However, when it has an equitable mortgage, the new bonus certificates will be sent to the mortgagor. The danger is that the mortgagor could sell these shares and so leave the bank with a residual shareholding of lower value.

(v) A rights issue is an issue by the company of shares to existing shareholders on a *pro rata* basis, at a price below the current market price. The effect on the share price is to reduce it, but to a lesser extent than applies with a bonus issue.

With a legal mortgage, all documentation is sent to the bank and the bank remains in control of the situation. With an equitable mortgage, all documentation is sent to the mortgagor, and it is the mortgagor who is in control, not the bank.

(b) The question relates to the position of a mortgagee when a tenancy has been created by the mortgagor after the date of the mortgage.

Section 99, Law of Property Act 1925 gives a mortgagor the power to grant agricultural or occupational leases, subject to certain conditions. This right can be excluded if there is a suitable clause in the mortgage form, except as regards leases of agricultural land, which cannot be excluded by the mortgage clause: Agricultural Holdings Act 1948.

In this case, as the mortgaged property is not agricultural land, the courts would uphold the mortgage's clause excluding s.99.

Once the bank has made formal demand, the mortgage form will specify a period of time (say one month) after which it may exercise its power of sale. (All bank mortgages exclude s.103, Law of Property Act.)

If necessary the bank could obtain a possession order against Fred once its power of sale was exercisable. If Fred did not then go willingly, the bank could obtain an eviction order from the court.

Index